翻译专业经典系列教材

Translation Appreciation and Criticism

翻译批评与赏析

李 明 编著

清华大学出版社
北京

版权所有，侵权必究。举报：010-62782989，beiqinquan@tup.tsinghua.edu.cn。

图书在版编目（CIP）数据

翻译批评与赏析 / 李明编著. —北京：清华大学出版社，2016（2025.1重印）
翻译专业经典系列教材
ISBN 978-7-302-44358-2

Ⅰ.①翻⋯　Ⅱ.①李⋯　Ⅲ.①英语—翻译—教材　Ⅳ.①H315.9

中国版本图书馆 CIP 数据核字（2016）第 167546 号

责任编辑：田　园
封面设计：平　原
责任校对：王凤芝
责任印制：宋　林

出版发行：清华大学出版社
　　　网　　址：https://www.tup.com.cn，https://www.wqxuetang.com
　　　地　　址：北京清华大学学研大厦 A 座　　　　邮　编：100084
　　　社 总 机：010-83470000　　　　　　　　　　邮　购：010-62786544
　　　投稿与读者服务：010-62776969，c-service@tup.tsinghua.edu.cn
　　　质量反馈：010-62772015，zhiliang@tup.tsinghua.edu.cn

印 装 者：三河市铭诚印务有限公司
经　　销：全国新华书店
开　　本：185mm×230mm　　印　张：19.5　　字　数：420 千字
版　　次：2016 年 8 月第 1 版　　　　　　　　印　次：2025 年 1 月第 9 次印刷
定　　价：76.00 元

产品编号：068661-03

前　言

翻译活动在我国可谓源远流长，从我国历史上出现最早的、具有较大规模的文字翻译活动即佛经翻译开始，至今已有一千余年的历史了。在这一千余年中，我们的前人不仅为我们留下了大量论述翻译的文字，更留下了大量可供我们慢慢阅读、细细品味，以及用以鉴赏和对比分析的翻译文字，这些翻译文字对于翻译学无疑是丰富的宝藏。

众所周知，对于译者而言，要提高翻译水平，除需进行大量的翻译实践之外，对前人所留下的翻译作品进行鉴赏和对比分析从而领悟翻译的真谛，也是一种行之有效的方法和途径。鉴赏和对比分析，既可以以对照原文和一个译文的形式进行，还可以以对照同一个原文和几个不同的译文进行，这些译文既可以是出自不同译家之手，也可以是出自相同译家之手。通过对照和对比，我们可以发现原文同译文之间、一种译文同其他译文之间在表达方面的差异。通过这种差异对比，我们可以评判译文质量的优劣，找出译文质量优劣的理据，从而得到可资我们借鉴的翻译方法。

自从有了翻译，人类就开始对译文进行评判和借鉴。这种评判和借鉴其实也就是所谓的翻译批评。翻译批评是翻译事业健康发展的源泉。尤其在我国翻译事业欣欣向荣、外译中和中译外进行得如火如荼的今天，翻译批评的重要性愈益彰显。对此，许钧教授在其著作《翻译概论》中作了很好的总结：翻译实践需要引导，翻译现象需要辨析，翻译作品需要评介，翻译队伍需要扶持，所有这些都离不开翻译批评。

对译文，尤其是翻译名家的译文展开翻译批评，不仅能够让批评者深入理解翻译作品、翻译过程及翻译现象，更能够有效实现翻译批评的根本任务，即"促使翻译在民族交流、文化传承、社会发展方面发挥应有的作用，促进翻译事业健康、理性地发展，保证翻译的价值得以实现，从而实现翻译批评自身的价值"（许钧，2009：226）。而在翻译这门学科方兴未艾的今天，翻译批评在培养高层次专业翻译人才的过程中更是发挥着非常积极的作用。

对翻译批评的重要作用，翻译教学界已达成共识。目前，全国各高等院校外语院系或翻译院系，均纷纷开设了适应英语专业翻译方向、翻译专业本科、硕士研究生、专业硕士等不同层次的"翻译批评与赏析"课程。

从广东外语外贸大学的情况来看，2003 年，英语语言文化学院便给英语专业翻译方向的学生开设了"译作赏析"这门课程。从 2005 年开始，高级翻译学院就给翻译学硕士研究生开设了"翻译批评与赏析"这门课程。它同时也成为高级翻译学院自 2008 年开始招收的翻译硕士专业学位（MTI）研究生的必修课程。

笔者长期教授这门课程，本教材正是笔者在"翻译批评与赏析"教学第一线上日积月累的成果。本教材于 2006 年第一次出版，并于 2007 年入选普通高等教育"十一五"国家级规划教材，并进行了重新印刷。在接下来的时间里，笔者根据教学需要和自己的不断研究和积累，对该教材进行了不断的完善和充实。2010 年，本教材出版了第二版。新的版次几乎完全翻新了原教材的编写模式和内容。自 2010 年至今，一晃又是五六年，在这五六年的时间里，笔者对其中尚未给出自己译文的章节进行了思考和探索，在该教材再次出版之际，为这些章节的原文提供了自己的译文，呈现在读者面前，希望读者从我的译文当中窥见我对其他译文的鉴赏和批评。

本教材共分七个部分、二十章。第一部分为"翻译批评与赏析概论"，第二部分为"小说翻译的批评与赏析"，第三部分为"散文翻译的批评与赏析"，第四部分为"诗歌翻译的批评与赏析"，第五部分为"演讲翻译的批评与赏析"，第六部分为"信函翻译的批评与赏析"，第七部分为"戏剧翻译的批评与赏析"。另外，书的附录中还附上了一些翻译批评与赏析方面的文章，供读者对译文进行批评与赏析时或者撰写翻译批评与赏析的论文时进行参考或借鉴。

在教学过程中，教师既可按照本书各部分的先后顺序（即按照小说、散文、诗歌、演讲、信函和戏剧的顺序）进行授课，也可先进行英汉翻译的批评与赏析，后进行汉英翻译的批评与赏析。另外，从第二部分开始，每一部分的各章当中均配有翻译批评与赏析练习。教师可根据学生的实际水平选择难易程度相当的材料进行鉴赏与批评。

本书的最大特点是：书中除信函和戏剧之外的所有原文材料均提供了笔者给出的译文。这些译文可以说是本人从事翻译批评与赏析教学、进行翻译批评与赏析过程的心得与体会。我们也可以将许钧先生的话换一种说法：翻译批评可以引导翻译实践，辨析翻译现象，扶持翻译队伍。这的确是翻译批评的根本目的。我们在批评与赏析他人的译文之后，会发现他人译文的长处和不足。而作为批评者和赏析者,应该在批评与赏析过后拿出自己更好的译文来,这样的批评与赏析才是更为深入的批评与赏析。新拿出的译文应该秉承他人译文的长处,避免他人译文的不足。这也是译者提高翻译水平的重要途径。我在教学中总是鼓励学生敢于挑战名家的译文,敢于拿出自己独创的译文。因为不管是谁的翻译,永远没有最好,只有更好。

本书得以再一次付梓出版,首先,我要感谢清华大学出版社领导及清华大学出版社外语分社郝建华社长对本书的出版所给予的关心和大力支持,感谢清华大学出版社外语分社田园编辑为此书的策划所作的一切努力和付出。其次,我要感谢书中所选译文的所有译者,感谢本书参考文献中引文的所有著作者,感谢所有在本书附录中撰写翻译批评与赏析文章的各位作者。

在目前翻译本科、翻译学硕士以及翻译专业硕士的招生规模不断扩大、"翻译批评与赏析"成为翻译这门新兴学科的重要课程的背景下,本教材无疑会为翻译学科的发展作出积极的贡献。本教材可用作翻译专业本科生、翻译学硕士研究生、翻译专业硕士研究生、英语语言文学专业翻译方向的学生、商务英语专业翻译方向的学生以及广大翻译爱好者的学习或自学教材。精力有限,学海无涯,译海无涯,书中由笔者所提供的译文的不足以及评析的不足在所难免,恳请广大译界专家、学者、同行及各方读者批评指正。

编 者

二〇一六年春于广东外语外贸大学高级翻译学院

目 录

第一部分 翻译批评与赏析概论 ·······································1
  一、关于翻译批评与赏析 ···3
  二、翻译批评的原则 ···5
  三、翻译批评的发展方向 ···5
  四、翻译批评的目的 ···6
  五、翻译批评所采用的准则 ···7
  六、翻译批评所涉及的因素 ···9
  七、翻译批评需探究文本功能 ······································10

第二部分 小说翻译的批评与赏析 ···································13
  一、关于小说体裁 ··15
  二、小说鉴赏方法 ··16
  三、关于小说翻译 ··18

第一章 Pride and Prejudice 汉译文片段的批评赏析 ················20
  一、关于 Pride and Prejudice ·····································20
  二、Pride and Prejudice 原文片段及四种汉译文 ·····················20
  三、小说翻译的批评与赏析练习 ····································32

第二章 Gone with the Wind 汉译文片段的批评赏析 ················36
  一、关于 Gone with the Wind ·····································36
  二、Gone with the Wind 原文片段及四种汉译文 ·····················36
  三、小说翻译的批评与赏析练习 ····································40

第三章 Jane Eyre 汉译文片段的批评赏析 ·························44
  一、关于 Jane Eyre ···44
  二、Jane Eyre 原文片段及四种汉译文 ······························44
  三、小说翻译的批评与赏析练习 ····································48

第四章 《骆驼祥子》英译文片段的批评赏析 ········· 50
一、关于《骆驼祥子》 ········· 50
二、《骆驼祥子》原文片段及四种英译文 ········· 50
三、小说翻译的批评与赏析练习 ········· 58

第五章 《红楼梦》英译文片段的批评赏析 ········· 59
一、关于《红楼梦》 ········· 59
二、《红楼梦》原文片段及四种英译文 ········· 60
三、小说翻译的批评与赏析练习 ········· 66

第六章 《一件小事》英译文的批评赏析 ········· 69
一、关于《一件小事》 ········· 69
二、《一件小事》原文及四种英译文 ········· 70
三、小说翻译的批评与赏析练习 ········· 78

第三部分 散文翻译的批评赏析 ········· 81
一、关于散文的基本特征 ········· 83
二、散文的"真""情"和"美" ········· 83
三、散文翻译的三个要义 ········· 84

第七章 "The Author's Account of Himself"汉译文的批评赏析 ······ 86
一、关于"The Author's Account of Himself" ········· 86
二、"The Author's Account of Himself"原文及四种汉译文 ······ 86
三、散文翻译的批评与赏析练习 ········· 96

第八章 "Of Studies"汉译文的批评赏析 ········· 99
一、关于"Of Studies" ········· 99
二、"Of Studies"原文及四种汉译文 ········· 100
三、散文翻译的批评与赏析练习 ········· 104

第九章 "Altogether Autumn"汉译文的批评赏析 ········· 106
一、关于"Altogether Autumn" ········· 106
二、"Altogether Autumn"原文及四种汉译文 ········· 106

三、散文翻译的批评与赏析练习 ··· 114

第十章　《落花生》英译文的批评赏析 ··· 118
　　一、关于《落花生》·· 118
　　二、《落花生》原文及四种英译文 ··· 118
　　三、散文翻译的批评与赏析练习 ··· 124

第十一章　《干校六记》英译文片段的批评赏析 ···································· 125
　　一、关于《干校六记》·· 125
　　二、《干校六记》原文片段及四种英译文 ·· 126
　　三、散文翻译的批评与赏析练习 ··· 132

第十二章　《荷塘月色》英译文的批评赏析 ·· 135
　　一、关于《荷塘月色》·· 135
　　二、《荷塘月色》原文及四种英译文 ·· 136
　　三、散文翻译的批评与赏析练习 ··· 146

第十三章　《桃花源记》英译文的批评赏析 ·· 148
　　一、关于《桃花源记》·· 148
　　二、《桃花源记》原文及四种英译文 ·· 148
　　三、散文翻译的批评与赏析练习 ··· 154

第四部分　诗歌翻译的批评与赏析 ··· 155
　　一、关于诗歌 ··· 157
　　二、诗歌翻译的原则 ··· 157
　　三、诗歌翻译批评 ··· 158

第十四章　"A Psalm of Life"汉译文的批评赏析 ································· 159
　　一、关于"A Psalm of Life" ··· 159
　　二、"A Psalm of Life"原文及四种汉译文 ···································· 160
　　三、诗歌翻译的批评与赏析练习 ··· 164

第十五章　"When You Are Old"汉译文的批评赏析 ······························ 165
　　一、关于"When You Are Old" ··· 165

二、"When You Are Old"原文及四种汉译文 ································ 166
　　三、诗歌翻译的批评与赏析练习 ·· 168

第十六章 《江雪》《清明》英译文的批评赏析 ························ 169
　　一、关于《江雪》 ·· 169
　　二、《江雪》原文及四种英译文 ·· 170
　　三、关于《清明》 ·· 170
　　四、《清明》原文及四种英译文 ·· 174
　　五、诗歌翻译的批评与赏析练习 ·· 174

第十七章 《再别康桥》英译文的批评赏析 ···························· 176
　　一、关于《再别康桥》 ·· 176
　　二、《再别康桥》原文及四种英译文 ······································· 178
　　三、诗歌翻译的批评与赏析练习 ·· 182

第五部分　演讲翻译的批评赏析 ··· 183
　　一、关于演讲及演讲词 ·· 185
　　二、演讲词翻译的原则 ·· 185

第十八章 "Gettysburg Address"汉译文的批评赏析 ················ 187
　　一、关于"Gettysburg Address" ··· 187
　　二、"Gettysburg Address"原文及四种汉译文 ··························· 188
　　三、演讲翻译的批评与赏析练习 ·· 190

第六部分　信函翻译的批评赏析 ··· 203
　　一、关于信函 ·· 205
　　二、书信的翻译 ··· 206

第十九章 "Letter to Lord Chesterfield"汉译文的批评赏析 ······ 207
　　一、关于"Letter to Lord Chesterfield" ···································· 207
　　二、"Letter to Lord Chesterfield"原文及四种汉译文 ·················· 208
　　三、信函翻译的批评与赏析练习 ·· 212

第七部分　戏剧翻译的批评赏析 ······ 221
一、关于戏剧 ······ 223
二、戏剧的翻译 ······ 223

第二十章　An Ideal Husband 汉译文的批评赏析 ······ 225
一、关于 An Ideal Husband ······ 225
二、An Ideal Husband 原文片段及四种汉译文 ······ 226
三、戏剧翻译的批评与赏析练习 ······ 232

附录：翻译批评与赏析文章 ······ 239
一、Pride and Prejudice 三种汉语译文对比赏析 ······ 241
二、Gone with the Wind 三种汉语译文对比赏析 ······ 247
三、"The Author's Account of Himself" 三种汉语译文对比赏析 ······ 253
四、对"Altogether Autumn"两种译文的比较评析
　　——兼论多种译本"批评"的方法论 ······ 259
五、翻译中的信息缺失与作用补偿 ······ 265
六、张培基先生的英译文《落花生》赏析 ······ 270
七、从原文作者内心出发，把握作者感情走向
　　——复译《荷塘月色》有感 ······ 273
八、"A Psalm of Life" 三种汉语译文对比赏析 ······ 282
九、"The Gettysburg Address" 三种译文的对比赏析 ······ 289
十、辜正坤对"Letter to Lord Chesterfield"两种译文的译注 ······ 292

参考文献 ······ 295

第一部分

翻译批评与赏析概论

一 关于翻译批评与赏析

本书所谓的"翻译批评与赏析",实际上也就是指"翻译批评"。为简便起见,本书多数时候使用"翻译批评"这一术语,它与"翻译批评与赏析"一样,是指同一概念。

在本书的第一部分,有必要就什么是"翻译批评"进行介绍。

"翻译批评"主要是针对具体的译作或与译作有关的某种翻译现象所发表的评论,因此,"批评"在这里的意思不是"批判",而是"评论"。对翻译进行评论,实际上既可以是鉴赏,也可以是指出错误式的批评,还可以是理论性的研究,即借评论某种翻译现象来说明某个翻译方面的问题。在英语中,"翻译批评"的对应语是 translation criticism 或者 critical reading of a translation or translations。(杨晓荣,2005)但不管是汉语中的"翻译批评",还是英语中的 translation criticism,其所指都是"以跨文化交际为背景,以内容、表达、风格、语言及生动性等为切入点的翻译批评和翻译欣赏的结合"①。

何谓"翻译批评"?根据《中国翻译词典》(林煌天,1997),"翻译批评"是指"参照一定的标准,对翻译过程及其译作质量与价值进行全面的评价"。它包括五个方面的内容:

1. 分析原作,着重了解原作者的意图和原作具有的功能;
2. 分析译者翻译原作的目的、所采取的翻译方法及其译作针对或可能吸引的读者对象;
3. 从原作与译作中选择有代表性的文字进行详细的对比研究;
4. 从宏观与微观的角度评价译作,包括译者采取的技巧与译作的质量等方面的内容;
5. 评价译作在译语文化或科学中的作用与地位。(周仪、罗平,2005)

许钧(转引自周仪、罗平,2005)将"翻译批评"界定为对诸如"信息再现活动、语言转变活动、符号转换活动和内容传达活动"的合理程度和转换结果的等值程度作出评价。他认为,就原作与译作而言,两者之间就等值程度的可比因素集中在以下几方面:

1. 译者在具体作品中所观感的世界与作者意欲表现的世界是否吻合(包括思想内容、思想倾向、思维程式)?
2. 译者所使用的翻译方法与手段与作者的具体创作方法与技巧(包括艺术安排、技巧、语言手段)是否统一?
3. 译作对读者的意图、目的与效果与原作对读者的意图、目的与效果是否一致(包括对读者审美的期待及读者的反应)?

翻译批评还可分为广义的翻译批评和狭义的翻译批评两种。前者是指理解翻译和评价翻译;后者是指如上所述的对翻译活动的理性反思与评价,既包括对翻译现象、翻译文本的具体评价与反思,也包括对翻译本质、过程、技巧、手段、作用、影响的总体评价与反思,而

---

① 英文原文为:Translation criticism is the combination of translation criticism and translation appreciation from the perspective of content, expression, style, language and vividness on the background of cross-cultural communication.

不论是具体评价与反思还是总体评价与反思，都依赖并取决于与翻译研究相关的理论和某种相对具有普遍意义的标准（许钧，2009：226，235）。

本书所说的翻译批评，是指狭义的翻译批评。我们认为，进行翻译批评，除需要依赖许钧所说的与翻译研究相关的理论和某种相对具有普遍意义的标准之外，还要采取某种论证方法（杨晓荣，2005；文军，2006），才能够对译者、翻译过程、译作质量与价值及其影响等进行中肯而客观的分析、评价（文军，2006）与反思。

翻译活动非常复杂，它涉及语言、思维、审美、心理、社会、交际、功能、信息传播、目的的实现等等，因此，对翻译活动以及翻译作品的质量和价值进行评价，就需要以语言学理论、哲学、文艺学、美学、心理学、社会学、跨文化交际学、功能主义理论、信息论、传播学等学科理论作为批评的视角。

与此同时，展开翻译批评还需依据一定的标准才能进行。许钧（2009：241）认为，就普遍意义而言，翻译标准就是翻译批评的典律，翻译标准不仅是翻译主体在翻译实践中遵循的原则和努力的方向，也是翻译批评主体用以鉴赏、阐释和评论译作的尺度，它对包括理论的建设和实践的开展在内的整个翻译活动起着重要作用。

在中国翻译界，产生深远影响的翻译标准有严复的"信、达、雅"，傅雷的"神似论"，钱钟书的"化境说"，许渊冲的"优势竞赛论"（即文学翻译中的"九论"——优化论、三势论、三似论、三美论、三化论、创译论、三之论、竞赛论、艺术论），林语堂的"忠实、通顺、美"，刘重德的"信达切"、辜正坤的"多元互补论"等。这些翻译标准均可作为翻译批评的准绳。

而至于翻译批评的论证方法，亦即翻译批评的方法论，根据杨晓荣（2005）的观点，可分为三个层次：最高层次的方法是属于哲学范畴的一般普遍性方法；中间层次是适用于翻译这一学科的方法，如自然科学方法、社会科学方法、跨学科方法等；第三层次是适用于翻译这门具体学科的个别性方法，如语言学的语义分析法等。许钧曾将翻译批评的方法归纳如下（转引自周仪、罗平，2005）：

1. 逻辑验证的方法；

2. 定量定性的分析方法；

3. 语义分析的方法；

4. 抽样分析的方法；

5. 不同翻译版本的比较；

6. 佳译赏析的方法。

这里面的不同翻译版本包括几种情况：东西方译者译品、不同时代或同一时代译品、不同地域或同一地域译品、同一译者不同时期之译品、同一原著不同译者多种译品。（奚永吉，2001）

二、翻译批评的原则

翻译批评到底如何进行？这是从事翻译批评的人们首先遇到的问题。要顺利地进行翻译批评，就必须确立翻译批评的原则。关于翻译批评的原则，国内有不少翻译家或翻译研究者均发表过真知灼见（许钧，1992，2009；喻云根，1996；刘宓庆，2001；杨晓荣，2005；文军，2006；王宏印，2006）。现将这些见解归纳如下：

1. 翻译批评的对象不应仅仅是翻译作品本身，还应是翻译过程和译者，但这里对译者进行翻译批评不是对其进行人身攻击，而是将其置于历史文化语境之下对其翻译立场、翻译方案以及翻译视界等进行考察；
2. 翻译批评应是主观印象和客观分析的综合，是感觉体味与理性检验的结合；
3. 翻译批评应是局部的、微观的评价同整体的、宏观的评价相结合，避免仅仅根据局部现象得出结论；
4. 翻译批评应是与译者为善的、实事求是的、本着探讨问题和解决问题的具有建设性的批评；
5. 翻译批评应是在充分借助与翻译过程或翻译文本相关的各种学科理论条件下的多视角、多维度、多学科的全面透视；
6. 翻译批评应有助于译者及翻译批评者本人对翻译过程的进一步认识，有助于进一步提高翻译作品质量，有助于翻译学科的建设与发展，充分发挥翻译批评对翻译实践的监督、指导和促进作用；
7. 翻译批评应具有开阔的历史文化视野，将翻译现象、翻译事件、翻译文本、翻译主体等置于一定的历史环境下予以考察，并从文化交流的视角来考察在具体翻译活动中的诸如翻译选择、文化立场、价值重构等重要问题。

翻译批评是"将翻译理论和翻译实践连接在一起的一个重要环节"（Peter Newmark）。只有在翻译批评过程中遵循以上原则，才能完成翻译批评的根本任务——促使翻译在民族交流、文化传承、社会发展方面发挥应有的作用，促使翻译事业健康、理性地发展，保证翻译价值得以实现，实现翻译批评的自身价值（许钧，2009：227），与此同时也实现翻译批评的监督功能（即对译者和读者的引导），最终为协调翻译理论与翻译实践的辩证关系，深化翻译理论研究，促进翻译学科的建构与发展，发挥应有的积极作用（许钧，2009：226-231）。

三、翻译批评的发展方向

人类社会进入21世纪，翻译工作进入专业化时代，翻译学也在逐渐往系统化的学科方向发展。作为翻译理论同翻译实践的桥梁和纽带，翻译批评若要满足译者及其评论者的需要，让他们真正从翻译批评中领会翻译的真谛，就需要从以下四个方面进行改进（周兆祥，2004）：

1. 提高系统性（systematicity）。不要让读者觉得赏析者是在东拉西扯的杂谈漫话或者随兴所至而拈出几个例子来大放厥词，而应该以学术的态度，从学术的角度，以建设整个翻译评估的方法架构，去认真耐心地、按部就班地对所涉及的翻译问题进行理论上的以及具有实践意义的探讨。这对翻译专业的学生尤其具有现实意义和理论意义。

2. 提高理论性（theoreticalness）。参照20世纪下半叶各种蓬勃发展的、与翻译工作有着直接或间接关系的学科，包括语言学、人类学、文化学、语言哲学、符号学、社会语言学、心理语言学、功能语言学、美学、文学批评、中西方文艺理论、修辞学等等，以这些学科的理论视角来建构有深度、有阐释力的翻译理论，并从这些理论的视角来对译文进行赏析和评价，而不是根据个人的直觉、随感或者主观尺度进行评判。

3. 提高切合性（appropriateness）。自20世纪下半叶开始，我国的翻译事业蓬勃发展。翻译越来越专业化、科技化，越来越以服务为本、以市场为导向。这样，过去两千年来以文艺作品和宗教文献为主的那种比较静态的、语文式的翻译工作，不再是翻译工作者所关注的焦点。翻译批评需要跟上时代步伐，将视点集中到目前翻译市场上最普遍的翻译任务（如商业、科技、公文、外交、新闻等文体的翻译）的赏析之上，还要关注专业译者、译文使用者、委托者等碰到的各种具体困难。只有这样，翻译批评才可能发挥它的最大效用，并给予翻译工作者充分的指导作用，最终得到行内外人士的认同和重视。

4. 提高整体意识（holisticness）。为了有效分析目前专业翻译工作的运作情况，也本着对译者、作者、译文使用者、委托者等负责的原则，翻译批评不但要像以往所做的大多数工作那样，要比较原文和译文在各个层面（词语、句法、语篇等）的特征，更要把翻译工作看成是一个系统工程（比如说翻译任务、翻译在某一历史阶段中的意义、翻译对于跨文化交际的意义、所翻译的文本同其他文本之间的关系等）中的一个环节来理解。这样的话，词语、句法、修辞等的表征无非是整个大的交际事件中的一部分。因此，翻译批评若能从比较全面、比较宏观的角度去理解翻译工作，我们对于翻译的本质就会有更为深入的理解。

四 翻译批评的目的

翻译批评的目的主要有以下几种（周兆祥，2004）：

1. 审校译文（proofreading translation）。翻译工作完成以后，交由其他人（最常见的是资深的译审等）校阅，检查有没有误译、漏译、不恰当的表达方式、错别字、语病等问题。审稿者担任把关员的角色，大多数时间往往用在保证不出错的消极检验方面。

2. 欣赏介绍（recommending for appreciation）。跟审校相反，有些翻译批评的重点在于推崇介绍，突出翻译工作的独到之处和所取得的成就，并分析其过人之处及其原因，这是积极的取向。

3. 为了评估（assessment）。为译文评分，判断优劣，例如翻译课程的习作、测验、毕业考试或者专业资格考试、翻译比赛、招聘中的笔试等等。在这些场合，都需要有系统的、公开的、明确的（有别于主观印象的）、全面的评分标准，供阅卷员使用。此时翻译批评的目的主要在于衡量译文的水准，以应考核和选拔人才之需。

4. 教学示范（demonstration）。在译员培训过程中，需要大量译例，来说明各种翻译方法的效果以及翻译功力的高低，让接受培训的译员能够从对译文的赏析中以及比较中领会到翻译的真谛，并在翻译实践中将所领会到的翻译理念予以实施，从而提高翻译能力，最终实现教学的目的。

五 翻译批评所采用的准则

翻译批评涉及价值判断，但这种价值判断不在于寻求绝对的真理，而只在于反映出译作批评者面对作品的态度和观点，它是作者、作品、翻译批评者之间相互作用的成果。

翻译批评与赏析往往遵循三种不同的准则（周兆祥，2004）：

1. 对等的准则（equivalence）

该准则蕴含一个假设，即译文是原文的复制品，应酷似原文，应尽量"存真"。因此，在赏析译文时，多注重比较原文和译文，找出二者之间的异同，两者之间越是相似，译文就越是成功。

总体来说，历来主流的翻译评论观点，都是采用这种以"对等"为金科玉律的法则："'信'可以说是翻译的天经地义；'不信'的翻译就不是翻译；不以'信'为理想的人可以不必翻译。"（转引自周兆祥，2004）

不过，对于"信"的本质，大家总有不同理解，正如林语堂所说："译者的第一责任，就是对原文或原著者的责任，换言之，就是如何才可以忠实于原文，不负著（作）者的才思与用意。在这个上面最重要的问题就是所谓忠实应做如何解释，是否应字字拘守原文，或是译者可有自由的权利，于译文时可自行其裁判力，于原文字句得斟酌损益，以求合于译文通顺明畅的本旨。"（转引自周兆祥，2004）

因此，对等有各种不同的层次，包括：(1) 语音的对等；(2) 词语的对等；(3) 意象的对等；(4) 功能的对等；(5) 神韵的对等。

2. 实效的准则（effectiveness）

这个标准背后的假设是：翻译工作作为一种消极服务，其成败主要视乎消费者（委托人、雇主等）的满意程度而定；消费者是否满意，则取决于译文能否达到其委托的目标。

换句话说，今天的翻译工作，往往是译者与委托者的一桩交易，委托者出钱，是为了达到某些目的，例如推销商品、掌握原文信息、影响他人、享受原文所给予的乐趣等，译员接受酬劳，须以专业态度提供服务，让委托者获得期望的效果。

若用这样的眼光来看翻译，任何合法而又合乎道德的手段只要达到委托人的目的，都是合理且应该的。于是历来被尊崇为金科玉律的种种翻译标准，有时都被弃之一旁。例如按照"忠信"的原则，译文应代表原文的全部信息，也没有原文本无的信息，按照"通达"的原则，译文应写得浅显易懂，可是，即使符合了这样的标准，译文未必就能达到委托人所期望的效果，反而不忠信又难以看得明白的译文，变成了好的译文。

因此，译得"好"的译文未必就是成功的译文。译文是否具有可读性，跟翻译任务的成败无必然联系，甚至有时译得"不好"的译文，反而达到了原定的目标。

至于如何衡量委托人的满意程度，则要视其期望而定。有些期望可以量化，如译文令委托人的生意赚了多少钱；有些期望可以验证，如译文使用者看了译文是否遵照其指示完成某些工作。但是相当大部分的译文成效还是要由译文的评论者或者译文赏析者按照可以得到的资料进行评估。

3. 再生的准则（revival）

还有一种"翻译哲学"，就是既不把译本当成原文的复制品或者替代品，也不斤斤计较译本对谁有什么"用"，而是把译本视作原文的"借尸还魂"，让读者及其意念得以在另一个时空里得到新的生命。

按照这个看法，每一次翻译都像音乐厅里的演奏家那样，凭着乐谱（score）里的指示再度为当场的听众演绎一遍该首作品。正如音乐演奏没有钦定的（authoritative）、唯一至尊的（definitive）、完美的演绎，翻译工作也无从追寻最正确的译法、最权威的解释，反而是译者透过原文跟作者心心相印，利用原著作为原料，演绎出新的作品，最终在另一个情景中以飨另一批读者。

若是这样，翻译评论或者赏析的标准则可能是 1) 译文本身作为艺术品的价值，例如译出来的诗有没有"诗味"、译出来的戏剧作为脚本在舞台上演出是否可行，也可能是 2) 译文使用者的期望是否得以满足。

至于译文跟原文酷似与否，译者行使了多大的自由来改变原文的本来面貌，译本对委托者、作者、社会大众、译本的语言文化产生什么影响等等，这些都不重要。在极端的例子中，原文只不过是一些灵感，甚至借口，让译者去发挥，去创造出跟原文具备"某种关系"的新作而已。

在这一点上，历来有不少翻译作品都出现了这种情形，尤以文艺、哲学、宗教领域较普遍，例如林纾取材于英法文学名著而写出的流行小说，Ezra Pound 取材于中国诗歌来创作的新的诗歌，20 世纪 60 年代多位"嬉皮士"（hippies）美国诗人借寒山的作品写自己的诗歌（但称之为翻译）、表达其人生观，都是突出的例子。

六 翻译批评所涉及的因素

从以上讨论可见，怎样评论翻译工作，取决于该翻译任务的本质，包括译者与委托人商定的目标、译文日后如何使用、翻译工作与整个翻译计划其他部分的关系等等。

就翻译工作本身而言，涉及以下因素（周兆祥，2004）：

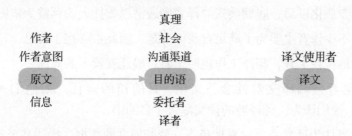

(1) 作者——撰写原文或发表谈话的人。

(2) 作者意图——作者心目中想表达的东西。

(3) 信息——原文表达出来的东西（往往跟作者意图并不完全一样，原因包括作者词不达意等）。

(4) 原文——翻译工作用来作为根据的那篇文章，有时它未必是作者所授权或有意撰写的，如孔子从未见过《论语》，莎士比亚也从未见过今天的莎剧英文本。

(5) 真理——就是作者所描述的事实真相（往往跟原文给人的印象有出入，原因包括作者词不达意、主观偏见、甚至故意歪曲等）。

(6) 社会——目的语的民族、社区、文化。

(7) 沟通渠道——指原来的传意过程使用的方法，如广播剧的渠道是电台，电话谈话记录的渠道是电话，报章专栏文字的渠道是报纸，情书的渠道是书信。

(8) 目的语——指翻译出来的那种语文。

(9) 委托者——译者提供服务的对象（可能亦是译文使用者，也可能不是），包括雇主、翻译社、客户等。

(10) 译者——可能是一个人（独译的情况）或一个翻译小组（合译的情况）。

(11) 译文使用者——通常都是直接阅读译文的人，但情况也有时较为复杂，如剧本翻译之后既由导演及演员"使用"，但间接也是为了观众；有些译文会被其他译者当作原文再翻译成第三种文字，于是译文使用者也包括其他的译者和他们的译本的读者。

(12) 译文——有时是指译者呈交给委托人的那个版本，但也可以较广义地指最后印刷出来的成品，或经过导演和演员的演绎念出来的台词。

七 翻译批评需探究文本功能

每项翻译任务，都可能有不同的目标，分别以上述十二个因素中的一个或多个作为服务重心。

历来大多数翻译评论，都以作者或原文为重心，假若翻译的任务主要是对作者负责，译文必须忠于原文本身、原文作者意图或原文信息。

自从翻译工作专业化以后，雇佣兵式的译者则通常以委托人的利益为依归。

古今中外也有不少译者主要为了满足自我而下笔，因此重心在于自己。

近年来读者的地位在上升，翻译工作也时常有百般迁就读者的倾向。

也有不少评论者强调译文对社会、文化、目的语的责任，如他们大声疾呼要抗拒"翻译腔"的译文，他们认为，翻译腔的译文危害了目的语。

有些翻译理论家认为译文亦要对真理负责，倘若原文的数据、描述甚至意念不符合事实，译者有责任予以更正。

翻译工作难免要有所舍弃，要完全满足上面所谈到的十二个因素是不可能的事情。其实，不论译者本人是否意识到，事实上他在下笔时早已心中有数。如果是较大规模的、较重要的翻译，还会事先跟委托人或者合作者进行深入讨论，以达成共识，如：

- 究竟是刻意保留原文的本来面貌，让读者多花一点功夫去认识作者，还是多换一些例子或多作一些补充解释，让作者迁就读者？
- 究竟是采用比较正式规范的文字来翻译（借此对目的语及目的语社会文化负责），还是采用较接近原文的本来面貌（"翻译腔"）的文字，来讨好某类读者？
- 究竟译者容许自己有多大的自由度，来"演绎"原文的信息？
- 究竟译者可否删去原文某些内容，来迁就委托人的需要或译文使用者的口味？

除了个别的任务有具体的要求之外，事实上原文的文体或多或少决定了翻译的态度和策略。不同的文体，翻译时都有不同的重心，一般来说，各类功能文体的着重点往往是这样的：

语篇功能	重心												文体
	作者	作者意图	信息	原文	真理	社会	沟通渠道	目的语	委托者	译者	译文使用者	译文	
1. 祈使功能							√		√		√		商业、演讲、宗教、公文
2. 表达功能	√	√	√	√									自传、诗歌、谈话
3. 描述功能					√	√							科技、新闻、法律
4. 美感功能							√	√		√		√	戏剧、诗歌、散文、小说

当然，语篇功能的划分并非泾渭分明，同一个语篇，往往有多重功能，如一本企业集团的年报，既有描述的成分（报告公司业绩及发展实况），也多少会有表达的成分（公司负责人向股东及公众吐露心声），更时常有祈使的效果（宣传政策、建立形象、改变读者的观点及态度），其中也可以甚至应该有美感的成分（部分文字有文采、艺术性的吸引力）。有些语篇可能具有隐藏的功能，如一篇医学报告表面上是描述性的科技文献，但当用于商业宣传文献之中时，实际上就变成了祈使功能的文本，即用于促销产品了。

翻译工作应该弄清楚原文的功能和译文所要求的功能（未必一样），翻译批评与赏析工作更应该依此行事。

翻译批评与赏析对于译员培训、翻译工作品质管理、翻译学的发展等都起着举足轻重的作用。翻译批评与赏析的水平如能提高，翻译事业也可以随之发扬光大。

第二部分

小说翻译的批评与赏析

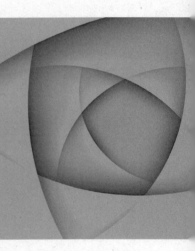

一 关于小说体裁

小说属于文学文体中的一种。除小说外，文学文体还包括散文、戏剧和诗歌等。那么，小说、诗歌和散文之间有何区别呢？这里我想引用北京大学史树生教授就此所打的比方。他说，一个人——姑且叫他为文人，吃过晚饭没有事情。他家门前有个池塘，于是一个人背着手在池塘边转，转啊转啊转，一不小心掉进池塘里了。他说这就叫小说，节外生枝。另一个人在继续转，他感到心中有一种情绪要释放，就大喊一声，这就是诗歌。还有一个人继续转，转了一圈又一圈，最后心中似乎有一种期待，但又不知期待什么，就像戴望舒的《雨巷》一样，遇到一个丁香一样的姑娘。于是，他在心中酝酿了一会儿，最后不转了，回到家泡上一壶香茗，铺开一张稿纸，若有所思地写下了一些东西，这就是散文。

但不管是散文、小说还是诗歌，虽然它们之间存在区别，但作为文学文体，在语言的使用上，它们均具有注重形象性、抒情性、含蓄性和象征性的特点。

就小说这种散文体叙事文学样式而言，其完整的"世界"由人物、情节、视角、环境、主题、基调等六个要素构成。正是这样的"世界"，使得小说能够充分展现出丰富多彩的旨趣、情境、人物性格、生活状况及至整个世界的广阔背景。

小说的特点主要体现在以下几个方面：

一是对人物进行丰富而细致的刻画。小说通过各种艺术手段，从各个角度对人物的肖像、心理、对话、行为、环境等进行描写，全方位地展现人物的音容笑貌、举止言行、衣着服饰、心理状况、思想情感以及人物同环境之间互为作用的关系。在现代小说叙事学中，小说的人物往往分为"扁型人物"和"圆型人物"。前者指"类型式人物"或"漫画式人物"，这类人物性格和心理发展比较单一，缺乏变化；后者则以其"复杂"见长，其性格、言行动机、内心世界、精神境界、气质性情等非常复杂，呈发展变化的状态，难以按照好恶标准进行简单归类（胡显耀、李力，2009：203）。

二是对情节进行完整而多变的铺叙。情节是作家对行为（即一个或一系列想象的事件）的组织安排方式，它包括开端、发展、高潮、逆转、结束等五个部分（胡显耀、李力，2009：202）。情节与故事有区别：故事主要以时间和因果的线性关系体现出来，而情节则关注言说的方式以及对线性故事行为的重新组织和安排。因不受时空限制，故在情节的铺叙方面，小说可在更大程度上做到更为完整，更具复杂性，更有连贯性（党争胜，2008：158）。这种情况在近现代小说中表现得尤其突出。

三是对叙述视角进行总体的把握。叙述视角是指"叙述时观察故事的角度"（申丹，2004）。按照人称，可分为第一人称、第二人称、第三人称叙述视角；按照视域范围，可分为全知型、参与者型、旁观者型、听众型等叙述视角（胡显耀、李力，2009：204）。第一人称叙述视角或参与者型叙述视角如《简·爱》《了不起的盖茨比》等；第三人称叙述视角、旁观者型或全知者型叙述视角如《飘》《名利场》《傲慢与偏见》等；这两种叙述视角较为常见。

在第二人称叙述视角或听众型叙述视角中,故事就是(或至少主要是)叙述者对他所称为"你"的受叙者所讲述的东西。这个"你"有可能是某一特定虚构人物,或者是故事的读者,又或者是叙述者本人,或者并非是明晰的、一以贯之的某个人(胡显耀、李力,2009:205),如美国小说家杰·麦卡爱内尼的《灯红酒绿》(*Bright Lights, Big City*)就是采用了第二人称的叙述视角。

四是对环境进行具体而独特的描写。小说中,对环境进行描写是为了拓展情节和刻画人物之需。小说中的典型环境包括人物所处时代的氛围、人与人之间的复杂关系所形成的社会环境(即文本外的大环境)、活动场所和自然景物等生活环境(即文本内的小环境),或简而言之的时间环境和空间环境。时间环境可以是现在、过去和未来,空间环境可以随着小说情节的发展和需要而不断变化。

五是对主题进行显性或隐性的揭示。主题是读者或批评家根据小说的人物、环境、情节、叙事手法等因素而概括出来的思想情感、道德价值判断、时代风貌等具有抽象化和普遍化特点的陈述(胡显耀、李力,2009:206)。作家对自己的主题有两种揭示方式,一是显性呈现,二是隐藏于作品的字里行间。前者如简·奥斯汀包括《傲慢与偏见》在内的六部以18世纪英国中产阶级青年女子的爱情、婚姻纠葛为主题的小说;后者如霍桑的《红字》,其主题是隐性的,因而晦涩、模糊、模棱两可。

六是对主基调的不断强化。任何小说都会有由小说人物、情节、环境、语言修辞、叙述策略等形成的感情综合效应,这种综合效应便是基调(英语为 mood 或 tone)。就像人的情感是多种多样的,小说的基调也是多种多样的,有悲怆的、忧郁的、荒凉的,也有明快的、欢愉的、浪漫的,还有昂扬的、幽默的、劝讽的等等。一部作品可以有不止一种次基调,但却只能有一种主基调或统摄基调。主基调往往是通过次基调得以强化。如《简·爱》的主基调是沉重却积极的,但有些章节也夹杂着欢乐或忧伤的基调。比如简和罗切斯特即将举行婚礼前的基调是欢乐明快的,但婚礼被意外取消后的基调则是悲沉的(胡显耀、李力,2009:208)。

正是小说的这些特点,使得读者在阅读的过程中能够品味到小说所塑造的人物美、所描写的环境美、所构建的情节美以及所赋予的修辞美等等。

二 小说鉴赏方法

小说是以刻画人物为中心,综合运用语言艺术的各种表现手法,通过完整的故事情节和具体的环境描写来反映社会生活的文学体裁。

小说有三个基本要素:一是通过对人物的外貌、对话、行为、心理等进行描写来对人物进行塑造;二是通过对社会生活的细致描写,来表现复杂的矛盾冲突,叙述故事的发生、发展、高潮和结局,来构筑故事情节,并在情节的发展中展现人物的性格变化;三是描写具体的社会环境,展现人物和事件产生的历史背景和社会条件,以此烘托人物、显示人物性格特征。

因此，作家总是通过他笔下的人物形象，依托其所构建的故事情节，来描绘其所处的时代，寄寓他所领悟的生活真理。而读者也只有通过人物形象的认识去把握作品所反映的生活本质。

对小说进行鉴赏可从品味其中的人物塑造美、环境描写美、情节构建美和文本修辞美等几个方面入手（党争胜，2008：159）。

一是解读故事，分析人物。

小说的独特艺术魅力体现在它塑造的具体感人的典型人物形象。这种典型的人物形象是指既具独特而鲜明的个性，又能反映一定社会的某些本质、具有某种共性的人物形象。

小说塑造人物的手段多种多样：既可正面描写，又可侧面烘托；既可进行语言、行动等直接描写，也可通过环境和细节的描写达到目的。

人物的性格和人物的行为是有机的统一，有什么样的性格就决定什么样的行为。所以，在分析人物形象时，应注意人物的行动描写。

语言是揭示人物性格特征的重要手段。俗话说：言为心声。各式各样的人物，都是通过自己独特的、个性化的语言来反映各自不同的性格。从人物语言入手，可以很好地把握人物形象的性格特征。

心理活动也是人物本性的再现，外貌描写也可反映人物内心，揭示人物性格，这些在分析人物时都应引起我们的重视。

另外，小说的故事情节又是由小说人物的性格、言行生发出来的一个个事件的有序组合。情节同性格的关系是：性格决定情节，情节表现性格并推动性格的发展。欣赏小说，就要在解读情节的基础上进一步分析和理解人物的性格和命运。

二是把握环境，感受氛围。

就像在现实中一样，小说中人物的存在也离不开环境。由于小说是时间和空间的艺术，这里的空间主要指的就是环境。环境是塑造人物性格，并驱使其行动的特定场所。环境包括自然环境和社会环境。

自然环境指人物活动的时间、地点、时令、气候、地理风貌等。它常常是为制造气氛，衬托人物的情趣、心境，表现人物的心理等而安排的，通常带有作者的感情色彩，被认为是社会环境的暗示。社会环境是指人物活动、事件发生、情节展开的社会背景、历史条件、风土人情、时代风貌、社会关系、政治经济等状况。描写社会环境的目的是交代故事的时代背景、渲染故事的环境气氛、烘托人物的突出特点、暗示人物的前途命运、推动情节的发展变化、深化小说的主题思想。

环境决定并影响人物的性格，同时，人物性格也对环境产生一定影响。在具体作品中，环境常常呈现出不同的表现形态。

另外，欣赏小说还要注意感受它的艺术氛围。所谓"艺术氛围"就是"主体心灵和客观对象相互交感而晕化出来，同时又渗透于各个构成部分之中并成为涵盖整个作品的一种意味、品性。"（蔡良骥，1996：36）它既是具体的，又是模糊的；既缺少形式感，却又是能够把握的；既可以感受到，却又不能置于眉睫；既可以意会，却又难以言传。（蔡良骥，1996：36）就一部小说而言，有了氛围，就能产生良好的艺术效应，就具有了情绪的渗透性和感应力。（蔡良骥，1996：37）

三是理解主题，欣赏技巧。

在把握小说中人物形象的刻画和环境描写的同时，领悟并体味作者在人物形象的描写和故事情节的展开中所寄寓的主题，这也是人物形象背后蕴含的艺术底蕴。小说的主题就是作家在描写和叙述人物性格及人物命运的过程中提炼出来的对生活的深入理解和理性认识，是从小说描写的具体内容中概括出来的思想意义。

欣赏小说就是要注意把握那些有因果关系的细节和事件，从而看出作家对生活的理解和认识，因为小说的主题就隐含在小说的因果情节和人物描写里面。这种对生活事件和人物命运的理性认识和小说作家的主观思想意图有直接联系，作家的思想认识和创作时的主观意图深刻地影响着小说主题的形成。但是，小说的主题又不直接等同于作家的创作意图。这两者有着既相互联系又相互区别的复杂关系。有时，小说主题艺术地传达了作家的主观意图，就使得这两者基本相同。有时，小说主题并没有完全传达作家的主观意图，就可以说是"小说主题小于主观意图"。有时，小说作品因写活了人物，写透了事件，小说的人物和事件便按照自己的生活逻辑发展，他们有了自己的艺术生命，显露了一些连作家自己都没有意识到的内涵底蕴，就可以说这是"小说主题大于主观意图"。小说主题与作家的创作意图之间的既联系又有区别的关系证明，小说主题包含着"形象客观"和"作家主观"两种成分。小说作家在表达主观意图时有参差不齐的艺术水平，这使得小说读者在鉴赏小说主题时会出现种种复杂的情形。

三 关于小说翻译

小说中所使用的语言丰富多彩。小说可以说是其他各种文学体裁话语形式的集大成者，比如小说中有诗歌，有书信，有口语体的对话，有书面体的散文式表达，有典雅华美之词，有粗俗龌龊之语，凡此种种。因此，小说翻译对译者提出了极高要求。

作为译者，要善于体味小说的艺术技巧，如人物塑造、情节设计、叙述角度、叙述节奏、结构形态、话语模式等等。

胡显耀、李力（2009：212-229）就小说翻译的基本方法进行了归纳。具体如下：

一是关注人物语言个性的翻译。小说中往往充满了对话。小说作者也是通过对话来揭示各个人物的形象的。俗话说：言为心声，言如其人。作为译者，就是要善于品味原作字里行间的信息，最大限度地再现小说人物各自独特的言说方式，从而将人物的性格和本质充分地揭示出来。

二是关注人物形象塑造的翻译。小说往往会塑造大量栩栩如生、风姿各异的人物形象。人物塑造包括肖像描写、行动描写和心理描写等方式。而这些人物形象的塑造,是通过最为灵动的文学语言来呈现的,小说也正是因为这些灵动的文学语言而魅力无穷。作为译者,就是要把握原文作者的意图,领会原文作者在进行人物塑造时所使用语言的各种意义,并进行充分传达,以便成功实现人物形象塑造的翻译。

三是关注小说修辞的翻译。小说是语言的艺术。作家在小说中往往会使用神韵皆备的语言艺术,这其中就包括修辞。修辞包括积极修辞和消极修辞。前者主要是对各种修辞格的有效运用,后者是为了传达特别用意而对各种句法结构的灵活运用。对小说修辞的翻译就是不仅仅应当译出原语文本的意义,更要传达出原语文本的韵味,使译文与原作形神毕肖。

四是关注小说文体风格的翻译。奈达曾将翻译定义为"在译语当中使用最贴近的自然对应语来再现原语信息,首先是在意义方面,其次是在风格方面"[2]。我们认为,对小说风格的翻译要高于意义层面的翻译。要在译文当中保留原作的风格是非常不易的,但作为译者,首先应该吃透原作的风格,进而在译文当中努力再现出来。

五是关注小说叙事视角的翻译。小说在叙述视角上常由单一的叙述视角转变为多种视角,由以全知视角为主的方式向多声部"复调"的方式转化。这种多视角叙述将各种叙述视角的优势兼收并蓄、有效组合,为读者提供了多维的阅读空间,使读者真切地感受到艺术世界的真实存在。作为译者,就应该在翻译过程中特别注意叙述视角的变化,将叙述视角看作是翻译过程中力求再现的重要内容。

---

[2] 英语原文为: Translation consists in reproducing in the receptor language the closest natural equivalent of the source language message, first in terms of meaning and secondly in terms of style.

第一章 Pride and Prejudice 汉译文片段的批评赏析

一 关于 Pride and Prejudice

美国著名文艺评论家埃德蒙·威尔逊曾说,最近一百多年以来,英国文学史上出现过几次趣味革命,文学口味的翻新影响了几乎所有作家的声誉,唯有莎士比亚和简·奥斯汀经久不衰。文艺评论家乔治·亨利·刘易斯也说,简·奥斯汀堪称是"散文中的莎士比亚"(Prose Shakespeare)。

简·奥斯汀(1775—1817)在其短促的一生中为后人留下了六部篇幅不大的小说。《傲慢与偏见》是其中的第二部。该小说虽然主要篇幅都是谈婚论嫁,但通常不被看作爱情小说,而被看作是世态(或风俗)小说。该小说历经两个多世纪的阅读和批评,却始终能够引起读者长盛不衰、雅俗共赏的兴趣,实属世界文库中不可多得的珍品。因其脍炙人口,毛姆将其列为世界十大小说名著之一。

小说写成于1796年,以伊丽莎白与达西的爱情为主线,讲述了四对男女不同类型的爱情

二 Pride and Prejudice 原文片段及四种汉译文

原 文	译文一	译文二
It is a truth universally acknowledged that a single man in possession of a good fortune must be in want of a wife. However little known the feelings or views of such a man may be on his first entering a neighborhood, this truth is so well fixed in the minds of the surrounding families, that he is considered as the rightful	凡是有钱的单身汉,总想娶位太太,这已经成了一条举世公认的真理。 这样的单身汉,每逢新搬到一个地方,四邻八舍虽然完全不了解他的性情如何,见解如何,可是,既然这样的一条真理早已在人们心目中根深蒂固,因此人们总是把他看作自己某一个女儿理所应得的一笔财产。	有钱的单身汉总要娶位太太,这是一条举世公认的真理。 这条真理还真够深入人心的,每逢这样的单身汉新搬到一个地方,四邻八舍的人家尽管对他的性情见识一无所知,却把他视为自己某一个女儿的合法财产。

与婚姻，深刻揭露了物质因素在婚姻关系、人际关系中所起的决定性作用。小说情节错综复杂，引人入胜；人物刻画惟妙惟肖。

　　小说中的语言都经过精心选择，处处透露着机智与幽默。这一切毫无疑问是作家本人才智的自然流露，这不仅表现在她对人物性格的把握上，更表现在作品的戏剧风格与对话安排上。小说的字里行间俯拾即是的都是基于她那过人的智力和才情而充分传达出的幽默与讽刺。这种幽默与讽刺也可称为整部小说的灵魂。

　　小说一开头，作者就直接用言语反讽把整部小说的主题烘托出来。接下来第二段这样描述道："每逢这样的未婚男子搬到一个新地方，不管左邻右舍的人们对于他的性情或者见识是多么地一无所知，但由于这一真理在周围人的心中早已根深蒂固，他就往往被看作是自己某个女儿理所应得的财产。"这样，言语层次上的反讽意味就更加昭然若揭了。于是乎，读者完全明白了：不是腰缠万贯的单身汉一定会娶一个媳妇儿，而是尚未婚嫁的女子一定要嫁个腰缠万贯的男子。从这个开头开始，作者就运用言语反讽来凸显小说的主题，把婚姻和财产紧密结合起来。随着情节的一步步展开，感情的纠葛随之发展，反讽的手法也一直如影随形，最终完成一桩又一桩的婚姻。

　　这里选取了小说的第一章，并将王科一和孙致礼两位译家的译文放在这里让读者进行对比。在小说的第一章当中，班纳特先生和班纳特太太之间的对话充满了浓烈的讽刺味道。对于译者来说，将这种讽刺意味充分再现出来应是着力达到的目标。

译文三	译文四	笔　记
有钱的单身汉必定想娶亲，这条真理无人不晓。	寰宇间有这样一条公认的真理：凡腰缠万贯的未婚男子一定会娶一个媳妇儿。	
这种人初到一地时，别看其喜好或想法如何谁都不甚了了，但由于这条真理在左邻右舍的头脑中根深蒂固，家家都会心想他理所当然应属于自己哪个女儿所有。	每逢这样的未婚男子搬到一个新地方，不管左邻右舍对于他的性情或者见识了解得是多么地不足，但由于这一真理在周围人们的心目中早已根深蒂固，他就往往被看作是自己某个女儿理所应得的财产。	

原 文	译文一	译文二
property of some one or other of their daughters.		
"My dear Mr. Bennet," said his lady to him one day, "have you heard that Netherfield Park is let at last?"	有一天，班纳特太太对她的丈夫说："我的好老爷，尼日斐花园终于租出去了，你听说过没有？"	"亲爱的贝纳特先生，"一天，贝纳特太太对丈夫说："你有没有听说内瑟菲尔德庄园终于租出去了？"
Mr. Bennet replied that he had not.	班纳特先生回答道，他没有听说过。	贝纳特先生回答道，没有听说。
"But it is," returned she, "for Mrs. Long has just been here, and she told me all about it."	"的确租出去了，"她说，"朗格太太刚刚上这儿来过，她把这件事的底细，一五一十地都告诉了我。"	"的确租出去了，"太太说道，"朗太太刚刚来过，她把这事一五一十地全告诉我了。"
Mr. Bennet made no answer.	班纳特先生没有理睬她。	贝纳特先生没有答话。
"Do not you want to know who has taken it?" cried his wife impatiently.	"你难道不想知道是谁租去的吗？"太太不耐烦地嚷起来了。	"难道你不想知道是谁租去的吗？"太太不耐烦地嚷道。
"You want to tell me, and I have no objection to hearing it."	"既是你要说给我听，我听听也无妨。"	"既是你想告诉我，我听也无妨。"
This was invitation enough.	这句话足够鼓励她讲下去了。	这句话足以逗引太太讲下去了。
"Why, my dear, you must know, Mrs. Long says that Netherfield is taken by a young man of large fortune from the north of England; that he came down on Monday in a chaise and four to see the place, and was so much delighted with it that he agreed with Mr. Mooris immediately; that he is to take possession before Michaelmas, and some of his servants are to be in the	"哦，亲爱的，你得知道，朗格太太说，租尼日斐花园的是个阔少爷，他是英格兰北部的人；听说他星期一那天，乘着一辆驷马大轿车来看房子，看得非常中意，当场就和莫里斯先生谈妥了；他要在"米迦勒节"以前般进来，打算下个周末先叫几个佣人来住。"	"哦，亲爱的，你应该知道，朗太太说，内瑟菲尔德让英格兰北部的一个阔少爷租去了；他星期一那天乘坐一辆驷马马车来看房子，看得非常中意，当下就和莫里斯先生讲妥了；他打算在米迦勒节以前搬进新居，下周末以前打发几个佣人先住进来。"

译文三

　　一天，贝内特先生的太太问他道：
　　"亲爱的，内瑟菲尔德园已经租出去了，你听说了么？"

　　贝内特先生说还没有。

　　太太接着道：
　　"当真租出去了。朗太太刚刚来过，我全是听她说的。"

　　贝内特先生没有吭声。

　　他太太忍不住提高嗓门说：
　　"是谁租了你就不想知道么？"
　　"是你想说给我听，我又没说不愿听。"

　　这一来贝内特太太上了劲。

　　"哼，告诉你吧，亲爱的，听朗太太说，租下内瑟菲尔德的是个年轻人，很有钱，原住在英格兰北边。星期一他坐了辆四匹马拉的车来看房子，中意得很，马上就与莫里斯先生谈定了。他本人准备搬来过米迦勒节[1]，有几个仆人下周末先住进来。"

译文四

　　"我说班纳特先生，"一天，班纳特太太对丈夫说，"您听说没有？内瑟菲尔德庄园终于租出去了。"

　　班纳特先生说没听说。

　　"但真的租出去了，"班纳特太太说，"因为朗格太太刚来过这儿，她把出租的事儿全都告诉我啦。"

　　班纳特先生没有理会。

　　"难道您不想知道是谁租去了吗？"班纳特太太不耐烦地嚷了起来。

　　"是你想告诉我的，我就听你讲给我听呗。"

　　这句话让她可来劲儿了。

　　"您知道吗班纳特先生，朗格太太说，内瑟菲尔德被一个阔少爷租去了，他是英格兰北部人；还说星期一那天他乘驷马大轿车来看了庄园，对庄园非常满意，当场就和莫里斯先生敲定了；还说他要赶在'米迦勒节'之前搬过来，几个仆人下周末之前就要住进来呢。"

第二部分　小说翻译的批评与赏析

原文	译文一	译文二
house by the end of next week."		
"What is his name?"	"这人叫什么名字？"	"他姓什么？"
"Bingley."	"彬格莱。"	"宾利。"
"Is he married or single?"	"有太太的呢，还是个单身汉？"	"成亲了还是单身？"
"Oh! Single, my dear, to be sure! A single man of large fortune; four or five thousand a year. What a fine thing for our girls!"	"噢！是个单身汉，亲爱的，确确实实是个单身汉！一个有钱的单身汉；每年有四五千镑的收入。真是女儿们的福气！"	"哦！单身，亲爱的，千真万确！一个有钱的单身汉，每年有四五千镑的收入。真是女儿们的好福气！"
"How so? How can it affect them?"	"这怎么说？关女儿们什么事？"	"这是怎么说？跟女儿们有什么关系？"
"My dear Mr. Bennet," replied his wife, "how can you be so tiresome! You must know that I am thinking of his marrying one of them."	"我的好老爷，"太太回答道，"你怎么这么叫人讨厌！告诉你吧，我正在盘算，他要是挑中我们的一个女儿做老婆，可多好！"	"亲爱的贝纳特先生，"太太答道，"你怎么这么令人讨厌！告诉你吧，我正在思谋他娶她们中的一个做太太呢！"
"Is that his design in settling here?"	"他住到这儿来，就是为了这个打算吗？"	"他搬到这里就是为了这个打算？"
"Design! Nonsense, how can you talk so! But it is very likely that he may fall in love with one of them, and therefore you must visit him as soon as he comes."	"打算！胡扯，这是哪儿的话！不过，他倒作兴看中我们的某一个女儿呢。他一搬来，你就得去拜访拜访他。"	"打算！胡扯，你怎么能这么说话！不过，他兴许会看中她们中的哪一个呢，因此，他一来你就得去拜访他。"
"I see no occasion for that. You and the girls may go, or you may send them by themselves, which perhaps will be still better, for as you are as handsome as any of them, Mr. Bingley	"我不用去。你带着女儿们去就得啦，要不你干脆打发她们自己去，那或许倒更好些，因为你跟女儿们比起来，她们哪一个都不能胜过你的美貌，你去了，彬格莱先生倒可能挑	"我看没有那个必要。你带着女儿们去就行啦，要不你索性打发她们自己去，这样或许更好些，因为你的姿色并不亚于她们中的任何一个，你一去，宾利先生倒作兴看中你呢。"

译文三	译文四
"这人姓什么？"	"他姓什么？"
"宾利。"	"彬格莱。"
"结了婚还是单身？"	"结婚了还是未婚？"
"哟，单身，亲爱的，这还用问？是个有钱的单身汉，一年四五千。我们几个女儿的福气来了！"	"噢，未婚啦亲爱的，千真万确！还是个腰缠万贯的未婚男呢，一年的收入就有四五千。这对我们的几个女儿可是大好事儿呀！"
"说到哪里去了！这跟她们有什么相关？"	"这话怎么讲？这与我们的几个女儿有什么关系？"
"哎呀呀，我的好先生，"贝内特太太说道，"你怎么这样讨人嫌？你明知故问，哪会不知道我在盘算着把哪个女儿嫁给他！"	"我亲爱的班纳特先生，"班纳特太太回答说，"您怎么就那么不开窍呢！您就没想到我正盘算着他能娶走我们的某个女儿吗？"
"难道他搬到这里来就是为了这桩事？"	"这就是他搬来庄园的用意？"
"为这桩事！胡说！你怎么讲出这种话来？不过呢，他看中我们的哪个女儿倒很可能。所以，等他一来，你非得拜访一趟不可。"	"用意？胡说八道！怎么能说用意呢？但很可能他会爱上我们的某个女儿嘛。也就是说，他一住到庄园里来，您就得去拜访拜访他。"
"我去一趟没有必要，你可以带着几个女儿去。要不然，你让她们自己去，说不定这样更好。要论长相漂亮，你跟她们哪个比都不差，你们一道去，宾利先生最看得中	"我看没这必要吧。你和女儿们去吧，或者你让她们自己去可能会更好些，因为你跟她们一样美丽动人，你跟她们去，彬格莱先生倒有可能喜欢上你呢。"

原文	译文一	译文二
might like you the best of the party."	中你呢。"	
"My dear, you flatter me. I certainly have had my share of beauty, but I do not pretend to be any thing extraordinary now. When a woman has five grown up daughters, she ought to give over thinking of her own beauty."	"我的好老爷,你太捧我啦。从前也的确有人赞赏过我的美貌,现在我可不敢说有什么出众的地方了。一个女人家有了五个成年的女儿,就不该对自己的美貌再转什么念头。"	"亲爱的,你太抬举我啦。我以前确实有过美貌的时候,不过现在却不敢硬充有什么出众的地方了。一个女人家有了五个成年的女儿,就不该对自己的美貌再转什么念头了。"
"In such cases, a woman has not often much beauty to think of."	"这样看来,一个女人家对自己的美貌也转不了多少念头喽。"	"这么说来,女人家对自己的美貌也转不了多久的念头啦。"
"But, my dear, you must indeed go and see Mr. Bingley when he comes into the neighbourhood."	"不过,我的好老爷,彬格莱一搬到我们的邻近来,你的确应该去看看他。"	"不过,亲爱的,宾利先生一搬到这里,你可真得去见见他。"
"It is more than I engage for, I assure you."	"老实跟你说吧,这不是我分内的事。"	"告诉你吧,这事我可不能答应。"
"But consider your daughters. Only think what an establishment it would be for one of them. Sir William and Lady Lucas are determined to go, merely on that account, for in general, you know they visit no new comers. Indeed you must go, for it will be impossible for us to visit him, if you do not."	"看女儿的分上吧。只请你想一想,她们不论哪一个,要是攀上了这样一个人家,够多么好。威廉爵士夫妇已经决定去拜望他,他们也无非是这个用意。你知道,他们通常是不会拜望新搬来的邻居的。你的确应该去一次,要是你不去,叫我们怎么去。"	"可你要为女儿们着想呀。请你想一想,她们谁要是嫁给他,那会是多好的一门亲事。威廉爵士夫妇打定主意要去,还不就是为了这个缘故,因为你知道,他们通常是不去拜访新搬来的邻居的。你真应该去一次,要不然,我们母女就没法去见他了。"
"You are over-scrupulous, surely. I dare say Mr. Bingley will be very glad to see you; and I will send a few lines by you to assure him of my hearty consent	"你实在过分心思啦。彬格莱先生一定高兴看到你的;我可以写封信给你带去,就说随便他挑中我哪一	"你实在多虑了。宾利先生一定会很高兴见到你的。我可以写封信让你带去,就说他随便想娶我哪位女儿,我都会欣然同意。不过,我要为小莉

译文三

的倒可能是你。"

"得了吧,你是想奉承我。当年我确实长得漂亮,可是现在我没什么可夸了。五个女儿都已长大成人,不该再想自己漂不漂亮。"

"到了这种地步,一个女儿大概也没多少漂亮好想了。"

"这事就别谈了吧,但是等宾利先生搬来了以后,无论如何你得去看看他。"

"老实说吧,这我可不会答应。"

"你就不为几个女儿着想?算计算计吧,哪个女儿嫁给他不是门好亲事。威廉爵士夫妇俩说定了要双双去走一趟,还不就打的那主意?你是知道的,新搬来了人,一般的他们都不登门。说正经话,你非去不可,你不去我们母女没法上他的门。"

"你也太顾虑重重了。我可以肯定,宾利先生见到你一定高兴。我写几行字让你带去,就告诉他,无论他挑中哪个女儿,我都打心底里乐意他娶过

译文四

"亲爱的,您这可太捧我啦!我的确也曾漂亮过,可如今,我可不能再装着自己有什么特别之处啦。毕竟,一个女人生了五个女儿,而且她们都长成大姑娘了,哪还敢对自己曾经的漂亮打什么主意呀?"

"这样呀,那这个女人也没有什么漂亮可言的。"

"不过亲爱的,彬格莱先生一搬过来,您的确要去看看他吧。"

"我告诉你,这可不是我的分内事儿。"

"可你也得看在女儿们的分上呀!你就想想,她们中哪一个嫁给他不会享尽荣华富贵的呀。威廉爵士夫妇决定去拜访他,就是这个意思。你知道的,他们一般是不会去拜访新近搬来的邻居的。的确你应该去,你去了,我们才能去拜访他呀。"

"你的心思可太足啦,真的太足啦。我敢说,彬格莱先生一定会很高兴看到你的;我可以写封信让你捎给他,向他保证:不论他选中我的哪个女

笔 记

第二部分 小说翻译的批评与赏析

原　文	译文一	译文二
to his marrying which ever he chooses of the girls; though I must throw in a good word for my little Lizzy." "I desire you will do no such thing. Lizzy is not a bit better than the others; and I am sure she is not half so handsome as Jane, nor half so good humoured as Lydia. But you are always giving her the preference." "They have none of them much to recommend them," replied he; "they are all silly and ignorant like other girls; but Lizzy has something more of quickness than her sisters." "Mr. Bennet, how can you abuse your own children in such way? You take delight in vexing me. You have no compassion on my poor nerves." "You mistake me, my dear. I have a high respect for your nerves. They are my old friends. I have heard you mention them with consideration these twenty years at least." "Ah! You do not know what I suffer." "But I hope you will get over it, and live to see many young men	个女儿，我都心甘情愿地答应他把她娶过去；不过，我在信上得特别替小丽萃吹嘘几句。" "我希望你别这么做。丽萃没有一点儿地方胜过别的几个女儿；我敢说，论漂亮，她抵不上吉英一半；论性子，好抵不上丽迪雅一半。你可老是偏爱她。" "她们没有哪一个值得夸奖的，"他回答道；"她们跟人家的姑娘一样，又傻，又无知；倒是丽萃要比她的几个姐妹伶俐些。" "我的好老爷，你怎么舍得这样糟蹋自己的亲生女儿？你是在故意叫我气恼，好让你自己得意吧。你半点儿也不体谅我的神经衰弱。" "你真错怪了我，我的好太太。我非常尊重你的神经。它们是我的老朋友。至少在最近二十年以来，我一直听到你郑重其事地提到它们。" "啊！你不知道我怎样受苦呢！" "不过我希望你这毛病会	齐美言两句。" "我希望你别做这种事。莉齐丝毫不比别的女儿强。我敢说，论漂亮，她远远及不上简；论性子，她远远及不上莉迪亚。可你总是偏爱她。" "她们哪一个也没有多少好称道的，"贝纳特先生答道。"她们像别人家的姑娘一样，一个个又傻又蠢，倒是莉齐比几个姐妹伶俐些。" "贝纳特先生，你怎么能这样糟蹋自己的孩子？你就喜欢气我，压根儿不体谅我那脆弱的神经。" "你怪错我了，亲爱的。我非常尊重你的神经。它们是我的老朋友啦。至少在这二十年里，我总是听见你郑重其事地说起它们。" "唉！你不知道我受多大的罪。" "我希望你会好起来，亲眼看见好多每年有四千镑收入

译文三

去，只不过在信里我得替小宝贝利齐[2]特地美言两句。"

"这种事我看你别干为好。与几个姐妹比，利齐没有哪点强。论漂亮，我看她绝对赶不上简一半，论活泼她又及不到莉迪亚一半，可是你总对她存着偏心。"

"她们没一个有多少值得夸的，"贝内特先生说，"全都傻乎乎，什么都不懂，跟别人家女孩儿没两样。姐姐妹妹几个就数利齐比起来有几分聪明。"

"你怎么能把自己亲生女儿贬得这样低？你就爱说惹我生气的话。明明知道我的神经受不起刺激，你偏不体贴我。"

"亲爱的，你别误会。我老惦挂着的就是你的神经。你那几根神经都成了我的老朋友了。你一谈起神经就心焦，至少这20年里我听得多。"

"哎，我的苦处你哪里会知道。"

"可是我总希望你的毛病会好，活着看到好些一年有

译文四

儿，我打心眼里都同意把她嫁给他。不过我要为我的小黎姿多美言几句。"

"我倒希望你别做这样的事儿。黎姿可不如她的其他几个姐妹；论美貌，我看她连简恩的一半都赶不上；论性子，她没有丽迪亚一半好。可你老是偏爱她。"

"她们当中没有一个值得夸奖的，"班纳特先生回答说，"她们同其他女孩儿一样，一个个既愚蠢，又无知，倒是黎姿比她的几个姐妹要更有些灵气。"

"班纳特先生！你怎么能这样损你的女儿？你这是有意要气我，自己爽吧。你对我那脆弱的神经有没有一点同情心啦！"

"你这可错怪我啦，亲爱的。我可高度尊重你的神经，它们可是我的老朋友啦。至少最近二十年，我听到你一再煞有介事地提到它们。"

"唉！你哪里知道我受的苦呀！"

"不过我倒希望你很快康复起来，你活着，就能看见一

笔 记

原　文	译文一	译文二
of four thousand a year come into the neighbourhood." "It will be no use to us if twenty such should come, since you will not visit them." "Depend upon it, my dear, that when there are twenty I will visit them all." Mr. Bennet was so odd a mixture of quick parts, sarcastic humour, reserve, and caprice, that the experience of three and twenty years had been insufficient to make his wife understand his character. Her mind was less difficult to develope. She was a woman of mean understanding, little information, and uncertain temper. When she was discontented, she fancied herself nervous. The business of her life was to get her daughters married; its solace was visiting and news. (Jane Austen, *Pride and Prejudice*, Vol. I, Chapter 1)	好起来，那么，像这种每年有四千镑收入的阔少爷，你就可以眼看着他们一个个搬来做你的邻居了。" "你既然不愿意去拜望他们，即使有二十个搬来，对我们又有什么好处！" "放心吧，我的好太太，等到有了二十个，我一定去一个个拜望到。" 班纳特先生真是个古怪人，他一方面喜欢插科打诨，爱挖苦人，同时又不苟言笑，变幻莫测，真使得他那位太太积二十三年之经验，还摸不透他的性格。太太的脑子是很容易加以分析的。她是个智力贫乏、不学无术、喜怒无常的女人，只要碰到不称心的事，她就自以为神经衰弱。她生平的大事就是嫁女儿；她生平的安慰就是访友拜客和打听新闻。 （王科一　译，1980）	的阔少爷搬到这一带。" "既然你不肯去拜访，即使搬来二十个，那对我们又有什么用。" "放心吧，亲爱的，等到搬来二十个，我一定去挨个拜访。" 贝纳特先生是个古怪人，一方面乖觉诙谐，好挖苦人，另一方面又不苟言笑，变幻莫测，他太太积二十三年之经验，还摸不透他的性格。这位太太的脑子就不那么难以捉摸了。她是个智力贫乏、孤陋寡闻、喜怒无常的女人。一碰到不称心的时候，就自以为神经架不住。她人生的大事，是把女儿们嫁出去；她人生的快慰是访亲拜友和打听消息。 （孙致礼　译，1990）

译文三

4 000镑收入的富家子弟搬到这地方来。"

"你不上他们的门,搬来20个也没用。"

"你放心好了,亲爱的,要是有20个搬来,我都要登门拜访。"

贝内特先生就是这么个怪物,头脑灵活,口舌尖酸,但又遇事能沉住气,且变化无常,所以他太太与他相处了23年都没有能够摸清楚他性格的底细。太太的头脑没那么顶用。这女人缺乏悟性,孤陋寡闻,肝火偏旺。一遇到不顺心的事,就以为神经出了毛病。她一生的大事是把几个女儿嫁出去,唯一的爱好是出门做客,打听新闻。

(张经浩 译)

[1] 米迦勒节(Michaelmas),在每年的9月29日,英国的四个结账日之一,租约多于此日履行。
[2] 利齐(Lizzy)是二女儿伊丽莎白(Elizabeth)的爱称。

译文四

个个年收入四千英镑的阔少爷搬来做你的邻居呀。"

"你又不去拜访他们,哪怕来二十个阔少爷,对我们又有什么用?"

"我给你打包票,亲爱的,如果有二十个阔少爷搬过来,我会一一造访的。"

班纳特先生就是这么怪里怪气的。他思维敏捷、好挖苦人、不苟言笑、难以捉摸。班纳特太太同他生活了二十三年,但这并不足以让她摸透他的性格。而她本人的心思倒并不那么难以琢磨。她这女人理解力差、见识短浅、喜怒无常,一不顺心,就自认为神经衰弱。她一生的事业就是把女儿们嫁出去,一生的快慰就是访亲拜友、打探消息。

(李明 译)

三 小说翻译的批评与赏析练习

原文

In consequence of an agreement between the sisters, Elizabeth wrote the next morning to her mother, to beg that the carriage might be sent for them in the course of the day. But Mrs. Bennet, who had calculated on her daughters remaining at Netherfield till the following Tuesday, which would exactly finish Jane's week, could not bring herself to receive them with pleasure before. Her answer, therefore, was not propitious, at least not to Elizabeth's wishes, for she was impatient to get home. Mrs. Bennet sent them word that they could not possibly have the carriage before Tuesday; and in her postscript it was added that, if Mr. Bingley and his sister pressed them to stay longer, she could spare them very well. —Against staying longer, however, Elizabeth was positively resolved—nor did she much expect it would be asked; and fearful, on the contrary, as being considered as intruding themselves needlessly long, she urged Jane to borrow Mr. Bingley's carriage immediately, and at length it was settled that their original design of leaving Netherfield that morning should be mentioned, and the

译文一

贝纳特家姐妹俩商定之后，第二天早晨伊丽莎白便给母亲写信，请她当天就派车来接她们。可是，贝纳特太太早就盘算让女儿们在内瑟菲尔德待到下星期二，以便让简正好住满一个星期，因此说什么也不乐意提前接她们回家。所以，她的回信写得也不令人满意，至少使伊丽莎白感到不中意，因为她急于回家。贝纳特太太在信里说，星期二以前不能派车去接她们。她在信后又补充了一句：如果宾利兄妹挽留她们多住几天，她完全没有意见。怎奈伊丽莎白坚决不肯再待下去——也不大指望主人家挽留她们。她只怕人家嫌她们赖在那里不走，便催促简马上去向宾利先生借马车。两人最后决定向主人家表明，她们当天上午就想离开内瑟菲尔德，而且提出了想借马车。

译文二

姐妹俩已经商量好了，第二天早晨，伊丽莎白就给母亲写了封信，恳求她当天派马车前来接她们。但由于班纳特太太原先就指望两个女儿在内瑟菲尔德呆到下星期二，那样的话，珍妮就刚好住满一星期，所以，她怎么也不愿意把她们提前接回家。因此，她回信时就没有答应派马车的事，至少没有像伊丽莎白所希望的那样派马车，因为她是归心似箭。班纳特太太回信说，星期二之前没可能派马车；同时她还在附言中补充道，如果彬格莱兄妹俩要留她们多住几天，她不会怪罪他们的。然而，伊丽莎白主意已定，不愿再呆下去。而且，她也没太指望主人挽留她们。相反，她还害怕别人嫌她俩住得太久而打乱了别人的生活，于是就催珍妮立马向彬格莱先生借马车。最后，她们决定当天上午向他们说明离开内瑟菲尔德的最初打算，然后再提借马车的事情。

原　文	译文一	译文二
request made.

The communication excited many professions of concern; and enough was said of wishing them to stay at least till the following day, to work on Jane; and till the morrow their going was deferred. Miss Bingley was then sorry that she had proposed the delay, for her jealousy and dislike of one sister much exceeded her affection for the other.

The master of the house heard with real sorrow that they were to go so soon, and repeatedly tried to persuade Miss Bennet that it would not be safe for her—that she was not enough recovered; but Jane was firm where she felt herself to be right.

To Mr. Darcy it was welcome intelligence—Elizabeth had been at Netherfield long enough. She attracted him more than he liked—and Miss Bingley was uncivil to her, and more teasing than usual to himself. He wisely resolved to be particularly careful that no sign of admiration should now escape him, nothing that could elevate her with the hope of influencing his felicity; sensible that if such an idea had | 主人家听到这话，表示百般关切，一再希望她们至少待到明天，简让他们说服了。于是，姐妹俩便推迟到明天再走。这时，宾利小姐又后悔自己不该挽留她们，因为她对伊丽莎白的嫉妒和厌恶，大大超过了对简的喜爱。

宾利先生听说这姐妹俩这么快就走，心里感到非常遗憾，再三劝告贝纳特小姐，说马上走不大稳妥——她还没有痊愈。可是简不管什么事，只要觉得对头，总是坚定不移。

在达西先生看来，这倒是条喜讯——伊丽莎白在内瑟菲尔德待得够久了。她太让他着迷了，迷得有些过分——再说，宾利小姐对她也不礼貌，而且越来越拿他自己开心。为了谨慎起见，他决定要特别小心，眼下决不要流露出任何爱慕之情，免得激起她的非分之想，以为她能左右他达西的终身幸福。他意识到，假若她真存有这种念头，那他最后一天的行为就至关重要了，不是起到助 | 这话一说出来，大家便纷纷关心备至。大家七嘴八舌，希望她们就是为珍妮的病情着想也要至少呆到第二天。于是就推迟到第二天她们才开始行程。彬格莱小姐这时则懊悔自己当时为什么要提出推迟行期，因为她嫉妒伊丽莎白，讨厌伊丽莎白，而对珍妮则倍加珍爱。

彬格莱先生听说她们这么快就要走，心里真的感到很难受，他一再劝班纳特小姐，这时走很危险，因为她还未完全康复；但珍妮对自己认准的事情总是坚定不移。

对达西先生来说，这可是利好的消息，因为伊丽莎白在内瑟菲尔德已经呆了够长的时间了。他现在与其说是喜欢她，不如说是垂青于她，可彬格莱小姐对她却毫不客气，而对他本人，则是一反常态地予以捉弄。于是他做出聪明的决定：一定要特别谨慎，现在决不能丝毫流露出对伊丽莎白的爱慕之情，决不能长她的志气，让她以为可以左右他的幸福。同时还要反应敏捷，如果先前让 |

第二部分　小说翻译的批评与赏析

原　文	译文一	译文二

原文：

been suggested, his behaviour during the last day must have material weight in confirming or crushing it. Steady to his purpose, he scarcely spoke ten words to her through the whole of Saturday, and though they were at one time left by themselves for half an hour, he adhered most conscientiously to his book, and would not even look at her.

On Sunday, after morning service, the separation, so agreeable to almost all, took place. Miss Bingley's civility to Elizabeth increased at last very rapidly, as well as her affection for Jane; and when they parted, after assuring the latter of the pleasure it would always give her to see her either at Longbourn or Netherfield, and embracing her most tenderly, she even shook hands with the former. —Elizabeth took leave of the whole party in the liveliest spirits.

They were not welcomed home very cordially by their mother. Mrs. Bennet wondered at their coming, and thought them very wrong to give so much trouble, and was sure Jane would have caught cold again. —But their father, though very laconic in his expressions of pleasure,

译文一：

长的作用，便是起到扼杀的作用。他心里打定了主意，行动上也能加以坚持，星期六一整天简直没跟她说上几句话，虽然他俩一度单独在一起待了半个钟头，他却在聚精会神地看书，瞧也没瞧她一眼。

星期日做过晨祷之后，贝纳特家两姐妹告辞了，大家几乎个个都很高兴。到了最后关头，宾利小姐对伊丽莎白骤然越发客气了，对简也越发亲热了。分手的时候，她先跟简说，希望以后能在朗伯恩或者内瑟菲尔德与她重逢，接着又十分亲切地拥抱了她一番，最后甚至还与伊丽莎白握了握手。伊丽莎白兴高采烈地告别了大家。

回到家里，母亲并不怎么热诚地欢迎她们。贝纳特太太奇怪她们怎么回来啦，埋怨她们不该惹那么多麻烦，硬说简一准又伤风了。那位做父亲的虽然没说什么欢天喜地的话，但是见到两个女儿还真感到高兴。他体会到了她俩在家里的分量。晚上一家人聚在一起聊

译文二：

她产生了这种想法，那他最后一天的表现就具有实质性的分量：要么让她吃一颗定心丸，要么让她的梦幻破灭。拿定主意后，星期六一整天他都没跟她讲几句话，而且尽管有一次他们单独呆了半小时，他也只顾专心致志地读他的书，连瞧都没瞧她一眼。

星期天做完晨祷后，姐妹俩就告别大家了，几乎人人都很高兴。到了最后一刻，彬格莱小姐由于对珍妮关爱有加，对伊丽莎白也突然倍加客气起来。分别时她对珍妮说，今后不管是在朗博恩还是在内瑟菲尔德与她相逢，她都会非常高兴的，接着她最为深情地拥抱了她，还同伊丽莎白握了手。伊丽莎白兴高采烈地告别了所有的人。

她们回到家，并没有受到母亲的热烈欢迎。班纳特太太看到她们回来，感到惊奇不已，她想，她们惹了那么多麻烦太不应该，还说珍妮一定又伤风着凉了。但她们的父亲却不一样，虽然只是三言两语地说他很高兴见到她们，但那是发自内心的高兴。他早已体会到了

原　文

was really glad to see them; he had felt their importance in the family circle. The evening conversation, when they were all assembled, had lost much of its animation, and almost all its sense, by the absence of Jane and Elizabeth.

They found Mary, as usual, deep in the study of thorough bass and human nature; and had some new extracts to admire, and some new observations of thread-bare morality to listen to. Catherine and Lydia had information for them of a different sort. Much had been done and much had been said in the regiment since the preceding Wednesday; several of the officers had dined lately with their uncle, a private had been flogged, and it had actually been hinted that Colonel Forster was going to be married.

(Jane Austen, *Pride and Prejudice*, Vol. I, Chapter 12)

译文一

天的时候，如果简和伊丽莎白不在场，那就没有劲，甚至毫无意思。

　　姐妹俩发觉玛丽像以往一样，还在埋头钻研和声学与人性问题，她拿出了一些新的札记给她们欣赏，还就迂腐的道德问题发表了一通议论。凯瑟琳和莉迪亚也告诉了她们一些新闻，只是性质截然不同。自上星期三以来，民兵团里又出了好多事，添了好多传闻：有几个军官最近跟她们的姨夫吃过饭，一个士兵挨了鞭打，还隐约听说福斯特上校就要结婚了。

（孙致礼　译）

译文二

女儿们在家庭生活中的重要作用。一家人晚上在一起时，如果没有珍妮和伊丽莎白在场，谈话就变得毫无生气，也几乎没有任何意义。

　　她们看到玛丽还同往常一样，专心研究声学和人性问题；她新近又摘录了一些用于欣赏的片断，还要去聆听就陈腐的道德问题所发表的见解。凯瑟琳和莉迪亚则给她们讲了一些截然不同的新闻。自上星期三以来，兵团里做了很多事情，也谈论了很多事情；有几位军官最近同他们的姨父一起吃过饭，有个大兵挨了鞭打，有人实际上已经暗示，福斯特上校就要娶太太了。

（李明　译）

第二章 Gone with the Wind 汉译文片段的批评赏析

一、关于 Gone with the Wind

美国作家玛格丽特·米切尔用了近十年时间写成的 Gone with the Wind（汉语译为《飘》）是一部具有浪漫主义色彩的、以南北战争为题材的小说。女主人公斯佳丽身上所表现出来的叛逆精神以及艰苦创业、自强不息的精神，一直令读者为之倾倒。在那个战火纷飞的年代，为了履行曾经答应过卫希礼照顾梅兰妮的一句承诺，在北军将要攻占亚特兰大之时，斯佳丽果断地替梅兰妮接生，并找到瑞特冲破重重阻碍和关卡，回到乡下老家——塔拉庄园。在又饥又饿之时，她又遭受母亲病亡、父亲痴呆、家里被劫、一贫如洗等多重打击，但她不屈不挠，带头种田干活，喝令妹妹下床摘棉花，并照顾梅兰妮和小波，支撑一家人的生计。面对巨大困难，

二、Gone with the Wind 原文片段及四种汉译文

原　文	译文一	译文二
Scarlett O'hara was not beautiful, but men seldom realized it when caught by her charm as the Tarleton twins were. In her face were too sharply blended the delicate features of her mother, a Coast aristocrat of French descent, and the heavy ones of her florid Irish father. But it was an arresting face, pointed of chin, square of jaw. Her eyes were pale green without a touch of hazel, starred with bristly black lashes and slightly tilted at the ends. Above them, her thick black brows slanted upward,	那郝思嘉小姐长得并不美，可是极富魅力，男人见了她，往往要着迷，就像汤家那一对双胞胎兄弟似的。原来这位小姐脸上显然混杂着两种特质：一种是母亲给她的娇柔，一种是父亲给她的豪爽。因为她母亲是个法兰西血统的海滨贵族，父亲是个皮色深浓的爱尔兰人，所以遗传给她的质地难免不调和。可是质地虽然不调和，她那一张脸蛋儿实在迷人得很，下巴颏儿尖尖的，牙床骨儿方方的。她的眼珠子是一味的淡绿色，不杂一丝儿的茶褐，周围竖着一圈儿粗黑的	斯佳丽·奥哈拉长得并不美，但是男人们一旦像塔尔顿家孪生兄弟那样给她的魅力迷住往往就不大理会这点。她脸蛋上极其明显地融合了父亲的容貌特征，既有母亲那种沿海地区法国贵族后裔的优雅，也有父亲那种肤色红润的爱尔兰人的粗野，不过这张脸还是挺引人注目，尖尖的下巴颏儿，方方的牙床骨儿。眼睛纯粹是淡绿色的，不带一点儿淡褐色，眼眶缀着浓密乌黑的睫毛，稍稍有点吊眼梢。上面是两道又浓又黑的剑眉，在木兰花似的洁白皮肤上勾画出两条触目惊

她没有选择逃避,而是勇敢挑起家里的重担,以常人难以企及的毅力同命运抗争,同时渴望安定、渴望生存、渴望富裕,并为此不择手段。自私、虚荣、贪婪,如果说这些形容词用在别人身上都是贬义词的话,那么它们用在斯佳丽身上却是褒义词。其实,就像白瑞德所说,"我们都是流氓,我们都是无赖。"他对自己和斯佳丽的分析是透彻的,也正因为他的这些分析,《飘》才会被无数人所拜读,斯佳丽也才成为一个完整的有血有肉的形象。

1936年6月,耗费作者近十年心血的小说《飘》终于问世。该书的出版使玛格丽特几乎一夜之间变成当时美国文坛的名人,也成为亚特兰大尽人皆知的"女英雄"。该小说的销售立即打破了美国出版界的多项纪录。随后,小说获1937年普利策奖和美国出版商协会奖。小说问世的当年,好莱坞将其改编成电影并于1939年上映。半个多世纪以来,这部厚达1 000多页的小说一直位居美国畅销书前列。截至20世纪70年代末期,小说已被译成27种文字,在全世界的销售量也逾2 000万册。被《时代》杂志收入"时代之1923—2005百部最佳英语小说"。

这里节选的部分是小说的开头。在开头部分,作者对女主人公的形象进行了描述。作为译者,应努力把握并突出小说人物的潜质,否则她在接下来所表现出的个性特点就会显得突兀,小说就不具有足够的感染力和说服力。因此,选择该小说的开头部分并提供几种汉语译文进行比较是非常有意义的。

译文三

思嘉·奥哈拉长得并不漂亮,但是男人们一旦像塔尔顿家那对孪生兄弟为她的魅力所迷住时,便看不到这一点了。她脸上混杂着两种特征,一种是她母亲的娇柔,一种是她父亲的粗犷,前者属于法兰西血统的海滨贵族,后者来自浮华俗气的爱尔兰人,这两种特征显得不太调和。不过这张脸,连同那尖尖的下巴和四四方方的牙床骨,是很引人注意的。她那双淡绿色的眼睛纯净得不带一丝褐色,配上刚硬乌黑的睫毛和稍稍翘起的眼角,显得别具风韵。上头是两撇墨黑的

译文四

斯佳丽·奥哈拉并不漂亮,但男人们,如果像塔尔顿这对孪生兄弟那样被她的魅力所迷倒的话,就很少能看得出这一点了。斯佳丽的脸上特别明显地融合了两种特征:一种是法国沿海地区贵族后裔的母亲留给她的眉目清秀,一种是皮肤红润的爱尔兰人的父亲留给她的浓眉大眼。但她的这张脸着实迷人:尖尖的下巴,方方的下颌,淡绿色的双眼无一丝淡褐色,又粗又黑的睫毛点缀着眼眶,并在眼角处微微上翘。眼睛上方是浓黑的眉毛,眉毛往上倾斜着,在她那木兰花般

笔 记

原文	译文一	译文二
cutting a startling oblique line in her magnolia-white skin—that skin so prized by Southern women and so carefully guarded with bonnets, veils and mittens against hot Georgia suns. Seated with Stuart and Brent Tarleton in the cool shade of the porch of Tara, her father's plantation, that bright April afternoon of 1861, she made a pretty picture. Her new green flowered-muslin dress spread its twelve yards of billowing material over her hoops and exactly matched the flat-heeled green morocco slippers her father had recently brought her from Atlanta. The dress set off to perfection the seventeen-inch waist, the smallest in three counties, and tightly fitting basque showed breasts well matured for her sixteen years. But for all the modesty of her spreading skirts, the demureness of hair netted smoothly into a chignon and the quietness of small white hands folded in her lap, her true self was poorly concealed. The green eyes in the carefully sweet face were turbulent, willful, lusty with life, distinctly at variance with her decorous demeanour.	睫毛，眼角微微有点翘，上面斜竖着两撇墨墨的蛾眉，在她那木兰花一般白的皮肤上，划出两条异常惹眼的斜线。就是她那一身皮肤，也正是南方女人最最喜爱的，谁要长着这样的皮肤，就要拿帽子、面罩、手套之类当心保护着，舍不得让那大热的阳光晒黑。 1861年4月一个晴朗的下午，思嘉小姐在陶乐垦植场的住宅，陪着汤家那一对双胞胎兄弟——一个叫汤司徒、一个叫汤伯伦的——坐在一个阴凉的走廊里。这时春意正浓，景物如绣，她也显得特别的标致。她身上穿着一件新制的绿色花布春衫，从弹簧箍上撑出波浪纹的长裙，配着脚上一双也是绿色的低跟鞋，是她父亲新近从饿狼陀买来给她的。她的腰围不过十七英寸，穿着那窄窄的春衫，显得十分合身。里面紧紧绷着一件小马甲，使得她胸部特别隆起。她的年纪虽只十六岁，乳房却已十分成熟了。可是不管她那散开的长裙显得多么端庄，不管她那梳得光滑的后髻显得多么老实，也不管她那叠在膝头上的一双雪白的小手显得多么安静，总都掩饰不了她的真性情。她那双绿色的眼睛虽然嵌在一张矜持的面孔上，却是骚动不宁的，慧黠多端的，洋溢着生命的，跟她那一副装饰起来的仪态截然不能相称。原来她平日受了	心的斜线。那种皮肤深受南方妇女珍视，而且她们总是戴上帽子、面纱和手套，小心翼翼地保护好，免得给佐治亚的烈日晒黑。 1861年4月，有一天下午阳光明媚，她在父亲的塔拉庄园宅前门廊的荫处，同塔尔顿家两兄弟斯图特和布伦特坐在一起，那模样真宛若画中人。她穿着那件绿花布的新衣，裙箍把用料十二码波浪形裙幅铺展开来，跟她父亲刚从亚特兰大给她捎来的平跟摩洛哥羊皮绿舞鞋正好相配。她的腰围只有十七英寸，三个县里就数她腰身最细，那身衣服把她腰肢衬托得更见纤细。虽说年方十六，乳房却长得非常成熟，熨贴的紧身上衣把她乳房裹得格外显眼。尽管她长裙舒展，显得仪态端庄，一头乌丝光溜溜地用发网拢成一个发髻，显得风度娴雅，一双雪白的纤手交叉搁在膝上，显得举止文静，但真正的本性却难以掩饰。精心故作娇憨的脸上那对绿眼睛爱动、任性、生气勃勃，和她那份端庄的态度截然不同。原来她一贯受到母亲的谆谆告诫和黑妈妈的严格管教才勉强养成这副礼

译文三	译文四	笔 记
浓眉竖在那里，给她木兰花一般白皙的皮肤划了一条十分惹眼的斜线。这样白皙的皮肤对南方妇女是极其珍贵的，她们常常用帽子、面纱和手套把皮肤保护起来，不让受到佐治亚炎热太阳的暴晒。	洁白的皮肤上划了一道十分显眼的斜线。这样洁白的皮肤南方的妇女们最为珍视，她们往往要戴上帽子、蒙上面纱、戴上手套来仔细保护它，不让佐治亚州那炎炎烈日暴晒。	

　　1861年4月的一个晴朗的下午，思嘉同塔尔顿家的孪生兄弟斯图尔特和布伦特坐在她父亲的塔拉农场阴凉的走廊上，她标致的模样儿使四周的一派春光显得更明媚如画了。她穿一件新做的绿花布衣裳，长长的裙子在裙箍上波翻浪涌般地飘展着，配上她父亲新近从亚特兰大给她带来的绿色山羊皮鞋，显得分外相称。她的腰围不过十七英寸，是附近三个县里最细小的了，而这身衣裳更把腰肢衬托得恰到好处，再加上里面那件绷得紧紧的小马甲，她的虽然只有十六岁但已成熟了的乳房便跃然显露了。不过，无论她散开的长裙显得多么朴实，发髻梳在后面的发型显得多么端庄，那双交叠在膝头上的白生生的小手显得多么文静，她的本来面目终归是掩藏不住的。那双绿色的眼睛尽管生在一张故作娇媚的脸上，却仍然是骚动的、任性的、生意盎然的，与她的装束仪表很不相同。她的举止是由她母

　　1861年4月的一个下午，春光明媚，斯佳丽同斯图尔特和布伦特一道坐在她父亲的农场——塔拉农场——门廊的阴凉处，她那模样宛如画中美人。她身穿一件新的绿色花棉布连衣裙，波浪形的裙幅有十二码宽，从裙箍处飘泻下来，这与她父亲最近从亚特兰大给她买回的绿色平跟摩洛哥皮拖鞋刚好相配。她腰身十七英寸，在几个县里都算最细小的。连衣裙把她的腰肢衬托得美妙绝伦。她的上衣紧贴着身子，虽然只有十六岁，可她那对乳房已经发育得非常成熟。尽管她穿着舒展的裙子，显得非常朴实，尽管她用发网将头发顺溜地拢进发髻中，显得非常端庄，尽管她将洁白的小手交叉着十指放在膝上，显得非常文静，但她的本性却几乎无法掩盖住。从她的脸上看，她非常贤淑，可那双绿色的眼睛却躁动不安、固执任性、充满活力，这与她那万千的仪态显然格格不入。她那优雅的举止是由于母亲循循善诱，还有那黑人嬷

原 文

Her manners had been imposed upon her by her mother's gentle admonitions and the sterner discipline of her mammy; her eyes were her own.

(Margaret Mitchell, *Gone with the Wind*, Part 1, Chapter I)

译文一

母亲的温和训诲和嬷嬷的严厉管教,这才把这副姿态勉强造成,至于那一双眼睛,那是天生给她的,决不是人工改造得了的。

(傅东华 译,1940)

译文二

貌;她那双眼睛才显出她的本色呢。

(陈廷良 译,1990)

三 小说翻译的批评与赏析练习

原 文

As the Manager of the Performance sits before the curtain on the boards, and looks into the Fair, a feeling of profound melancholy comes over him in his survey of the bustling place. There is a great quantity of eating and drinking, making love and jilting, laughing and the contrary, smoking, cheating, fighting, dancing, and fiddling: there are bullies pushing about, bucks ogling the women, knaves picking pockets, policemen on the lookout, quacks (other quacks, plague take them!) bawling in front of their booths, and yokels looking up at the tin-shelled dancers and poor old rouged tumblers, while the light-fingered folk are operating upon their pockets behind. Yes, this is VANITY FAIR: not a moral place certainly; nor a

译文一

领班的坐在戏台上幔子前面,对着底下闹哄哄的市场,瞧了半晌,心里不觉悲惨起来(悲从中来——思果改译)。市场上的人有的在吃喝,有的在调情,有的得了新宠就丢了旧爱,有在笑的,也有在哭的,还有在抽烟,打架的,跳舞的,拉提琴的,诓骗哄人的。有些是到处横行的强梁汉子;有些是对女人飞眼儿的花花公子,也有扒儿手和到处巡逻的警察,还有走江湖吃十方的,在自己摊子前面扯起嗓子嚷嚷(这些人偏和我同行,真该死!),跳舞的穿着浑身发亮的衣服,可怜的翻筋斗老头儿涂着两腮帮子胭脂,引得那些乡下佬睁着眼瞧,不提防后面就有三只手的家伙在掏他们的口袋。是了,这就是我们的名利场。这里虽然是个热闹去处,却是道德沦亡,说不上有什么快活。你瞧瞧戏子们丑角

译文二

舞台监督坐在戏台上的帷幕前,注目着市场,看到那闹哄哄的场面,不由得忧心忡忡。市场上,有人在大吃大喝,有人在打情骂俏、另寻新欢,有人在大笑不止,有人在哭得死去活来,有人在猛抽烟,有人到处行骗,有人在大打出手,有人在手舞足蹈,有人在到处胡闹。有些人横行霸道、恃强凌弱,有些人花花心肠,对女人挤眉弄眼,有些人是十足的流氓,扒窃你没商量,有些人是警察,眼观六路耳听八方,有些人是江湖医生(另一批行骗者,真该死!),在自己的摊子前大叫大嚷,有些人是乡巴佬,看着舞台上浑身穿着发亮衣服的人跳着舞蹈,看着可怜的老头儿涂着胭脂翻着筋斗,津津乐道,全然没有意识到身后的三只手在掏他们的钱包。可不是,这就是名利场:虽然热闹非凡,却是个彻头彻

译文三

亲的谆谆训诫和嬷嬷的严厉管教强加给她的，但她的眼睛属于自己。

（戴侃、李野光 译）

译文四

嬷的严加管教才好不容易形成的，可她的那双眼睛折射出了她的心灵。

（李明 译）

笔 记

原 文

merry one, though very noisy. Look at the faces of the actors and buffoons when they come off from their business; and Tom Fool washing the paint off his cheeks before he sits down to dinner with his wife and the little Jack Puddings behind the canvas. The curtain will be up presently, and he will be turning over head and heels, and crying, "How are you?"

A man with a reflective turn of mind, walking through an exhibition of this sort, will not be oppressed, I take it, by his own or other people's hilarity. An episode of humor or kindness touches and amuses him here and there; —a pretty child looking at a gingerbread stall; a pretty girl blushing whilst her lover talks to her and chooses

译文一

们下场以后的脸色——譬如那逗人发笑的傻小子汤姆回到后台洗净了脸上的油彩，准备和老婆儿子（一群小傻小子）坐下吃饭时候的情景，你就明白了。不久开场做戏，汤姆又会出来连连翻筋斗，嘴里叫唤着说："您好哇？"

我想，凡是有思想的人在这种市场上观光，不但不怪人家兴致好，自己也会跟着乐。他不时的会碰上一两件事，或是幽默得逗人发笑，或是显得出人心忠厚的一面，使人感动。这儿有一个漂亮的孩子，眼巴巴的瞧着卖姜汁面包的摊儿；那儿有一个漂亮的姑娘，脸红红的听她的爱人说话，瞧他给自己挑礼物；再过去是可怜的

译文二

尾的道德沦丧之所，彻头彻尾的令人伤心之地。瞧瞧演员和小丑们表演完后的那一张张的脸，那个傻冒儿汤姆要洗掉脸上的油彩才能到后台坐到老婆和一群小的小丑们那里一起吃饭。很快帷幕就要升起，汤姆就要连连翻筋斗，并且大叫一声："你们好！"

我想，只要是善于思考的人，在这种市场上走一遭，都会尽自己的兴致取乐，或者跟着他人一起取乐。不时地，他会为一件幽默的趣事，或者一件善意的趣事所感动，所逗乐：一个漂亮的小孩儿直盯着姜饼摊儿；一个漂亮的女孩儿听着爱人谈话、看着爱人给自己买礼物时红着脸；那可怜的傻冒儿汤姆躲在货车后面同老老实

原文	译文一	译文二
her fairing; poor Tom Fool, yonder behind the wagon, mumbling his bone with the honest family which lives by his tumbling; but the general impression is one more melancholy than mirthful. When you come home, you sit down, in a sober, contemplative, not uncharitable frame of mind, and apply yourself to your books or your business.	小丑汤姆躲在货车后头带着一家老小啃骨头，这些老实人就靠他翻筋斗赚来的钱过活，可是话又说回来，大致的印象还是使人愁而不是逗人乐的。等你回到家里坐下来读书做事的时候，玩味着刚才所见的一切，就会冷静下来，对于别人的短处也不太苛责了。	实的一家人啃着骨头，这家人就靠他翻筋斗赚来的钱过活。当然，市场给人的印象与其说是让人捧腹，不如说是让人忧郁。等你回到家里时，你坐下来读书也好，做事也好，会陷入冷静的沉思，心里充满无限的同情。
I have no other moral than this to tag to the present story of "Vanity Fair". Some people consider Fairs immoral altogether, and eschew such, with their servants and families: very likely they are right. But persons who think otherwise, and are of a lazy, or a benevolent, or a sarcastic mood, may perhaps like to step in for half-an-hour, and look at the performances. There are scenes of all sorts: some dreadful combats, some grand and lofty horse-riding, some scenes of high life, and some of very middling indeed; some love-making for the sentimental, and some light comic business; the whole accompanied by appropriate scenery, and brilliantly illuminated with the Author's own candles.	我这本小说《名利场》就只有这么一点儿教训。有人认为市场上人口混杂，是个下流的地方，不但自己不去，连家眷和佣人也不准去。大概他们的看法是不错的。不过也有人生就懒散的脾气，或是仁慈的心肠，或是爱取笑讽刺的性格，他们看法不同一些，倒愿意在市场上消磨半个钟头，看看各种表演，像激烈的格斗，精彩的骑术，上流社会的形形色色，普通人家生活的情形，专为多情的看客预备的恋爱场面，轻松滑稽的穿插等等。这场表演每一幕都有相称的布景，四面点着作者自己的蜡烛，满台照得雪亮。	《名利场》这个故事就只有这么一个寓意。有些人认为，凡市场，都龌龊下流，遇之连同佣人和家眷都要退避三舍。很可能他们有道理。但持相反观点的人，处于懒散状态、有着菩萨心肠或者爱挖苦讽刺的人，也许愿意走进市场溜达个把小时，看看各种表演。各种情景应有尽有：激烈的格斗，宏观的场面，威风凛凛的骑术，上流社会生活的情景，再普通不过的人生活的情景，为多情的看客上演的打情骂俏，还有轻松滑稽的小品。所有表演都有相应的布景，所有表演都用作者自己的蜡烛，照得整个舞台灯火辉煌。
What more has the Manager of the Performance to say? —To acknowledge the kindness with	领班的还有什么可说的呢？他带着戏班子在英国各大城市上演，多承各界惠顾，	舞台监督还有什么好说的呢？对于各界对他的戏班子到英国各大城市上演所作的良好

原 文	译文一	译文二
which it has been received in all the principal towns of England through which the Show has passed, and where it has been most favorably noticed by the respected conductors of the Public Press, and by the Nobility and Gentry. He is proud to think that his Puppets have given satisfaction to the very best company in this empire. The famous little Becky Puppet has been pronounced to be uncommonly flexible in the joints, and lively on the wire; the Amelia Doll, though it has had a small circle of admirers, has yet been carved and dressed with the greatest care by the artist; the Dobbin Figure, though apparently clumsy, yet dances in a very amusing and natural manner; the Little Boys' Dance has been liked by some; and please to remark the richly dressed figure of the Wicked Nobleman, on which no expense has been spared, and which Old Nick will fetch away at the end of this singular performance.	报的编辑先生们也都有好评，又蒙各位大人先生提拔，真是不胜感激。他的傀儡戏被英国最高尚的人士所赏识，使他觉得面上很有光彩。那个叫蓓基的木偶人儿非常有名，大家一致称赞她的骨节特别的灵活，线一牵就活泼泼的手舞足蹈。那个叫爱米丽亚的洋娃娃虽然没有这么叫座，卖艺的倒也费了好些心血刻画她的面貌，设计她的服装。还有一个叫都宾的傀儡，看着笨手笨脚的，跳起舞来却很有趣，很自然。也有人爱看男孩子们跳的一场舞。请各位观众注意那"黑心的贵人"，他的服饰非常华丽，我们筹备的时候真实不惜工本；这次表演完毕以后，它马上会给"魔鬼老爹"请去。	反应，尤其是各大报纸尊敬的编辑先生们所作的好评，还有各位贵人的提携，他真是感激不尽。一想到自己的木偶戏得到英国最高阶层人士的赏识，他就感到无比自豪。大家都一致称赞那个出了名的小木偶人蓓基的骨节特别灵活，线一牵就生龙活虎；那个洋娃娃艾米丽亚虽然没有那么叫座，可卖艺人对它做了最精心的雕琢和最细心的打扮；幽灵都宾尽管看上去笨手笨脚，但跳起舞来却特别有趣，特别自然；小男孩儿们的舞蹈有些人也一直非常喜欢。但请各位注意一下那位"恶毒的贵人"雍容华贵的服饰，这套服饰可没少花钱，在这次非凡的表演之后妖魔还要请它去呢。
And with this, and a profound bow to his patrons, the Manager retires, and the curtain rises.	领班的说到这儿，向各位主顾深深的打了一躬退到后台，接下去就开幕了。	舞台监督说到这儿，向各位主顾深深鞠了一躬退到台后，接着就开幕了。
LONDON, June 28, 1848	1848年6月28日于伦敦	1848年6月28日于伦敦
(William Thackeray, *Vanity Fair*)	（杨必 译）	（李明 译）

第二部分　小说翻译的批评与赏析

第三章 *Jane Eyre* 汉译文片段的批评赏析

一 关于 *Jane Eyre*

  Jane Eyre 是英国 19 世纪著名女作家夏洛蒂·勃朗特（1816—1855）的代表作。尽管作者在世上仅仅生活了 39 年，可她的小说 *Jane Eyre* 却一直生活在人世间，成为千千万万青年人的朋友。由于该小说深入读者内心，读者们往往将作者本人同该小说中的主人公 Jane Eyre（简·爱）的形象联系在一起，永远纪念并一直追寻着这位一代才女。

  小说的梗概是这样的：简·爱自小失去父母，寄住在舅妈家，不平等的待遇让她饱受欺凌，小小的年纪就承受了别人无法想象的委屈和痛苦。成年后，她成了桑菲尔德贵族庄园的家庭教师，她以真挚的情感和高尚的品德赢得了主人的尊敬和爱恋，谁料命运对她如此残忍，她又为这段婚姻付出了惨重代价，但自始至终，她却一直坚持着自己的信念，执着自己的理想。

二 *Jane Eyre* 原文片段及四种汉译文

原文	译文一	译文二
There was no possibility of taking a walk that day. We had been wandering, indeed, in the leafless shrubbery an hour in the morning; but since dinner (Mrs. Reed, when there was no company, dined early) the cold winter wind had brought with it clouds so sombre, and a rain so penetrating, that further outdoor exercise was now out of the question. I was glad of it: I never liked	那一天是没有散步的可能了。不错，早晨我们已经在无叶的丛林中漫游过一点钟了；但是午饭后——在没有客人的时候，里德太太是早早吃午饭的——寒冷的冬风刮来的云这样阴阴沉沉，吹来的雨这样寒透内心，再做户外运动是不可能的了。 　　我觉得高兴：我从来不喜	那一天不可能去散步了。不错，我们早上已经在片叶无存的灌木林中逛了一个钟头；但是，自从吃午饭的时候起（如果没有客人，里德太太是很早吃午饭的），冬日的凛冽寒风就送来了那样阴沉的云和那样透骨的雨，这就不可能再在户外活动了。 　　我倒是很高兴，我素来不

与追求,并最终争取到了平等、自由和幸福。

Jane Eyre 被普遍认为是夏洛蒂·勃朗特"诗意的生平"的写照,是一部具有自传色彩的作品。作者夏洛蒂·勃朗特与其两个妹妹艾米莉·勃朗特和安妮·勃朗特一起合称"勃朗特三姐妹"(The Family Brontë),享誉当时英国文坛,她们同勃朗宁夫人一道构成那个时代英国妇女最高荣誉的完美的三位一体。

夏洛蒂·勃朗特虽然一生仅仅写了四部小说,即《教师》(*The Professor*, 1857)、《简·爱》(*Jane Eyre*, 1847)、《谢利》(*Shirley*, 1849)和《维莱特》(*Villette*, 1853)(其中《教师》在她去世后才出版),但她在文学史上却占据着相当重要的地位。在她的小说中,最突出的主题就是女性要求独立自主的强烈愿望。这一主题可以说在她的所有小说中都顽强地表现了出来,而将女性的呼声作为小说主题,这在她之前的英国文学史上是不曾有过的——她是表现这一主题的第一人。此外,她的小说还有一个特点,那就是人物和情节都与她自己的生活息息相关,因而具有浓厚的抒情色彩。女性主题加上抒情笔调,这是夏洛蒂·勃朗特创作的基本特色,也是她对后世英美作家的影响所在。后世作家在处理女性主题时,都不同程度地受到她的影响,尤其是关心女性自身命运问题的女作家,更是尊她为先驱,并把她的作品视为"现代女性小说"的楷模。

这里选取的是 Jane Eyre 这一小说开头的三个自然段。原文文字洗练优美,但译文却犹如千人千面。到底为何会如此这般?请仔细评析。

译文三

那一天是没法再出去散步了。不错,那天上午我们还在光秃秃的灌木林间漫步了一个钟头,但是从吃午饭的时候起(只要没有客人,里德太太总是很早吃午饭),就刮起了冬日凛冽的寒风,一时天空阴霾密布,风雨交加,寒气透骨,这样一来,自然谈不上再到外面去活动了。

这倒正合我的心意,我一

译文四

那天外出散步是不可能的了。那天上午我们在光秃秃的灌木林中漫步已经整整一小时了。但是从午饭(如果没有人陪伴,里德太太就早早地吃完午饭)后开始,冬日里那凛冽的寒风就刮起来了,带来的云阴阴沉沉,带来的雨刺骨寒心,此时要做户外活动也是不可能的事情了。

我倒是挺高兴的。我向来

笔 记

原文

long walks, especially on chilly afternoons: dreadful to me was the coming home in the raw twilight, with nipped fingers and toes, and a heart saddened by the chidings of Bessie, the nurse, and humbled by the consciousness of my physical inferiority to Eliza, John, and Georgiana Reed.

The said Eliza, John, and Georgiana were now clustered round their mama in the drawing-room: she lay reclined on a sofa by the fireside, and with her darlings about her (for the time neither quarrelling nor crying) looked perfectly happy. Me, she had dispensed from joining the group; saying, "She regretted to be under the necessity of keeping me at a distance; but that until she heard from Bessie, and could discover by her own observation, that I was endeavouring in good earnest to acquire a more sociable and childlike disposition, a more attractive and sprightly manner—something lighter, franker, more natural, as it were—she really must exclude me from privileges intended only for contented, happy, little children."

(Charlotte Bronte, *Jane Eyre*, Chapter 1)

译文一

欢路远时长的散步，尤其在寒冷的下午；手指和足趾都冻坏，怀着被保姆贝西骂得忧伤的心，觉得身体不及伊莱扎、约翰和乔治亚娜·里德而感到自卑，在湿冷的黄昏回家，在我看来是可怕的。

说到的伊莱扎、约翰和乔治亚娜，这时正在会客室里围绕着他们的妈妈：她偎卧在炉旁的沙发上，她宠爱的爱儿爱女在她周围（暂时既没有争吵，也没有哭嚷），看来是十分快乐。她没有让我加入这个团体；她说她抱歉不得不疏远我；又说要不等到贝西告诉她，并且凭她自己的观察看出，我在认真努力使自己有更合群的和跟小孩子一般的脾气，有更可爱和活泼的态度（大概是一种更轻松，更坦率，更自然的态度吧），那么，只让满意快乐的小孩享受的好处，她就不得不把我排除在外了。

（李霁野 译）

译文二

爱远距离的散步，特别是在寒冷的下午。对我来说，在阴冷的黄昏回家实在可怕，手指和脚趾都冻僵了，还得听保姆白茜的责骂，弄得心里很不痛快，而且自己觉得体质不如伊丽莎、约翰和乔奇安娜·里德，又感到低人一等。

上面提到的伊丽莎、约翰和乔奇安娜·里德，这时候都在休憩室里，正簇拥在他们的母亲周围，她斜靠在炉边的沙发上，心爱的儿女都在身旁（这忽儿既不争吵，又不哭闹），看上去很是快活。她没让我和他们在一起；她说她很遗憾，不得不叫我离他们远一点；她真的不能把只给知足快乐的小孩的那些特权给我，除非是白茜告诉了她，而且还要她自己亲眼看到，我确实是在认认真真地努力培养一种更加天真随和的性情，一种更加活泼可爱的态度——大概是更轻快、更坦率、更自然的一种什么吧。

（祝庆英 译）

译文三	译文四
向不喜欢漫长的散步,尤其是在午后寒冷的天气里。在我看来,在阴冷的黄昏时分回家实在可怕,手脚都冻僵了不说,还得挨保姆贝茜的训斥,弄得心里挺不痛快。再说我自觉身体不及伊丽莎、约翰和乔治亚娜·里德健壮,因此不免感到自卑。	不喜欢长时间的散步,尤其在寒冷的下午。对我来说,在阴冷的黄昏时分回家实在可怕:手指头和脚趾头全都冻得发麻,还要受保姆贝西责骂一番,令我伤心不已;再说,知道自己的身体不如伊丽莎、约翰,还有乔治亚娜·里德,自觉低人一等。
我刚才提到的伊丽莎、约翰和乔治亚娜这时都在客厅里,正团团围在他们的妈妈身边。她斜靠在炉旁的沙发上,被几个宝贝儿女簇拥着(这会儿既不争吵,也不哭闹),看上去非常快活。她从来不让我加入他们的圈子,她为自己不得不让我离他们远一点感到遗憾。她说,除非她从贝茜那里听到并且亲眼目睹,发现我确实在努力养成一种更加天真随和和更加活泼可爱的举止,也就是说,一种更优雅、更坦率、更自然的品性,否则她真的没法让我享受到只有那些知足快乐的孩子才配享受的待遇。	说到伊丽莎、约翰和乔治亚娜,现在他们正在客厅里围着他们的妈妈里德太太。她斜靠在壁炉旁边的沙发上,身边围着自己心爱的儿女,他们此时既不争吵,也不哭闹,她真是快乐无比。我呢,她就是不让同他们在一起。她说她很遗憾,不得不让我同他们保持距离。但她又说,她一定要等到保姆贝西告诉她,并且通过自己的观察真正了解到,我是真心实意地在努力培养起一种更加随和而天真的性情,更加可爱而活泼的行为方式——也就是一种更加轻松、更加直率、更加自然的一种处世方式——她才真正让我去享受那些原本只让那些富足而快乐的小孩子们才享受的特权。
(凌雯 译)	(李明 译)

三 小说翻译的批评与赏析练习

原文

The chamber looked such a bright little place to me as the sun shone in between the gay blue chintz window curtains, showing papered walls and a carpeted floor, so unlike the bare planks and stained plaster of Lowood, that my spirits rose at the view. Externals have a great effect on the young: I thought that a fairer era of life was beginning for me—one that was to have its flowers and pleasures, as well as its thorns and toils. My faculties, roused by the change of scene, the new field offered to hope, seemed all astir. I cannot precisely define what they expected, but it was something pleasant: not perhaps that day or that month, but at an indefinite future period.

I rose; I dressed myself with care: obliged to be plain—for I had no article of attire that was not made with extreme simplicity—I was still by nature solicitous to be neat. It was not my habit to be disregardful of appearance or careless of the impression I made: on the contrary, I ever wished to look as well as I could, and to please as much as my want of beauty would permit. I sometimes regretted

译文一

太阳从鲜艳的蓝印花布的窗幔间照射进来时,显出纸糊的墙和铺地毯的地板,和罗沃德的光板同褪色的粉墙很是不同,使得这房子在我看来是一个很愉快的小地方:一看它我的精神就振作起来了。外表对于年轻的人很有影响:我想一个更美好的生活时代为我开始了——一个既有荆棘和劳苦,也有鲜花和欢乐的时代。我的才智被这种情景,这种令人满怀希望的新地方所刺激,似乎全活动起来了。我的才智究竟希望得到什么东西,我无法准确说明,不过是一种令人愉快的东西:并不就在那一天或在一个不明确的未来的时期。

我起来了;我细心替自己穿着:虽然不得不朴素——因为我没有一件衣服不是做得非常简朴的——我却天生的满心想要整洁。不修边幅或不留心给人的印象如何,并不是我的习惯;反之,我总愿尽力显得好看一点,愿尽力在我不美的限度之内讨人喜欢。我有时惋惜我没有更漂亮一些;我有时愿意有玫瑰的面颊,直梁的鼻子和一张樱桃小口;我渴望发展得端庄美好的高身材;我觉

译文二

太阳从鲜艳的蓝色印花窗帘缝隙间照进来,照亮了糊着墙纸的四壁和铺着地毯的地板,这跟劳渥德的光秃秃的木板和玷污的灰泥墙完全不同。这个房间看上去是个如此明亮的小地方,我一看见它就精神振奋起来。外表对于青年人是有强烈的影响的。我想,对于我来说,生活中一个比较美好的时期正在开始,一个有着荆棘和劳苦,同时也有鲜花和欢乐的时期。由于场景有了变动,由于有希望出现一个新天地,我的官能被唤醒,似乎完全都活跃起来。我不能确切地说明它们在期待什么,不过那总是一种愉快的东西:也许不只是在那一天或者那一个月,而是在一个不明确的未来时期。

我起身了,细心地穿着衣服;不得不穿得朴素——因为我没有一件衣服不是做得极其简单的——可是我却天生酷爱清洁。不修边幅,不管自己给人家留下什么印象,这些都不是我的习惯;相反,我一直希望:尽可能使自己显得好看些,在缺少美貌所许可的范围内尽可能使自己讨人喜欢。我有时候惋惜自己没长得再漂亮一点;有时候希望有红喷喷的脸蛋,挺直的鼻子和樱桃般的

原 文

that I was not handsomer; I sometimes wished to have rosy cheeks, a straight nose, and small cherry mouth; I desired to be tall, stately, and finely developed in figure; I felt it a misfortune that I was so little, so pale, and had features so irregular and so marked. And why had I these aspirations and these regrets? It would be difficult to say: I could not then distinctly say it to myself; yet I had a reason, and a logical, natural reason too. However, when I had brushed my hair very smooth, and put on my black frock—which, Quakerlike as it was, at least had the merit of fitting to a nicety—and adjusted my clean white tucker, I thought I should do respectably enough to appear before Mrs. Fairfax, and that my new pupil would not at least recoil from me with antipathy. Having opened my chamber window, and seen that I left all things straight and neat on the toilet table, I ventured forth.

(Charlotte Bronte, *Jane Eyre*, Chapter 11)

译文一

得我这样小，这样苍白，这样五官引人注目的不端庄，是一种不幸。为什么我有这些愿望和惋惜呢？要说明是困难的：那时候我连对自己也说不明白；然而我也有一个理由，而且是一个合乎逻辑的，自然的理由。不论怎样，当我把头发梳得很平，穿上我的黑衣裙——这虽然像教友派一样朴素，至少有一种非常合身的好处——并戴好干净的白颈饰的时候，我想我总可以满体面地到费尔法克斯太太前露面，我的新学生至少也不会厌恶地避开我了吧。我打开房里的窗子。看梳妆台上一切都放得整齐干净了，我就大胆走出去了。

（李霁野 译）

译文二

小嘴；希望自己长得高，庄严，身材丰满；我觉得自己长得那么矮小，那么苍白，五官长得那么不端庄、那么特征显著，真是一种不幸。为什么我会有这些渴望、这些惋惜呢？那是很难说的；当时我就没法对自己说清楚；不过，我是有个理由，而且是个合乎逻辑的、自然的理由。不管怎样，我还是把头发梳得很平服，穿上黑上衣——这看来虽然像贵格会教徒，但至少有非常合身的好处——把干净的白色领饰整整好，我想我总可以够体面地去见菲尔费克斯太太，我的新学生至少总不会厌恶地躲开我了吧。我把这卧房的窗户打开，注意让梳妆台上我所有的东西都放得整整齐齐，就鼓起勇气去了。

（祝庆英 译）

第四章 《骆驼祥子》英译文片段的批评赏析

一 关于《骆驼祥子》

《骆驼祥子》讲述的是旧中国北平城里一个人力车夫祥子的悲剧故事。祥子来自乡间，日益凋敝衰败的农村使他无法生存下去，他来到城市，渴望以自己的诚实劳动，开始新的生活。他尝试过各种工作，最后选中拉洋车。这一职业选择表明祥子尽管离开了土地，但其思维方式仍然是农民的。他习惯于个体劳动，同时又渴望有一辆像土地那样靠得住的车。买车，做个独立的劳动者，"这是他的志愿、希望，甚至是宗教。"城市似乎给了祥子实现志愿的机遇，经过三年奋斗，他买上了车，但不到半年，竟被人抢去；但祥子仍然不肯放弃拥有自己的一辆车的梦想，尽管他对自己的追求不无怀疑，几度动摇，但仍然不断振作起来，再度奋斗。应该说，祥子以坚韧的性格和执拗的态度与生活展开搏斗，而搏斗的结局，是以祥子的失败

二 《骆驼祥子》原文片段及四种英译文

原　文	译文一	译文二
祥子在海甸的一家小店里躺了三天，身上忽冷忽热，心中迷迷忽忽，牙床上起了一溜紫泡，只想喝水，不想吃什么。饿了三天，火气降下去，身上软得像皮糖似的。恐怕就是在这三天里，他与三匹骆驼的关系由梦话或胡话中被人家听了去。一清醒过来，他已经是"骆驼祥子"了。	For three days, Xiangzi rested in a small inn at Haidian, now burning with fever, now shivering with cold, his mind a blank. Purple blisters had appeared along his gums. He was racked by thirst but had no appetite. After fasting for three days, the fever abated and he felt as limp as taffy. It was probably during this time that people got to know about the three camels from his delirious raving, for when he finally came to his senses he was already "Camel Xiangzi".	Happy Boy lay for three days in a little inn in the town called Seas Domain, to the west of Peking. His body would suddenly become hot and then as suddenly cold again; his mind was confused and his gums were covered with blisters. He didn't want to eat anything, but only to drink water. After three days of fasting his fever subsided, leaving his body as soft and weak as taffy. At times during those three days, people must have heard Happy Boy talking in his sleep or in delirium about his relation to the three cam-

而告终的,他终于未能做成拥有自己一辆车的梦。这部小说的现实主义深刻性在于,它不仅描写了严酷的生活环境对祥子的物质剥夺,而且还刻画了祥子在生活理想被毁坏后的精神堕落。"他没了心,他的心被人家摘去了。"一个勤劳善良的农村青年,就这样被改塑成一个行尸走肉般的无业游民。

通过这部小说,作者老舍深刻揭露了旧中国的黑暗,控诉了统治阶级对劳动者的剥削和压迫,表达了作者对劳动人民的深切同情,向人们展示了军阀混战以及黑暗统治下的北京底层贫苦市民生活于痛苦深渊中的图景。

这里选取的是小说的第四章。祥子回到北平在海甸的一家小店住了三四天,梦话被人们听了去,从此得了一个"骆驼"的外号,他花了些钱将自己整顿好,又再次干起了拉车的营生,这一次他将家安在了刘四爷的人和车厂。透过刘四爷的车厂,老舍将笔墨展开,开始写到了车厂中其他的洋车夫,而祥子也在这里遇到了之后影响他一生的虎妞。祥子将花剩的30元大洋交给刘四爷保存,希望着有一天攒够了钱再次买上属于自己的车。

这里所选的英译文有三个版本,分别摘自由旅美华人翻译家施晓菁翻译的 *Camel Xiangzi*、美国翻译家 Even King 翻译的 *Rickshaw Boy* 和美国翻译家 Jean M. James 翻译的 *Rickshaw: the novel Lo-t'o Hsiang Tzu*。

译文三

　　Hiang Tzu lay for three days in a small inn in Hai Tien, his body shaking with chills and fever. He was delirious at times and had great purple blisters on his gums. Water was all he wanted, not food. Three days of fasting brought his temperature down and left his body flaccid as soft taffy. It was probably during these three days that, either by talking in his sleep or babbling deliriously, he let others find out about the camels. He was Camel Hiang Tzu even before he recovered.

译文四

　　Xiangzi lay in a small inn for three days at Haidian to the west of Peiping. Now burning with fever and now shivering with cold, he fell into a coma from time to time. With purple blisters all along his gums, he didn't want to have anything but only water. After going hungry for three days, his fever abated and he felt himself as soft as taffy. Perhaps it was just during these three days that people got to know from his talk or babble in his dreams his relationship with those three camels. So when he came to his senses, he

笔　记

原　文	译文一	译文二

els, because when he came to he already had the name "Happy Boy Camel".

自从一到城里来，他就是"祥子"，仿佛根本没有个姓；如今，"骆驼"摆在"祥子"之上，就更没有人关心他到底姓什么了。有姓无姓，他自己也并不在乎。不过，三条牲口才换了那么几块钱，而自己倒落了个外号，他觉得有点不大上算。

Since coming to town he had been known only as "Xiangzi" as if he had no surname. Now with "Camel" tacked on, people cared even less about his family name. He had never worried about his name before, but now he felt he had got the worst of the bargain, getting so little for those animals yet landing himself with this nickname.

From the time that he had first come to Peking he had been known as "Happy Boy", as if originally he had never had a surname. Now, with Camel added to his name, people cared less than ever to inquire what his surname was. He himself didn't care whether he had a last name or not. But to have sold three great big animals for such a trifling sum of money, and to have had a new nickname tacked to him as well, seemed to be a poor trade altogether.

刚能挣扎着立起来，他想出去看看。没想到自己的腿能会这样的不吃力，走到小店门口他一软就坐在了地上，昏昏沉沉的坐了好大半天，头上见上凉汗。又忍了一会儿，他睁开了眼，肚中响了一阵，觉出点饿来。极慢的立起来，找到了个馄饨挑儿。要了碗馄饨，他仍然坐在地上。呷了口汤，觉得恶心，在口中含了半天，勉强的咽下去；不想再喝。可是，待了一会儿，热汤像股线似的一直通到腹部，打了两个响嗝。他知道自己又有了命。

As soon as he could stand, he decided to go out and look around, but his legs were unbelievably weak and when he reached the door of the inn they suddenly gave way and he collapsed on the ground. He sat there in a daze for a long time, beads of cold sweat on his brow. He bore it stoically, then opened his eyes and heard his stomach rumbling. He felt a little hungry. Slowly he stood up and made his way to a peddler selling dumpling soup from a portable stove. He bought a bowl and sat down on the ground again. The first sip made him want to retch and he kept the liquid in his mouth for some time before finally forcing himself to swallow it. He didn't feel like having any more. However,

He had hardly struggled to his feet when he thought of going out to look around. He wouldn't have believed it possible that his legs could become so weak. When he got to the door of the little inn he had to sit down on the ground, and he stayed squatting there stupidly for a long while, his forehead covered with cold sweat. When the dizziness had passed, he opened his eyes again. His stomach made a noise and he began to feel a little hungry. Slowly he raised himself up and dragged himself along to a little stand where a peddler was selling steamed cakes. He bought a bowl of them and sat down again on the ground. The first mouthful of the soup made him sick and he held it

译文三

He had been simply Hiang Tzu, as if he had no family name, ever since he came to the city. Now that Camel was put before Hiang Tzu, no one would care what his family name was. Having or not having a family name didn't bother him, but to have sold three animals for only thirty-five dollars and then been stuck with a nickname to boot was nothing to brag about.

He decided to take a look around once he struggled to his feet, but he never expected his legs to be so weak. He collapsed feebly onto the ground when he got to the front door of the inn. He sat there, dizzily, for a long time, his forehead covered with cold sweat. He put up with it and then opened his eyes. His stomach rumbled; he felt a little hungry. He stood up very slowly and went over to a won ton peddler. Then, with a bowl of won ton soup, he sat down on the ground again. He took a mouthful and felt nauseated, but held the soup in his mouth awhile and forced it down. He didn't want any more. After a short wait it finally went straight down to his belly and he belched loudly

译文四

already got the nickname "Camel Xiangzi".

The first time he came to Peiping, he only got the name "Xiangzi", as if he simply had no family name. Now, with the nickname "Camel" placed before "Xiangzi", people would care even less about his family name. Whether he had a family name or not, he himself didn't care at all. However, selling three camels for such a small sum of money and at the same time getting a nickname was indeed not worthwhile, he thought.

As soon as he could struggle to his feet, he wanted to have a look around him. However, it never occurred to him that he felt so weak that when he reached the door of the inn, he suddenly gave way and collapsed onto the ground. He sat there in a daze for a long while, with cold sweat on his forehead. After quite another while, he opened his eyes, and hearing the noise from his stomach, he felt a little hungry. Very slowly, he came to his feet and edged toward a peddler selling wonton from a portable stove. He bought a bowl of wonton and sat back on the ground. He took a sip of the soup and the soup made him sick. He kept the soup in his mouth for a long while before he finally

原 文

肚中有了点食，他顾得看看自己了。身上瘦了许多，那条破裤已经脏得不能再脏。他懒得动，可是要马上恢复他的干净利落，他不肯就这么神头鬼脸的进城去。不过，要干净利落就得花钱，剃剃头，换换衣服，买鞋袜，都要钱。手中的三十五元钱应当一个不动，连一个不动还离买车的数儿很远呢！可是，他可怜了自己。虽然被兵们拉去不多的日子，到现在一想，一切都像个噩梦。这个噩梦使他老了许多，好像忽然的一气增多了好几岁。看着自己的大手大脚，明明是自己的，可是又像忽然由什么地方找到的。他非常的难过。他不敢想过去的那些委屈与危险，虽然不去想，可依然的存在，就好像连阴天的时候，不去看天也知道

译文一

a second later, the soup seemed to have threaded its way down to his stomach and he belched loudly twice. At that he knew he was going to survive.

With a little food in his stomach, he took stock of himself once more. He was much thinner and his tattered trousers were as filthy as could be. He didn't feel like moving yet was in a hurry to regain his old spruceness, not wanting to arrive in town looking so down and out. But that meant spending money. A shave, change of clothes, new shoes and socks all would cost money, yet he shouldn't touch a cent of the thirty-five dollars, already nowhere near enough to buy a rickshaw. However, he felt sorry for himself. Though he had not spent many days with the troops, it already seemed like a nightmare, a nightmare which had aged him considerably, as if overnight he had added years to his age. His big hands and feet were obviously his own yet it was as if he had suddenly found them somewhere. He felt very bad and dared not recall his past wrongs and dangers, though conscious of them all the time, just as one knows during a rainy period that it's a grey day

译文二

in his mouth a long while before he could force himself to swallow it. He didn't feel like taking any more, but in a moment the hot liquid made its way like a warm thread through his insides to the bottom of his stomach, and he belched a couple of times. He knew from that familiar sound that he had come back to life.

With a little food in his stomach, he had time to look himself over. His body was much thinner; the ragged old trousers he was wearing were already as dirty as they could ever become. He felt too lazy to move but he had to restore as quickly as he could his cleanliness and tidiness: he could not go into Peking looking like a shoddy old ghost. The only thing was that if he wanted to be clean and tidy he'd have to spend money. Getting his head shaved, changing his clothes, buying shoes and stockings—all these things would mean money. He shouldn't touch the thirty-five dollars he had in his pocket: even without spending a penny of it, it was still a long way from enough to buy a richshaw with. But he felt sorry for himself. Although the soldiers had not held him for long, it all seemed like a nightmare now—a nightmare that had made him much older, as if he had suddenly and in one breath added many years to his age. (Note: What follows in the

译文三	译文四
twice. He knew he still had life in him.	forced himself to swallow it. He didn't feel like it any more. But a moment later, the soup seemed to have warmly threaded its way down to his stomach. He belched loud twice. He knew that he was still alive.
He looked himself over after getting a little food in his stomach. He had lost a lot of weight and his ragged trousers couldn't have been dirtier. He was too tired to move but he had to get himself cleaned up immediately; he refused to enter the city looking like a wreck. Only he'd have to spend money to make himself clean and neat. It would take money to get his head shaved and buy a change of clothes and shoes and socks. He ought not to disturb the thirty-five dollars he had in hand. But after all, even if he didn't, wasn't it still a long way from enough to buy a richshaw? He took pity on himself.	With a little food in his stomach, he was energetic enough to take a look at himself: he was much thinner than before and his ragged old trousers could never be so dirty. He wanted to make no move at all, yet he was aware that he should instantly make himself as clean and tidy as before, for how could he go to town looking so down and out? However, to be made clean and tidy means spending money. A haircut, a change of clothes, and a pair of shoes and socks all mean money. Not a single cent of those thirty-five silver dollars that he had at the moment should be spent. Even without spending a single cent of them, the sum was still far from enough to buy a rickshaw. He, then, began to take pity on himself. Though he had been detained by the soldiers for only a couple of days, it all seemed like a nightmare whenever he thought about it now. The nightmare aged him considerably as if he had taken on many years in one single breath. Looking at his own
Although it wasn't so long ago that he had been captured by the soldiers, it was all like a nightmare when he thought about it now. This nightmare had aged him considerably; it was as if he'd taken on many years in a single breath. When he looked at his big hands and feet it was obvious they were his, but	

原 文	译文一	译文二
天是黑的。他觉得自己的身体是特别的可爱，不应该再太自苦了。他立起来，明知道身上还很软，可是刻不容缓的想打扮打扮，仿佛只要剃剃头，换件衣服，他就能立刻强壮起来似的。 （老舍《骆驼祥子》）	without looking at the sky. His body seemed to him particularly precious, he really shouldn't be so hard on it. He stood up. Though he knew he was still very weak, he must lose no time in sprucing up, for once his head was shaved and he'd changed his clothes he was sure he would recover his strength right away. （施晓菁 译）	source text has been omitted from the translation.) （Evan King 译）

译文三

they looked like they might have been picked up any old place. He didn't dare think of all the hardship and danger he'd just gone through, but it was still there even though he didn't think about it. It was like knowing the sky is overcast during a succession of dark days, even though you do not go out to look at it. He knew his body was especially precious; he should not make himself suffer. He stood up, aware that he was still very weak, intending to go get properly dressed without another minute's delay—as if all he needed was to get his head shaved and his clothes changed to be strong again instantly.

(Jean M. James 译)

译文四

big hands and feet which obviously belonged to him, he suddenly felt as if they were picked up from somewhere unknown. It was indeed very miserable of him. He didn't dare to recall all the wrongs he had suffered and all the dangers he had experienced. Though he might not think about them, they were still there. It remained just like that during a span of several dark days: you knew it very well that it was overcast outside even if without going out for a look. He knew that he had a particularly lovely body which should not be too much exploited. He came to his feet, though fully aware that he was still very weak. To him, what admitted no delay was that he should get himself properly dressed. It seemed that right away, only a haircut or a change of clothes would enable him to recover his strength.

（李明 译）

三 小说翻译的批评与赏析练习

原 文

互 助

　　L君跻身文坛，盖有年矣，但总是红不起来，颇感寂寞。于是，他找到了各种关系，以盛宴重礼把著名的评论家J君招待了一次。J君有感于其情之盛，慨然允诺说："现在他们对你太冷落了，就是不公平！我一定要写一篇推荐你的作品的文章，登到大报上，你的作品的优点是……"

　　L君不等J君说完，慌忙摆手摇头，他说："千万不必！千万不必！我只祈求您写一篇义正词严的文章把我批一个狗血淋头！积数十年之经验，我深知凡被您批了的，都可以风行全国，名震环球！而您也可以获得另一方面的美誉和利益，那才叫相反相成，相得益彰！

译文一

Mutual Help

　　It had been several years since Mr. Yi had climbed up in the literary world, but he was still not very popular. Through various connections, he managed to meet the famous critic Mr. Jiang and invite him to a sumptuous banquet.

　　"They neglect you unfairly," said Mr. Jiang, moved by Yi's hospitality. "I will write a laudatory essay and publish it in an influential newspaper. Your work is characterized by …"

　　But before Mr. Jiang could finish, Mr. Yi shook his head and said, "Please do not compliment my work. I implore you to write an article denouncing me. According to my observations over the past ten years, the works that you criticize become popular both at home and abroad. You, in turn, build your reputation and earn a nice income. That's what we call 'mutual help'".

（冯庆华，1997：462）

译文二

Helping Each Other

　　Mr. L. had been a member of the literary circles for years without attracting any public attention. He felt deserted, but he managed through various personal connections to invite Mr. J., a famous literary critic, to an elaborate dinner. Mr. J. was quite moved by Mr. L.'s hospitality and promised right away, "It's not fair that you have been so ignored! I must write an article for a key newspaper to recommend your works. The merits of your works are …"

　　Mr. L. cut in, shaking his head and waving his hands, "No! No! I only beg you to write a very severe criticism against me. From my years of experience, I have come to the conclusion that all work criticized by you will become popular not only in our country but also in the world. Meanwhile, you win greater fame through your criticism. This is indeed mutual help and profit!"

（夏乙琥 译）

第五章 《红楼梦》英译文片段的批评赏析

一 关于《红楼梦》

曹雪芹的《红楼梦》是我国古典小说艺术的最高峰。以贾、史、王、薛四大家族为背景，以贾宝玉、林黛玉的爱情悲剧为中心，表现了具有叛逆倾向的青年与传统思想的尖锐冲突，揭示了封建社会走向没落的必然趋势。在总的思想倾向上，打破了传统的大团圆的结局，写了一部彻头彻尾的悲剧。在爱情婚姻问题上，突破了传统的郎才女貌、一见钟情的才子佳人俗套，提倡以思想倾向的一致作为爱情基础的知己之爱，并对爱情这一题材进行了丰富深入的描写。在题材选取上，一反传统小说题材因袭的现象，比以前任何作品都更发扬了以现实生活作为创作基础的现实主义原则。在人物塑造上，打破了传统的传奇式的写法，以写实的手法塑造出一大批多侧面、立体化、个性化的典型形象，如凤姐、宝玉、黛玉、宝钗等，"和从前小说叙好人完全是好，坏人完全是坏的，大不相同，所以其中所叙的人物，都是真的人物"（鲁迅语）。在情节上，摆脱了传统小说追求曲折离奇的故事情节的倾向，善于从平凡的日常生活中挖掘出不寻常的审美意义；在结构上，一反传统小说的线形结构形式，采用了纵横交织的网状结构形式。《红楼梦》具有高度的思想性和卓越的艺术成就，不愧为中国小说难以征服的顶峰。

这里选取了《红楼梦》这部小说的第六回"贾宝玉初试云雨情 刘姥姥一进荣国府"中的一部分。这里描写了刘姥姥一大早起床带着板儿到荣国府找王夫人求助。在太太的陪房周瑞家的引荐下，刘姥姥先见到平儿，误以为凤姐。终于，刘姥姥见到了凤姐，凤姐的态度不热不冷。

这里选了三个英译文，分别是杨宪益、戴乃迭翻译的 *A Dream of Red Mansions*、David Hawkes 翻译的 *The Story of the Stone* 和 Chi-Chen Wang 翻译的 *Dream of the Red Chamber*。

二 《红楼梦》原文片段及四种英译文

原 文

次日天未明,刘姥姥便起来梳洗了,又将板儿教训了几句。那板儿才五六岁的孩子,一无所知,听见带他进城逛去,便喜的无不应承。于是刘姥姥带他进城,找至宁荣街。来至荣府大门石狮子前,只见簇簇轿马,刘姥姥便不敢过去,且掸了掸衣服,又教了板儿几句话,然后蹲到角门前。只见几个挺胸叠肚指手画脚的人,坐在大板凳上,说东谈西呢。刘姥姥只得蹭上来问:"太爷们纳福。"众人打量了他一会,便问:"那里来的?"刘姥姥陪笑道:"我找太太的陪房周大爷的,烦那位太爷替我请他老出来。"那些人听了,都不瞅睬,半日方说道:"你远远的在那墙角下等着,一会子他们家有人就出来的。"内中有一老年人说道:"不要误他的事,何苦耍

译文一

The next day Granny Liu got up before dawn to wash and comb her hair and to coach Baner. Being an ignorant child of five or six, he was so delighted at the prospect of a trip to the city that he agreed to everything he was told.

In town they asked their way to Rong Ning Street. But Granny Liu was too overawed by the crowd of sedan-chairs and horses there to venture near the stone lions which flanked the Rong Mansion's main gate. Having dusted off her clothes and given Baner fresh instructions, she timidly approached the side entrance where some arrogant, corpulent servants were sunning themselves on long benches, engaged in a lively discussion.

Granny Liu edged forward and said, "Greetings, gentlemen."

The men surveyed her from head to foot before condescending to ask where she had come from.

"I've come to see Mr. Zhou who came with Lady Wang when she was married," she told them with a smile. "May I trouble one

译文二

Next day Grannie Liu was up before dawn. As soon as she had washed and done her hair, she set about teaching Ban-er a few words to say to the ladies at the great house—an exercise to which he submitted cheerfully enough, as would any little boy of four or five who had been promised an outing to the great city. That done, she set off on her journey, and in due course made her way to Two Dukes Street. There, at each side of the stone lions which flanked the gates of the Rong Mansion, she saw a cluster of horses and palanquins. Not daring to go straight up, she first dusted down her clothes and rehearsed Ban-er's little repertoire of phrases before sidling up to one of the side entrances.

A number of important-looking gentlemen sat in the gate-way sunning their bellies and discoursing with animated gestures on a wide variety of topics. Grannie Liu waddled up to them and offered a respectful salutation. After looking her up and down for a moment or two, they asked her business, Grannie Liu smiled ingratiatingly.

"I've come to see Old Zhou that used to be in service with Her Ladyship before she married. Could I trouble one of you gentlemen to fetch him out for me?"

The gentlemen ignored her request and returned to their discussion. After she had waited there for some considerable time one of them said, "If you stand at that gate along there on the corner, someone from inside the house

译文三	译文四	笔 记

译文三

The next morning, Liu Lao-lao got up before dawn, combed her hair and washed her face, and coached Pan-er, who was to accompany her, in what he was to say. She went into the city and inquired her way to the Yungkuofu. After waiting a while by one of the stone lions, she went timidly to the side gate and greeted in very humble terms the servants sitting around there. They surveyed grandmother and child from head to foot, then asked what she wanted. "I have come to see Chou Ta-yeh[1], Tai-tai's pei-fang," Liu Lao-lao answered with a smile. "Would one of you gentlemen be kind enough to ask him please to come out?"

It was some time before one of them answered, "Go over there in the corner and wait. He may come out by and by."

Liu Lao-lao was about to comply when an older man admonished the first speaker, saying, "You shouldn't make her waste her time like that," and then turning to Liu Lao-lao, he added, "Chou Ta-yeh is on a trip to the south. But his wife is at home. If you want to see her, you can go to the back street and inquire at the

译文四

Before dawn the next day, Granny Liu got up to freshen herself up and taught Ban'er a few words to say to the ladies at the great house. Ban'er, a five- or six-year-old child who knew nothing about the world, was but only too pleased to follow her instructions as he had been promised a trip to the city. When everything was ready, Granny Liu took Ban'er towards the city and found her way to the Ning-Rong Street. In due time, they arrived before the stone lions at the gate to the Rong Mansion. With sedan-chairs and horses before her, Granny Liu did not dare to venture near them. Having whisked away the dust off her clothes and taught Ban'er a few more words to say, she crouched down before the side entrance where she saw some arrogant-looking men sitting on the benches and discoursing on a wide variety of topics with animated gestures. Granny Liu could do nothing but edged forward and said, "Good day, dear sirs!" The men looked her up and down for a while before they asked about her business. With an ingratiating smile, Granny Liu said, "I've come to see Mr. Zhou who came with Lady Wang when she was married. May I trouble one of you to fetch him for me?" None of those men paid any attention to her and went on with their talk. After a long while, one of them said to her, "You just wait at the far corner of the wall and someone from his family would come to see you in no time." One elderly man from them interposed, "Why make fun of her

原　文	译文一	译文二
他。"因向刘姥姥道："那周大爷已往南边去了。他在后一带住着，他娘子却在家。你要找时，从这边绕到后街上后门上去问就是了。" 刘姥姥听了谢过，遂携了板儿，绕到后门上。只见门前歇着些生意担子，也有卖吃的，也有卖玩耍物件的，闹吵吵三二十个小孩子在那里厮闹。刘姥姥便拉住一个道："我问哥儿一声，有个周大娘可在家么？"孩子们道："那个周大娘？我们这里周大娘有三个呢，还有两个周奶奶，不知是那一行当的？"刘姥姥道："是太太的陪房周瑞。"孩子道："这个容易，你跟我来。"说着，跳蹭蹭的引着刘姥姥进了后门，至一院墙边，指与刘姥姥道："这就是他家。"又叫道："周大娘，有个老奶奶来找你呢，我带了来了。"	of you gentlemen to fetch him out for me?" The men ignored her for a while, but finally one of them said, "Wait over there by that corner. One of his family may come out by and by." An older man interposed, "Why make a fool of her and waste her time?" He told Granny Liu, "Old Zhou has gone south but his wife is at home. His house is at the back. Go round to the back gate and ask for her there." Having thanked him, Granny Liu took Baner round to the back gate. Several peddlars had put down their wares there and about two dozen rowdy servant boys had crowded round those selling snacks and toys. The old woman caught hold of one of these youngsters and asked, "Can you tell me, brother, if Mrs. Zhou is at home?" "Which Mrs. Zhou?" he retorted. "We have three Mrs. Zhous and two Granny Zhous. What's her job?" "She's the wife of Zhou Rui who came with Lady Wang." "That's easy then. Come with me." He scampered ahead of her through the back gate and pointed	should be coming out presently." But a more elderly man among them protested that it was "a shame to send her on a fool's errand", and turning to Grannie Liu he said, "Old Zhou is away in the South at the moment, but his missus is still at home. She lives round at the back. You'll have to go from here round to the back gate in the other street and ask for her there." Grannie Liu thanked him and trotted off with little Ban-er all the way round to the rear entrance. There she found a number of sweetmeat vendors and toy-sellers who had set their wares down outside the gate and were being besieged by a crowd of some twenty or thirty noisy, yelling children. She grabbed a small urchin from their midst and drew him towards her. "Tell me, sonny, is there a Mrs Zhou living here?" The urchin stared back at her impudently. "Which Mrs Zhou? There are several Mrs Zhous here. What's her job?" "She's the Mrs Zhou that came here with Her Ladyship when she was married." "That's easy," said the urchin. "Follow me!" He led Grannie Liu into a rear courtyard. "That's where she lives," he said, pointing in the direction of a side wall. Then, bawling over the wall, "Mrs Zhou, there's an old woman come to see you!" Zhou Rui's wife came hurrying out

译文三

gate there."

　　Liu Lao-lao thanked the man and made her way with Pan-er to the back gate. She saw there a number of peddlers, some selling food and some selling toys and other things, and a score or so of servant boys. She caught hold of one of the latter and asked, "Would you tell me, little brother, where I can find Chou Ta-niang[2]?"

　　"Which Chou Ta-niang?" the boy asked impatiently. "We have several of them here."

　　"I want the one who is Tai-tai's pei-fang," Liu Lao-lao said.

　　"That's easy," the boy said. "You come along with me."

　　He led Liu Lao-lao inside and, pointing to one of the small compounds, said to her, "That's where she lives." Then he called, "Chou Ta-niang, someone here is to see you."

　　When Chou Jui's wife finally recognized her caller, she said, "So it is you, Liu Lao-lao. I am sorry I did not recognize you immediately. It is so long since we saw each other. Please come in."

译文四

and waste her time?" He then turned to her, saying, "That Mr. Zhou has gone south on business. His house is at the back quarters. Only his wife is at home now. Just go round from here to the back gate in the back street and find her there."

　　Granny Liu thanked him for his kind help and took Ban'er all the way round to the back gate. There she saw that outside the gate were set wares of some vendors who sell either snacks or toys. Around the vendors were crowded about two dozens of children making a huge commotion.

　　Granny Liu grabbed one of them and asked, "Tell me, little brother, is Mrs. Zhou at home?"

　　The child looked at her in a puzzle. "Which Mrs. Zhou? We have three Mrs. Zhous and two Granny Zhous here. Which family does she belong to?"

　　Granny Liu said, "Oh, she's the wife of Zhou Rui who came with Lady Wang."

　　The child then said, "Oh, that's easy. Please follow me."

　　With that, he scampered ahead of Granny Liu through a back gate to the wall of a compound and pointed to Granny Liu, "That's where she lives." Meanwhile, he called at the top of his voice, "Auntie Zhou, here's a granny coming to see you."

　　When Zhou Rui's wife heard about

笔　记

原文

周瑞家的在内听说，忙迎了出来，问："是那位？"刘姥姥忙迎上来问道："好呀，周嫂子！"周瑞家的认了半日，方笑道："刘姥姥，你好呀！你说说，能几年，我就忘了。请家里来坐罢。"刘姥姥一壁里走着，一壁笑说道："你老是贵人多忘事，那里还记得我们呢。"说着，来至房中。周瑞家的命雇的下丫头倒上茶来吃着。周瑞家的又问板儿道："你都长这们大了！"又问些别后闲话。又问刘姥姥："今日还是路过，还是特来的？"刘姥姥便说："原是特来瞧瞧嫂子你，二则也请请姑太太的安。若可以领我见一见更好，若不能，便借重嫂子转致意罢了。"

（曹雪芹《红楼梦》）

译文一

out a compound. "That's where she lives." Then he called, "Auntie Zhou! Here's a granny asking for you."

Mrs. Zhou hurried out to see who it was while Granny Liu hastened forward crying, "Sister Zhou! How are you?"

It took the other some time to recognize her. Then she answered with a smile, "Why, it's Granny Liu! I declare, after all these years I hardly knew you. Come on in and sit down."

Smiling as she walked in, Granny Liu remarked, "The higher the rank, the worse the memory. How could you remember us?"

Once indoors, Mrs. Zhou told a maid to pour tea. Then looking at Baner she exclaimed, "What a big boy he is!" After a short exchange of polite inquiries, she asked Granny Liu whether she just happened to be passing or had come with any special object.

"I came especially to see you, sister, and also to inquire after Her ladyship's health. If you could take me to see her, that would be nice. If you can't, I'll just trouble you to pass on my respects."

（杨宪益、戴乃迭　译）

译文二

and asked who it was.

"How are you, my dear?" said Grannie Liu, advancing with a smile. Zhou Rui's wife scrutinized her questioningly for some moments before finally recognizing her.

"Why, it's Grannie Liu! How are you? It's so many years since I saw you last, I'd forgotten all about you! Come in and sit down!"

Grannie Liu followed her cackling.

"You know what they say: 'Important people have short memories.' I wouldn't expect you to remember the likes of us!"

When they were indoors, Zhou Rui's wife ordered her little hired help to pour out some tea.

"And hasn't Ban-er grown a big boy!" said Zhou Rui's wife; then, after a few inquiries about the various things that had happened since they last met, she asked Grannie Liu about her visit.

"Were you just passing by, or have you come specially?"

"Well, of course, first and foremost we came to see you," replied Grannie Liu mendaciously, "but we were also hoping to pay our respects to Her Ladyship. If you could take us to see her, that would be very nice; but if that's not possible, perhaps we could trouble you just to give her our regards."

(David Hawkes　译)

译文三

After exchanging polite inquiries, Chou Jui's wife asked Liu Lao-lao whether she was just passing by or had come on some special business. "I have come just to see you," the latter answered. "But I would like to present my greetings to our Ku Tai-tai [Madame Wang] as long as I am here. If Sao-sao[3] can arrange an interview for me, it would be a great honor, but if it is not convenient, just mention my visit when you have the opportunity."

(Chi-Chen Wang 译)

[1] Ta-yeh ("big father", or "uncle older than one's father") is here used merely as an honorific.

[2] Ta-niang ("big mother", or "wife of an uncle older than one's father") is here used as an honorific for a married woman.

[3] Sao-sao: "wife of an older brother".

译文四

that, she came hurrying out and asked who it was. Granny Liu hastened forward and greeted her, saying, "How are you, Sister Zhou?"

When Zhou Rui's wife heard about this, she came hurrying out and asked who it was. Granny Liu hastened forward and greeted her, saying, "How are you, Sister Zhou?" It took Mrs. Zhou quite a while to recognize her before she said, "Why, it's Granny Liu. How are things with you? You can't imagine I can hardly recognize you after only a few years! Do come in and take a seat." By following her closely, Granny Liu said with a smile, "Oh, that's natural. Important people forget things easily. How is it possible for you to remember us?" As they talked, they entered her house. Mrs. Zhou urged her maid to serve them some tea. She then turned to Ban'er and said, "What a big boy you are now!" After some exchange of polite remarks, she asked Granny Liu, "Are you just passing through or do you come for a special purpose?" Granny Liu said, "First, I've come specially to see you. Second, I've come to pay respects to Her Ladyship. It would be better if you could be so kind as to bring me before her. If that's not possible, could I possibly trouble you to give my best regards to her?"

(李明 译)

三 小说翻译的批评与赏析练习

原　文

余忆童稚时，能张目对日，明察秋毫，见藐小微物，必细察其纹理，故时有物外之趣。夏蚊成雷，私拟作群鹤舞空。心之所向，则或千或百，果然鹤也。昂首观之，项为之强。又留蚊于素帐中，徐喷以烟，使其冲烟飞鸣，作青云白鹤观，果如鹤唳云端，怡然称快。于土墙凹凸处，花台小草丛杂处，常蹲其身，使与台齐；定神细视，以丛草为林，以虫蚁为兽，以土砾凸者为丘，凹者为壑，神游其中，怡然自得。

一日，见二虫斗草间，观之正浓，忽有庞然大物拔山倒树而来，盖一癞虾蟆也。舌一吐而二虫尽为所吞。余年幼方出神，不觉呀然惊恐。神定，捉虾蟆，鞭数十，驱之别院。年长思之，二虫之斗，盖图奸不从也。古语

译文一

I remember that when I was a child, I could stare at the sun with wide, open eyes. I could see the tiniest objects, and loved to observe the fine grains and patterns of things, from which I derived a romantic, unworldly pleasure. When mosquitoes were humming round in summer, I transformed them in my imagination into a company of storks dancing in the air. And when I regarded them that way, they were real storks to me, flying by the hundreds and thousands, and I would look up at them until my neck was stiff. Again, I kept a few mosquitoes inside a white curtain and blew a puff of smoke round them, so that to me they became a company of white storks flying among the blue clouds, and their humming was to me the song of storks singing in high heaven, which delighted me intensely. Sometimes I would squat by a broken, earthen wall, or by a little bush on a raised flower-bed, with my eyes on the same level as the flower-bed itself, and there I would look and look, transforming in my mind the little plot of grass into a forest and the ants and insects into wild animals. The little elevations on the ground became my hills, and the depressed areas became my valleys, and my spirit wandered in that world at leisure.

译文二

When I was small I could stare directly at the sun with my eyes wide open. I could see the smallest things clearly and often took an almost mystic pleasure in making out the patterns on them.

During the summer, whenever I heard the sound of mosquitoes swarming, I would pretend they were a flock of cranes dancing across the open sky, and in my imagination they actually would become hundreds of cranes. I would look at them so long my neck became stiff. At night I would let mosquitoes inside my mosquito netting, blow smoke at them, and imagine that what I saw were white cranes soaring through blue clouds. It really did look like cranes flying among the clouds, and it was a sight that delighted me.

I would often squat down by unkempt grassy places in flower beds or by niches in walls, low enough so that my head was level with them, and concentrate so carefully that to me the grass became a forest and the insects became animals. Imagining that small mounds of earth were hills and that shallow holes were valleys, I let my spirit wander there in happiness and contentment.

Once while I was concentrating

原　文	译文一	译文二
云："奸近杀"，虫亦然耶？贪此生涯，卵为蚯蚓所哈（吴俗呼阳曰卵），肿不能便。捉鸭开口哈之，婢妪偶释手，鸭颠其颈作吞噬状，惊而大哭；传为话柄。此皆幼时闲情也。 及长，爱花成癖，喜剪盆树。识张兰坡，始精剪枝养节之法，继悟接花叠石之法。花以兰为最，取其幽香韵致也，而瓣品之稍堪入谱者不可多得。兰坡临终时，赠余荷瓣素心春兰一盆，皆肩平心阔，茎细瓣净，可以入谱者。余珍如拱璧。值余幕游于外，芸能亲为灌溉，花叶颇茂。不二年，一旦忽萎死。起根视之，皆白如玉，且兰芽勃然。初不可解，以为无福消受，浩叹而已。事后始悉有人欲分不允，故用滚汤灌杀也。从此誓不植兰。 （沈复《浮生六记·闲情记趣》）	One day, I saw two little insects fighting among the grass, and while I was all absorbed watching the fight, there suddenly appeared a big monster, overturning my hills and rearing up my forest—it was a little toad. With one lick of his tongue, he swallowed up the two insects. I was so lost in my young imaginary world that I was taken unawares and quite frightened. When I had recovered myself, I caught the toad, struck it several dozen times and chased it out of the courtyard. Thinking of this incident afterwards when I was grown up, I understood that these two little insects were committing adultery by rape. "The wages of sin is death." So says an ancient proverb, and I wondered whether it was true of the insects also. I was a naughty boy, and once my ball (for we call the genital organ a "ball" in Soochow) was bitten by an earthworm and became swollen. Believing that the duck's saliva would act as an antidote for insect bites, they held a duck over it, but the maid-servant, who was holding the duck, accidentally let her hand go, and the duck was going to swallow it. I got frightened and screamed. People used to tell this story to make fun of me. These were the little incidents of my childhood days. When I was grown up, I loved flowers very much and was very fond of training pot flowers and pot plants.	all my attention on two insects battling in the grass, a giant suddenly appeared, knocking down the mountains and pulling up the trees. It was nothing but a toad, but with one flick of his tongue he swallowed both the insects. I was small, and because I had been so caught up in the scene I could not help being frightened. When I had calmed down, I caught the toad, spanked it severely, and expelled it to a neighbor's yard. Since growing up I have sometimes thought that the battle of the two insects was probably an attempted rape. The ancients said, "Rapists deserve death." I wonder, was this why the insects were eaten by the toad? One day while I was absorbed in my imaginary world, my egg was bitten by an earthworm (in Soochow we call the male organs eggs), so that it swelled up and I could not urinate. The servants caught a duck, and were forcing it to open its mouth over the wound, when suddenly one of them let go of the bird. The duck stretched out its neck as if to bite me there, and I screamed with fright. This became a family joke. These were all things that happened to me when I was small. When I was a little older I became obsessed with a love of flowers, and found much delight in pruning miniature potted trees to make them look like real ones. It was not until I met Chang Lan-po, however, that

原文

译文一

When I knew Chang Lanp'o, I learnt from him the secrets of trimming branches and protecting joints, and later the art of grafting trees and making rockeries. The orchid was prized most among all the flowers because of its subdued fragrance and graceful charm, but it was difficult to obtain really good classic varieties. At the end of his days, Lanp'o presented me with a pot of orchids, whose flowers had lotus-shaped petals; the center of the flowers was broad and white, the petals were very neat and even at the "shoulders", and the stems were very slender. This type was classical, and I prized it like a piece of old jade. When I was working away from home, Yün used to take care of it personally and it grew beautifully. After two years, it died suddenly one day. I dug up its roots and found that they were white like marble, while nothing was wrong with the sprouts, either. At first, I could not understand this, but ascribed it with a sigh merely to my own bad luck, which might be unworthy to keep such flowers. Later on, I found out that some one had asked for some off-shoots from the same pot, had been refused, and had therefore killed it by pouring boiling water over it. Thenceforth I swore I would never grow orchids again.

（林语堂 译）

译文二

I began really to learn how to prune branches and care for sprouts, and later to understand grafting and the creation of miniature rock formations in the pots. My favorite flower was the orchid, because of its elegant fragrance and charming appearance, though it is difficult to obtain ones that can be considered truly classic.

Shortly before Lan-po died he presented me with a pot of orchids that looked like lotus flowers. The centers were white and broad, and the edges of the petals were straight. They had thin stems, and the petals themselves were quite pale. This was a classic flower, and I treasured mine like a piece of old jade. When I was away from home Yün would water it herself, and its flowers and leaves grew luxuriantly. After I had had it for almost two years, however, it suddenly dried up and died. I dug it up and found the roots in good condition, white as jade with many new shoots. At first I could not understand it, and could only sigh at the thought that I was simply not luck enough to raise so fine a flower. Only later did I learn that someone who had asked for a cutting and been refused had poured boiling water over it and killed it. I swore that from that time on I would never grow orchids again.

(Leonard Pratt and Chiang Su-hui 译)

第六章 《一件小事》英译文的批评赏析

一 关于《一件小事》

在鲁迅先生所创作的众多小说之中,《一件小事》是较为经典的一篇。虽然小说篇幅不长,但给人的印象最为深刻。《一件小事》主要围绕着我、车夫、老太太、巡警四人展开。鲁迅先生将我从一开始对老太太被撞一事表示的冷漠与后来车夫对此事表示的热心进行对照,突出了《一件小事》中的人性之美。尤其是通过"毫不理会""扶起""挽着臂膊立定""却毫不踌躇"等细致入微的动作描写,刻画了车夫渐渐变得高大的形象,一改我们印象之中车夫对富商的唯唯诺诺的形象。可以说,在鲁迅先生的笔下,车夫这个最为平凡却又最难于描写的人物变得栩栩如生,更贴近于生活。从小说末尾"我"的一番自责:"以前的事姑且搁起,这一大把铜元又是什么意思?奖他么?我还能裁判车夫么?"中,我们看到了鲁迅先生的寓意已大白于众。在此,他不仅赞赏了车夫的正义行为,而且也寄托了他的另类情怀:在封建社会的阴影之下,人与人之间也应当充满热情,和睦相处。

鲁迅的小说写的是平凡人的平凡的生活,没有离奇的故事,没有引人入胜的情节,却充满了无穷的艺术魅力。读鲁迅的小说,时时有一种"发现的喜悦"。画面是普通的画面,人物是普通的人物,但却在这么普通的画面和普通的人物身上,随时都能注意到我们平时注意不到的特征,觉察到平时觉察不到的人物的心理活动,体会到被我们忽视了的可贵品质。多少年来,他的作品、他的思想启蒙着一代又一代的炎黄子孙,为中华民族的伟大复兴作出了不朽的贡献。

一 《一件小事》原文及四种英译文

原文

一件小事

我从乡下跑到京城里，一转眼已经六年了。其间耳闻目睹的所谓国家大事，算起来也很不少；但在我心里，都不留什么痕迹，倘要我寻出这些事的影响来说，便只是增长了我的坏脾气，——老实说，便是教我一天比一天的看不起人。

但有一件小事，却于我有意义，将我从坏脾气里拖开，使我至今忘记不得。

这是民国六年的冬天，大北风刮得正猛，我因为生计关系，不得不一早在路上走。一路几乎遇不见人，好容易才雇定了一辆人力车，教他拉到S门去。不一会，北风小了，路上浮尘早已刮净，剩下一条洁白的大道来，车夫也跑得更快。

刚近S门，忽而车把上带着一个人，慢慢地倒了。

译文一

A Small Incident

Six years have slipped by since I came from the country to the capital. During that time the number of so-called affairs of state I have witnessed or heard about is far from small, but none of them made much impression. If asked to define their influence on me, I can only say they made my bad temper worse. Frankly speaking, they taught me to take a poorer view of people every day.

One small incident, however, which struck me as significant and jolted me out of my irritability, remains fixed even now in my memory.

It was the winter of 1917, a strong north wind was blustering, but the exigencies of earning my living forced me to be up and out early. I met scarcely a soul on the road, but eventually managed to hire a rickshaw to take me to S-Gate. Presently the wind dropped a little, having blown away the drifts of dust on the road to leave a clean broad highway, and the rickshaw man quickened his pace. We were just approaching S-Gate when we knocked into someone who slowly toppled over.

译文二

An Incident

Six years have slipped by since I came from the country to the capital. During that time I have seen and heard quite enough of so-called affairs of state; but none of them made much impression on me. If asked to define their influence, I can only say they aggravated my ill temper and made me, frankly speaking, more and more misanthropic.

One incident, however, struck me as significant, and aroused me from my ill temper, so that even now I cannot forget it.

It happened during the winter of 1917. A bitter north wind was blowing, but, to make a living, I had to be up and out early. I met scarcely a soul on the road, and had great difficulty in hiring a rickshaw to take me to S-Gate. Presently the wind dropped a little. By now the loose dust had all been blown away, leaving the roadway clean, and the rickshaw man quickened his pace. We were just approaching S-Gate when someone crossing the road was entangled in our rickshaw and slowly fell.

It was a woman, with streaks

译文三

A Little Incident

Six years have gone by, as so many winks, since I came to the capital from the village. During all that time there have occurred many of those events known as "affairs of state", a great number of which I have seen or heard about. My heart does not seem to have been in the least affected by any of them, and recollection now only tends to increase my ill-temper, and cause me to like people less and less as the day wears on. But one little incident alone is deep with meaning to me, and I am unable to forget it even now.

It was a winter day in the Sixth Year of the Republic, and a strong northerly wind blew furiously. To make a living I had to be up early, and on the way to my duties I encountered scarcely anyone. After much difficulty I finally succeeded in hiring a rickshaw. I told the puller to take me to the South Gate.

After a while the wind moderated its fury, and in its wake the streets were left clean of the loose dust. The puller ran quickly. Just as we approached the South Gate somebody ran in front of us, got entangled in the rickshaw, and tumbled to the ground.

译文四

An Incident

It has been six years since I came from the country to the capital. During this period, I have heard or witnessed countless numbers of the so-called affairs of the state, but I can find no trace of them in my mind. If asked to decide on their impact on me, I can only say that they have sharpened my ill-temper. —Or to be frank, they have caused me to become more and more disdainful.

One incident, however, meant a great deal to me and drew me away from my ill temper. It lingers on in my mind till even today.

It was in the winter of 1917. A strong north wind was blustering. In order to make a living, I had to get up and go out early. I scarcely met a single soul on the road and eventually managed to hire a rickshaw to take me to the S-Gate. Presently the wind dropped a little. By now the loose dust had all been blown away, leaving the roadway very much clean so that the rickshaw man could quicken his steps. We were just approaching the S-Gate when someone crossing the road was caught in our rickshaw and slowly fell.

It was a woman, grey-haired

笔 记

原文

跌倒的是一个女人，花白头发，衣服都很破烂。伊从马路边上突然向车前横截过来；车夫已经让开道，但伊的破棉背心没有上扣，微风吹着，向外展开，所以终于兜着车把。幸而车夫早有点停步，否则伊定要栽一个大斤斗，跌到头破血出了。

伊伏在地上；车夫便也立住脚。我料定这老女人并没有伤，又没有别人看见，便很怪他多事，要自己惹出是非，也误了我的路。

我便对他说，"没有什么的。走你的罢！"

车夫毫不理会，——或者并没有听到，——却放下车子，扶那老女人慢慢起来，搀着臂膊立定，问伊说：

"您怎么啦？"

"我摔坏了。"

我想，我眼见你慢慢倒地，怎么会摔坏呢，装腔作势罢了，这真可憎恶。车夫多

译文一

It was a grey-haired woman in ragged clothes. She had stepped out abruptly from the roadside in front of us, and although the rickshaw man had swerved, her tattered padded waistcoat, unbuttoned and billowing in the wind, had caught on the shaft. Luckily the rickshaw man had slowed down, otherwise she would certainly have had a bad fall and it might have been a serious accident.

She huddled there on the ground, and the rickshaw man stopped. As I did not believe the old woman was hurt and as no one else had seen us, I thought this halt of his uncalled for, liable to land him in trouble and hold me up.

"It's all right," I said. "Go on."

He paid no attention—he may not have heard—but set down the shafts, took the old woman's arm and gently helped up.

"Are you all right?" he asked.

"I hurt myself falling."

I thought: I saw how slowly you fell, how could you be hurt? Putting on an act like this is simply disgusting. The rickshaw man asked for trouble, and now he's got it. He'll have to find his own way out.

译文二

of white in her hair, wearing ragged clothes. She had left the pavement without warning to cut across in front of us, and although the rickshaw man had made way, her tattered jacket, unbuttoned and fluttering in the wind, had caught on the shaft. Luckily the rickshaw man was already pulling up quickly, otherwise she would certainly have had a bad fall and been seriously injured.

She lay there on the ground, and the rickshaw man stopped. I did not think the old woman was hurt, and there had been no witnesses to what had happened, so I resented this officiousness which might land him in trouble and hold me up.

"It's all right," I said. "Go on."

He paid no attention, however—perhaps he had not heard—for he set down the shafts, and gently helped the old woman get up. Supporting her by one arm, he asked:

"Are you all right?"

"I'm hurt."

I had seen how slowly she fell, and was sure she could not be hurt. She must be pretending, which was disgusting. The rickshaw man had asked for trouble, and now he had got it. He would have to find his

译文三

It was a woman, with streaks of white in her hair, and she wore ragged clothes. She had darted suddenly from the side of the street, and crossed directly in front of us. My puller had tried to swerve aside, but her tattered jacket, unbuttoned and fluttering in the wind, caught in the shafts. Fortunately, the puller had slowed his pace, otherwise she would have been thrown head over heels, and probably seriously injured. After we halted the woman still knelt on all fours. I did not think she was hurt. No one else had see the collision, and it irritated me that the puller had stopped and was apparently prepared to get himself involved in some foolish complication. It might delay and trouble my journey.

"It's nothing," I told him. "Move on!"

But either he did not hear me or did not care, for he put down the shafts and gently helped the old woman to her feet. He held her arms, supporting her, and asked:

"Are you alright?"

"I am hurt."

I thought, "I saw you fall, and it was not at all rough. How can you be hurt? You are pretending. The whole business is distasteful, and

译文四

and dressed in rags. She stepped out from the roadside all of a sudden and cut across in front of us. Although the rickshaw man had already swerved to avoid her, her tattered padded waistcoat, unbuttoned and fluttering in the wind, got caught on the shaft. Fortunately, the rickshaw man had slowed down. Otherwise, she would doubtlessly have had a bad fall and have got herself seriously injured.

She lay there on the ground. The rickshaw man halted. I did not suppose this old woman was hurt. What's more, since there had been no one around, this halt of his was completely uncalled for, I thought. On the other hand, it would land him in trouble and hold me up.

"It's all right," I said, "Go on our way."

He ignored what I said, however—or perhaps he had not heard what I said. He set down the shafts, and gently helped the old woman to stand up, asking:

"Are you all right?"

"I'm badly hurt."

I have seen you fall down slowly. How can you hurt yourself? I thought. You are just pretending.

原文	译文一	译文二
事,也正是自讨苦吃,现在你自己想法去。	But the rickshaw man did not hesitate for a minute after hearing the old woman's answer. Still holding her arm, he helped her slowly forward. Rather puzzled by this I looked ahead and saw a police station. Because of the high wind, there was no one outside. It was there that the rickshaw man was taking the old woman.	own way out.
车夫听了这老女人的话,却毫不踌躇,仍然搀着伊的臂膊,便一步一步的向前走。我有些诧异,忙看前面,是一所巡警分驻所,大风之后,外面也不见人。这车夫扶着那老女人,便正是向那大门走去。		But the rickshaw man did not hesitate for a minute after the old woman said she was injured. Still holding her arm, he helped her slowly forward. I was surprised. When I looked ahead, I saw a police station. Because of the high wind, there was no one outside, so the rickshaw man helped the old woman towards the gate.
我这时突然感到一种异样的感觉,觉得他满身灰尘的后影,刹时高大了,而且愈走愈大,须仰视才见。而且他对于我,渐渐的又几乎变成一种威压,甚而至于要榨出皮袍下面藏着的"小"来。	Suddenly I had the strange sensation that his dusty retreating figure had in that instant grown larger. Indeed, the further he walked the larger he loomed, until I had to look up to him. At the same time he seemed gradually to be exerting a pressure on me which threatened to overpower the small self hidden under my fur-lined gown.	Suddenly I had a strange feeling. His dusty, retreating figure seemed larger at that instant. Indeed, the further he walked the larger he loomed, until I had to look up to him. At the same time he seemed gradually to be exerting a pressure on me, which threatened to overpower the small self under my fur-lined gown.
我的活力这时大约有些凝滞了,坐着没有动,也没有想,直到看见分驻所里走出一个巡警,才下了车。	Almost paralyzed at that juncture I sat there motionless, my mind a blank, until a police man came out. Then I got down from the rickshaw.	My vitality seemed sapped as I sat there motionless, my mind a blank, until a policeman came out. Then I got down from the rickshaw.
巡警走近我说,"你自己雇车罢,他不能拉你了。"	The policemen came up to me and said, "Get another rickshaw. He can't take you any further."	The policeman came up to me, and said, "Get another rickshaw. He can't pull you any more."
我没有思索的从外套袋里抓出一大把铜元,交给巡警,说,"请你给他……"	On the spur of the moment I pulled a handful of coppers from my coat pocket and handed them to the policeman. "Please give him this," I said.	Without thinking, I pulled a handful of coppers from my coat pocket and handed them to the policeman. "Please give him these," I said.

译文三	译文四

译文三

the rickshaw man is merely making difficulties for himself. Now let him find his own way out of the mess."

But the puller did not hesitate for a moment after the old woman said she was injured. Still holding her arm, he walked carefully ahead with her. Then I was surprised as, looking ahead, I suddenly noticed a police-station, and saw that he was taking her there. No one stood outside, so he guided her in through the gate. As they passed in I experienced a curious sensation. I do not know why, but at that moment it suddenly seemed to me that his dust-covered figure loomed enormous, and as he walked farther he continued to grow, until finally I had to lift my head to follow him. At the same time I felt a bodily pressure all over me, which came from his direction. It seemed almost to push out from me all the little-ness that hid under my fur-lined gown. I grew weak, as though my vitality had been spent, as though the blood had frozen in me. I sat motionless, stunned and thoughtless, until I saw an officer emerged from the station. Then I got from the rickshaw as he approached me.

"Get another rickshaw," he advised. "This man can't pull you anymore."

Without thinking I thrust my

译文四

How disgusting of you! And the rickshaw man, too, you are asking for trouble. I now want to see how you can find a way out yourself!

But not for a single moment did the rickshaw man hesitate after hearing what the woman had said. He continued to hold her arm and helped her slowly forward. With quite some surprise, I looked ahead and saw a police station. Due to the high wind, there was no one outside. It was towards the police station that the rickshaw man was taking the old woman.

A strange sensation suddenly welled up in me that his dusty retreating figure seemed in that instant to have grown larger and larger to such an extent that I had to look up at him. At the same time, he gradually became such a pressure on me as to threaten to overpower the "small self" hidden under my fur-lined gown.

I felt as if my vitality had sapped to a certain extent. I sat there motionless, blank-minded, until a policeman came out. Then I got off the rickshaw.

The policeman came up to me and said, "Hire another rickshaw. He cannot pull you any further."

Without thinking, I grabbed

原文

风全住了,路上还很静。我走着,一面想,几乎怕敢想到我自己。以前的事姑且搁起,这一大把铜元又是什么意思?

奖他么?我还能裁判车夫么?我不能回答自己。

这事到了现在,还是时时记起。我因此也时时熬了苦痛,努力的要想到我自己。几年来的文治武力,在我早如幼小时候所读过的"子曰诗云"一般,背不上半句了。独有这一件小事,却总是浮在我眼前,有时反更分明,教我惭愧,催我自新,并且增长我的勇气和希望。

一九二〇年七月

译文一

The wind had dropped completely, but the road was still quiet. As I walked along thinking, I hardly dared to think about myself. Quite apart from what had happened earlier, what had I meant by that handful of coppers? Was it a reward? Who was I to judge the rickshaw man? I could give myself no answer.

Even now, this incident keeps coming back to me. It keeps distressing me and makes me try to think about myself. The politics and the fighting of those years have slipped my mind as completely as the classics I read as a child. Yet this small incident keeps coming back to me, often more vivid than in actual life, teaching me shame, spurring me on to reform, and imbuing me with fresh courage and fresh hope.

(Yang Xianyi and Gladys Yang 译)

译文二

The wind had dropped completely, but the road was still quiet. I walked along thinking, but I was almost afraid to turn my thoughts on myself. Setting aside what had happened earlier, what had I meant by that handful of coppers? Was it a reward? Who was I to judge the rickshaw man? I could not answer myself.

"Even now, this remains fresh in my memory. It often causes me distress, and makes me try to think about myself. The military and political affairs of those years I have forgotten as completely as the classics I read in my childhood. Yet this incident keeps coming back to me, often more vivid than in actual life, teaching me shame, urging me to reform, and giving me fresh courage and hope.

(杨宪益、戴乃迭 译)

译文三

hand into my pocket and pulled forth a big fistful of coppers. "Give the fellow these," I said.

The wind had ceased entirely, but the street was still quiet. I mused as I walked, but I was almost afraid to think about myself. Leaving aside what had happened before, I sought an explanation for the fistful of coppers. Why had I given them? As a reward. And did I think myself, after my conduct, fit to pass judgment upon a rickshaw-puller? I could not answer my own conscience.

Even now that experience burns in my memory. I recall it often with pain and effort. The dramas of the political and military events of all those years are to me like the classics I read in childhood and quickly forgot. Now, I can't even recite half a line. But always, standing before my eyes, purging me with shame, impelling me to improve, invigorating my hope and courage; I re-enact this little incident—each detail distinct and clear as that day when all this happened.

(Edgar Snow 译)

译文四

a handful of coppers from my pocket and handed them to the policeman, "Please give him these."

By now the wind had stopped completely and it was still very quiet along the road. Walking along, I turned over the whole matter in my mind but I was hardly bold enough to think about myself. If not to mention what had happened before, what did I mean by giving him that handful of coppers? Was it a reward? Or was I in the very position to judge the rickshaw man? I could not figure out an answer.

Even till now, this incident keeps coming back to me afresh. It tortures me very often and makes me think hard about myself. I have forgotten the military and political affairs of all those years as completely as the classics I had read as a child. Only this incident keeps leaping up before my eyes, often more vivid than ever. It makes me know what shame is. It urges me on to start anew and imbues me with fresh courage and hope.

July 1920

（李明 译）

三 小说翻译的批评与赏析练习

原文

梦 想

我母亲和我都是耽于梦想的人。我们常常坐在海滩上，把脚趾插进沉重而潮湿的沙里，看又大又慢、又绿又白的碎浪滚滚而来，脑子里尽在遐想。当时我10岁，母亲34岁。我想的是海边有幢房子。母亲想的是钻石耳环。

母亲是矮身材，那时胖胖的。容貌端庄秀美，鼻梁笔直，鼻尖微翘。头发古铜色，光可鉴人。我黑发细眼，长得矮，矮到比不上弟弟约翰。我们常常坐下来梦想，一面看约翰和小妹妹阿黛尔在海滩上赛跑。

我梦想的是在防波堤后面有一幢华厦。可以坐在大门口看邮船在海上行驶，船上满载逍遥自在、有说有笑的阔客。我憧憬家里

译文一

Dreams

My mother and I liked to dream a lot. It had become a custom with us to sit on the beach and dig our toes into the wet heavy sand and then watch the big blue and white slow-moving waves crash into shore while our minds wandered off to some wild and fanciful thoughts. I was ten and mother was thirty-four by then. My fantasy consisted of living in a splendid seaside mansion while my mother's was to dream of a pair of diamond earrings.

By build, although my mother was both short and stout, she had that dignified and elegant countenance in her, a nose that slid down to a fine point and hair that had a sheen of aged copper. As for me, I had black hair and a rather unremarkable pair of eyes. I was short then, even shorter than my younger brother, John. While my mother and I would sit and while our thoughts away, John and my little sister Adele, would race along the lengths of the placid shore.

In my daydreams, I would be living in a mansion overlooking the breakwaters of the day. At the gates of the mansion, I could see luxury liners plying the ocean with their load of rich passengers. Some of those on board would be talking while some other would be laughing.

译文二

Dreams

We were dreamers my mother and I. We would sit on the beach, digging our toes into the heavy, wet sand, and watch the big, slow breakers come curling in, green and white, and we would dream. I was 10. She was 34. I dreamed that I wanted to own a house by the sea. She dreamed that she wanted real diamond earrings.

She was a short, plump woman in those days. She had a calm exquisite face and a straight nose with a tiny tilt on the end. There was bronze in her hair. I was short, shorter than my younger brother John, and I had black hair and slit eyes. We used to sit and dream, and watch John and little Adele race each other up and down the beach.

In my dream, I owned a big, beautiful house behind the sea wall. I could sit on my imaginary front porch and see the big ocean liners—the Leviathan, the Berengaria, the Olympic—as they sailed loaded with rich people who were always

原文	译文一	译文二
仆从如云，他们手托银盘，以巧克力、冰激凌侍候我们。 母亲并不知道怎样放胆做大梦。她想的是一副每只大约有半克拉钻石的小耳环。耳朵早给外婆穿了孔，她告诉我，有了耳环绝不会丢掉。	Then, a battalion of servants would come up to me to serve silver plates of chocolates and ice cream. My mother had an imagination of the milder kind, she had often told me of her desire for just a set of small half-karat earrings. She had had her ears pierced by my grandmother, so she told me, so those earrings would never get lost. （陈开顺　用例）	laughing and gay. In my imaginary house, servants went around with silver trays loaded with chocolate bars and jelly beans and ice cream. Jenny Tier Bishop didn't really know how to dream well. She dreamed of small earrings, about half a carat apiece. Her ears had been pierced long before by her mother and she knew that if she ever got those earrings she would not lose them. So she told me. (Jim Bishop　译)

第三部分

散文翻译的
批评赏析

一 关于散文的基本特征

散文有广义与狭义之分。广义的散文是指除韵文、骈文等讲求韵律的诗歌之外的所有不押韵、不排偶的文学作品,也包括一般的科学著作、论文及应用文等。狭义的散文则是指与文学文体中的小说、戏剧、诗歌并列的一种文学体裁。这里所说的散文是指狭义的散文。根据其形式的不同特点,散文可分为抒情散文、叙事散文、杂文、小品、随笔、游记等等。从其内容看,散文可分为以记人叙事为主的散文和以咏物抒情为主的散文两类(党争胜,2008:6)。

散文的基本特征是"形散而神不散"。

"形散"是就"外在形式"而言的,即散文取材范围广泛,其形式、技巧等表现手法自由灵活、不拘成法,它运笔如风,"时而勾勒描绘,时而倒叙联想,时而感情激发,时而侃侃议论"(方道,2004:71),时而谈古论今,时而说东道西,时而天南海北,时而上下左右,虚虚实实,时而小题大做,时而大题小作,时而微言大义,时而言近旨远,等等。总之,散文可以冲破时空界限,"现实的、历史的、未来的、自然的,只要能触发作者的思想感情,经过作者的精心构思,都可以纳入作家的笔下"(党争胜,2008:6)。

"神不散"中的"神"所代表的是"散文的思想"。"神不散"是指散文所要表达的主题必须明确而集中,即不管取材范围多么广泛,不管表现手法多么灵活,不管时空的变换多么自由,但自始至终,其"内在的联系很紧密,总有一条明确的线索贯穿始终,严谨而统一"(胡裕树,1985)。

关于"形散"与"神不散"的辩证关系,翁世荣(1984)曾有过这样的论述:散文的"主要任务是抒情述志,只要有利于情和志的抒发,什么样的内容、手法、技巧都可运用,这就决定了它的创作有一定的随意性。具体表现在作品中,一篇散文的材料可跳跃,可断续,可松动,可散漫;但不管怎样跳跃、断续、松动、散漫,总得还要遵循一条无形的轨迹——作者的'情'和'志',这就是'凝'。'情'和'志'是散文'凝'的最好的粘合力,散文的'散'和'凝'最终也就统一在作者的'情'和'志'上,这就是'散'和'凝'的辩证关系"。这里所谓的"凝"也就是指"神凝",即"神不散"(方道,2004:74)。

二 散文的"真""情"和"美"

真正的散文,都必须充分表现作家自己的个性、感情、思想和精神(方道,2004:88)。换言之,真正的散文就是要讲究"真"。散文的"真"体现在文字表达上的"不假雕饰、不施铅华、全凭本色的真实和直接"(胡显耀、李力,2009:172),体现在作家说真话、直抒胸臆、裸露心灵,抒真情、流露自然情感与性情,写实景、以景语传达情语。因此,散文不需要像诗歌那样含蓄,也不需要像许多小说、戏剧那样讲究语言艺术技巧。

散文所表现的均是作者的感受,"感受"者,情也。"写景、写人、写事,其目的还是在于抒写自己的主观感情;发挥思想,议论道理,也是抒情的一法,归根结蒂,思想、道理也是'情',只不过是一种'理智'化、'规范'化、'条理'化了的'情'"(佘树森,1986)。

那么,"真"和"情"到底是何关系?弄清这个问题,我们首先要看看散文的类别。裴显生(1987)将散文分为叙事型散文、状物型散文和议论型散文三大类。对于这三类散文他是这样描述的:

叙事型散文可以以写人为主,可以以写事为主,也可以以完整的情节取胜,侧重于以情驭事、融情于事,将作者的主观诗情流溢于叙写文字中间,形成一股内在的抒情魅力。

状物型散文是指状物绘景、叙写风情风物一类。此时,作者的诗情间接地附丽于山川名胜、自然景物之中,托物言志、情景交融,往往形成诗一般的意境;或者借物借景,直接让主观诗情从文字中流涌出来。

议论型散文"由具体的事物和现象引起感兴,围绕某种诗意感受,放开笔墨,纵横议论,形成融情于理、情理交融的境界;或者采取形象化的手法,即借助于可感触的人、事、景、物的叙写来进行议论。这一类散文以议论为主,仍归结为主观的抒情。"(方遒,2004)

由散文的三个类别不难看出,"无论是写景、叙事、咏物,抑或是论理,散文的真都融于情和理这两个因素当中。专事抒情的,就情真意切;专事说理的,情就隐于理中。即使是叙事和咏物的散文,也不会只干巴巴地作清冷的陈述或毫无情感的描写,而总是把情和理寓于其中。"(胡显耀、李力,2009:175)

但同时,正如西方的哲人波瓦洛所说:"真实的才是美的;只有真实的才是可爱的"。西方哲人克罗齐还说:"表达本身就是一种美"。既然散文体现真,散文就体现美。既然散文旨在表达,散文就传达美。因此,语言的美,文辞的美,便成为散文的一大特色,散文也因此而常被称为"美文"。散文之美,体现在其情味、韵致、意境之美,体现在其叙述语言的朴素、自然、流畅、平实之美。同诗歌语言相比,散文的确平淡无奇,但因散文经过了作者"情感的渗透、写意的磨练"(胡显耀、李力,2009:178),其中的一个个文字,必沁润着作者的心绪,宛如烟雾,轻轻地环绕,纠缠着读者的心扉,因而它有着无限的美,并让读者去充分领略其中的功夫、其中的品味以及其中的语言运用的高超技艺和巧夺天工。

"真""情""美"乃散文之本色。

三 散文翻译的三个要义

既然"真""情""美"乃散文之本色,那么,散文翻译则应围绕"真""情""美"的传达来进行。

上面讲过,散文在文字表达上"不假雕饰、不施铅华、全凭本色的真实和直接"(胡显耀、李力,2009:172),作家在其中说的是真话、抒的是胸臆、裸露的是真实的心灵,流露的是自然情感与性情，写的是实景等。因此，作为译者，翻译散文的第一要义就是要充分领会原文作者的这份"真"，并将这份"真"充分地在译文当中再现出来。

具体来讲，就是"要求译文在意义、形式、趣味、格调等方面力求与原文等质等量"（胡显耀、李力，2009：182）。要做到这一点，译者必须对原文从所使用词语的语音、字形，到所使用词语的各种意义（如内涵意义、外延意义、联想意义、比喻意义、象征意义等），到句子信息结构和各种修辞手法，再到整个语篇的主题意义等，要有充分的理解和把握，并在译文当中将这些信息充分再现出来。

散文翻译的第二要义就是要传达出原文的"情"。所谓的"传情达意"在散文当中体现得最为充分。不管是叙事型散文、状物型散文，还是议论型散文，它们的"真都融于情和理这两个因素当中。专事抒情的，就情真意切；专事说理的，情就隐于理中。即使是叙事和咏物的散文，也不会只干巴巴地作清冷的陈述或毫无情感的描写，而总是把情和理寓于其中。"（胡显耀、李力，2009：175）可见，"情"是散文翻译当中应该着力再现的元素。散文的"情"不是虚的，对字、词、句以及修辞、逻辑等的传达要围绕散文的整体效果。因此，对散文的"情"进行传达必须从微观层面的各种选择入手，最终将散文的整体效果传达出来。

散文翻译的第三要义就是要传达出原文之"美"。散文旨在表达"真"，旨在传达"情"，散文的"真"和"情"共同演绎出散文之"美"，因而散文常被称作"美文"。散文之"美"不仅体现在其意境和情趣的审美效果，更体现在其形式（包括其音韵节奏、遣词造句、修辞手段、说理方式、语言的凝练等）所蕴含和体现的美。因此，翻译散文就是要以精湛的语言艺术和巧夺天工的语言技巧来不仅再现散文的意境和情趣，更再现散文的各种形式，以充分传达出散文之美。

第七章 "The Author's Account of Himself" 汉译文的批评赏析

一 关于 "The Author's Account of Himself"

《作者自叙》一文出自美国久负盛名的早期浪漫主义作家华盛顿·欧文（1783—1859）之笔。欧文是美国文学的奠基人，被誉为"美国文学之父"，是第一个得到欧洲人承认的美国作家。他的作品反映了美国文学从18世纪理性主义到19世纪浪漫主义的转变。他文笔优美，语言生动，在描述中能够恰如其分地运用幽默与夸张的艺术手法，其中所反映出的浪漫主义气息为作品增添了无穷魅力。他的许多优秀作品已成为典范，作品的风格对埃德加·爱伦·坡、霍桑等美国作家均产生了重要影响。欧文遍游英国、苏格兰、爱尔兰的名胜古迹，怀着"对英国古老文明的仰慕和对前资本主义社会的向往"（喻云根，1996：29），他于1820年写成了作品集《见闻杂记》。此书出版后不久便在欧洲大陆竞相出版，书中收有散文、杂感、故事等共34篇，《作者自叙》便是其中的首篇。

自少年时代起，欧文就喜爱阅读英国作家司各特、拜伦、彭斯等人的作品。中学毕业后，他遵从父命在律师事务所学习法律，但他的志趣却在文学方面。1815年他渡洋赴英，旅居英国17年，由于其家父的企业倒闭，所以在英国一直意志消沉，心神不定，但由于爱好写作，便以写文章为生。他的代表作有《纽约外史》《见闻札记》《布雷斯勃列奇田庄》《哥伦

二 "The Author's Account of Himself" 原文及四种汉译文

原　文	译文一	译文二
I am of this mind with Homer, that as the snaile that crept out of her shel was turned eftsoones into a toad I and thereby was forced to make a stoole to sit on; so the traveller that stragleth from his owne country is in a short time transformed into so monstrous a shape, that he is		

布传》《攻克格拉纳达》和《阿尔罕伯拉》等。他的足迹遍及英国各个角落，他喜欢观察风土人情，研究英国人的内心世界。由于欧文来自被认为是荒蛮的、未开化的新大陆，他对英国充满了向往，他所写文章的字里行间都流露着他对英国的热爱，并加进了英国浪漫主义的怀旧之情。

虽然欧文蜚声欧洲，而且美国人也认为他的作品标志着美国文学的开端，但是真正反映美国生活、具有美国民族特色的美国文学作品还需要至少一代人的努力才会出现。这主要是因为欧文的作品多以欧洲为题材，具有较明显的模仿的痕迹。欧文由于经常模仿写作英国风格的散文、杂文等，所以，其写作风格和技巧往往带有浓厚的欧洲作家的气息。他对日常琐事和人物景观都有得天独厚的洞察力。他的散文幽默诙谐，例如他在《作者自叙》第一段中，就用了很多大词来描绘童年时的经历，如 observe、converse、terra incognita 等，通过用词和思想上的反差取得一种幽默效果。他的文章不拘泥于形式，而且富有音乐感。这篇脍炙人口的《作者自叙》之所以能受到广大读者的喜爱，是由于"欧文的音乐性和有律拍的风格，娴静的幽默和梦幻的魅力。"（戴婉平，2003：80）。

《作者自叙》是一篇游记，可看作是写景抒情类散文。全文从一个"游"字写起，娓娓道来，意趣横生，情景人物都写得极有情致。另外，欧文在散文中善于运用"朴实的英文和美国式的名词和动词"（戴婉平，2003：78），如在《作者自叙》中他用典型的美国式的名词 humor 和 traveler 代替英国式的名词 humour 和 traveller。整篇文章显得匀称而不流于牵强，舒卷自然而富于隐喻。他善于运用不虚饰又不过分的文体，文字简洁优美，清丽妩媚。他用词不事雕琢，句式参差有致，结构如行云流水，风格涉笔成趣，其文字风格既幽雅又浅近。正如喻云根所评价的：欧文的散文"行文从容不迫，抑扬有致，笔触轻盈而趣味盎然"（喻云根，1996：28）。《作者自叙》与其说是一篇优美的散文，倒不如说是一首歌咏自然风光的乡村民谣。

译文三　　　　**译文四**　　　　**笔　记**

"鄙人与荷马所见略同：脱壳之蛇随即变为蟾蜍，因而不得不另觅栖处；游历者去国辞乡，亦随即变为畸形之怪物，因而不得不徙其居处，易其习惯，不得不居之所能，而非居之所愿。"——李利《攸

原文	译文一	译文二

faine to alter his mansion with his manners, and to live where he can, not where he would. — LYLY'S *EUPHUES*.

I was always fond of visiting new scenes, and observing strange characters and manners. Even when a mere child I began my travels, and made many tours of discovery into foreign parts and unknown regions of my native city, to the frequent alarm of my parents, and the emolument of the town-crier. As I grew into boyhood, I extended the range of my observations. My holiday afternoons were spent in rambles about the surrounding country. I made myself familiar with all its places famous in history or fable. I knew every spot where a murder or robbery had been committed, or a ghost seen. I visited the neighboring villages, and added greatly to my stock of knowledge, by noting their habits and customs, and conversing with their sages and great men. I even journeyed one long summer's day to the summit of the most distant hill, whence I stretched my eye over many a mile of terra incognita, and was astonished to find how vast a globe I inhabited.

This rambling propensity strengthened with my years. Books of voyages and travels became my passion, and in devouring their contents, I neglected the regular exercises of the school.

译文一

我喜欢游历，见识各地的奇风异俗。我的旅行从童年时候就开始，本城范围以内的"穷乡僻壤"，我很小就去"考察"，因此我常常失踪，害得家长很着急，镇上的地保把我找回来了，常常因此受到奖赏。我这个小孩子长成大孩子，观察范围也日益扩大。每逢假日下午，我总到附近乡村去漫游。有些地方是历史名胜，有些地方是有神话传说的，我都亲加勘察，把它们摸熟了。什么地方发生过盗窃案或者凶杀案的，什么地方有过鬼魂出现的，我都知道。邻近各村我常去观光，当地的耆老硕德我总去踵门求教，因此我的智识也大为增加。有一天——那是漫长的夏天——我爬上了很远很远地方的一个山头，纵目四望，一哩之内的地方我是大多不认识的，我想起我们这个地球是多么的大，心里不免吃惊。

岁月增添，游兴更盛。我最爱读的书是游记旅行之类，废寝忘餐读这种闲书，把学校里的正课练习都给耽误了。风和日丽之日，我到码头四周去游荡，看见船只一艘一艘的开向远方，不禁心向往之——船帆渐渐远渐小，岸上的我，以目

译文二

我平生最喜欢游览新境，考察种种异地人物及其风习。早在童稚时期，我的旅行即已开始，观察区域之广，遍及我出生城镇的各个偏僻之所与罕至之地；此事固曾使我的父母饱受虚惊，市镇报讯人却也赖以而沾益颇丰。及长，我观察的范围更续有扩大。无数假日下午尽消磨在郊垌的漫游之中。那里一切在历史或传说上有名的地方，我无不十分熟悉。我知道那里的每一处杀人越货之所与鬼魂出现之地。我继而访问了许多邻村，观察其地的风俗习惯，并与当地的圣贤与伟人接谈，因而极大增加了我的原有见闻。一次，在一个漫长的夏日天气，我竟漫游到一座远山之巅，登临纵目，望见了数不尽的无名广土，因而惊悟所居天地之宽。

这种浪游的习性在我竟随着年齿而俱增。描写海陆的游记成了我的酷嗜，寝馈其中，致废课业。在天气晴和的日子里，我往往怀着多么渴慕的心情

译文三

　　余生平好采风而问俗，凡有奇事，必稔闻之。自少时恒乐外出，即就我生长之城中，搜寻幽僻之地、犹探险然。二亲颇为我忧，辄倩人四出侦我，受倩者转用以取资于我家。吾年既长，旅行之范围亦渐展拓。当午后放学，辄作郊行，于故典有关之陈迹，余必至而考验。于有人遇盗或见鬼之区，余必亲涉其地，相其原隰。并入邻村访问故老，审其风俗。曾于夏假长日中，登高山四望，觉吾生所履地局，而地球博也，而好游之心，遂与吾年竞长。迨既能读，尤嗜读古人之游记，屏正书弗读。有时至商埠，见贾舶张帆，而余一缕游魂，竟逐此船至于天涯地角。

　　后此读书既博，而意念亦端，惟远游之心，尚勃勃然。余之在本国，所经亦不谓少。若云风物之佳，似吾美洲

译文四

菲斯》

　　我平素总喜欢游历新的景点，喜欢见识异地的人物、了解他乡的习俗。还是童稚时我就开始旅游，多次造访我所在城镇的罕至之地、未名之域。为此我父母经常担心受怕，而街头公告员则借此获利良多。进入少年时代，我所观察的人和物的范围扩大了。一个又一个假日的下午，我漫步于周围的乡村，去熟悉了解历史上和传说中的有名之地。我悉数知道凶杀案、抢劫案的发生之地，也知道鬼魂出没之所。我造访了附近的村庄，通过观察当地的风俗习惯，通过与那里的德高望重者以及大人物进行交谈，我大大拓宽了自己的知识面。在一个漫漫的夏日，我甚至旅行到最远处一座山的山顶。站在山顶，极目远眺，周围绵延数英里都是未知的世界，不禁惊叹自己所居地球之广阔。

　　随着年龄的增长，这种游历异域的爱好与日俱增。有关海上和陆地的游记成了我的至爱，我如饥似渴地读着其中每一章每一节，完全忘记了自己每天要做的课业。我多么渴望在晴朗的日子里漫步于码头边，多么渴望去观察那驶向迢迢远方的一艘艘船只——我会以怎样渴望

笔　记

原文

How wistfully would I wander about the pier-heads in fine weather, and watch the parting ships bound to distant climes—with what longing eyes would I gaze after their lessening sails, and waft myself in imagination to the ends of the earth!

Further reading and thinking, though they brought this vague inclination into more reasonable bounds, only served to make it more decided. I visited various parts of my own country; and had I been merely a lover of fine scenery, I should have felt little desire to seek elsewhere its gratification, for on no country have the charms of nature been more prodigally lavished. Her mighty lakes, like oceans of liquid silver; her mountains, with their bright aerial tints; her valleys, teeming with wild fertility; her tremendous cataracts, thundering in their solitudes; her boundless plains, waving with spontaneous verdure; her broad deep rivers, rolling in solemn silence to the ocean; her trackless forests, where vegetation puts forth all its magnificence; her skies, kindling with the magic of summer clouds and glorious sunshine; —no, never need an American look beyond his own country for the sublime and beautiful of natural scenery.

But Europe held forth the charms of storied and poetical association. There were to be seen the masterpieces of

译文一

远送，我的灵魂已经随着我的幻想到了地球的不知哪一个角落了。

以后读书更多，思想日开，我这种好玩的性情，自然也渐渐的纳入理性的规范；但是本来只是空泛的憧憬，现在变成确定的心愿了。在自己本国，我也算游历了不少地方；假如我只想欣赏自然风景，那么美国风景之美，品类繁多，我已经目不暇接，无遑他求了。美国有大湖，银波闪翻，浩瀚汪洋；有高山，空灵缥缈，上接苍空；有草木横生鸟兽繁殖的山谷，有在荒山中彭湃直泻的大瀑布；有一望无际满目绿色的大平原；美国的大河，身阔水深，庄严的静静的流向海洋；美国的森林，古木参天，绵延千里，至今没有樵径可循；美国的天空，阳光普照，夏云过处，光彩奇丽；举凡天地之美，不论是宏伟的，或是优美的，均尽萃于此，美国有景如斯，美国人实在用不着舍近就远，到外国去游山玩水的了。

但是欧洲也有它的美，欧洲的美较之美国的美更富于历史与诗意的联想。艺术巨著，高尚社会的文雅生活，各地古老相传的奇风异俗，这种种为欧洲所有，而美国所未必有者。美国固然朝气蓬勃，前途无穷，可是欧洲历史久远，历代累积下来的文物之盛，却为美国所

译文二

漫步在码头周围，凝视着一艘艘离去的船只驶赴迢递的远方；我曾以何等希冀的眼神目送着那渐渐消逝的桅帆，并在想象之中自己也随风飘越至地角天边！

此后进一步的阅读与思考虽使这种渺茫的向往稍就理性之范，却适足使之更其固定。我游历了自己国土的各个地方；而如果我的爱好仅限于妍丽景物的追逐，则快心悦目，尽可以无须远求，因为纯以大自然的妩媚而论，此邦确可谓得天独厚，世罕其俦。试想她那银波荡漾、与海相若的浩渺湖面；那晴光耀眼、顶作天青的巍峨群山；那粗犷而富饶盈衍的峡岸溪谷；那雷鸣喧豗于阒寂之中的巨大飞瀑急湍；那绿色葱茏、好风阵阵的无际平原；那庄严静谧、滚滚入海的深广江流；那万木争荣、无径可循的茂密森林；那夏云丽日、诡谲幻变的灿烂天空；——不，在自然景物的壮丽方面，美国人从不需要舍本土而远求。

然而在传奇与诗意的联想方面，欧洲却具有着它特殊的魅力。那里人们则可以见到艺术上的名作巨制，上流社会的精致娴

译文三

较人为胜。以天然景物，熟则类此富庶者？湖身广博如海，山色如画，山中产物至夥，而巨瀑之声，乃震数里以外。平原旷壤，有同碧海。长江大河，日夜奔流入海，至若林光云物，在在咸足饱饫。试问美国人乃反嗜他国烟水耶？

唯欧洲古迹多，不能不往；而美术产品亦多，足备观览，且先正典型，尤宜瞻仰，至于风俗异同，更当一考。若吾美洲，特新造之国，基桢纵立，然非古国也。至欧罗巴洲，则万古菁华所聚，断瓦颓垣，其中咸有史迹，即残碑一片，其中亦足凭吊英雄。余凝望至久，欲一临观古人建功垂统之地，循迹而行，登彼古堡废垛，低徊于圮塔斜阳之下。

舍此外，尚望过访彼伟人。虽然，吾美人物夥也，一城之中，多者逾数

译文四

的双眼去凝视那些渐远渐小的船帆，并想象着自己随着船帆飘向海角天涯！

通过进一步阅读和更深入的思考，我的这一爱好更加确定无疑了——尽管这种阅读和思考使得这种道不清、说不明的爱好趋于理性化。我游历了祖国的各个地方。假如我只喜欢美丽的景色，我就不会想到要去其他地方一饱眼福了，因为没有哪个国度能像我的祖国那样得到大自然如此的垂青和厚爱，处处都是鬼斧神工的迷人风光。她那烟波浩渺的湖泊，犹如银光闪烁的大海；她那绵延不绝的群山，巍峨挺立，苍翠欲滴；她那沟壑纵横的山谷，草木茂盛，鸟兽欢腾；她那飞流湍急的大瀑布，雷鸣于阒寂之中；她那一望无际的平原，绿草茵茵，随风起伏；她那水深面阔的河流，庄严静谧，滔滔流入大海；她那人迹罕至的森林，枝繁叶茂，苍翠葱茏；她那天空，在夏日的云彩和万丈光芒的诡谲之下，光彩夺目；——的确，美丽又壮观的自然景色在美国应有尽有，美国人永远也用不着舍近求远，去国外寻觅这一切。

当然，欧洲也有着自己的迷人之处，它那历史传奇，它那诗歌传统都让人遐

笔 记

原文

art, the refinements of highly-cultivated society, the quaint peculiarities of ancient and local custom. My native country was full of youthful promise: Europe was rich in the accumulated treasures of age. Her very ruins told the history of times gone by, and every moldering stone was a chronicle. I longed to wander over the scenes of renowned achievement—to tread, as it were, in the footsteps of antiquity—to loiter about the ruined castle—to meditate on the falling tower—to escape, in short, from the common-place realities of the present, and lose myself among the shadowy grandeurs of the past.

I had, besides all this, an earnest desire to see the great men of the earth. We have, it is true, our great men in America: not a city but has an ample share of them. I have mingled among them in my time, and been almost withered by the shade into which they cast me; for there is nothing so baleful to a small man as the shade of a great one, particularly the great man of a city. But I was anxious to see the great men of Europe; for I had read in the works of various philosophers, that all animals degenerated in America, and man among the number. A great man of Europe, thought I, must therefore be as superior to a great man of America, as a peak of the Alps to a highland of the Hudson; and in this idea I was confirmed, by observ-

译文一

不及。你到了欧洲,不必进博物院,就是普通的废墟,就可以激发你怀古的幽情:每一块腐蚀的石头,都好像是一本历史读物。有什么地方,是以纪念古代的丰功伟绩的,我最喜欢在它左右徘徊——那时候我觉得我是"踏在历史的脚迹上面"——我看见了一片瓦砾的古堡遗迹,就流连不舍,看见了摇摇将坠的古塔巨楼,就低回凭吊——总而言之,我那时候避开了现实的庸俗,置身于迷离恍惚的古代盛世,我也就忘了我自己了。

我除了游览之外,又喜欢拜会当代伟大人物。美国自然也有大人物,我们每一个城市都叫得出几个响当当的名字。我尽量找机会和他们来往,在他们的身影底下,我总觉得自己的渺小;因为小人物在大人物(尤其是城市里的大人物)的脚底下,总觉得自己抬不起头来的。可是我见识了本国大人物之余,更想认识欧洲的大人物;因为好几位哲学家都这么说过:任何动物到了美洲都要退化,人也不是例外。因此我想:咱们赫德逊河流域的土丘既然比不上人家阿尔卑斯山的高峰,咱们的大人物比起欧洲的伟人来,至少也得矮一个头;我这个见地也不无理由,只要看看人家英国人到敝邦来的游客就可明白的了;那辈英国人在他们本国,据我看来,

译文二

雅以及古今风尚的种种特点。我的本国充满着青年的远大前程;欧洲却蕴蓄着世代聚集的珍奇宝藏。就连那里的遗址废墟也尽是过去历史的记载,每块残砖烂石都是一部史册。我渴望到那些有过丰功伟业的故地去漫游——仿佛是去步履一下往古的足迹——流连于废堡颓垣之侧,低徊于圮塔欹楼之中——总之,暂时忘情于眼前的凡庸现实,而沉湎在过去繁华胜事的幻影里去。

除此之外,我还殷切期望有幸去瞻仰瞻仰世上的伟人。诚然,美国自有它自己的伟人:这种人物广布各个城中,不知凡几。我平生也颇厕身其间,而且常被他们弄得黯无颜色;因为一位伟人——尤其是一位城市的伟人——的光焰往往有为小人物所难堪者。但是欧洲的伟人我却久思一睹丰采;因为我就曾在不止一个哲学家的著作里读到过这种说法,即,大凡动物一入美洲,即有出现退化之患,当然连人也不例外。因此我想,欧洲的伟人之于美国的伟人,大概也犹如阿尔卑斯山的高峰之于哈得孙河边的高地那样,而这种认识,在饱看了不少英

译文三

十人。余恒与过从，觉此伟人，阳光也，余身见曝，如槁鱼矣。今将更谒欧洲之所谓伟人者。余尝诵哲学家言，言各种动物，一至美洲，其种立变。然则人亦类是矣。余挈美、欧人物互较，则直挈阿尔迫司山与黑逞河频培塿比耳。后此参以阅历，乃益信。该观英人之游美者，意气张王，傲然自名为大人。然而是大人者，在彼中特小人耳，余故更欲觇其所谓大者。且吾美之人，欧之变种也，今当审验其未变者如何。

后此吾愿果慰，正不知于吾生命运，为吉为凶。余足迹所经，凡越数国，目光所到，无不周瞩。虽不类哲学家之穷窥天奥，然亦颇同懒人闲行，对画肆窗外，内瞩山水人物及俳优之画本也。在旅行人公例，行必挟一铅笔，随时记载，归时稿本盈箧。余亦窃窃有所涂抹，将归示

译文四

思。那里可以读到艺术名著，那里可以享受到贵族阶层的高雅生活，那里可以体验到古朴、独特、离奇而有趣的地方风俗。我的祖国充满朝气，前途无量；欧洲历史悠久，积聚了丰富的瑰宝。在欧洲，即使是废墟也能讲述逝去的历史，那里的每一块烂石都是一部编年史。我渴望着徜徉于取得瞩目成就的地方——渴望着步古人之后尘——渴望着漫步于废弃的城堡——渴望着冥思苦想在欹塔前——渴望着暂时避开眼前的凡庸之事，渴望着沉浸于对往昔那恍惚迷离的繁华盛世的遐想。

此外，我还热切地希望去见识世上的伟人。诚然，美国有着自己的伟人：每个城市都拥有无数的伟人。在我一生中，我一直厕身其间，在他们高大的形象面前，我几乎黯然失色，因为对于小人物来说，再也没有什么比站在伟人面前，尤其是一座城市的伟人面前，更令他感到难堪的了。但我渴望去见识欧洲的伟人，因为我从无数哲学家的著作中读到，所有动物在美国都会退化，人类也不例外。因此我想，欧洲的伟人一定比美国的伟人高贵，就像阿尔卑斯山的山顶要比哈德逊河的高地高贵一样。对此我深信不疑，因

笔 记

原　文

ing the comparative importance and swelling magnitude of many English travelers among us, who, I was assured, were very little people in their own country. I will visit this land of wonders, thought I, and see the gigantic race from which I am degenerated.

It has been either my good or evil lot to have my roving passion gratified. I have wandered through different countries, and witnessed many of the shifting scenes of life. I cannot say that I have studied them with the eye of a philosopher; but rather with the sauntering gaze with which humble lovers of the picturesque stroll from the window of one print-shop to another; caught sometimes by the delineations of beauty, sometimes by the distortions of caricature, and sometimes by the loveliness of landscape. As it is the fashion for modern tourists to travel pencil in hand, and bring home their port-folios filled with sketches, I am disposed to get up a few for the entertainment of my friends. When, however, I look over the hints and memorandums I have taken down for the purpose, my heart almost fails me at finding how my idle humor has led me aside from the great objects studied by every regular traveler who would make a book. I fear I shall give equal disappointment with an unlucky landscape painter, who had traveled on the continent, but, following the bent of his vagrant in-

译文一

也没有什么了不起，可是一到美国，就趾高气扬，不可一世了。我既然也忝为一个身居美国的"退化"之人，我自然极想观光上国，见识见识尚未退化的人类的真面目了。

我的"游历欲"居然常常能够实现，这不知道是我的好运气还是坏运气了。我游历过好几个国家，人生的变迁也见识了不少。我不敢说我有抉隐发微的哲学家的眼光；我至少像一个普通爱好艺术的人，走过一家一家图书店的时候，不得不驻足浏览一下，有些画是画得真美，有些画却是奇形怪状的诙谐画，可是它们能吸引我的注意则初无二致，至于可爱的山水画，那是我更要击节称赏的了。近代人旅行，都喜欢一手执铅笔，一手拿画册，速写留影，我因此也喜欢乱涂几笔，作为诸亲好友茶余饭后谈笑之助。可是我把这些杂记随笔重读一遍，心中不免起一种惶恐之感，因为通常出门旅行回来写书的人，总要讨论几项大题目，可是我信手写来，偏偏把大题目都给遗漏了。我像是个不幸的风景画家，也算到欧洲大陆去旅行写生过，可是他心有偏好，专找冷僻角落去作画；他的画集里因此也满是些普通山水以及荒村茅屋穷乡古墟之类，至于圣彼得大教堂或者罗马圆剧场，透尔尼的大瀑布或者那不勒斯的海湾他

译文二

国旅客在我们中间所流露的那种优越神情与倨傲态度之后，乃益信其不妄；而其实这些人，据我听说，在其本国之中也不过是凡庸之辈而已。因此我立志要恭游上国，亲历奇境，以便见见我这已经凋残的后裔所自出的那个巨人种族。

不管好运厄运，我这漂泊的热望总算宿愿得偿了。我漫游了许多不同的国家，阅历了不少变动不定不居的人生世相。我绝不敢妄称我对于这形形色色曾以哲人的目光作了观照；而仅仅是徘徊于众多版画店窗前的探幽寻胜的谦卑癖嗜者的一种闲眺：时而美物写生，勾勒微妙；时而戏谑漫画，突梯滑稽；时而山水风景，意境悠悠，因而令人迷恋不置。既然当今的旅行家一出门便须画笔在手，地不虚至，以便将来图稿盈箧，满载而归，因此我也不免要捡出几件，以博友人一粲。然而当我重检自己为此而作的种种札记日志时，我却发现，由于素性疏懒，我对每位立志著述的正规旅行家照例列入其研究范围的种种重大事物，竟然多有脱漏，因而惶惧无已。我担心，我之必然令人失望，将不下于下述之不幸

译文三

吾友。殆归而检阅，则凡大而足记者咸缺，存者直零星不足齿数之事。盖余性质怪特，往往于蚁封中取材，狗窦中伺间，无大笔墨也。以故余之游记，多记村庄风物及幽僻无人规仿之残碑。若圣彼得之礼拜寺及罗马之大戏场、与奈百而司海湾风物，皆屏弗录。遍余纪中，亦无一语涉及火山冰河也。

（林纾、魏易 译）

译文四

为我发现，很多英国旅游者一来到我们中间就优越感十足，而且不可一世。这些人，我敢肯定，在他们本国只不过是无名小卒而已。我一直在想，我一定要去游历这片充满神奇的土地，一定要去见见已经退化了的我所诞生于斯的这个伟大民族。

　　说我运气好也罢，歹也罢，我游历欧洲的热望是得到满足了。我游历了不同的国家，见证了许许多多人生的变迁。我不能说我以哲人的眼光研究了这一切，但却以普普通通的热爱如画的事物的那些人在从一家版画店闲逛到另一家版画店时的那种悠闲的目光观察了这一切（他们时而被对美的描绘所吸引，时而被漫画的过分夸张所吸引，时而被风景的秀美所吸引）。如今，很多旅行者在旅行时手中拿着铅笔，等回到家里，就有了沓沓的速记随笔了，这种做法已成为一种时尚。我也可以拿出几样速记随笔供朋友鉴赏。可是，当我对自己因此而做的速记随笔进行审视时，我发现，由于自己天性懒散，对许多重要的东西多有疏漏，而这些东西却正是每个想写游记的真正旅行者所密切关注的。想到这里，我心里不觉惶恐起来。我想，我跟一个不幸的山水画家一样，非

笔　记

原　文	译文一	译文二
clination, had sketched in nooks, and corners, and by-places. His sketch-book was accordingly crowded with cottages, and landscapes, and obscure ruins; but he had neglected to paint St. Peter's, or the Coliseum; the Cascade of Terni, or the Bay of Naples; and had not a single glacier or volcano in his whole collection. (Washington Irving, "The Author's Account of Himself")	根本没有收集在内，他整本画册里，你找不到一幅冰川或是火山的伟观。读者诸君假如感到失望，作者只好在这里告罪了。 （夏济安　译）	山水画家。其人也确曾旅游过欧陆，然而终不胜其烟霞癖之驱遣，每有所作，辄得之于穷乡僻壤之中。因而充溢其画册的东西则茅屋也，山水也，无名之故地废墟也，但是圣彼得大堂他却漏掉；迦利辛斗兽场他却漏掉；特尔尼瀑布或那波里海湾他也都漏掉；甚至连冰川与火山之巨观，他的全部作品中也都没有一笔提到。 （高健　译）

三　散文翻译的批评与赏析练习

原　文	译文一	译文二
Youth is not a time of life; it is a state of mind; it is not a matter of rosy cheeks, red lips and supple knees; it is a matter of the will, a quality of the imagination, a vigor of the emotions; it is the freshness of the deep springs of life. Youth means a temperamental predominance of courage over timidity, of the appetite for adventure over the love of ease. This often exists in a man of 60 more than a boy of 20. Nobody grows old merely by a number of years. We grow old by deserting our ideals.	青春不是指生命的一段时间，而是指一种精神状态；它并不是指红润的面颊、透红的嘴唇和灵便的腿脚，而是指坚强的意志、丰富的想象和强烈的感情。它是指生命的源头，活水的清新之感。 　　青春意味着在气质上勇敢多于怯懦，冒险进取多于舒适苟安。这在60岁的老年人中往往比在20岁的青年人中更为常见。人之变老不仅由于年岁的增长，我们之变老常常是因为放弃了对理想的追求。	青春并非指年龄，而是指心境；并非指红润的面颊、鲜红的嘴唇、柔韧的双膝，而是指坚强的意志、丰富的想象、强烈的情感。青春是生命的始源，充满活力。 　　青春意味着天性勇敢而不怯懦，喜好冒险而不图安逸。图安逸多在60岁而非20岁。一个人失去青春并非只是因为岁月的增长，而是由于放弃了理想。

| 译文三 | 译文四 | 笔 记 |

常令人失望。这个山水画家游遍了欧洲大陆，但由于天性喜好漫游，他只挑那些隐蔽之地、偏僻角落、罕见之所来作画。因此，他的写生簿里画的满是村舍和风景点，还有那朝代久远的废墟。可是，他却恰恰遗漏了圣·彼得大教堂，遗漏了古罗马圆剧场，遗漏了特尔尼瀑布，还有那那不勒斯海湾；在他的整本画册中，既没有一条冰河，也没有一座火山。

（李明 译）

原 文

Years may wrinkle the skin, but to give up enthusiasm wrinkles the soul. Worry, fear, self-distrust bows the heart and turns the spirit back to dust.

Whether 60 or 16, there is in every human being's heart the lure of wonder, the unfailing childlike appetite of what's next and the joy of the game of living. In the center of your heart and my heart there is a wireless station: so long as it receives messages of beauty, hope, cheer, courage and power from men and from the Infinite (= God), so long are you young.

译文一

年岁也许会使皮肤增添皱纹，可是一旦丧失热忱，灵魂上的皱纹就会随即出现。忧虑、恐惧和缺乏自信会使人心灰意冷、意志消沉。

无论是60岁，还是16岁，新奇事物对每个人都有吸引力；只要童心不泯，就会对未来有好奇心和享受人生的乐趣。在你的心中和我的心中都有一个无线电台：只要它总在接收人类和上帝发出的美、希望、鼓励、勇气和力量的信息。

译文二

岁月会弄皱皮肤，可失去热情会弄皱灵魂。忧虑、恐惧、缺乏信心会让人心灰意冷，会让人意志消沉。

不管是60岁还是16岁，每个人都有一颗好奇之心，都有一颗探求未来、享受生活乐趣的永不泯灭的童心。在你我内心深处，都有一座无线电台：只要它一直在接收着人类和上帝发出的美好、希望、喝彩、勇气、力量等信息，你就会永远青春。

原 文

When the aerial are down, and your spirit is covered with snows of cynicism and the ice of pessimism, then you are grown old, even at 20, but as long as your aerials are up, to catch waves of optimism, there is hope you may die young at 80.

(Samuel Ullman, *Youth*)

译文一

假若你将天线收起,使你的心灵蒙上玩世不恭的霜雪和悲观厌世的冰层,那么即使你年方20,你也老气横秋;然而只要你将天线竖起,去接受乐观主义的电波,那么你就有希望即使活到80岁死去,也仍然年轻。

(隋荣谊,2004:72)

译文二

当天线收起,当你的心灵蒙上玩世不恭的积雪和悲观主义的冰层,那么你就失去了青春,即使你只有20岁,但只要你将天线竖起,去接受乐观主义的电波,你就有希望,即使80岁死去,你也仍然青春。

(李明 译)

第八章 "Of Studies" 汉译文的批评赏析

一 关于 "Of Studies"

本章批评赏析的是英国散文家培根的散文 "Of Studies" 的几种汉语译文。"Of Studies" 一文属于说理性散文。说理性散文即议论文。西方的说理性散文起源于古代雅典元老院雄辩的演说，其主要特点为深思熟虑的逻辑推理，目的在于让元老们信服发言者观点的正确性与合理性而加以采纳。今日的说理性散文同样具有真诚、客观、合乎逻辑的特征。一般说来说理性散文由以下四个部分组成：

首先，提出问题并对问题作简短的介绍和分析。介绍必须中肯，分析必须客观。如果问题本身就有谬误，那么就失去了议论的前提。其次，应明确、概括地摆出解决问题的办法，既可紧跟在提出问题后立刻说明，然后再仔细分析，也可在文章最后作为总结性的归纳提出。应尽可能用一两句话简练明确地表达出来，利于读者领会。第三，任何观点都必须有充分的事实作为依据，即必须举出有关的典型例证来支持自己的论点。事例越具体越实在就越好。决不可使用无关的或不典型的例证，也不可仅仅根据个别例证而得出一般性的结论，否则将犯逻辑错误。第四，在肯定自己论点的同时，必须对对方的论点进行批驳。批驳时应记住不能绝对化。任何问题都有其两面性。不可能一方绝对正确，另一方完全错误。只能衡量优劣，以此作为选择的标准。辩论的态度应公正而宽宏大度，对方的正确方面需予以承认，而对其谬误也应采取宽容的态度，才能赢得读者的信任与支持。

为了使自己的文章有征服人心的力量，作者往往一方面用逻辑推理的方法来诉诸读者的理性和智力，而另一方面也用打动人心的论点来诉诸读者的知觉与情感。逻辑推理的主要方式为归纳、演绎与类比。而要打动人心则必须充满感情，塑造形象，做到文情并茂。总之，说理性散文具有用词讲究、结构严谨、逻辑性强、风格凝重、说理透彻等特点。

翻译说理性散文要求译者注意措词和结构的严谨性，用简洁明快的语言来翻译。尤其对文中所提出的问题、解决的办法和得出的结论等都要用简练明确的文字翻译出来。严谨、精练、准确、逻辑性强是翻译说理性散文必须遵守的原则。但同时也不能忽略文字所包含的情感因素，以便更好地打动读者的心。

一 "Of Studies" 原文及四种汉译文

原 文

Studies serve for delight, for ornament, and for ability. Their chief use for delight is in privateness and retiring; for ornament, is in discourse; and for ability, is in the judgment and disposition of business. For expert men can execute, and perhaps judge of particulars, one by one; but the general counsels, and the plots and marshalling of affairs come best from those that are learned.

To spend too much time in studies is sloth; to use them too much for ornament is affectation; to make judgment wholly by their rules is the humor of a scholar. They perfect nature and are perfected by experience: for natural abilities are like natural plants, that need pruning by study, and studies themselves do give forth directions too much at large, except they be bounded in by experience.

Crafty men contemn studies, simple men admire them, and wise men use them, for they teach not their own use; but that is a wisdom without them and above them, won by observation. Read not to contradict and confute; nor to believe and take for granted; nor to find talk and discourse; but to weigh and consider.

Some books are to be tasted, others to be swallowed, and some few to be chewed and digested; that is, some books are to be read only in parts; others to be read, but not curiously; and

译文一

读书为学的用途是娱乐、装饰和增长才识。在娱乐上学问的主要的用处是幽居养静；在装饰上学问的用处是辞令；在长才上学问的用处是对于事务的判断和处理。因为富于经验的人善于实行，也许能够对个别的事情一件一件地加以判断；但是最好的有关大体的议论和对事务的计划与布置，乃是从有学问的人来的。在学问上费时过多是偷懒；把学问过于用作装饰是虚假；完全依学问上的规则而断事是书生的怪癖。学问锻炼天性，而其本身又受经验的锻炼；盖人的天赋有如野生的花草，他们需要学问的修剪；而学问的本身，若不受经验的限制，则其所指示的未免过于笼统。多诈的人渺视学问，愚鲁的人美慕学问，聪明的人运用学问；因为学问的本身并不教人如何用它们；这种运用之道乃是学问以外，学问以上的一种智能，是由观察体会才能得到的。不要为了辩驳而读书，也不要为了信仰与盲从；也不要为了言谈与议论；要以能权衡轻重、审察事理为目的。

有些书可供一尝，有些书可以吞下，有不多的几部书则应当咀嚼消化；这就是

译文二

读书足以怡情，足以傅彩，足以长才。其怡情也，最见于独处幽居之时；其傅彩也，最见于高谈阔论之中；其长才也，最见于处世判事之际。练达之士虽能分别处理细事或一一判别枝节，然纵观统筹、全局策划，则舍好学深思者莫属。读书费时过多易惰，文采藻饰太盛则矫，全凭条文断事乃学究故态。读书补天然之不足，经验又补读书之不足，盖天生才干犹如自然花草，读书然后知如何修剪移接；而书中所示，如不以经验范之，则又大而无当。

有一技之长者鄙读书，无知者羡读书，唯明智之士用读书，然书并不以用处告人，用书之智不在书中，而在书外，全凭观察得之。读书时不可存心诘难作者，不可尽信书上所言，亦不可只为寻章摘句，而应推敲细思。

书有可浅尝者，有可吞食者，少数则须咀嚼消化。换言之，有只须读其部分者，有只须

译文三

读书之用有三：一为怡神旷心，二为增趣添雅，三为长才益智。怡神旷心最见于蛰伏幽居，增趣添雅最见于高谈雄辩，而长才益智则最见于处事辨理。虽说有经验者能就一事一理进行处置或分辨，但若要通观全局并运筹帷幄，则还是博览群书者最能胜任。读书费时太多者皆因懒散，寻章摘句过甚者显矫揉造作，全凭书中教条断事者则乃学究书痴。天资之改善须靠读书，而学识之完美须靠实践；因天生资质犹如自然花木，需要用学识对其加以修剪，而书中所示则往往漫无边际，必须用经验和阅历界定其经纬。讲究实际者鄙薄读书，头脑简单者仰慕读书，唯英明睿智者运用读书，这并非由于书不示人其用法，而是因为乃一种在书之外并高于书本的智慧，只有靠观察方可得之。读书不可存心吹毛求疵，不可尽信书中之论，亦不可为己言掠词夺句，而应该斟酌推敲，钩深致远。有些书可浅尝辄止，有些书可囫囵吞枣，但有些书则须细细咀嚼，慢慢消化；换言之，有些书可只读其章节，有

译文四

读书赐人欢愉，赋人光彩，长人才干。欢愉多显于独处幽居之时；光彩多展于高谈阔论之中；才干多表于判别处事之际。经验丰富者虽能对具体问题一一处理或判别，然唯有学识之士方能高屋建瓴、通观全局、运筹帷幄。

读书耗时过多乃怠惰，炫耀所读之书乃造作，判断事理按章行事乃迂腐。读书可使人之天性臻于完善，经验又使所读之书臻于完美：因天生能力犹如自然花草，需通过学习加以"修剪"；书中所示，如不以经验定其方圆，则过于空泛。

耍小聪明者鄙读书，头脑简单者羡读书，明智之人士善读书，因所读之书本身不会告人其用处。其用处需用智慧寻觅，而智慧不在书中，而在书外，唯有观察方可得之。阅读时不可对书中内容万般诘难，不可尽信书中所言，不可只为寻章摘句，而应悉心斟酌、仔细推敲。

有些书需品尝，有些书需吞食，少数书需细嚼，慢慢消化。换言之，有些

笔 记

原 文	译文一	译文二
some few to be read wholly, and with diligence and attention. Some books also may be read by deputy and extracts made of them by others; but that would be only in the less important arguments, and the meaner sort of books; else distilled books are, like common distilled waters, flashy things. Reading maketh a full man; conference a ready man; and writing an exact man. And therefore, if a man write little, he had need have a great memory; if he confer little, he had need have a present wit; and if he read little, he had need have much cunning to seem to know that he doth not. Histories make men wise; poems witty; the mathematics subtle; natural philosophy deep; moral grave; logic and rhetoric able to contend. *Abeunt studia in mores*. Nay, there is no stond or impediment in the wit, but may be wrought out by fit studies: like as diseases of the body may have appropriate exercises. Bowling is good for the stone and reins; shooting for the lungs and breast; gentle walking for the stomach; riding for the head; and the like. So if a man's wit be wandering, let him study the mathematics; for in demonstrations, if his wit be called away never so little, he must begin again. If his wit be not apt to distinguish or find differences, let him study the schoolmen; for they are *symini sectores*. If he be not apt to beat over matters, and to call up one	说，有些书只要读读他们的一部分就够了，有些书可以全读，但是不必过于细心地读；还有不多的几部书则应当全读，勤读，而且用心地读。有些书也可以请代表去读，并且由别人替我作出摘要来；但是这种办法只适于次要的议论和次要的书籍；否则录要的书就和蒸馏的水一样，都是无味的东西。阅读使人充实，会谈使人敏捷，写作与笔记使人精确。因此，如果一个人写得很少，那末他就必须有很好的记性；如果他很少与人会谈，那么他就必须有很敏捷的机智；并且假如他读书读得很少的话，那么他就必须要有很大的狡黠之才，才可以强不知以为知。史鉴使人明智；诗歌使人巧慧；数学使人精细；博物使人深沉；伦理之学使人庄重；逻辑与修辞使人善辩。"学问变化气质"。不特如此，精神上的缺陷没有一种是不能由相当的学问来补救的：就如同肉体上各种的病患都有适当的运动来治疗似的。踢球有益于结石和肾脏；射箭有益于胸肺；缓步有益于胃；骑马有益于头脑；诸如此类。同此，如果一个人心志不专，他顶好研究数学；因为在数学的证理之中，如果他的精神稍有不专，他就非从头再做不可。如果他的精神不善于辨别异同，那么他最好研	大体涉猎者，少数则须全读，读时须全神贯注，孜孜不倦。书亦可请人代读，取其所作摘要，但只限题材较次或价值不高者，否则书经提炼犹如水经蒸馏，淡而无味矣。 读书使人充实，讨论使人机智，笔记使人准确。因此不常做笔记者须记忆特强，不常讨论者须天生聪颖，不常读书者须欺世有术，始能无知而显有知。 读史使人明智，读诗使人灵秀，数学使人周密，科学使人深刻，伦理学使人庄重，逻辑修辞之学使人善辩：凡有所学，皆成性格。人之才智但有滞碍，无不可读适当之书使之顺畅，一如身体百病，皆可借相宜之运动除之。滚球利睾肾，射箭利胸肺，慢步利肠胃，骑术利头脑，诸如此类。如智力不集中，可令读数学，盖演题须全神贯注，稍有分散即须重演；如不能辨异，可令读经院哲学，盖是辈皆吹毛求疵之人；如不善求同，不善以一物阐证另一物，可令读律师之案卷。

译文三

些书可大致浏览，有些书则须通篇细读并认真领悟。有些书还可以请人代阅，只取代阅人所做摘录节要；但此法只实用于次要和无关紧要的书，因浓缩之书如蒸馏之水淡而无味。读书可使人充实，讨论可使人敏锐，笔记则可使人严谨；故不常做笔记者须有过目不忘之记忆，不常讨论者须有通权达变之天资，而不常读书者则须有狡诈诡谲之伎俩，方可显其无知为卓有见识。读史使人明智，读诗使人灵透，数学使人精细，物理学使人深沉，伦理学使人庄重，逻辑修辞则使人善辩，正如古人所云：学皆成性；不仅如此，连心智上的各种障碍都可以读适当之书而令其开豁。身体之百病皆有相宜的调养运动，如滚球有益于膀胱和肾脏，射箭有益于肺部和胸腔，散步有益于肠胃，骑马有益于大脑等等；与此相反，若有人难聚神思，可令其研习数学，因在演算求证中稍一走神就得重来一遍；若有人不善辨异，可令其读经院哲学，因该派哲学家之条分缕析可令人不胜其烦；而若有人不善由果溯因之归纳，或不善于由因及果之演绎，则可令其阅读律师之卷；如

译文四

书只需读其部分，有些书只需大体涉猎，少数书则需如饥似渴、集中精力整篇阅读。有些书可请人代读，有些书读他人之摘要则已足够，但这种书只限无关紧要或价值不高者。否则，好书经提炼，犹如经蒸馏之水，淡而无味。

　　阅读让人充实，讨论让人机智，记录让人准确。故不常记录者需有强健之记忆；不常讨论者需天生聪慧；不常阅读者需善耍小聪明，对己不知佯装知之。

　　历史使人睿智，诗歌使人灵秀，数学使人缜密，物理学使人深刻，伦理学使人庄重，逻辑修辞学使人善辩。此所谓"读书铸就性格者也"。是故才智之任何阻滞，无不可以读适当之书加以疏通。此犹如体内之百病，均可经适当运动予以消除。滚球有益睾肾，射箭有益胸肺，慢步有益肠胃，骑术有益大脑，如此等等。是故注意力难以集中者，可令其学数学，因演算时稍不留神，须重新开始。不善甄别者，可令其读经院哲学，因经院哲学家善辨毫厘之差异。不善由此及彼、举一反三者，可令其研读律

原文

thing to prove and illustrate another, let him study the lawyers' cases. So every defect of the mind may have a special receipt.

Abeunt studia in mores: Studies pass into the character.
symini sectores: dividers of cumin seeds, or hair-splitters.

(Francis Bacon, "Of Studies")

译文一

究经院学派的著作,因为这一派的学者是条分缕析的人;如果他不善于推此知彼,旁征博引,他顶好研究律师们的案卷。如此看来,精神上各种的缺陷都可以有一种专门的补救之方了。

(水天同　译)

译文二

如此头脑中凡有缺陷,皆有特药可医。

(王佐良　译)

三 散文翻译的批评与赏析练习

原文

When I try to understand what it is that prevents so many Americans from being as happy as one might expect, it seems to me that there are two causes, one of which goes much deeper than the other. The one that goes least deep is the necessity for subservience in some large organizations. If you are an energetic man with strong views as to the right way of doing the job with which you are concerned, you find yourself invariably under the orders of some big man at the top who is elderly, weary and cynical. Whenever you have a bright idea, the boss puts a stopper on it. The more energetic you are and the more vision you have, the

译文一

　　我对是什么使得众多的美国人不如人们所想象的那样开心进行了分析,认为原因有二,一个原因要更令人深思,另一个则显而易见,那就是在一些大机构供职者不得不对上司唯命是从。即使你活力十足,对如何做好自己的工作富于创见,仍然免不了要受制于某个年长资深、精力不支(济)、不纳贤言的高层大人物,难以有所作为。每当你提出什么意见,你的上司会立时让你缄口。你越有活力,越有创见,你就因不能按照自己的想法行事而越感抑郁。

译文二

　　在我设法弄清到底是什么使得那么多美国人不如人们所想象的那么开心时,我突然发现这似乎有两个原因,其中一个原因要比另一个原因体现得更为深刻。而相对表层的原因是,在有些大公司中供职,唯命是从非常必要。即使你精力充沛,并对如何做好自己的工作胸有成竹,你会发现,自己却总难免要听命于某位年龄稍长、体力不支、愤世嫉俗的高层大人物。不管你何时有何高见,上司马上会让你缄口无言。你越是精力充沛,越是有先见,你就越是不可能做成你觉得应该做的任何

译文三

此心智上之各种毛病皆有特效妙方。

（曹明伦　译）

译文四

师策卷。综而观之，凡心智之不足，均可以特别良方医治。

（李思伊、李明　译）

笔　记

原　文

more you will suffer from the impossibility of doing any of the things that you feel ought to be done. When you go home and moan to your wife, she tells you that you are a silly fellow and that if you became proper sort of yes-man your income would soon be doubled. If you try to divorce or remarry it is very unlikely that there will be any change in this respect. And so you are condemned to gastric ulcers and premature old age.

译文一

你若是回到家里向妻子诉苦，她反倒会说你是傻冒一个，还会说若是你学乖一点，在上司面前点头称是、唯命是从，薪水说不定很快翻番。即使你离婚另娶何人，你的再婚妻子也还会是这个态度，不可能对你有何安慰。因此，你注定要抑郁成疾，未老先衰。

（曾利沙　译）

译文二

事情。

当你回到家里向妻子抱怨时，她反倒会说你是傻瓜一个，还会说如果你乖巧一些，在上司面前唯唯诺诺，点头称是，薪水一定很快翻番。如果你想离婚再娶，这种景况也不可能有何改变。因此，你注定要得胃溃疡，注定要未老先衰。

（李明　译）

第九章 "Altogether Autumn" 汉译文的批评赏析

一、关于"Altogether Autumn"

"Altogether Autumn"据闻是刊登在美国知名杂志 Reader's Digest 上的一篇叙事型散文，作者身份现无从考究。在散文开头，作者从一年一度在秋季栽种球茎植物这一事件入手，进入主题，继而描写花园里的烂漫秋光。接着作者笔锋一转，回忆起同小女儿共同栽种球茎植

二、"Altogether Autumn"原文及四种汉译文

原 文	译文一	译文二
Altogether Autumn It's time to plant the bulbs. But I put it off as long as possible because planting bulbs means making space in borders which are still flowering. Pulling out all the annuals which nature has allowed to erupt in overpowering purple, orange and pink, a final cry of joy. That would almost be murder, and so I'll wait until the first night frost anaesthetizes all the flowers with a cold, creaky crust that causes them to wither; a very gentle death. Now I wander through my garden indecisively, trying to hold on to the last days of late summer.	**人间尽秋** 到了栽种球茎植物的时候了。我却是能拖则拖，因为栽种球茎得在园篱处腾出空间，而此时篱上仍开着朵朵鲜花。把一年生植物强行拔起，掐死造化恩赐的绛紫、橘黄和浅红这一片烂漫，阻断自然界的最后欢声，简直无异于谋杀。所以我要等待第一个霜降之夜，等待花瓣全部沾上一层冷冽的霜晶，蒙无知觉中自行凋零，和婉地寿终正寝。我在园中徜徉，拿不定主意，只求留住残夏的最后几天。	**挡不住的秋天** 是种球茎植物的时候了，但我却尽量推迟种花的时间。种球茎花就得在仍然盛开着各色花卉的花坛中开出地盘，就得把那些欢畅地绽放着紫色、橙色、粉红色的花朵给拔除掉，大自然一年只许诺了它们一次生机，拔除它们无异于谋杀。因此我得等待，等到夜晚的第一次寒霜用清冷的嚓嚓作响的冰衣将所有的花朵麻醉，使它们慢慢凋零，温柔地死去。此时，我徜徉在花园里，试图让夏季为时不多的光阴再停留些时候。

物的时日,并在此过程中不断转换场景,借以描写光阴的转瞬即逝,女儿在不知不觉中从懵懂小儿长成亭亭玉立的少女。最后以母女俩共同期盼着能够再一次拥有过去作结。文章以"Autumn"为主线串起全文,虽然表面上作者是在感叹秋天,实际上是在感叹岁月的无情流逝。

整篇散文行文自由、简洁、晓畅,笔法细腻、亲切、感人,语言朴实、真挚、清新,既有对秋日景物的描写,又有对母女深情的叙述,兼具景物之美和亲情之美,两种美交相辉映,互为表里。文章的节奏紧凑,结构分明,前半部分写景,后半部分写情,并围绕"秋"字做文章,通篇文章自然天成。

翻译该文的难点在于:一是要努力对应原文的结构,使得前后两个部分(写景与抒情)既互为表里,又层次分明;二是要充分传达出原文的意切情深和真挚感人,将母女间的亲情和深情在译文中充分再现出来。

译文三

秋忆满园

又到了栽种球茎植物的时候了,然而我却是能拖则拖,因为要种植球茎植物就不得不在花园周边腾出地方来。那里花儿依旧盛放着,这些一年生植物在大自然的恩宠下喷薄开出大片大片的紫色、橙色和粉色,那是凋零前最后的欢声。要是拔除这些植物则无异于谋杀,所以我一直等到第一场夜霜将这些花儿染上一层冷冽的冰衣,让它们在无知无觉之中枯萎凋谢,温柔地死去。此时此刻,我漫步徜徉在我的花园里,努力想要抓住夏季的尾巴。

译文四

秋天感怀

眼下到了栽种球茎的好时光,但我却能拖则拖,因为要栽种球茎的话,就意味着要在开满鲜花的狭长花坛中腾出空地,就意味着要把这些一年生植物连根拔起,而这些植物此时正受大自然的恩赐而在尽情绽放各种色彩——紫色、橙色、粉红等,这是它们最后的欢声。连根将它们拔掉无异于谋杀。所以我要等到第一个霜降之夜,那时,所有的花儿将被寒霜麻醉,那冰冷的、嘎吱作响的霜层会让它们慢慢凋零,会让它们温柔地逝去。此刻的我,犹疑不决,徜徉在花园中,多想留住这夏末里的最后时日。

笔 记

原文	译文一	译文二
The trees are plump with leafy splendor. The birch is softly rustling gold, which is now fluttering down like an unending stream of confetti. Soon November will be approaching with its autumn storms and leaden clouds, hanging above your head like soaking wet rags. Just let it stay like this, I think, gazing at the huge mysterious shadows the trees conjure up on the shinning green meadows, the cows languidly flicking their tails. Everything breathes an air of stillness, the silence rent by the exuberant colors of asters, dahlias, sunflowers and roses. The mornings begin chilly. The evenings give you shivers and cold feet in bed. But in the middle of the day the sun breaks through, evaporating the mist on the grass, butterflies and wasps appear and cobwebs glisten against windows like silver lace. The harvest of a whole year's hard work is on the trees and bushes: berries, beech mast, chestnuts, acorns. Suddenly I think of my youngest daughter, living now in Amsterdam. One day soon she will call and ask, "Have you planted the bulbs yet?" Then I will answer teasingly that actually I'm waiting until she comes to help me. And then we will both be overcome by	树叶犹盛，光鲜可人。白桦婆娑轻摇，一片片金色的叶子飘飘落地，有如一溜不绝如缕的庆典彩纸。十一月行将降临，带来秋的凄风苦雨和铅灰色阴云，像浸水的抹布一样压在你的头顶。但愿眼下的好天气会持续下去，我这样想，一边注视着树木在绿油油的草地上投下的幢幢诡谲黑影，还有倦慵地甩动尾巴的牛群。一片静谧，唯有紫苑、大丽菊、向日葵和玫瑰的浓艳色彩似在撕裂四下的沉寂。 清晨时分，天气凛冽，到了夜晚，你打起了哆嗦，躺在床上双脚冰凉。但在正午时分，阳光拨开云层，将暮霭化作蒸汽，在草地上升腾。蝴蝶和黄蜂开始出没。蛛网犹如丝带，挂在窗前闪出银光。树梢上和灌木丛里凝结了整整一年的辛劳，浆果、毛栗、板栗和橡实等着收获归仓。 突然，我想到如今客居阿姆斯特丹的幼女。这两天，她定会打电话来问："球茎植物种下了吗？"随即我会用打趣的口吻回答说，老妈正等着她来帮忙下种呢。接着母女双双陷入怀旧的情思，因为从前有段时间我们总是合作下种的。她才三岁半那年，一个秋阳万里的午后，	树儿郁郁葱葱的，丰满而气派。白桦树轻轻摇落着金黄色的叶子。落叶飘啊飘，像不停飞舞的彩纸屑。要不了多久，11月就会来临，连同秋天的风暴和铅灰色的云朵，如浸了水的破布高悬在你的头上。光阴要能凝滞于此刻该多好啊，我想，一边呆望着懒洋洋地摇动着尾巴的牛儿。万物都在呼吸着恬静的空气，静谧中穿透着紫苑花、大丽菊、太阳花和玫瑰花浓郁的芳香。 清晨开始变得寒冷。夜晚，在被窝里也不由得浑身战栗，双脚冰凉。但中午时分，太阳得以冲出重围，将笼罩在草丛上的雾气蒸发一空；蝴蝶、黄蜂出来了；窗棂上，蜘蛛网如同银色的花边在闪闪发光。一年辛苦过后，树上、灌木丛里到处是这一年的收成，有浆果，有板栗，有橡子，有山毛榉实。 突然想起了我在阿姆斯特丹的小女儿。不用多久，有一天她会打电话来问，"球茎花种上了么？"到时，我会逗乐地回答：在等你回来帮忙呢。随后我们双方都会沉浸在怀旧的情绪中。从前我们可一直是一块儿干这活儿的。只有三岁半那么大的时候，一个阳光明媚的秋日，她曾经带着浓厚的兴趣和欢

翻译批评与赏析 Translation Appreciation and Criticism

译文三

　　树儿们枝繁叶茂，桦树轻轻摇曳着枝条，金黄的树叶飘落下来，像不停飞舞的五彩纸屑。十一月就要到了，随之而来的将是秋日的暴风雨。铅灰色的阴云如一团浸湿的破布般压在头顶。凝望着绿油油的草地上投影下的婆娑树影，还有懒洋洋轻甩着尾巴的牛群，一派祥和宁静，我仿佛听见紫苑，大丽花和玫瑰怒放的声音。多想让夏日就此长留！

　　正值秋日，早晨凉意丝丝，夜晚则是冷颤连连，睡下了也是双脚冰凉。然而正午时分，阳光却拨开云层，将草地上弥漫的薄雾蒸发散去；蝴蝶和黄蜂开始飞舞，窗檐上的蛛网像银丝带般闪闪发光。枝头和灌木上凝结了一整年沉甸甸的果实：有浆果，毛果，板栗，还有橡皮果。

　　我忽然就想起了如今远在阿姆斯特丹的小女儿。过不多久，她一定会打电话来问："球茎植物种上了吗？"然后我就会打趣地告诉她，我正等她来帮我一起种呢，然后我们就会一起被回忆淹没，怀念曾经一起种植球茎植物的日子。那是一个秋阳高照的午后，她还只有三岁半，带着孩童的热情与欢快和我一起种下了球茎植物。

译文四

　　周围的树木枝繁叶茂，茁壮成长。白桦树在婆娑地摇曳着一片片金色，这一片片金色飘然而下，犹如源源不断的五彩纸屑。很快，十一月就要来临，随之而来的便是秋雨，还有那犹如浸湿的抹布般悬挂在头顶上铅灰色的云。多么想让时光凝固在此刻，我思忖着，同时还注视着树木在绿得发光的草地上所投下的巨大而诡谲的黑影，还有那倦怠地甩动着尾巴的牛儿。周围的一切一片静谧，唯有紫苑花、大丽菊、向日葵、玫瑰花那五彩斑斓的浓艳色彩在侵蚀四周的沉寂。

　　清晨从一开始就冷飕飕的。到了夜晚，即使躺在被窝里也会打哆嗦，也会双脚冰凉。但在正午时分，阳光透过云层照射过来，将草地上的雾气蒸发。此时，蝴蝶和黄蜂都出来了，蜘蛛网衬着窗户闪着光，犹如银色的丝带。一棵棵树上、一簇簇灌木上，都挂满了辛劳整整一年后的收成：浆果、山毛榉实、板栗、橡树果实等等。

　　突然，我想起了此时正生活在阿姆斯特丹的小女儿。过一两天，她一定会打电话来问："球茎种好了吗？"我会打趣地告诉她，我正等着她来帮忙呢。接着，我们俩就会沉浸在怀旧的思绪中，因为那时，我们总是在一起种球茎。在一个阳光灿烂的秋日下午（那时她刚过

笔　记

原文	译文一	译文二
nostalgia, because once we always did that together. One entire sunny autumn afternoon, when she was just over three and a half years old, she helped me with all the enthusiasm and joyfulness of her age. It was one of the last afternoons I had her around because her place in school had already been reserved. She wandered around so happily carefree with her little bucket and spade, covering the bulbs with earth and calling out "Night nigh" or "Sleep tight", her little voice chattering constantly on. She discovered "baby bulbs" and "kiddie bulbs" and "mummy and daddy bulbs" —the latter snuggling cozily together. While we were both working so industriously I watched my child very deliberately. She was such a tiny thing, between an infant and a toddler, with such a round little tummy. Every autumn, throughout her childhood, we repeated the ritual of planting the bulbs together. And every autumn I saw her changing; the toddler became a schoolgirl, a straightforward realist, full of drive. Never once dreamy, her hand in her pockets; no longer happily indulging her fantasies. The schoolgirl developed long legs, her jawline changed, she had her hair cut. It was autumn again	女儿曾怀着她那年龄特有的全部踊跃和欢乐,做过我的帮手。 生活中女儿绕膝的下午不多了,因为学校已给她留出一个名额。她带着自己的小桶和铲子,兴高采烈又无忧无虑地满园子跑,给球茎培掩泥土的同时,用尖细的嗓子一遍又一遍聒噪着"晚安,晚安"或是"睡个好觉"。她还分别发现了"贝贝种"和"娃娃种",还有"爸爸妈妈种",后者指的是那些亲密依偎的球茎种。两人辛苦劳作的同时,我曾留意审视孩子:真是个小不点儿,出了襁褓,挺着个圆滚滚的小肚子刚开始蹒跚学步。 在女儿童年期的每个秋季,我们履行仪式似的种下球茎植物,而每个秋季我都注意到女儿身上发生的变化。学步小儿长成了女学生,成为一个充满进取心而又坦率直面现实的人,从不把双手插在口袋里想入非非,再不依靠恣意幻想而自得其乐。女学生的双腿变得修长,下颌的轮廓线变了,要上理发店剪发了。秋季再次来临时,我在心里默念:"别了,玫瑰;别了,蝴蝶;别了,女学生。"当我们使劲在泥土里掘洞,种下明春的希望时,我在倾听女儿述说她的	呼雀跃的心情整整一个下午帮着我栽种球茎花。 这个下午是我得以有小女儿陪伴的最后几个下午时光之一,因为小女儿已经在学校里报了名。她兴高采烈、无忧无虑地四处转悠着,提着小桶、拿着小铲,在给球茎花埋土;嘴里还念念有词"宝宝,宝宝,睡个好觉",稚嫩的声音不停地传过来。她发现了"球茎花宝宝""球茎花娃娃"和"球茎花爸爸妈妈"——那温情地拥抱在一块儿的就是"球茎花爸爸妈妈"。我们俩都非常辛勤地干着活。我顺便特别观察了一下小女儿。她是如此如此的纤小,个头介乎于不会走路的婴孩和蹒跚学步的儿童之间;她还有一个溜圆溜圆的小肚子呢。 小女儿的整个童年时期,每年秋天,我们都要重复在一块儿栽种球茎花的仪式。每年秋天我都发现小女儿在发生着变化。学步童变成了学龄童,变成了一个直率干脆的现实主义者,浑身干劲十足。双手插在衣袋里,一副从不沉迷幻想的模样;也不热衷于沉浸在遐思之中。她双腿变得修长,下巴轮廓发生了变化,头发也剪短了。秋天又来临了,我想,"再见吧,玫瑰;再见吧,蝴蝶;再见吧,我的学龄童。"一边

译文三

那一年，她已报了名即将入学，女儿陪伴左右的下午已经不多了。她无忧无虑，欢快地满院子晃悠，带着她的小水桶和小铲子，一边给球茎植物盖上土，一边用她稚嫩的声音一遍又一遍叫唤着"天黑啦，快快睡吧"。她还发现了"球茎宝宝""球茎娃娃"和"球茎爸爸妈妈"，"球茎爸爸妈妈"总是惬意地依偎在一起。趁着两个人一同辛苦劳作的时候，我仔细观察着我的孩子。这个小不点儿，走路尚摇摇晃晃的，小肚子还圆滚滚地挺在外面！

她童年时代的每年秋天，我们都会照例一同栽种球茎植物。我也看着她一年一年地改变，从蹒跚学步的孩子长成了小学生，成为一个正直坦率又上进的现实主义者。她从不会两手一摊不劳动而只做不切实际的梦，也不再耽于幻想自娱自乐。她有了修长的双腿，下巴轮廓也改变了，还剪了头发。又是一年秋天，我心里想着，"再见了，玫瑰；再见了，蝴蝶；再见了，我的小女生"。我一边听着她的故事，一边和她一起用力挖土，种下来年春天的希望。

转眼间，她已经出落成我身边高挑的少女，快得出

译文四

三岁半），她带着她那个年纪所具有的满腔热情和全部欢乐帮我种下了球茎。

当时她已报到准备上学了，她能伴我身边只剩最后几个下午了。那是其中一个下午的事情。她提着小桶，拿着铲子，兴高采烈、无忧无虑地满园子里跑，一会儿给球茎掩土，一会儿喊着"夜晚要来了"或"睡个好觉吧"。那稚嫩的声音一遍又一遍地传来。她还会区分"茎宝宝""茎娃娃""茎爸妈"。"茎爸妈"是指那些亲密相依的球茎。在我们母女辛勤劳作的同时，我曾有意观察自己的孩子：她是个小不点儿，个头比婴孩大，比刚学步的儿童小，肚肚小小的、圆圆的。

在她童年时代的每个秋季，我们都要一起种球茎，那仿佛是在重复某种仪式。而每个秋季，我都注意到了她的变化。蹒跚学步的幼儿渐渐长成一个女学生，长成一个勇敢地直面现实的人，浑身充满活力。她从不双手插兜儿地沉溺于梦幻之中，也不再沉浸于遐想之中而自得其乐。女学生的双腿变得修长了，下颌变得有轮廓了，也注意理头发了。又是一年的秋季，我心里默念着："再见吧，玫瑰花；再见吧，花蝴蝶；再见吧，女学生。"当我们精心地在泥土中挖坑，并播下春天的希望时，我倾听着女儿讲述的各种故事。

笔 记

原 文	译文一	译文二
and I thought "Bye roses; bye butterflies; bye schoolgirl." I listened to her stories while we painstakingly burrowed in the earth, planting the promise of spring. Suddenly, much quicker than I had expected, a tall teenage was standing by my side; she had grown taller than me. The ritual became rather silent, we no longer chattered away from one subject to another. I thought about her room full of posters and knick-knacks, how it had been full of treasures in bottles and boxes, white pebbles, a copper brooch, colored drawings, the treasures of a child who still knew nothing of money, who wanted to be read aloud to and who looked anxiously at a spider in her room and asked, "Would he want to be my friend?" Then came the autumn when I planted the bulbs alone, and knew that from then on it would always be that way. But every year, in autumn, she talks about it. Full of nostalgia for the security of childhood, the seclusion of a garden, the final moments of a season. How both of us would dearly love to have a time machine. To go back. Just for a day.	故事。 突然，站在我身旁的女儿成了大姑娘，变化之神速远胜我的预料。随后，她的身高超过了我。下种成了相对无言的程式，不再有天南海北的闲聊。我不由得想起她那挂满大幅招贴以及充斥各种小摆设的房间，而先前这儿多的是瓶子和纸盒，白色的卵石，一枚铜制胸针，彩色图画。这些都是一个尚不知晓金钱为何物的幼儿的珍藏品，一个要大人读书给她听的稚女，见了屋里的蜘蛛会忧心忡忡的发问："蜘蛛愿跟我做朋友吗？" 接着就是我独自下种的那个秋天，我还知道从此就是单干的命了。但每到秋天，她总要提下种的事，口气里充满怀旧的意味，缅想事事都有保障的童年，幽闭的庭院，一个季节的最后时刻。父女俩（应为"我们母女俩"——编者注）多么衷心希望有一台时间机器，能回到往昔，即便过上一天也好。 （陆谷孙 译）	听着关于她的故事，我们一边辛勤地在地上挖着土窝，种上春天的希望。 突然，大大出乎我的意料，一个高大的少女站在了我的身旁。她已经出落得比我高大。种球茎花的仪式变得很沉默，我们不再是一个话题接一个话题地聊个没完。我想起她那间贴满了海报摆满了小玩意的卧室。那里曾经满是孩子的宝贝，有瓶子盒子有白色的卵石有铜制的胸针有彩色的图画。孩子没半点金钱意识，老吵着要听故事，还曾经不安地看着屋子里的蜘蛛问："他愿意做我的朋友吗？" 然后，秋天来了，只剩下我独自栽种球茎花，我知道从此以后都得这个样子了。但每年，秋天的时候，小女儿都会谈到种球茎花的事儿。谈话中充满了怀旧的心情：怀念孩提时代的安全感，怀念花园远离尘嚣的宁静，怀念一个季节的最后时光。我们俩是多么多么地希望能够拥有一台科幻传说中的时间机器啊！让它带我们回到从前，只一天就行。 （周仁华 译）

译文三

乎我的意料,她的个头已经高过我了。种球茎植物时也沉默多了,我们不再从一个话题扯到另一个话题。我不禁想起了她满是海报和小摆设的房间,那里曾是她的宝库,有她装满宝贝的瓶子和盒子,白色卵石,铜胸针,还有彩色的图画。那时的她还只是个不知金钱为何物的孩子,会想要听故事,会不安地看着房里的蜘蛛问,"他会愿意同我做朋友吗?"。

之后的秋天,我就开始独自种球茎植物了。我知道,以后也都会是我独自一人。但是年年秋天,她都会说起这事,怀念着童年时的安全感,想念那宁静恬然的花园,和秋末的最后时光。我们是多么深切地希望有一架时光穿梭机,带我们回到过去,哪怕只有一天也好!

(盛吉 译)

译文四

转眼间,一位亭亭玉立的大姑娘站到了我的身边,其速度之快超出了我的预料。她长得比我高很多。栽种球茎的仪式变得沉寂了,我们不再是一个话题接一个话题地聊个没完。我又想起她曾住过的房间,里面贴满了海报,摆满了各种小饰物;想起了里面曾堆积在一起的那些用瓶子和盒子装着的各种宝物:白色的鹅卵石,铜制的胸针,彩色的图画等等。这些宝物竟然出自一位甚至连钱都不知为何物的小孩之手,出自一位需要别人朗读故事给她听的小孩之手,出自一位见了房间里的蜘蛛便忧心忡忡地问:"它愿做我的朋友吗?"的小孩之手。

在那之后的秋天里,只有我一个人种球茎了。我知道,自此以后,我将永远一个人种球茎了。但每年秋天,她总会谈起种球茎的事。一想到童年时所具有的安全感,一想到园子里所充满的幽静,一想到夏季里最后的时刻,她便充满了怀念。我们母女俩多么想望着拥有一台时间机器呀!多么想望着回到从前!哪怕只有一天!

(李明 译)

笔 记

散文翻译的批评与赏析练习

原文	译文一	译文二
In Memoriam: Rena C. Hayden Diane Fortune From 1908 to 1948, a remarkable woman, Rena C. Hayden, ran the John Lewis Childs' Elementary School, K-8, with impeccable taste and, albeit, an iron hand. As principal, she hired and fired the staff for its classrooms as well as for its kitchen; personally policed the schoolyards at recess, making miscreants walk single file behind her; disciplined, and on occasion, expelled unruly students; and came knocking loudly on parents' doors in her capacity as sometime truant officer. She stood no more than 5'1", was stocky, with an enormous chest and delicate, small limbs. No animal rights activist, she wore hats with birds on them, tailored suits with a stole of little foxes draped over her shoulders and sensible leather shoes. Her voice, when she had to raise it, sounded to her pupils like the wrath of God Himself, and her bulging blue eyes commanded attention. Awestruck teachers referred to her as R. C. H; awestruck children whispered her name. Both teachers and pupils withered under her terrible gaze.	缅怀雷娜·C·海登 1908年到1948年，一位杰出的女性，雷娜·C·海登，管理着约翰·路易斯·查尔兹小学学前预备班到八年级的教育。她有毋庸置疑的明鉴力，但管理方式颇为严厉。身为校长，她掌管着聘用、解雇教师和炊事人员的大权；课间休息时，她亲自督察校园，责令捣乱的学生排成一路纵队跟在她后面；她惩罚那些难以管教的学生，有时甚至开除他们；她时而还会以劝学员的身份，去砰砰地敲击逃学、旷课学生家长的门。她身高不过5英尺1英寸，身体结实，胸部丰满，四肢纤细。她不是动物权利保护主义者，因而头上戴着印有小鸟图案的帽子，身上穿着定做的套装，披着绣有小狐狸图案的披肩，脚上穿着朴实耐用的皮鞋。她不得不提高嗓门的时候，她的声音在学生们听来就像上帝在发怒，她那双蓝眼睛瞪得圆鼓鼓的，让学生不敢走神。敬畏她的老师称她为R. C. H.；敬畏她的学生说起她的名字得压低声音。不管老师还是学生，在她咄咄逼人的目光下都会感	怀念雷娜·C·海顿 1908至1948年间，一位杰出的女性管理着约翰·路易斯·查尔兹这所从事学前预备班至八年级教育的小学。虽然她以铁的手腕管理着该校，她的管理却有着无懈可击的风范。这位女性就是雷娜·C·海顿。身为校长，她凡事亲历亲为，从教师到厨师的聘用和解雇，她都要一一过问。课间休息时，她还亲自维持校园秩序，让捣蛋的学生排成一列纵队跟在自己身后；对那些目无校纪的学生更是严加管教，有时甚至逐出校园。她不时还以劝导员的身份兴致勃勃地走进那些逃学或旷课学生家的大门。 海顿身高只有5英尺1英寸，身体结实，胸部丰满，四肢纤细。她不是动物权利保护的激进分子，所以头戴的帽子上嵌有鸟儿图案，身着的定做的套装披肩上绣有小狐狸图案，脚穿的皮鞋是由实用耐穿的动物皮制成。提高嗓门时，她那嗓音让学生听了觉得是上帝在怒吼，她那双瞪得圆鼓鼓的眼睛让人根本不敢走神。老师们都敬畏她，管她叫R. C. H.；孩子们也敬畏她，提到她的名字都不敢大声念出。老

原 文

For forty years, Mrs. Hayden personally oversaw the education of nearly every kid in town. They learned English grammar by diagramming sentences, writing by practicing the Palmer method; they learned to read by sounding out their letters, arithmetic by working with flash cards at school and at home. Those that would not or could not master these skills were remanded to summer school, and if that did not help, they were unceremoniously left back. She commanded so much respect that few parents ever disagreed with her judgments. Strong in character and social in purpose, she led the Pledge of Allegiance and the 23rd Psalm at assemblies, headed the John Lewis Childs' contingent to the Mummer's Parade at Thanksgiving and marched in the very first ranks of every Memorial Day celebration. During the early years, many of her charges left school upon completing eighth grade; she had only nine brief years to teach them to think clearly and independently, to polish the many diamonds in the rough she believed them to be, to inspire them with the highest ideals of American culture.

That was her public persona; in

译文一

到诚惶诚恐。

　　四十年间，海登夫人亲自督管了镇上几乎所有孩子的教育。孩子们用图解句子的方法学习英语语法，用帕默尔默氏法学习写字。不管在家里还是在学校里，他们通过大声念出字母来学识字，用抽认卡来学算术。那些不愿或不能掌握这些技能的孩子被送到暑假班，如果到暑假班还不奏效，就毫不客气地抛下他们不管。她深受人们敬重，很少有家长对她的决断持有异议。她性格坚强，又热心社会活动，曾带领学生在集会上做效忠宣誓，唱第二十三首圣歌。她还在感恩节时带领约翰·路易斯·查尔兹小学的队伍参加过化装游行；在每年阵亡将士纪念日游行中，她总是走在队伍的最前列。早年间，她的许多学生上完八年级就离开学校了；她只有短短的九年时间来培养他们独立清晰思考的能力，来打磨那许多她认为有待雕琢的钻石，用美国文化中的崇高理想激励他们。

　　这是她在公众面前的形象。在私人交往中，她却是另外一个样子：心地善良，为人谨慎。我了解一桩轶事，

译文二

师也好，学生也好，看到她那威严的目光，个个都要畏缩三分。

　　四十年来，海顿夫人亲自督促了镇上几乎每个孩子的学习。这些孩子通过图解句子的方法学习英语语法，通过帕默尔氏书法练习写字。在学校也好，在家里也好，他们通过高声朗读字母来学识字，通过抽认卡来学算术。有不愿意或者不能够掌握这些技巧的学生，她都要责令他们进暑假班。如果暑假班还不奏效，她就毫不客气地让他们留级。她的威严赢得了人们无限的敬仰，很少有学生家长对她的决断有什么异议。海顿夫人性格坚强，一心为着社会。她曾带领学生在集会上做效忠宣誓，朗诵《圣经》第23首赞美诗，带领查尔兹小学队参加感恩节期间举行的化装游行，并在每年举行的阵亡将士纪念日游行活动中走在队伍的最前排。可惜的是，她的很多学生在读完八年级之后就早早地离开了学校。毕竟，要培养学生清晰、独立的思维，要磨光那许许多多未经琢磨的"钻石"，要用美国文化中最崇高的理想激励他们，九年的时间的确是太短暂的一瞬。

　　这就是海顿夫人给予公

原 文	译文一	译文二
private, she acted otherwise, with kindness and discretion. I know one anecdote about her spontaneous generosity; there must have been others. In 1927, Robert C. —one of six children—lost his mother. He was nine years old. His older brother and sisters quit school. So Bobby quit too. An enterprising youngster, he began handing around the coal yards, going out on the deliveries, running errands, now and then getting tips. He was doing pretty well, when one fine morning, Mrs. Hayden came looking for him. In her severest voice, she asked, "Robert C., why are you not in school?" "I've quit school," he replied bravely. "You can't quit school at age nine," she thundered. Thinking quickly for some kind of excuse, he stammered, "I haven't got any clothes to wear to school." Mrs. Hayden looked down at him—his shirt was worn, his pants ripped. Without hesitation, she opened her pocketbook and gave the boy a twenty-dollar bill. "Now you have money for clothes for school. I expect you to be there." Bobby's father, who was working from early in the morning to dusk, hadn't realized that his son was truant or why. Ever grateful to Mrs. Hayden for her intercession, Mr. C. paid back the twenty dollars. Thereafter when she saw the boy in the halls of John Lewis Childs, she	足以显示她那慷慨的天性；当然这种事肯定还有不少。1927年，身为家中六个孩子之一的罗伯特·C失去了母亲。他当时才9岁。他的哥哥和姐妹们都辍学了。于是，鲍比也不上学了。他是个很有进取心的孩子，开始在煤场附近辗转，出去送送货，跑跑腿，不时挣点小费。他干得很不错，不想一个晴朗的早晨，海登夫人来找他了。夫人以极其严厉的口气问他："罗伯特·C，你为什么不去上学？""我退学了。"罗伯特了无惧色地答道。"你才9岁，不能退学。"海登夫人大声斥责道。罗伯特灵机一动找了个理由，吞吞吐吐地说："我没有上学穿的衣服。"海登夫人低头看了看他，只见他衬衫破旧，裤子也撕破了。她毫不犹豫打开钱包，给了他一张20元的钞票。"现在你有钱买上学的衣服了。我等着你去上学。"鲍比的父亲起早贪黑地工作，不知道儿子逃学了，也不知道他为什么逃学。C先生对海登夫人出面劝儿子上学始终抱有感激之情，便把20元钱还给了她。后来，海登夫人每次在学校的走廊里遇到鲍比时，都会主动跟他打招呼，但从不提起新衣服的事。罗伯特·C一直读完了八年级。现在他已是80多岁的老人了，这个故事是他亲口讲给	众的形象。但在私人生活中，她完全是另一副样子：她心地善良、为人谨慎。这里有件轶事，完全可以昭示出她天性慷慨大方。当然这样的轶事一定还有很多。1927年，身为家中六个孩子之一的罗伯特失去了母亲。当时罗伯特只有九岁，他的一个哥哥和几个姐妹都辍学了，小罗伯特也辍学了。这个小伙儿进取心十足，他开始转悠于煤场附近，外出送送货、跑跑腿，不时赚点小钱。他干得正有滋有味，突然，一个晴朗的早晨，海顿夫人找到他了。她用最严厉的声音问道，"罗伯特，为什么不上学？""我弃学了。"他大着胆子说。"你不能九岁就弃学。"她大声喝道。罗伯特灵机一动，找个借口吞吞吐吐地说，"我上学没衣服穿。"海顿夫人俯视了他一眼——他衣衫破烂，裤子也被撕裂。海顿夫人毫不犹豫打开钱包给了他二十元钱："现在该有钱买衣服上学了吧。我在学校等你。"小罗伯特的父亲起早摸黑在外做工，根本不知道儿子逃学或为什么要逃学。C先生对海顿夫人出面规劝儿子上学感激不尽，将二十元钱还给了她。那以后，每次看到小罗伯特在学校走廊里，海顿夫人就会同他打招呼，但她从不提新衣服的事。罗伯特最终读完了八年级。如今已80高龄的罗伯特将这个故事亲口讲给我听。他敬佩海顿，

原文

would greet him, but never did she make mention of his new clothes. Robert C. told me that story himself. He reveres the memory of Rena C. Hayden.

Mayors and fire chiefs came and went; she remained, through World War I, through the roaring Twenties, through the Great Depression, through World War II. In April, 1945, when F. D. R. died, she turned out the entire school on the lawn in front of the original bell-topped school building. Solemnly, she lowered the flag to half-mast. Her eyes filled with tears; many of the teachers openly wept. Some of her pupils realized, perhaps for the first time, that like the fallen President, Mrs. Hayden had provided them with an example of commitment, strength and self-reliance. For an even longer time than he, through dark and difficult years, she had led the way. It was her finest hour. In 1948, she retired to the house on Jericho Turnpike by the Long Island Railroad trestle; for a few more years she continued to march in the holiday parades. And then she passed indelibly into our recollections even as she receded into the town's history.

She was as much a founder of the town of Floral Park as John Lewis Childs, who had owned all the land originally.

译文一

我听的。一想起雷娜·C·海登，他心里总是充满敬意。

镇长和消防队长换了一任又一任，她却始终待在校长的岗位上，先后经历了第一次世界大战、喧嚣的20年代、大萧条时期，以及第二次世界大战。1945年4月，罗斯福总统去世的时候，她把全校师生招集到学校原来的钟楼前的草坪上。她极其庄严地降下了半旗。她的眼里噙满了泪水。许多教师当众失声恸哭。有些学生意识到，也许是第一次意识到：海登夫人就像已故的总统一样，为他们树立了奉献、坚强、自立的榜样。在那黑暗和艰难的岁月里，她引领着前进的方向，甚至比罗斯福总统引领的时间还要长。这是她人生中最美好的时刻。1948年，她退休后回到了长岛铁路高架桥与耶利哥公路交汇口的家中；此后的几年里，她继续参加节日游行。后来她去世了，即使在她淹没在小镇历史中的时候，还依然留在我们的记忆中，永远不会磨灭。

与曾拥有这片土地的约翰·路易斯·查尔兹一样，海登夫人也是弗洛尔帕克镇的缔造者。

（孙致礼 译）

译文二

对海顿永远不会忘怀。

小镇上的镇长和消防队长换了一个又一个，但海顿却从未离开过校长的职位。她历经了第一次世界大战，历经了喧嚣的20年代，历经了20年代末30年代初的经济大萧条，历经了第二次世界大战。1945年4月罗斯福总统去世时，她把全校师生招集到学校原来钟楼前的草坪上。她非常庄严地降下半旗。她的双眼噙满了泪水，许多老师失声痛哭。她的一些学生这才意识到，也许是第一次意识到，海顿夫人就像刚刚倒下的总统，为他们树立了榜样：奉献、坚强、自立。是她带领他们走过黑暗而艰苦的岁月，在时间上甚至比罗斯福总统还要长。那是她最辉煌的岁月。1948年，她退休了，回到了自己位于长岛铁路高架桥同耶利戈公路交汇处的家中。在接下来的许多年里，她仍然行进在节日游行的队伍中。后来，她离我们而去，永远留在了我们的记忆之中——尽管她渐渐淡出了我们镇的历史。

同当时拥有我们镇全部土地的约翰·路易斯·查尔兹一样，海顿夫人同样缔造了作为花园式公园的我们这座小镇。

（李明 译）

第十章 《落花生》英译文的批评赏析

一 关于《落花生》

《落花生》是许地山（1893—1941）先生的作品。许地山，名赞，字地山，笔名落华生。祖籍台湾省台南市，落籍福建龙溪（今龙海），生于台湾一个爱国志士的家庭。现代小说家、散文家。早年就读于燕京大学，后赴美国哥伦比亚大学、英国牛津大学研究文学、宗教和哲学，回国后在燕京大学、清华大学、北京大学、香港中文大学执教。曾积极参加五四运动，合办《新社会》旬刊。抗日战争开始后，任中华全国文艺界抗敌协会香港分会常务理事，为抗日救国事业奔走呼号，展开各项组织和教育工作。他的创作虽不丰硕却独树一帜，作品具有爱国、进步的思想倾向。他以"落华生"为笔名（在古文中，"华"同"花"），表明了他的人生态度和高尚品格。

《落花生》这篇散文发表于20世纪20年代。由于其"质朴淳厚、意境深远"的风格，被誉为现代散文的经典。该文较为真实地记录了许地山小时候所接受的家教。其父亲许南英，

二 《落花生》原文及四种英译文

原 文	译文一	译文二
落花生 我们屋后有半亩隙地。母亲说，"让它荒芜着怪可惜，既然你们那么爱吃花生，就辟来做花生园罢。"我们几姊弟和几个小丫头都很喜欢——买种的买种，动土的动土，灌园的灌园；过不了几个月，居然收获了！	**Peanuts** Behind our house there lay half a *mu* of vacant land. Mother said, "It's a pity to let it lie waste. Since you all like to eat peanuts so much, why not have them planted here." That exhilarated us children and our servant girls as well, and soon we started buying seeds, ploughing the land and watering the plants. We gathered in a good harvest just after	At the back of our house there was half a *mu* of unused land. "It's a pity to let it lie waste like that," Mother said, "Since you all enjoy eating peanuts, let us open it up and make it a peanut garden." At that my brother, sister and I were all delighted and so were the young housemaids. And then some went to buy seeds, some began to dig the

曾是清朝政府驻台湾筹防局统领。中日"甲午战争"爆发后，许南英率部奋起抗击侵略军，但由于清政府腐败，终因寡不敌众，台湾招致陷落，并沦为日本殖民地。许南英出于爱国之心，毅然抛弃全部家产，携带家眷在福建龙溪定居，过着清贫的生活。许地山小时，父亲曾以"落花生"作比，要求子女们为人做事要脚踏实地，不求虚荣。这给许地山留下了深刻印象。因此，许地山在自己的创作生涯中，不仅写了《落花生》一文追忆父亲的教诲，而且以"落华生"为笔名勉励自己。其著作有《许地山选集》。

散文《落花生》以"讲故事"的方式，运用独具匠心的叙事表达，使得整篇散文：1) 语言浅显平实、简明精当，但旨趣深远、寓理于物；2) 布局详略得当，主次分明。

文章简略地描述了一家人过花生收获节的经过，通过对花生好处的谈论，揭示了花生不图虚名、默默奉献的品格，说明人要做有用的人，不要做只讲体面或只追求外表华美而对别人或社会没有用的人，表达了作者不为名利，只求有益于社会的人生理想。这也是全文的主旨所在。

根据这一主旨，作者在文章的布局上，把种花生、收花生作为次要内容，写得比较简略；把在过收获节过程中对花生的谈论作为文章的主要内容，写得比较详细。正是由于围绕着文章的主旨，使得文章的主次分明。因此，文章篇幅虽然简短，但却给人以非常清晰明了的印象，使人从平凡的事物中悟出了耐人寻味的道理。

这里选取了张培基、刘士聪的译文各一篇，魏志成基于张培基和刘士聪的译文而给出的译文一篇，最后还给出了本人的英译文。

译文三	译文四	笔记
Behind our house lay half a *mu* of vacant land. My mother said, "It's a pity to let it lie waste. Since you all like to eat peanuts so much, why not open it up and make it a peanut garden?" We children and the little maidservants were all delighted—some of us started buying seeds, some digging up the land and others watering the	Behind our house there lay half a *mu* of open field. "It's a pity that it lies waste like that," Mother said one day. "Since you all like peanuts, why not plant some over there?" At that, all of us children, together with our servant girls, were greatly overjoyed. Instantly, some of us went to buy seeds, others began to	

原　文	译文一	译文二
妈妈说:"今晚我们可以做一个收获节,也请你们爹爹来尝尝我们的新花生,如何?"我们都答应了。母亲把花生做成好几样的食品,还吩咐这节期要在园里的茅亭举行。 那晚上的天色不大好,可是爹爹也到来,实在很难得!爹爹说:"你们爱吃花生么?" 我们都争着答应:"爱!" "谁能把花生的好处说出来?" 姊姊说:"花生的气味很美。" 哥哥说:"花生可以制油。" 我说:"无论何等人都可以用贱价买它来吃;都喜欢吃它。这就是它的好处。" 爹爹说:"花生的用处固然很多;但有一样是很可贵的。这小小的豆不像那好看的苹果、桃子、石榴,把它们的果实悬在枝上,鲜红嫩绿的颜色,令人一望而	a couple of months! Mother said, "How about giving a party this evening to celebrate the harvest and invite your Daddy to have a taste of our newly-harvested peanuts?" We all agreed. Mother made quite a few varieties of goodies out of the peanuts, and told us that the party would be held in the thatched pavilion on the peanut plot. It looked like rain that evening, yet, to our great joy, father came nevertheless. "Do you like peanuts?" asked Father. "Yes, we do!" We vied in giving the answer. "Which of you could name the good things in peanuts?" "Peanuts taste good," said my elder sister. "Peanuts produce edible oil," said my elder brother. "Peanuts are so cheap," said I, "that anyone can afford to eat them. Peanuts are everyone's favourite. That's why we call peanuts good." "It's true that peanuts have many uses," said Father, "but they're most beloved in one respect.	ground and others watered it and, in a couple of months, we had a harvest! "Let us have a party tonight to celebrate," Mother suggested, "and ask Dad to come for a taste of our fresh peanuts. What do you say?" We all agreed, of course. Mother cooked the peanuts in different styles and told us to go to the thatched pavilion in the garden for the celebration. The weather was not very good that night but, to our great delight, Dad came all the same. "Do you like peanuts?" Dad asked. "Yes!" We all answered eagerly. "But who can tell me what the peanut is good for?" "It is very delicious to eat," my sister took the lead. "It is good for making oil," my brother followed. "It is inexpensive," I said with confidence. "Almost everyone can afford it and everyone enjoys eating it. I think this is what it is good for." "Peanut is good for many things," Dad said, "but there is

译文三

plants; and in just a few months we gathered in a good harvest!

My mom said, "How about having a party this evening to celebrate the harvest and inviting your dad to taste our newly-harvested peanuts?" We all agreed. Mom made quite a few varieties of goodies out of the peanuts, and told us that the party should be held in the thatched pavilion in the garden.

The weather was not very good that evening, but to our great joy, our dad came all the same.

"Do you like peanuts?" asked Dad.

"Yes, we do!" We vied for the answer.

"But who can tell me what the peanut is good for?"

"Peanuts taste good," said my elder sister.

"Peanuts can be made into edible oil," said my elder brother.

"Everybody, whoever he might be, can afford to buy peanuts since they are so cheap; and everyone likes them. I think this is what the peanut is good for." said I.

译文四

dig up the field and still others helped water it. In only a few months, we gathered in a good harvest!

Mother said, "Tonight, let's have a harvest party and invite your father to share with us the newly-harvested peanuts, shall we?"

We all agreed. And out of the peanuts, Mother made quite a few varieties of goodies and urged that the party be held in the thatched pavilion in the field.

It was overcast that evening, but Father came all the same. That was a great joy to all of us.

"Do you like peanuts?" Father asked.

"We do!" answered we in clamour.

"But who can tell us the good things in peanuts?"

"They taste nice," Elder Sister said.

"We can make oil out of them," responded Elder Brother.

"Everyone can afford to eat them. Everyone likes them. These are the good things in peanuts." I added.

Father said, "Surely, peanuts can

笔　记

原文	译文一	译文二
发生美慕的心。它只把果子埋在地底，等到成熟，才容人把它挖出来。你们偶然看见一棵花生瑟缩地长在地上，不能立刻辨出它有没有果实，非得等到你接触它才能知道。" 我们都说："是的。"母亲也点头。爹爹接下去说："所以你们要像花生，因为它是有用的，不是伟大、好看的东西。"我说："那么，人要做有用的人，不要做伟大、体面的人了。"爹爹说："这是我对于你们的希望。" 我们谈到夜阑才散，所有花生食品虽然没有了，然而父亲的话现在还印在我心版上。	Unlike nice-looking apples, peaches and pomegranates, which hang their fruit on branches and win people's instant admiration with their brilliant colours, tiny little peanuts bury themselves underground and remain unearthed until they're ripe. When you come upon a peanut plant lying curled up on the ground, you can never immediately tell whether or not it bears any nuts until you touch them." "That's true," we said in unison. Mother also nodded. "So you must take after peanuts," Father continued, "because they're useful though not great and nice-looking." "Then you mean one should be useful rather than great and nice-looking," I said. "That's what I expect of you," Father concluded. We kept chatting until the party broke up late at night. Today, though nothing is left of the goodies made of peanuts, father's words remain engraved in my mind. （张培基 译）	one thing that is particularly good about it. Unlike apples, peaches and pomegranates that display their fruits up in the air, attracting you with their beautiful colors, peanut buries its seeds in the earth. They do not show themselves until you dig them out when they are ripe and, unless you dig them out, you can't tell whether it bears seeds or not just by its frail stems above ground." "That's true," we all said and Mother nodded her assent. "So you should try to be like the peanut," Dad went on, "because it is useful, though not great or attractive." "Do you mean," I asked, "we should learn to be useful but not seek to be great or attractive?" "Yes," Dad said, "This is what I wish you to be." We stayed up late that night, eating all the peanuts Mother had cooked for us. But Father's words remained vivid in my memory till this day. （刘士聪 译）

译文三

"It's true that peanuts have many uses," said Dad, "but the most valuable thing about them is: While nice-looking apples, peaches and pomegranates hang their fruit on branches and win people's instant admiration with their brilliant colors, tiny little peanuts bury themselves underground and remain unearthed until they're ripe. When you come upon a peanut plant lying curled up on the ground, you can never immediately tell whether or not it bears any nuts until you touch them."

"That's true," we all agreed. Mom also nodded. "So you must take after peanuts," Dad went on, "because they're useful though not great and nice-looking.""Then you mean one should be useful rather than great and nice-looking," I wondered. "That's what I expect of you," Dad concluded.

We kept chatting until the party broke up late at night. Today, though nothing is left of the goodies made of peanuts, my father's words still remain engraved in my memory.

（魏志成 译）

译文四

serve many purposes. But it has one quality that is the most admirable. While nice-looking apples, peaches and pomegranates hang their fruits on branches and win people's instant admiration with brilliant colours, the little peanuts remain buried in the ground till they are ripe before they are unearthed. So, only when you dig them out instead of an occasional glimpse at their curling up on the ground can you instantly tell whether they bear any fruits at all."

We all agreed with what Father had said and Mother also nodded in consent.

"Then," continued Father, "You should all acquire the qualities of peanuts by being useful instead of being great and nice-looking."

"What you mean is that," I explained, "One should try to be a useful person rather than just trying to be great or decent."

"Yes. That's what I expect of you all," Father concluded.

We chatted till very late that evening. Though we can now no longer taste the goodies for that night, what Father had said still remains etched in our minds.

（李明 译）

笔 记

三 散文翻译的批评与赏析练习

原文

"达则兼济天下，穷则独善其身"，这是中国古代知识分子最基本的价值观念和人生理想，也决定了他们人格中最深刻的矛盾。"庙堂之上"的读书人会时常想要悠然隐退、寄情山水；"山林之中"的读书人却无时不盼望晋身官场、踏入仕途。士人心灵深处的矛盾决定了书院精神宗旨的矛盾：它以反对科举之学为旗帜，力倡独立的学术研究、学术传播，但它从来没有真正摆脱科举的影响和控制。毕竟，科举考试是他们步入政界、治国平天下的唯一一途径。

千年学府，千年书香，书院的存在，对中国教育史、学术史的发展有着不可替代的作用和意义，它永远是中国文化史上一颗灿烂的明珠。

译文一

"If prominent, I shall spread my benevolence to all the people; if impoverished, I shall keep my destitution to myself." That expressed the basic values and ideals of China's ancient intellectuals. Yet, at the same time, such a code of conduct also generated the most profound contradiction in their personality. When they were "at the court", they would long to retire to the quiet mountains and rivers; when they actually fell from grace and retreated to the mountains and rivers, they would yearn for officialdom. As a result, the academies also suffered from the same contradiction. Although they advocated independent academic study and disseminating knowledge while opposing the imperial examination system, they were never able to shake off the latter's impact and control. After all, the imperial examination system was the only way through which they could enter officialdom to realize their grand ideals.

China's ancient academies, with their history of more than one thousand years, played a significant role in the country's education and academic history. They were bright pearls that will shine forever in the history of Chinese culture.

（丁树德　用例）

译文二

"When in office, I will work for the well-being of the people in the whole world and when out of office, I will try to maintain my own personal integrity." That was the expression of the most basic values and ideals that ancient Chinese intellectuals cherished. It at the same time nourished the most profound contradiction in their personality. While intellectuals who were "in the imperial court" would long to retire to the quiet mountains and rivers, those who "did retire to the mountains and rivers" would yearn for officialdom at any moment. This contradiction in the innermost of their hearts generated the similar contradiction in the tenets of the academies. On the one hand, the academies opposed the imperial examination system and advocated independent academic research and academic communication. On the other hand, they could never shake off the impact and control exerted by the imperial examination system. After all, the system was the only way through which they could enter officialdom to realize their grand ideals.

China's ancient academies, with a history of over one thousand years, played an irreplaceable and significant role in the country's education and academic history. They constituted a resplendent pearl that will shine forever in the history of Chinese culture.

（李明　译）

第十一章 《干校六记》英译文片段的批评赏析

一 关于《干校六记》

《干校六记》是杨绛的作品。杨绛（1911—2016），原名杨季康，江苏无锡人，中国社会科学院外国文学研究所研究员，作家、评论家、翻译家、剧作家、学者，既从事创作，又从事理论研究及翻译实践。主要作品有剧本《称心如意》《弄假成真》和《风絮》，长篇小说《洗澡》，短篇小说集《倒影集》，散文集《干校六记》和《将饮茶》等。其中享有最高声誉的有《干校六记》和《洗澡》，翻译出版过的作品包括《一九三九年以来英国散文作品》、西班牙名著《小癞子》《堂·吉诃德》、法国名著《吉尔·布拉斯》等。

《干校六记》于1981年出版，畅销整个20世纪80年代，在港澳台均出版了繁体字单行本，并被译成多种外国文字在国外出版。该散文集包括《下放记别》《凿井记劳》《学圃记闲》《"小趋"记情》《冒险记事》《误传记妄》等六篇，其中《学圃记闲》记述了作者在干校期间，学习种菜的经历。在不动声色的描写里，作者流露出鲜明的爱憎。尽管只是三言两语、一个细节，抑或是几句对话，但它们却勾勒出丰富复杂的思想感情，引起读者强烈的共鸣。

整部散文集，用的委实是井旁圃中的家常言语，记的也不过是下放之别、凿井之劳、种圃之闲、冒险之幸、小狗的人情世故和由传闻而生的妄思，以及由此引发出的种种感慨。然而，这些看似闲常之笔，仔细想来却微言大义，颇为耐人寻味。

《干校六记》的艺术特色体现在：

1. 《干校六记》记叙的是作者1970年7月至1972年3月在"五七"干校劳动改造的一段生活。作者将这段时光描写得恬淡自然，避开了社会政治的人生观照，以边缘人的达观诙谐，表现了作家在逆境中的洒脱与镇静，体现出学者式的智慧与风范。

2. 作品中并没有正面描写干校里的大事件，只是通过衣食住行、同志之谊、夫妻之情等琐碎之事，以个性化的审视角度反映出那个特殊的年代以及知识分子的命运。作品以轻盈空灵的笔调，刚柔相济的情思，漫不经意但却浑然天成的结构，平淡朴素但却耐人寻味的语言，展现出独具特色的艺术魅力，展示出一位老作家的赤子之心和善良情怀，也为散文创作提供了新的审美样式。

3. 作品的另一显著特色是其既幽默又泰然的艺术格调。作者在追忆过往的经历时，处处带着"回头一笑"的宽容，以如话家常般的从容，娓娓道来，妙语连珠，涉笔成趣，在凝重的生活底色上呈现出纯朴、动人的光彩，显示了真正审美意义上发达的智慧与宽厚的境界。作者写到在干校时编的门帘、积的肥、沤的绿肥、种的菜被当地百姓连偷带拾去时，既让人感受到当地人民生活的贫困，又令人忍俊不禁。而当我们读到作

二 《干校六记》原文片段及四种英译文

原文

我在菜园里拔草间苗，村里的小姑娘跑来闲看。我学着她们的乡音，可以和她们攀话。我把细小的绿苗送给她们，她们就帮我拔草。她们称男人为"大男人"；十二三岁的小姑娘，已由父母之命定下终身。这小姑娘告诉我那小姑娘已有婆家；那小姑娘一面害羞抵赖，一面说这小姑娘也有婆家了。她们都不识字。我寄居的老乡家是比较富裕的，两个十岁上下的儿子不用看牛赚钱，都上学；可是他们十七八岁的姊姊却不识字。她已由父母之命、媒妁之言，和邻村一位年貌相当的解放军战士订婚。两人从未见过面。那位解放军给

译文一

When I was pulling out weeds some of the young girls from the village came to watch. I imitated their local accent and struck up a conversation with them. I gave them some green seedlings and they helped me with the weeding. They called all males "big men", and though none of them were old enough to be married—they were all about twelve or thirteen—their parents had already chosen their future mates. One girl pointed to a friend who, she said, already had "in-laws". The girl in question blushed shyly and denied it, claiming that it was actually the girl who had been speaking who had the in-laws. Neither of them could read. The family I had been staying with was relatively well off—neither of their two ten-year-old boys had to earn their pocket money by herding cows, and both of them were still going to school, though their eighteen-year-old sister was illiterate. Her parents had used a matchmaker to find a husband for her and she was engaged. The young man was a People's Liberation Army soldier

译文二

Once, as I was weeding in the vegetable garden, two young girls from the village came to visit me. I carried on a conversation with them by imitating their native dialect, albeit imperfectly. I gave them some surplus young seedlings and they in return helped me in the weeding. They referred to their men folk as "big daddies". Their marriages were arranged by their parents; even girls as young as twelve or thirteen were promised in future marriages. One girl pointed a finger at the other one, saying, "She has been engaged and is expecting to be married soon." Embarrassed, the latter retaliated and said, "She has been promised in marriage to a family too." Both were illiterate.

The family with which I stayed when I first arrived was comparatively well-to-do. Two boys about ten years old were attending school, as there was no need for them to herd cows for a little extra income. However, their sister, about seventeen or eighteen years old, was illiterate. She had been engaged to a soldier of the Liberation Army from a neighboring village through a marriage

者去收获他们精心培育的"象牙萝卜"时,也几乎要如同作品中的"我"一样,笑得"跌坐地下"。正因如此,《学圃记闲》等反映干校生活的纪实散文,以其无穷的韵味,赢得了读者广泛的欣赏和好评。

译文三

Whenever I was weeding and pruning in the vegetable plot, some of the village girls would run over to watch me work. Once I had mastered their local speech I passed the time of day with them. I gave them some of the smaller twigs and they helped me do the weeding. They referred to their men folk as "the big guys". They were all young girls of twelve or thirteen whose future marriages had been arranged by their parents. One of them told me that one of the others had already been accepted by her in-laws. This comment obviously embarrassed the girl referred to, who denied the charge and turned it right back to the first girl. Neither of them was literate. The family I had lived with for a while in another village was better off than the families of these girls; their two sons, who were in the neighborhood of ten years of age, didn't need to tend oxen to make a little money, but were both in school. Their seventeen- or eighteen-year-old sister, on the other hand, was illiterate. Her parents had enlisted the aid of a matchmaker, and the girl was already engaged to be married to a PLA soldier

译文四

While I was pulling out weeds or making space for seedlings, some village girls came to watch me working. By imitating their local accent, I could strike up a conversation with them. I gave them some seedlings and they in return helped me with the weeding. To them, men were "great gallants". Though they were only twelve or thirteen years of age, they were already made a match in marriage under their parents' command. One girl told me that the other girl had been engaged already. The said girl, who tried hard to deny it with embarrassment, said that the other party had also been engaged. Neither of them was literate.

The family with which I had been living was relatively better off. Their two sons, at the ages of ten or so, didn't have to herd cows for extra income and were attending school. Their seventeen- or eighteen-year-old sister, however, didn't receive any education. She was already engaged under

原 文	译文一	译文二
未婚妻写了一封信，并寄了照片。他小学程度，相貌是浑朴的庄稼人。姑娘的父母因为和我同姓，称我为"俺大姑"；他们请我代笔回信。我举笔半天，想不出一句合适的话；后来还是同屋你一句，我一句拼凑了一封信。那位解放军连姑娘的照片都没见过。 村里十五六岁的大小子，不知怎么回事，好像成天都闲来无事的，背着个大筐，见什么，拾什么。有时七八成群，把旁边不及胳膊粗的树拔下，大伙儿用树干在地上拍打，"哈！哈！哈！"粗声訇喝着围猎野兔。有一次，三四个小伙子闯到菜地里来大吵大叫，我忙赶去，他们说菜畦里有"猫"。"猫"就是兔子。我说：这里没有猫。躲在菜叶底下的那头兔子自知藏身不住，一道光似的直窜出去。兔子跑得快，狗追不上。可是几	from a neighboring village who was about the same age as she was. They had never met, and he wrote her a letter with a picture of himself inside; he only had a primary-school education and had the solid honest look of a peasant. Her parents called me "elder sister" because we had the same surname, and they asked me to write a reply to the boy from their daughter. I asked for some suggestions from my room-mates as to what to write, and then sat, pen in hand, staring at the paper in front of me for a long time. Her future husband had never seen her picture. I was constantly amazed that the young boys in the village, all of them in their mid-teens, never seemed to have anything better to do than wander around with large wicker baskets tied to their backs, throwing into them whatever they laid their eyes on. Sometimes seven or eight of them would band together to hunt rabbits by beating the ground with sticks made from small stripped saplings, screaming and shouting all the while. Once, when a few of them came stomping into the vegetable garden making a great commotion, I rushed over to see what was going on. They told me they were after "cats" — "cats" being the word they used for rabbit. I had barely finished telling them that our vegetable garden didn't have any "cats" in it when	broker at the insistence of her parents. The couple had never met. The young man had sent his fiancée a letter and a photograph of himself. From the photograph, he looked like a person of solid peasant stock and had received a primary school education. The girl's parents happened to share the same surname with us so I was addressed as "cousin". It therefore became the "cousin's" duty to write a reply to the future son-in-law. I held the pen for a long time without putting down a single appropriate word. Finally, the people who shared the dwelling with me made their contributions—one sentence here and another sentence there. The letter was thus haphazardly patched together. But the soldier was not favored with a picture of his fiancée. Surprisingly, young men of fifteen or sixteen from the villages didn't seem to have regular work to do. They spent much of their time in small groups loitering around. With big baskets hanging on their backs, they searched for kindling here and there. Occasionally they pulled up trees of considerable size and beat the ground with them, yelling in unison, "Ha…Ha…Ha…" in order to scare up wild jack rabbits. Once, three or four youngsters rushed into my vegetable garden, yelling at the top of their lungs, "A cat! …a cat!" In their dialect, cat and rabbit were synonymous. I went out to have a look and told them there was no cat in the vegetable garden. But the rabbit hiding there knew that he had

译文三	译文四
whose age and appearance were just right. The two of them had never laid eyes on one another, but the soldier had written his fiancée a letter and sent her a photograph. Both his level of education and his appearance were those of a simple farmer. The girl's family and I shared the same surname, so they called me "Auntie"; they asked me to write a letter for them in reply. But I sat there, pen in hand, for the longest time without coming up with a single appropriate line, until finally my roommate and I put our heads together and managed to compose a letter. The soldier had to do without a photograph of his intended. For some reason, the fifteen-and-sixteen-year-old boys from the village seemed to loaf around all day long with nothing to do. With large baskets slung over their shoulders, whenever they saw something that interested them, they picked it up. Sometimes they went out in groups of seven or eight and uprooted young trees alongside the road that were no bigger around than a man's arm. Then they would smack the ground with them and shout loudly—"Ha! Ha! Ha!" as they hunted around for wild rabbits. Three or four of them came rushing into our vegetable plot one day, clamoring and yelling for all they were worth. They said there was a "cat" in one of the vegetable beds. "Cats" were	her parents' command and upon the matchmakers' word to a PLA soldier of a similar age and of a matching appearance from a neighboring village. They had never seen each other. When the PLA soldier wrote a letter to her, he enclosed in it a photo of himself. He only received primary school education and had a solid stock of an honest peasant. As the girl's parent had the same family name as I, they called me "Dear Auntie" in the way their daughter called me. They asked me to write for them a letter in reply to the soldier. With pen in hand for a long time, I just couldn't figure out what to write. Later, my roommates each added something which helped me with the completion of a letter. The soldier didn't even see the photo of her. Surprisingly enough, boys of fifteen or sixteen in the village seemed to loaf around all day long without anything to do. With large bamboo baskets on their backs, they throw into them whatever they saw on the way. Sometimes in groups of seven or eight, they would pull off a tree nearby as wide as an arm in diameter and beat the ground with tree trunks in hunt for a hare by yelling "ha, ha, ha!" at the top of their voice. Once, three or four kids trespassed into the vegetable plot and shouted

原 文

条狗在猎人指使下分头追赶,兔子几回转折,给三四条狗团团围住。只见它纵身一跃有六七尺高,掉下地就给狗咬住。在它纵身一跃的时候,我代它心胆俱碎。从此我听到"哈!哈!哈!"粗哑的訇喝声,再也没有好奇心去观看。

(杨绛《干校六记》之"学圃记闲")

译文一

a rabbit that had been hiding under a leafy vegetable nearby suddenly sprinted for safety. It was so fast that they had to send their dogs to hunt it down. For a few moments, there was some furious running and dodging before the rabbit was cornered by the four yelping animals. After a final, desperate leap into the air it fell to the ground and was savaged. When it pounced into the air my heart seemed to jump into my throat. From that time on, when I heard the boys screaming and beating their sticks, I never had the slightest interest in watching the hunt.

("The Vegetable Garden: On Idleness" from *A Cadre School Life: Six Chapters*)

(Geremie Barmé 译)

译文二

been detected and rushed out like a flash of lightning. Several dogs pursued him relentlessly at the command of their masters and soon he was surrounded. In a desperate effort to escape, the rabbit jumped six or seven feet into the air, but when he landed, he was caught by the dogs. My heart ached for this unfortunate creature. From then on, when I heard "Ha … Ha … Ha…," I knew what was going on and refused to look further.

("Leisure Between Chores at the Vegetable Garden" from *Six Chapters of Life in a Cadre School*)

(章楚 译)

译文三

what they called rabbits. I told them there were no cats here. The rabbit that was hiding among the cabbage leaves knew instinctively that there wasn't enough cover to protect him, so he darted out like a flash. He was much too fast for any of the dogs chasing him, but under the direction of the young hunters, they split up and went after from different directions. The rabbit changed course several times until he was surrounded by the dogs. He jumped into the air, as high as six or seven Chinese feet, and when he hit the ground he was set upon by the dogs. I felt so frightened and sorry for him when he jumped that my heart nearly broke. From then on, the coarse, loud shouts of "Ha! Ha! Ha!" held no attraction for me to go take a look.

("Leisure: Tending a Vegetable Plot" from *Six Chapters From My Life*)

(Howard Goldblatt 译)

译文四

loudly. I rushed over to see what was happening. They said that there was a "cat" in the vegetable bed. By "cat", they mean "hare". I said that there wasn't any cat here. Knowing it could no longer hide itself, the hare under the vegetable leaves rushed out in a flash of light. It ran so fast that even dogs couldn't catch up with it. But at the command of their masters, the dogs split up and continued to run after the hare. After several changes of its course, the hare was besieged by three or four dogs. In desperate efforts to escape, it jumped into the air more than two meters high. When it fell onto the ground, it was set upon by the dogs. The moment it pounced into the air, my heart nearly got broken. Since then, whenever I heard the yelling at the top of the voice "ha, ha, ha" again, no longer had I had any interest in watching the hunt.

（李　明　译）

三 散文翻译的批评与赏析练习

原　文

燕子去了，有再来的时候；杨柳枯了，有再青的时候；桃花谢了，有再开的时候。但是，聪明的，你告诉我，我们的日子为什么一去不复返呢？——是有人偷了他们罢：那是谁？又藏在何处呢？是他们自己逃走了：现在又到了哪里呢？

我不知道他们给了我多少日子；但我的手确乎是渐渐空虚了。在默默里算着，八千多日子已经从我手中溜去；像针尖上一滴水滴在大海里，我的日子滴在时间的流里，没有声音也没有影子。我不禁头涔涔而泪潸潸了。

去的尽管去了，来的尽管来着，去来的中间，又怎样的匆匆呢？早上我起来的时候，小屋里射进两三方斜斜的太阳。太阳他有脚啊，轻轻悄悄地挪移了；我也茫茫然跟着旋转。于是——洗手的时候，

译文一

Swallows may have gone, but there is a time of return; willow trees may have died back, but there is a time of regreening; peach blossoms may have fallen, but they will bloom again. Now, you the wise, tell me, why should our days leave us, never to return? —If they had been stolen by someone, who could it be? Where could he hide them? If they had made the escape themselves, then where could they stay at the moment?

I do not know how many days I have been given to spend, but I do feel my hands are getting empty. Taking stock silently, I find that more than eight thousand days have already slid away from me. Like a drop of water from the point of a needle disappearing into the ocean, my days are dripping into the stream of time, soundless, traceless. Already sweat is starting on my forehead, and tears welling up in my eyes.

Those that have gone have gone for good, those to come keep coming; yet in between, how swift is the shift, in such a rush? When I get up in the morning, the slanting sun marks its presence in my small room in two or three oblongs. The sun has feet, look, he is treading on, lightly and furtively; and I am caught, blankly,

译文二

If swallows go away, they will come back again. If willows wither, they will turn green again. If peach blossoms fade, they will flower again. But, tell me, you the wise, why should our days go by never to return? Perhaps they have been stolen by someone. But who could it be and who could be hide them? Perhaps they have just run away by themselves. But where could they be at present moment?

I don't know how many days I am entitled to altogether, but my quota of them is undoubtedly wearing away. Counting up silently, I find that more than 8,000 days have already slipped away through my fingers. Like a drop of water falling off a needle point into the ocean, my days are quietly dripping into the stream of time without leaving a trace. At the thought of this, sweat oozes from my forehead and tears tickle down my cheeks.

What is gone is gone, what is to come keeps coming. How swift is the transition in between! When I get up in the morning, the slanting sun cast two or three squarish patches of light into my small room. The sun has feet too, edging away softly and stealthily. And, without knowing it, I am

原 文	译文一	译文二
日子从水盆里过去；吃饭的时候，日子从饭碗里过去；默默时，便从凝然的双眼前过去。我觉察他去的匆匆了，伸出手遮挽时，他又从遮挽着的手边过去，天黑时，我躺在床上，他便伶伶俐俐地从我身边跨过，从我脚边飞去了。等我睁开眼和太阳再见，这算又溜走了一日。我掩着面叹息。但是新来的日子的影儿又开始在叹息里闪过了。	in his revolution. Thus—the day flows away through the sink when I wash my hands, wears off in the bowl when I eat my meal, and passes away before my day-dreaming gaze as reflect in silence. I can feel his haste now, so I reach out my hands to hold him back, but he keeps flowing past my withholding hands. In the evening, as I lie in bed, he strides over my body, glides past my feet, in his agile way. The moment I open my eyes and meet the sun again, one whole day has gone. I bury my face in my hands and heave a sigh. But the new day begins to flash past in the sigh.	already caught in its revolution. Thus the day flows away through the sink when I wash my hands; vanishes in the rice bowl when I have my meal; passes away quietly before the fixed gaze of my eyes when I am lost in reverie. Aware of its fleeting presence, I reach out for it only to find it brushing past outstretched hands. In the evening, when I lie on my bed, it nimbly strides over my body and flits past my feet. By the time when I open my eyes to meet the sun again, another day is already gone. I heave a sign, my head buried in my hands. But, in the midst of my sighs, a new day is flashing past.
在逃去如飞的日子里，在千门万户的世界里的我能做些什么呢？只有徘徊罢了，只有匆匆罢了；在八千多日的匆匆里，除徘徊外，又剩些什么呢？过去的日子如轻烟却被微风吹散了，如薄雾，被初阳蒸融了；我留着些什么痕迹呢？我何曾留着像游丝样的痕迹呢？我赤裸裸来到这世界，转眼间也将赤裸裸地回去罢？但不能平的，为什么偏要	What can I do, in this bustling world, with my days flying in their escape? Nothing but to hesitate, to rush. What have I been doing in that eight-thousand-day rush, apart from hesitating? Those bygone days have been dispersed as smoke by a light wind, or evaporated as mist by the morning sun. What traces have I left behind me? Have I ever left behind any gossamer traces at all? I have come to the world, stark naked; am I to go back, in a blink, in the same stark nakedness? It is not fair though: why should I have made such a trip for nothing!	Living in this world with its fleeting days and teeming millions, what can I do but waver and wander and live a transient life? What have I been doing during the 8,000 fleeting days except wavering and wandering? The bygone days, like wisps of smoke, have been dispersed by gentle winds, and, like thin mist, have been evaporated by the rising sun. What traces have I left behind? No, nothing, not even gossamer-like traces. I have come to this world stark naked, and in the twinkling of an eye, I am go to back as stark naked as ever. However, I am taking it very much to heart: why should I be made to pass

原文	译文一	译文二
白白走这一遭啊？ 你聪明的，告诉我，我们的日子为什么一去不复返呢？ （朱自清《匆匆》）	You the wise, tell me, why should our days leave us, never to return? (Zhu Ziqing, *Rush*) （朱纯深 译）	through this world for nothing at all? O you the wise, would you tell me please: why should our days go by never to return? (Zhu Ziqing, *Transient Days*) （张培基 译）

第十二章 《荷塘月色》英译文的批评赏析

一 关于《荷塘月色》

读散文重要的是要抓住线索，抓住了线索，就能理清作者的思路，准确把握文章的立意。所谓线索，就是串联文章内容的一根"红线"，它在文章结构中起着举足轻重的作用，没有恰当的线索，文章就变成一盘散沙。抓住散文中的线索，不仅有助于理解作者的写作意图，还能充分地欣赏作者的谋篇布局。（党争胜，2008：7）散文《荷塘月色》就是以游踪为线索的。

除了线索之外，散文中还有表达作者思想感情，反映作品主旨的词句。这种词句便是"文眼"。"文眼"是散文的"点睛"之笔，是文章"心灵"的透视，是读者窥见作者写作意图和主题思想的窗口，是理清全文脉络的筋节，是掌握文章各部分相互联系的关键。清代学者刘熙载说："揭全文之旨，或在篇首，或在篇中，或在篇末。在篇首则后者必顾之，在篇末则前者必注之，在篇中则前注之，后顾之。顾注，抑所谓文眼者也。"换言之，"文眼"乃提示文章主旨的词句。

那么，《荷塘月色》这篇散文的"文眼"到底为何？对此，不同读者可能会有不同的理解和阐释。有人说，文章开头的"颇不宁静"便是该散文的文眼。但仔细思之便会发现，"颇不宁静"这一词句无法透视该篇散文的"心灵"，无法成为让读者窥见作者写作意图和主题思想的窗口，无法让人理清全文脉络的筋节，无法让人掌握文章各部分相互联系的关键。因此，我同意将"惦着江南"作为全文"文眼"的说法。而对于"惦着江南"，朱自清在写完此文后的两个月，曾说过这样的话："在北京住了两年多了，一切平平常常地过去。要说福气，这也是福气了。因为平平常常，正像'糊涂'一样'难得'，特别是'这年头'。但不知怎的，总不时想着在那儿过了五六年转徙生活的南方。转徙无常，诚然算不得好日子；但要说到人生味，怕倒比平平常常时候容易深切地感着。"这表明在白色恐怖的年头，作者深感世态的炎凉，因而特别向往过去在江南生活的"人生味"。

因此，将"惦着江南"作为全文的"文眼"恐怕是更具理据性的。

另外，在赏析这篇散文时，还要注意全文中的两个"忽然想起"。第一个"忽然想起"引出的是荷塘夜游。而第二个"忽然想起"引出的是江南采莲的习俗，这为全文的"文眼"——"惦着江南"作了铺垫。这样，我们也就可以弄清楚《荷塘月色》的主旨了：全文记叙了夜游荷塘的经过，描绘了一幅恬淡幽美、富有诗情画意的荷塘月色图，含蓄地表达了对时局的忧虑，希望能够再次过上过去曾经在江南过的那种具有"人生味"的和平而安宁的生活。

二 《荷塘月色》原文及四种英译文

原 文

这几天心里颇不宁静。今晚在院子里坐着乘凉，忽然想起日日走过的荷塘，在这满月的光里，总该另有一番样子吧。月亮渐渐地升高了，墙外马路上孩子们的欢笑，已经听不见了；妻在屋里拍着闰儿，迷迷糊糊地哼着眠歌。我悄悄地披了大衫，带上门出去。

沿着荷塘，是一条曲折的小煤屑路。这是一条幽僻的路；白天也少人走，夜晚更加寂寞。荷塘四面，长着许多树，蓊蓊郁郁的。路的一旁，是些杨柳，和一些不知道名字的树。没有月光的晚上，这路上阴森森的，有些怕人。今晚却很好，虽然月光也还是淡淡的。

路上只我一个人，背着手踱着。这一片天地好像是我的；我也像超出

译文一

I have felt quite upset recently. Tonight, when I was sitting in the yard enjoying the cool, it occurred to me that the Lotus Pond, which I pass by everyday, must assume quite a different look in such moonlit night. A full moon was rising high in the sky; the laughter of children playing outside had died away; in the room, my wife was patting the son, Run'er, sleepily humming a cradle song. Shrugging on an overcoat, quietly, I made my way out, closing the door behind me.

Alongside the Lotus Pond runs a small cinder footpath. It is peaceful and secluded here, a place not frequented by pedestrians even in the daytime; now at night, it looks more solitary, in a lush, shady ambience of trees all around the pond. On the side where the path is, there are willows, interlaced with some others whose names I do not know. The foliage, which, in a moonless night, would loom somewhat frighteningly dark, looks very nice tonight, although the moonlight is not more than a thin, grayish veil.

I am on my own, strolling, hands behind my back. This bit of the universe seems in my possession now; and I myself seem to have been uplifted from my ordinary self into another world. I like a serene and peaceful life, as much as a

译文二

The last few days have found me very restless. This evening as I sat in the yard to enjoy the cool, it struck me how different the lotus pond I pass every day must look under a full moon. The moon was sailing higher and higher up the heavens, the sound of childish laughter had died away from the lane beyond our wall, and my wife was in the house patting Run'er and humming a lullaby to him. Quietly I slipped on a long gown, and walked out leaving the door on the latch.

A cinder-path winds along by the side of the pool. It is off the beaten track and few pass this way even by day, so at night it is still more quiet. Trees grow thick and bosky all around the pool, with willows and other trees I cannot name by the path. On nights when there is no moon the track is almost terrifyingly dark, but tonight it was quite clear, though the moonlight was pale.

Strolling alone down the path, hands behind my back, I felt as if the whole earth and sky were mine and I had stepped outside my usual self into another world. I like both excitement and stillness, under the full moon, I could think of whatever I pleased or of nothing at all, and that gave me a

136 翻译批评与赏析 Translation Appreciation and Criticism

译文三

The last few days I have been quite troubled in my mind. Tonight as I sat in the yard enjoying the cool of evening I suddenly thought of the lotus pond I passed every day: it must surely look different now in the light of the full moon. The moon was mounting high in the sky, and the sounds of the children at play in the road outside had died away. Indoors my wife was putting our little Runer to sleep, drowsily humming a lullaby. I quietly slipped on my gown and went out, pulling the gate to behind me.

At the edge of the pond is a winding narrow cinder path. This path, being out of the way, is little used even in the daytime, and at night is all the more deserted. All around the pond grow many trees, lush and dense, while on one side of the path there are some willows, and other trees whose names are unknown to me. On moonless nights the path is overcast and gloomy, somewhat eerie. But tonight all was well, even though the moonlight was only dim.

I was the only person on the path, pacing along with my hands

译文四

These days have found me quite in turmoil. Tonight as I was sitting in my yard, cooling off in the night air, I suddenly thought of the lotus pond I pass by every day: on such a fully-moonlit night, it must assume a different outlook.

As the moon was rising higher and higher up in the sky, we could no longer hear the laughter of children playing in the alleys beyond our wall. Inside our home, my wife was patting our son—Run'er, sleepily humming a cradle song. And quite quietly, I put on my long gown, left the door on the latch and made my way towards the pond.

Along the pond winds a narrow cinder footpath. The footpath, peaceful and secluded, is not much frequented by pedestrians in the daytime and at night, it is even more solitary. Around the pond grows a huge profusion of trees, exuberant and luxuriant. On one side of the path are willows and some other trees whose names are unknown to me. On a moonless night, it is somewhat somber here, looking rather forbidding. But it has a cheerful outlook tonight, though the moonlight is in a thin, whitish veil.

Strolling along the path I am, all alone, with my hands behind my back. I seem to have this bit of the universe all in my possession. What's more, it seems that I have overreached my usual self to such an extent

笔 记

原 文	译文一	译文二
了平常的自己, 到了另一世界里。我爱热闹, 也爱冷静; 爱群居, 也爱独处。像今晚上, 一个人在这苍茫的月下, 什么都可以想, 什么都可以不想, 便觉是个自由的人。白天里一定要做的事, 一定要说的话, 现在都可不理。这是独处的妙处, 我且受用这无边的荷香月色好了。	busy and active one; I like being in solitude, as much as in company. As it is tonight, basking in a misty moonshine all by myself, I feel I am a free man, free to think of anything, or of nothing. All that one is obliged to do, or to say, in the daytime, can be very well cast aside now. That is the beauty of being alone. For the moment, just let me indulge in this profusion of moonlight and lotus fragrance.	sense of freedom. All daytime duties could be disregarded. That was the advantage of solitude: I could savour to the full that expanse of fragrant lotus and the moonlight.
曲曲折折的荷塘上面, 弥望的是田田的叶子。叶子出水很高, 像亭亭的舞女的裙。层层的叶子中间, 零星地点缀着些白花, 有袅娜地开着的, 有羞涩地打着朵儿的; 正如一粒粒的明珠, 又如碧天里的星星, 又如刚出浴的美人。微风过处, 送来缕缕清香, 仿佛远处高楼上渺茫的歌声似的。这时候叶子与花也有一丝的颤动, 像闪电般, 霎时传过荷塘的那边去了。叶子本是肩并肩密密地挨着, 这便宛然	All over this winding stretch of water, what meets the eye is a silken field of leaves, reaching rather high above the surface, like the skirts of dancing girls in all their grace. Here and there, layers of leaves are dotted with white lotus blossoms, some in demure bloom, others in shy bud, like scattering pearls, or twinkling stars, or beauties just out of the bath. A breeze stirs, sending over breaths of fragrance, like faint singing drifting from a distant building. At this moment, a tiny thrill shoots through the leaves and flowers, like a streak of lightning, straight across the forest of lotuses. The leaves, which have been standing shoulder to shoulder, are caught trembling in an emerald heave of the pond. Underneath, the exquisite water is covered from view, and none can tell its color; yet the leaves on top project themselves all the more attractively.	As far as eye could see, the pool with its winding margin was covered with trim leaves, which rose high out of the water like the flared skirts of dancing girls. And starring these tiers of leaves were white lotus flowers, alluringly open or bashfully in bud, like glimmering pearls, stars in an azure sky, or beauties fresh from the bath. The breeze carried past gusts of fragrance, like the strains of a song faintly heard from a far-off tower. And leaves and blossoms trembled slightly, while in a flash the scent was carried away. As the closely serried leaves bent, a tide of opaque emerald could be glimpsed. That was the softly running water beneath, hidden from sight, its color invisible, though the leaves looked more graceful than ever.
	The moon sheds her liquid light silently over the leaves and flowers,	Moonlight cascaded like water over the lotus leaves and flowers and a light blue mist floating from the pool made them seem washed in milk or caught in a gauzy dream. Though the moon was full, a film of pale clouds in the sky would not allow its rays to shine through brightly; but I felt this was all to the good—though refreshing sleep is indispensable,

译文三

clapsed behind my back. It was as if this domain belonged to me; and also as if I had transcended my normal self, had crossed into another dimension. I like excitement, and also like calm; I like to be in crowds, and also love to be on my own. On a night like this, alone in the all-pervading moonlight, one could think about everything, or about nothing, and so believe oneself to be a free man. One's daytime obligations, in terms of what one had to do and say, could be entirely ignored. This was the beauty of solitude. I resolved to make the best of this abundance of lotus and moonlight.

On the surface of the serpentine lotus pond all one could see was fields of leaves. The leaves stood high above the water, splayed out like the skirts of a tall slim ballerina. Here and there among the layers of leaves were sown shining white flowers, some blooming glamorously, some in shy bud, just like unstrung pearls, or stars against a blue sky. Their fresh fragrance wafted on the faint breeze, like snatches of song from some distant tower. At each breath of wind the leaves and flowers also gave a shiver, which passed over the entire breath of the pond in a

译文四

as to have entered another world. I enjoy a tranquil life as well as a bustling one; I enjoy being in solitude as well as being in company. On such a night as this, bathing in the mist-like moonlight, I can think of anything or nothing, which makes me feel that I have complete freedom. Also, all that I have to do, or to say, in the daytime, can be totally cast aside at the moment. This is the best feeling that I have when being alone. And I can now immerse myself fully in this profusion of moonlight and fragrance.

All over the pond with its winding margin what meets the eye was a field of trim leaves. The leaves rise high out of the water, looking like the flared skirts of fair lasses dancing gracefully. Upon layers of leaves are dotted with white lotus flowers, some blooming gracefully while others budding bashfully. They are just like pearls shining bright, or stars twinkling high in an azure sky. They are also like fair ladies coming fresh out of a bath. When a breeze passes, it wafts breaths of fragrance, which are like faint singing drifting from a far-away building. Instantly, a slight tremble thrills through the leaves and flowers, like a streak of lightning, flashing across the whole field. And the leaves, which have been jostling and overlapping, are caught trembling in an emerald heave of the pond. Underneath the leaves is the rippling water, which is hidden from view and whose color cannot be seen. But the leaves project themselves all the more enchantingly.

The moonlight, like a cascade, was

原文

有了一道凝碧的波痕。叶子底下是脉脉的流水，遮住了，不能见一些颜色；而叶子却更见风致了。

月光如流水一般，静静地泻在这一片叶子和花上。薄薄的青雾浮起在荷塘里。叶子和花仿佛在牛乳中洗过一样；又像笼着轻纱的梦。虽然是满月，天上却有一层淡淡的云，所以不能朗照；但我以为这恰是到了好处——酣眠固不可少，小睡也别有风味的。月光是隔了树照过来的，高处丛生的灌木，落下参差的斑驳的黑影，峭楞楞如鬼一般；弯弯的杨柳的稀疏的倩影，却又像是画在荷叶上。塘中的月色并不均匀；但光与影有着和谐的旋律，如梵婀玲上奏着的名曲。

荷塘的四面，远远近近，高高低低都是树，而杨柳最多。这些树将一

译文一

which, in the floating transparency of a bluish haze from the pond, look as if they had just been bathed in milk, or like a dream wrapped in a gauzy hood. Although it is a full moon, shining through a film of clouds, the light is not at its brightest; it is, however, just right for me—a profound sleep is indispensable, yet a snatched doze also has a savor of its own. The moon light is streaming down through the foliage, casting bushy shadows on the ground from high above, dark and checkered, like an army of ghosts; whereas the benign figures of the drooping willows, here and there, look like paintings on the lotus leaves. The moonlight is not spread evenly over the pond, but rather in a harmonious rhythm of light and shade, like a famous melody played on a violin.

Around the pond, far and near, high and low, are trees. Most of them are willows. Only on the path side can two or three gaps be seen through the heavy fringe, as if specially reserved for the moon. The shadowy shapes of the leafage at first sight seem diffused into a mass of mist, against which, however, the charm of those willow trees is still discernible. Over the trees appear some distant mountains, but merely in sketchy silhouette. Through the branches are also a couple of lamps, as listless as sleepy eyes. The most lively creatures here, for the moment, must be the cicadas in the trees and the frogs in

译文二

short naps have a charm all their own. As the moon shone from behind them, the dense trees on the hills threw checkered shadows, dark forms loomed like devils, and the sparse, graceful willows seemed painted on the lotus leaves. The moonlight on the pool was not uniform, but light and shadow made up a harmonious rhythm like a beautiful tune played on a violin.

Far and near, high and low around the pool were trees, most of them willows. These trees had the pool entirely hemmed in, the only small clearings left being those by the path, apparently intended for the moon. All the trees were somber as dense as smoke, but among them you could make out the luxuriant willows, while faintly above the treetops loomed distant hills—their general outline only. And between the trees appeared one or two street lamps, listless as the eyes of someone drowsy. The liveliest sounds at this hour were the cicadas chirruping on the trees and the frogs croaking in the pool, but this animation was theirs alone, I had no part in it.

Then lotus-gathering flashed into my mind. This was an old custom south of the Yangtze, which apparently originated very early and was most popular in the period of the Six Kingdoms, as we see from the songs

译文三

flash, like lightning. The leaves being so densely massed together, this gave the impression of an emerald wave. Beneath the leaves were channels of flowing water, but they were hidden from view, not even a hint being visible; but that only served to give the leaves more presence.

The moonbeams spilled placidly onto this expanse of leaves and flowers like living water. A thin mist floated up from the lotus pond. The leaves and flowers seemed to be washed in milk, and at the same time trapped in a dream of flimsy gauze. Although the moon was full, there was a veil of light cloud, which prevented it from shining brightly; but to me this was just right—we cannot do without deep sleep, admitted, but a quiet doze also has its pleasures. The moonlight was filtered through the trees, while the clumps of bushes on the high ground cast heavy irregular mottled shadows. The spare silhouettes of the arching willows appeared to be painted on the lotus leaves. The moonlight on the pond was not all smooth and even, but the rhythm of light and shade was harmonious, like a musical masterpiece played on a violin.

译文四

flowing down quietly to the leaves and flowers and a light blue mist shrouded the pond, which made the leaves and flowers look like being washed in milk or being caught in a gauzy dream. Though there was a full moon tonight, as the sky was covered with a veil of thin clouds, it could not shed its brightest brilliance. But to me, it was the moment of perfection—a sound sleep is certainly necessary, but a nap also has its own flavor. As the moon shed its light from behind the trees, the dense shrubs high above cast down checkered shadows which looked gloomy and ghost-like. But the sparsely-mapped beautiful shadows of the weeping willows looked as if they were painted on the lotus leaves. The moonlight was not evenly distributed over the pond but there was a harmonious combination of light and shade, which was as rhythmic as a famous melody played on a violin.

Around the lotus pond could be seen trees here and there, anywhere and everywhere, most of them willows. These trees had the pond entirely enveloped, with only a few small clearings left on one side of the path, as if purposefully reserved for the moon to shed light. The trees were all enshrouded in such heavy gloom that they looked like a heavy mass of mist at first sight, but the charm of the willows could still be prominently discernible. Above the treetops loomed faintly distant hills—their shapes were rather sketchy, though. Through the branches could be seen some light from a couple of street-lamps, which was as listless as the eyes of someone who is drowsy.

原 文	译文一	译文二
片荷塘重重围住；只在小路一旁，漏着几段空隙，像是特为月光留下的。树色一例是阴阴的，乍看像一团烟雾；但杨柳的丰姿，便在烟雾里也辨得出。树梢上隐隐约约的是一带远山，只有些大意罢了。树缝里也漏着一两点路灯光，没精打采的，是渴睡人的眼。这时候最热闹的，要数树上的蝉声与水里的蛙声；但热闹是它们的，我什么也没有。 忽然想起采莲的事情来了。采莲是江南的旧俗，似乎很早就有，而六朝时为盛；从诗歌里可以约略知道。采莲的是少年的女子，她们是荡着小船，唱着艳歌去的。采莲人不用说很多，还有看采莲的人。那是一个热闹的季节，也是一个风流的季节。梁元帝《采莲赋》里说得好： 于时妖童媛女，荡舟心许。鹢首徐	the pond. But the liveliness is theirs, I have nothing. Suddenly, something like lotus-gathering crosses my mind. It used to be celebrated as a folk festival in the South, probably dating very far back in history, most popular in the period of Six Dynasties. We can pick up some outlines of this activity in the poetry. It was young girls who went gathering lotuses, in sampans and singing love songs. Needless to say, there were a great number of them doing the gathering, apart from those who were watching. It was a lively season, brimming with vitality, and romance. A brilliant description can be found in "Lotus Gathering" written by Yuan Emperor of the Liang Dynasty: So those charming youngsters row their sampans, heart buoyant with tacit love, pass on to each other cups of wine while their bird-shaped prows drift around. From time to time their oars are caught in dangling algae, and duckweed float apart the moment their boats are about to move on. Their slender figures, girdled with plain silk, tread watchfully on board. This is the time when spring is growing into summer, the leaves a tender green and the flowers blooming, —among which the girls are giggling when evading an outreaching stem, their	of the time. The lotuses were picked by girls in small boats, who sang haunting songs as they padded. They turned out in force, we may be sure, and there were spectators too, for that was a cheerful festival and a romantic one. We have a good account of it in a poem by Emperor Yuan of the Liang Dynasty called "Lotus Gatherers": Deft boys and pretty girls Reach an understanding while boating; Their prows veer slowly, But the winecups pass quickly; Their oars are entangled, As they cut through the duckweed, And girls with slender waists Turn to gaze behind them. Now spring and summer meet, Leaves are tender, flowers fresh; With smiles they protect their silks, Drawing in their skirts, afraid lest the boat upset. There we have a picture of these merry excursions. This must have been a delightful event, and it is a great pity we cannot enjoy it today. I also remember some lines from the poem "West Islet": When they gather lotus at Nantang in autumn The lotus blooms are higher than their heads;

译文三

On all sides of the pond, near and far, high and low, were trees, the majority being willows. These trees ringed the pond like a fortress. Only on the side where the path was were a few gaps left, as if on purpose for the moonlight. The trees were all of somber hue, and at first sight looked like a bank of fog; but the grace of the willows could still be perceived. Above the crests of the trees a range of far hills could be dimly seen, but only in outline. A few gleams from streets lights also leaked through the interstices of the trees, but they were wan and lifeless, eyes heavy with sleep. At this time the most animated of things were the thrumming of the cicadas in the trees and the croaking of the frogs in the water. But animation was their affair: it had nothing to do with me.

I suddenly bethought myself of the business of gathering lotuses. This was an old custom in the lower Yangtze region, apparently of very early origin, and most popular during the Six Dynasties. A rough idea of it can be got from poetry. I went on to recall these lines from "Song of the Western Eyot":

We gather lotus from the

译文四

The creatures that were full of vitality at the moment, however, were the cicadas that were chirping on the trees and the frogs that were croaking in the water. But this vitality belongs to them; I have nothing in my possession.

Then I was suddenly reminded of the lotus-seed plucking, which was an old custom in areas south of the Changjiang River. The custom, as can be seen from clues in some poetry, could be dated far back in history but was the most prevalent during the Six Dynasties Period. It was the young girls who went plucking lotus seeds in a boat with the singing of love songs. There were doubtlessly a huge number of them doing the plucking apart from those who were watching. That was a busy season, full of vitality as well as of romance. About that, a description was brilliantly made in "Lotus-seed Plucking" written by Emperor Yuan of the Liang Dynasty:

> Charming boys and fair maidens
> Row their boats in mutual understandings;
> They veer their prows slowly,
> But pass the wine cups swiftly;
> When they pull the oars,
> They are easily caught in algae;
> When they row their boats,
> The duckweed apart floats;
> The maidens with slender waists
> Are girdled with plain silk
> And turn round watchfully and with grace.
> It is late spring and early summer

笔记

原文

回，兼传羽杯。櫂将移而藻挂，船欲动而萍开。尔其纤腰束素，迁延顾步。夏始春余，叶嫩花初，恐沾裳而浅笑，畏倾船而敛裾。

可见当时嬉游的光景了。这真是有趣的事，可惜我们现在早已无福消受了。

于是又记起《西洲曲》里的句子：

采莲南塘秋，莲花过人头；低头弄莲子，莲子清如水。今晚若有采莲人，这儿的莲花也算得"过人头"了；只不见一些流水的影子，是不行的。这令我到底惦着江南了。——这样想着，猛一抬头，不觉已是自己的门前；轻轻地推门进去，什么声息也没有，妻已睡熟好久了。

译文一

skirts tucked in form fear that the sampan might tilt.

It must have been fascinating, but unfortunately we have long been denied such a delight.

Then I recall those lines in "Ballad of Xizhou Island": "Gathering the lotus, I am in the South Pond, / The lilies in autumn reach over my head; / Lowering my head I toy with the lotus seeds. / Look, they are as fresh as the water underneath."

If there were somebody gathering lotuses tonight, she could tell that the lilies here are high enough to reach over her head; but one would certainly miss the sight of the water. So my memories drift back to the South after all.

Deep in my thought, I looked up, just to find myself at the door of my own house. Gently I pushed the door open and walked in. Not a sound inside, my wife had been asleep for quite a while.

（朱纯深　译）

译文二

They stoop to pick lotus seeds,
Seeds as translucent as water.

If any girls were here now to pick lotus, the flowers would reach above their heads too—ah, rippling shadows alone are not enough! I was feeling quite homesick for the south, when I suddenly looked up to discover I had reached my own door. Pushing it softly open and tiptoeing in, I found all quiet inside, and my wide fast asleep.

（杨宪益、戴乃迭　译）

译文三

South Pond in autumn
The lotus flowers are higher than a man's head
We bend to get the lotus seeds up
The lotus seeds are as green as water.

If those lotus gatherers had been here tonight, they would have been satisfied that the lotuses were "higher than a man's head", but disappointed that there was not even a glimpse of flowing water. This led me to feel thoroughly nostalgic for the country south of the Yangtze. Absorbed in such thoughts, I suddenly raised my head, and found mylself back at my own gate. I opened the door quietly and went in. Not a sound was to be heard. My wife had long since fallen asleep.

(David E. Pollard 译)

译文四

When leaves are tender green and flowers blooming;
They giggle for fear of wetting their silk,
They draw in their skirts lest the boats tilt.

It can be seen that they had a merry life then. It must have been a very fascinating life, but unfortunately we have long been denied the chance to enjoy it.

And then I could recall several lines from the "Ballad of the West Islet":

In autumn I pluck lotus seeds in the South Pond
With lotus flowers high above my head.
Lowering my head, I pluck lotus seeds
Which are as green as the water underneath.

If there were someone plucking lotus seeds tonight, the lotus flowers would certainly be higher above their heads. But it was a pity that the rippling water was hidden from view. This reminded me of the scenes in areas south of the Changjiang River. —Deep in such thoughts, I suddenly looked up, only to find myself at the door of my house. I gently pushed the door in, with quietness all around me. My wife had long fallen fast asleep.

（李明 译）

三 散文翻译的批评与赏析练习

原 文

读书的状态大致分为三种：一是为别人而读，二是为有用而读，三是为兴趣而读。

处在第一种状态是最痛苦的，自己本不想读，但迫于外界压力却不得不读。好多中小学生就属于这种情形。在这样的状态下，读书真是苦不堪言。有不少学生曾咬牙切齿地发誓：毕业考试一结束，一定把××书烧掉。

一些为了拿文凭、评职称而读书的亦在此列，对于他们而言，读书实在是件苦差事。

第二种是为有用而读书。处在此列的人已知书中自有黄金屋和颜如玉，已经能从烟波浩渺的书海中有所取舍，读书很有目的性。或为提高专业技术水平，或为丰富知识，学电脑的看电脑书籍，学文学的看小说，当老师的读教育心理，做生意的看经济，搞行政的读政治、管理……为获得某方面的知识而读书，以

译文一

Readers fall roughly into three groups. One group reads for others, another for use, and still another for interest.

The first group of readers feels sad, because they are forced to read while they don't like to. Many of the primary and secondary school students belong to this group. Their reading is really a suffering. A great number of students swear bitterly the burning of some kind of books after they pass the graduation examination. It is also true of those who read for diploma or titles. They are indeed doing a hard job.

The second group reads for use. These people know that they can benefit a lot from books and that they are well aware what they should read. They have clear purposes of improving their professional ability or widening their knowledge. For instance, computer people read computer books, literary people read novels, teachers read educational psychology, businessmen read economics and administrators read politics and management. They read for obtaining some knowledge so that they can make

译文二

Reading can be done for roughly three purposes: for others, for use and for pleasure.

Reading for others is the most painful. Readers with this purpose are compelled to read because they just hate reading. Many of the primary and secondary school students are in such a state of mind. To them, reading is utterly suffering. That is why quite a large number of students often swear bitterly that they will burn the damned books the moment they have had the graduation examinations. Those who read for diplomas or for titles of technical posts also feel the same. To them, reading means drudgery.

Reading for use is the most practical. Readers with this purpose know very well that reading enables them to gain success and fortunes, and that they are able to make their own choices according to their needs. To acquire more expertise or to enrich their knowledge, computer people read computer books, literary people read novels, teachers read educational psychology, businessmen read economics, and administrators read politics and management… Thus they read in order to acquire knowledge of a certain field so that they can obtain the basic skills to earn the family's living and to

原文

具备养家糊口的基本技能，凭真才实学立足于社会。

第三种是为兴趣而读书。这是读书的自觉状态，更是一种境界。不为有用，只因喜欢。这些读者把读书当做生存的基本需要，读书已和吃饭睡觉一样必不可少。三日不读书，则自觉面目可憎，心里就空虚、失落、不踏实。

（李娇《读书的三种状态》）

译文一

a living and do something constructive.

The third group reads for interest. They are on their own initiative and in a realm of doing something not for use but for pleasure. These readers take reading as their basic requirements for living, which is as necessary as eating and sleeping. They cannot do without reading and if they do not read for some time they will feel shame, meaningless and uneasy.

("Three Groups of Reading")
（马秉义 译）

译文二

survive in the society with their own genuine ability and learning.

Reading for pleasure is consciousness-driven. Or rather, it is the acme of the state of mind. Reading in this way is not for practical use but merely for enjoyment. Readers of this sort simply take reading as their basic needs for a living, and it is considered as indispensable as eating and sleeping in daily life. If they do not read for a single day, they would have a sense of shame, of loss, of emptiness and of uneasiness.

("Three Purposes for Reading")
（李明 译）

第十三章 《桃花源记》英译文的批评赏析

一 关于《桃花源记》

《桃花源记》的作者陶渊明（约365—427年），东晋末期南朝宋初期诗人、文学家、辞赋家、散文家；字元亮，谥号靖节先生，别号五柳先生，后改名潜，字渊明。曾做过几年小官，后辞官回家，从此隐居，田园生活是陶渊明诗的主要题材，故被称为"田园诗人"。作品有《饮酒》《归园田居》《桃花源诗》《五柳先生传》《归去来兮辞》等。尤长于诗文辞赋，诗多描绘自然景色及农村生活的情景，其中的优秀作品寄寓着对官场与世俗社会的厌倦，表露出洁身自好，不愿屈身逢迎的志趣。其艺术特色，兼有平淡与爽朗之胜，语言质朴自然，而又极为精练，具有独特风格。

《桃花源记》中的"记"，是一种文体。它可以分为游记和碑记（或铭记）两类。游记是

二 《桃花源记》原文及四种英译文

原　文	译文一	译文二
晋太原中，武陵人捕鱼为业，缘溪行，忘路之远近。忽逢桃花林，夹岸数百步，中无杂树，芳草鲜美，落英缤纷，渔人甚异之。复前行，欲穷其林。 林尽水源，便得一山，山有小口，仿佛	During the reign of Taiyuan of Chin, there was a fisherman of Wuling. One day he was walking along a bank. After having gone a certain distance, he suddenly came upon a peach grove which extended along the bank for about a hundred yards. He noticed with surprise that the grove had a magic effect, so singularly free from the usual mingling of brushwood, while the beautifully grassy ground was covered with its rose petals. He went further to explore, and when he came to the end of the grove, he saw a spring	In the year of Taiyuan[1] of the Jin Dynasty, there lived a man in Wuling[2] jun who earned his living by fishing. One day, he rowed his boat along a stream, unaware of how far he had gone when all of a sudden, he found himself in the midst of a wood full of peach blossoms. The wood extended several hundred footsteps along both banks of the stream. There were no trees of other kinds. The lush grass was fresh and beautiful and peach petals fell in riotous profusion. The fisherman was so curious that he rowed on, in hopes of discovering where the trees ended. At the end of the wood was the foun-

收在文集中记叙游览山川名胜、描写景物并抒发感情的文字。碑记尽管也是一种叙述兼议论的文体,但它不同于游记,有些像现在的记叙式散文,其中夹杂着一些议论。

《桃花源记》约作于永初二年(公元421年),即南朝刘裕弑君篡位的第二年。该文以武陵渔人进出桃花源的行踪为线索,按时间先后顺序,把发现桃源、小住桃源、离开桃源、再寻桃源的曲折离奇的情节贯穿起来,描绘了一个没有阶级,没有剥削,自食其力,自给自足,和平恬静,人人自得其乐的社会。这样的社会同当时的黑暗社会形成鲜明的对照,是作者及广大劳动人民所向往的一种理想社会,体现了人们的追求与想往,也反映出人们对现实世界的不满与反抗。

文章构思精巧,结构巧妙。作者借用小说笔法,以一个捕鱼人的经历为线索展开故事的铺陈。开头交代的所处时代以及渔人的籍贯,都写得十分肯定,给人很强的真实感。这就缩短了读者同作者之间的心理距离,把读者从现实世界引入到虚拟的桃花源。而文末南阳刘子骥规往不果一笔,又使全文有着余意无穷之趣。

全文语言生动、简练、隽永,看似轻描淡写,但所描写的景物历历在目,令人神往。文章详略得当,中心突出。正是这篇散文所具有的这些特点,吸引了一代代读者对它的关注。在翻译界,更是有众多翻译名家纷纷将它翻译成外文。这里我们选取了四种英语译文,供大家鉴赏。

译文三

During the reign of Tai Yuan of Tsin Dynasty, a certain fisherman of Wuling, who had followed up one of the river branches without taking note whither he was going, came suddenly upon a grove of peach-trees in full bloom, extending some distance on each bank, with not a tree of any other kind in sight. The beauty of the scene and the exquisite perfume of the flowers filled the heart of the fisherman with surprise, as he proceeded onwards, anxious to reach the limit of this lovely grove. He found that the peach trees ended where the

译文四

During Taiyuan's reign in the Jin Dynasty, a man from Wuling Prefecture made a living as a fisherman. One day as the fisherman was rowing his boat along a stream, he became unaware of how far he had gone when suddenly he found himself in the midst of a grove full of peach blossoms. For several hundred steps on both banks of the stream could be seen no other trees but the peach ones with fresh and beautiful green grass and fallen petals. This made the fisherman so astonished that he decided to go farther to see where on earth the grove would end.

笔 记

原　文	译文一	译文二
若有光，便舍船，从口入。初极狭，才通人，复行数十步，豁然开朗。土地平旷，屋舍俨然，有良田美池桑竹之属。阡陌交通，鸡犬相闻。其中往来种作，男女衣著，悉如外人。黄发垂髫，并怡然自乐。 见渔人，乃大惊，问所从来。具答之。便要还家，设酒杀鸡作食。村中闻有此人，咸来问讯。自云先世避秦时乱，率妻子邑人，来此绝境，不复出焉，遂与外人间隔。问今是何世，乃不知有汉，无论魏晋。此人一一为具言所闻，皆叹惋。余人各复延至其家，皆出酒食。停数日，辞去。此中人语云，"不足为	which came from a cave in the hill. Having noticed that there seemed to be a weak light in the cave, he tied up his boat and decided to go in and explore. At first the opening was very narrow, barely wide enough for one person to go in. After a dozen steps, it opened into a flood of light. He saw before his eyes a wide, level valley, with houses and fields and farms. There were bamboos and mulberries; farmers were working and dogs and chickens were running about. The dresses of the men and women were like those of the outside world, and the old men and children appeared very happy and contented. They were greatly astonished to see the fisherman and asked him where he had come from. The fisherman told them and was invited to their homes, where wine was served and chicken was killed for dinner to entertain him. The villagers hearing of his coming all came to see him and to talk. They said that their ancestors had come here as refugees to escape from the tyranny of Tsin Shih-huang (builder of Great Wall) some six hundred years ago, and they had never left it. They were thus completely cut off from the world, and asked what was the ruling dynasty now. They had not even heard of the Han Dynasty (two centuries before to two centuries after Christ), not to speak of the Wei (third century A.D.) and the Chin (third and fourth centuries). The fish-	tainhead of the stream. The fisherman beheld a hill, with a small opening from which issued a glimmer of light. He stepped ashore to explore the crevice. His first steps took him into a passage that accommodated only the width of one person. After he progressed about scores of paces, it suddenly widened into an open field. The land was flat and spacious. There were houses arranged in good order with fertile fields, beautiful ponds, bamboo groves, mulberry trees and paths crisscrossing the fields in all directions. The crowing of cocks and the barking of dogs were within everyone's earshot. In the fields the villagers were busy with farm work. Men and women were dressed like people outside. They all, old and young, appeared happy. They were surprised at seeing the fisherman, who, being asked where he came from, answered their every question. Then they invited him to visit their homes, killed chickens, and served wine to entertain him. As the words of his arrival spread, the entire village turned out to greet him. They told him that their ancestors had come to this isolated haven, bringing their families and the village people, to escape from the turmoil during the Qin Dynasty and that from then onwards, they had been cut off from the outside world. They were curious to know what dynasty it was now. They did not know the Han Dynasty, not to mention the Wei and the Jin dynasties. The fisherman told them all the things they wanted to know. They sighed. The villagers offered him one feast after another. They entertained him with wine and delicious food.

译文三

water began, at the foot of a hill; and there he espied what seemed to be a cave with light issuing from it. So he made fast his boat, and crept in through a narrow entrance, which shortly ushered him into a new world of level country, of fine houses, of rich fields, of fine pools, and of luxuriance of mulberry and bamboo. Highways of traffic ran north and south; sounds of crowing cocks and barking dogs were heard around; the dress of the people who passed along or were at work in the fields was of a strange cut; while young and old alike appeared to be contented and happy.

One of the inhabitants, catching sight of the fisherman, was greatly astonished; but, after learning whence he came, insisted on carrying him home, and killed a chicken and placed some wine before him. Before long, all the people of the place had turned out to see the visitor, and they informed him that their ancestors had sought refuge here, with their wives and families, from the troublous times of the house of Chin, adding that they had thus become finally cut off from the rest of the human race. They then enquired about the politics of the day, ignorant of the establishment of Han dynasty, and of course of the later dynasties which had succeeded it. And when the fisherman told them the story, they grieved over

译文四

The grove ended at the fountainhead of the stream where a hill came into view. On the hill could be spotted a small cave with some light glimmering inside. He stepped ashore from his boat and entered the cave. The cave was so narrow at first that only one person could pass through. With a few dozen more steps, a bright open plain suddenly came in sight. On the plain could be seen a stretch of flat and wide land with houses built in good order and surrounded by fertile fields, beautiful ponds, and mulberry and bamboo groves. Between the fields could be seen crisscross footpaths and within one's earshot could be heard roosters' crows and dogs' barks. On the fields, men and women were busy doing their farm work with dresses exactly like those of the people in the outside world. All of them, old and young, lived a happy and contented life.

When they saw the fisherman, they felt greatly surprised and asked where he had come from. After hearing the fisherman's whole story, they invited him to their homes and treated him with the best wine and the most delicious food. When other villagers learned about his coming, they all came for some inquiries. At the same time, they told the fisherman that their ancestors, by taking refuge from the chaos of war, brought their wives and children with their neighbors to this place and they were then isolated from the outside world. Since then, they forever stayed in this place and lost contact with the people outside. Next, they asked him what

原文

外人道也"。

　　既出，得其船，便扶向路，处处志之。及郡下，诣太守，说如此。太守即遣人随其往，寻向所志，遂迷不复得路。

　　南阳刘子骥，高尚士也。闻之，欣然规往，未果。寻病终。后遂无问津者。

（陶渊明《桃花源记》）

译文一

erman told them, which they heard with great amazement. Many of the other villagers then began to invite him to their homes by turn and feed him dinner and wine. After a few days, he took leave of them and left. The villagers begged him not to tell the people outside about their colony. The man found his boat and came back, marking with signs the route he had followed. He went to the magistrate's office and told the magistrate about it. The latter sent someone to go with him and find the place. They looked for the signs but got lost and could never find it again. Liu Tsechi of Nanyang was a great idealist. He heard of this story, and planned to go and find it, but was taken ill and died before he could fulfill his wish. Since then, no one has gone in search of this place.

（"The Peach Colony"）

（林语堂　译）

译文二

After several days, the fisherman took his leave. The village people entreated him not to let others know of their existence.

　　Once out, the fisherman found his boat and rowed homeward, leaving marks all the way. When he came back to the jun, he reported his adventure to the prefect, who immediately sent people to look for the place, with the fisherman as a guide. However, the marks he had left could no longer be found. They got lost and could not find the way.

　　Liu Ziji of Nanyang[3] jun, a learned scholar of high repute, was excited when he heard the fisherman's story. He devised a plan to find the village, but it was not carried out. Liu died soon afterwards, and after his death, no one else made any attempt to find it.

（"A Tale of the Fountain of the Peach Blossom Spring"）

（罗经国　译）

[1] Taiyuan was the title of the reign of Emperor Xiaowu of the Eastern Jin Dynasty (376-396).
[2] Wuling is today's Changde City, Hunan Province.
[3] Nanyang is today's Nanyang City, Henan Province.

译文三

the vicissitudes of human affairs.

Each in turn invited the fisherman to his home and entertained him hospitably, until at length the latter prepared to take his leave. "It will not be worth while to talk about what you have seen to the outside world," said the people of the place to the fisherman, as he bade them farewell and returned to his boat, making mental notes of his route as he proceeded on his homeward voyage.

When he reached home, he at once went and reported what he had seen to the Governor of the district, and the Governor sent off men with him to seek, by the aid of the fisherman's notes, to discover this unknown region. But he was never able to find it again. Subsequently, another attempt to pierce the mystery was planned by a famous scholar named Liu Tse-kee, but the plan was not carried out. Liu soon died, and from that time on no further attempts to locate the place were made.

（"The Peach-Blossom Fountain"）
(Herbert A. Giles 译)

译文四

the present dynasty was and even knew nothing about the Han Dynasty, let alone the Wei and the Jin Dynasties. The fisherman told them everything he knew and they all felt greatly sympathetic about the lives of the people outside. The other villagers also invited him to their homes for a treat with good wine and delicious food. After several days' stay, the fisherman was ready to go. Before he was leaving, people urged him never to say anything about this place to the outside world.

As soon as the fisherman got outside, he found his boat and went home along the way he first came, making marks wherever necessary. He went to Wuling Prefecture and reported to the magistrate what he had seen. Immediately, the magistrate sent some people to find the place together with the fisherman by following the marks he had made. They got lost, however, and never found the way.

When Liu Ziji, a man of noble character from Nanyang Prefecture, heard about this, he instantly made a plan to find the place but came to no result. Soon afterwards he died. Since then, no further attempts had been made to find it.

（"The Peach Blossom Fountainhead"）
(李明 译)

三 散文翻译的批评与赏析练习

原文

环滁皆山也。其西南诸峰，林壑尤美。望之蔚然而深秀者，琅琊也。山行六七里，渐闻水声潺潺而泄于两峰之间者，酿泉也。峰回路转，有亭翼然临于泉上者，醉翁亭也。作亭者谁？山之僧智仙也。名之者谁？太守自谓也。太守与客来饮于此，饮少辄醉，而年又最高，故自号曰醉翁也。醉翁之意不在酒，在乎山水之间也。山水之乐，得之心而寓之酒也。

（欧阳修《醉翁亭记》）

译文一

The district of Chu is enclosed all round by hills, of which those in the southwest boast the most lovely forests and dales. In the distance, densely wooded and possessed of a rugged beauty, is Mount Langya. When you penetrate a mile or two into this mountain you begin to hear the gurgling of a stream, and presently the stream—the Brewer's Spring—comes into sight cascading between two peaks. Rounding a bend you see a hut with a spreading roof hard by the stream, and this is the Roadside Hut of the Old Drunkard. This hut was built by the monk Zhi Xian. It was given its name by the governor, referring to himself. The governor, coming here with his friends, often gets tipsy after a little drinking; and since he is the most advanced in years, he calls himself the Old Drunkard. He delights less in drinking than in the hills and streams, taking pleasure in them and expressing the feeling in his heart through drinking.

（"The Roadside Hut of the Old Drunkard"）

（杨宪益、戴乃迭 译）

译文二

Surrounding the Prefecture of Chu are mountains whose peaks to the southwest boast forests and valleys which are especially beautiful. The one with luxuriance of trees and picturesque beauty when seen from afar is Langya Mountain. Several miles further away into the mountain where the brook can be gradually heard murmuring between the peaks is Brewers' Spring. Then, after a few twists and turns can be seen a pavilion called Old Drunken Man's Pavilion, perching by the Spring with its wings outstretched. Who was it that built the pavilion? It was Monk Zhi Xian who built it. Who was it that gave this name? It was the magistrate who gave this name by referring to himself. The magistrate used to have a drink here with his friends and often got drunk though drinking a drop in the bucket. Advanced in years, he called himself "Old Drunken Man". Actually, his interest was not in the cup, but rather in the landscape around him. (Actually, it was not the cup that attracts him so much as the landscape around him does.) His pleasure in the landscape was felt within, but resided in the cup.

（李明 译）

第四部分

诗歌翻译的批评与赏析

一 关于诗歌

　　诗歌是高度集中地概括并反映社会生活的一种文学体裁。它通过凝练而形象的语言以及鲜明的节奏与和谐的音韵，充满音乐美地将诗人丰富的想象和感情充分地传达出来。

　　诗歌具有同小说不同的特点。当代著名作家曹文轩曾以比喻的方式对诗歌和小说进行了区别。他说："诗写了我们的感觉，而小说写了我们的经验。诗是对经验的提炼，而不在经验本身。而小说则呈现经验本身，将提炼——即对经验的感受留给读者。这就好比是：小说呈现一幢住宅，而诗歌却只有对这幢住宅的感叹而没有住宅。"

　　美国诗人弗罗斯特也对诗歌作过一个非同寻常的定义：诗歌就是在翻译中丢失的东西。从翻译的角度看，这句话充分地道出了许多诗歌译者的无奈和尴尬。

　　廖四平和张瑜（2007：51-52）认为，诗歌是雕琢后的语言，是人类语言的雕塑品。而这种字斟句酌、精雕细刻并非是华丽的辞藻使然，而是简练、自然、朴素所致。

　　诗歌同生活紧密相连。袁可嘉曾说："诗是生活的再精致，是生活的升华和结晶。"

　　诗歌的独特形式体现在它以分行进行排列。这样，一首诗就由并列的诗行组成，若干诗行组成一个诗节，若干诗节组成一个整体（胡显耀、李力，2009：286）。诗歌的这种结构形式的美，再加上音韵节奏的美、意境意象的美，构成了诗歌总体的美。

二 诗歌翻译的原则

　　有人说，翻译难，翻译文学作品尤其难，而翻译诗歌则更是难上加难。这从诗歌的特点中便可以看出，诗歌翻译是翻译艺术的顶峰，它需要意美、音美、形美融于一体。因此，诗歌翻译是一门复杂的综合性艺术。

　　就如何译诗的问题上，翻译大家们均已各陈己见，各抒其理，见仁见智。比如，郭沫若提出了"以诗译诗"，闻一多提出了以"诗笔"译诗等诗歌翻译原则。诗歌是思想感情、意境形象、音韵节奏和风格神韵等几个方面的统一体，即所谓音美、意美、形美的统一体。诗歌翻译，就应从这几个方面去把握，在达意的同时，还须力求传神并将音韵充分传达出来。（宁会勤，2009：34）

　　这也就是袁可嘉所认为的，译诗一要避免语言的"一般化"，即，若以平板的语言追踪原诗的字面，既不考虑一般诗歌语言的应有特点，也不照顾个别诗人的语言特色，就会既不能够保护原诗的真正面貌，更谈不上传出原诗的神味。（廖四平、张瑜，2007：53）二要避免诗歌形式的"民族化"，即把外国诗歌硬性汉译成整齐划一的五言、七言或者民歌体。如果硬要民族化，便是将异域民族的诗改成中国化的东西了，结果作品不伦不类，甚至庸俗化。（廖四平、张瑜，2007：53-54）

　　再者，译诗还需有诗才的译者去进行。正如著名作家老舍所说：有诗才的译者应以诗译诗地去译这些作品，使读者不但知道书中说了什么，而且知道怎么说的（老舍，1984：131）。这正说明翻译诗歌除达意之外，再现原著的文体特征尤为重要。

最后一点是，译诗是一种有根据的再创造。这意味着译诗时，既要保持原状，又要适当地灵活变通（廖四平、张瑜，2007：53）。对此，台湾宋颖豪教授曾说，译诗要"入于诗，出于诗，只见诗，不见人（译者）"。诗是一种有机组织，其本身就是一个生命体。所以译诗亦应是一个有机体，要承原诗之形，协原诗之声，生动再现原诗的意境。偏废音、形、意三美之中的任何一个方面都会有损于诗的意境（宁会勤，2009：39）。

三 诗歌翻译批评

著名诗人闻一多在谈论诗歌的翻译时曾说：译诗是一种文学翻译，是把一种文学转变为另一种文学；译者负有特别的责任，那就是以"诗笔"去翻译原来的诗籍，要以"'诗'的文字"而不是"用平平淡淡的字句一五一十地"去翻译原作（转引自袁锦翔，1990：271）。闻一多在这里所倡导的是"以诗译诗"。"以诗译诗"也是诗歌翻译的标准。而要做到"以诗译诗"，译者就不可能采用逐字对等式的直译法，不能够只是进行简单的语言上的等值变换，而应"捉住原诗的精神"（袁锦翔，1990：274）。而这种"精神"，大体上就是鲁迅所说的"原作的丰姿"、郭沫若所说的"内在的韵律"，或茅盾所说的"神韵"，即做到"词句圆活，意旨畅达"（袁锦翔，1990：276）。

因此，好的译诗第一就是要能够体现原诗的神韵，其次是要使译诗的文字醒豁，第三是所译诗歌的音乐要铿锵（袁锦翔，1990：273-276）。好的译诗就是将原诗中所包含的审美艺术与价值传递出来，并使译文读者能够获得与原文读者近似审美感受的诗，也是意美、音美、形美等三美密切结合的诗。

第十四章　"A Psalm of Life" 汉译文的批评赏析

一 关于 "A Psalm of Life"

"A Psalm of Life" 出自美国浪漫主义文学时期杰出诗人亨利·沃兹沃思·朗费罗（Henry Wadsworth Longfellow）（1807—1882）之手。1836 年始，朗费罗在哈佛大学讲授语言、文学，致力于介绍欧洲文化和浪漫主义作家的作品，成为新英格兰文化中心剑桥文学界和社交界的重要人物。1839 年他出版了第一部诗集《夜吟》（Voices of the Night）（亦有人译为《夜籁集》），其中包括著名的《夜的赞歌》《人生礼赞》《群星之光》等音韵优美的抒情诗。1841 年又出版诗集《歌谣及其他》（Ballads and Other Poems）。这两部诗集在大西洋两岸风靡一时，他也从此以诗人闻名，一生创作了大量抒情诗、歌谣、叙事诗和诗剧，享有"美国牧歌之花"的美誉。

朗费罗的诗歌在语言上以优美、质朴、清新见长，做到了雅俗共赏。他的诗歌在 19 世纪美国主流诗坛占据着主导地位，影响深远，在美国广为传颂，在欧洲亦受赞赏，被译成 20 多种文字。朗费罗逝世后，伦敦威斯敏斯特教堂诗人之角安放了他的胸像，他是获得这种尊荣的第一位美国诗人。

朗费罗所创作的诗歌中，深受人们喜爱的 "A Psalm of Life" 写于 1838 年，匿名发表于 1839 年。当时正值美国资本主义进入蓬勃发展时期，诗人以积极乐观的态度讴歌人生，反映出当时美国人民的心声。

该诗的汉语译文，据钱钟书先生考证，是第一首被翻译成中文的西方诗歌。由清朝咸丰年间的户部尚书董恂以七言诗的形式率先译出。可惜当时的译文非常蹩脚，还因此激起了当时中国旧知识分子对西方文学的鄙视。之后，新的译文相继不绝，有旧体，有新体，有格律体，也有自由体，在中国广为流传。

该诗短小精悍、结构严谨。虽然篇幅短小，但内容丰富，条理清晰，层次感强。全诗每四句一节，共九节三十六句。分四个部分来讨论诗人眼中的人生。第一、二节主要纠正 "life is but an empty dream" 的颓废论调，大声告诉人们 "Life is real! Life is earnest!"。第三至第六节探讨了应如何度过人生，进一步指出人生苦短，奉劝人们要把握现在，赶快行动，只争朝夕。在这一部分，诗人强调了一个行动的人生，这也是本诗的主旨。第七、八节强调了人生的价值和意义。以伟人的榜样来激励人们，要在"时间的沙滩上"留下脚印，只有实干的人生才能流芳万世，才能给后来者以鼓舞。这同时也呼应了第二节中所说的：人死去的仅仅是肉体，而绝不是精神，灵魂会因为你人生的辉煌而不朽。最后一节是对全诗的总结与升华。诗人号召人们要行动起来，要勇于面对生命中的挑战，并以更为激昂的声调总结全诗："Still achieving, still pursuing"，与主题相呼应。

因此，该诗充满了饱满的激情和乐观的精神，唱出了对人生的热爱，对美好生活的追求，

三 "A Psalm of Life" 原文及四种汉译文

原　文	译文一	译文二
A Psalm of Life	**生命的礼赞**	**生 之 颂**
Tell me not in mournful numbers, Life is but an empty dream! For the soul is dead that slumbers, And things are not what they seem.	别用悲伤的语调对我低吟， "人生不过是梦幻一场"！ 因为沉睡中的灵魂已经死去， 万物并非它们显示的模样。	别用悲切的诗句对我唱： "人生只是虚幻的梦一场！" 因为昏睡的灵魂已死亡， 而事物不是看来那模样。
Life is real! Life is earnest! And the grave is not its goal; Dust thou art, to dust returnest, Was not spoken of the soul.	生命是真实的！生活是严肃的！ 它们的终点决不是坟场； "你来自尘土，必归于尘土"， 但这是指肉体，灵魂并未死亡。	人生多真切！它决非虚度！ 一抔黄土哪里会是它归宿； "你来自泥尘，得重归泥尘，" 这话所指的并不是灵魂。
Not enjoyment, and not sorrow, Is our destined end or way; But to act, that each to-morrow Finds us farther than to-day.	我们注定的结局和道路， 既不是享乐，也不是悲伤； 而是行动，为了每一个明天， 使我们比今天走得更远更长。	我们命定的终点和道路 既不是享乐，也不是悲苦； 行动吧；要让每一个明天 发现我们比今天走得远。
Art is long, and time is fleeting, And our hearts, though stout and brave, Still, like muffled drums, are beating Funeral marches to the grave.	艺术长久，韶光飞逝， 我们的心尽管英勇而坚强， 却仍像阵阵低沉的鼓声， 正朝着坟墓把哀乐敲响。	学艺费光阴，时日去匆忙， 任我们的心勇敢又坚强， 依然像一些蒙住的鼙鼓—— 敲打着哀乐走向那坟墓。
In the world's broad field of battle,	在世界的辽阔的战场上，	在风云世界的广阔战场，

以积极进取、奋发向上的人生态度，鞭挞了人生如梦的悲观态度，是一首极富感染力的诗歌，使读者与之产生强烈的共鸣。

在语言的运用上，该诗非常讲究用词、句式、节奏、韵脚和形象。这些也是翻译中需要着力予以再现和保留的。

译文三

人 生 颂

别用忧伤的韵调向我哀叹：
人生不过是一场空虚的梦！
灵魂睡去就如同死去一般，
肉体也不再是原来的姿容。

人生是实在的，人生不是虚无；
坟墓并非就是它的终极地。
"你本是尘土，复归于尘土"——
那不是说灵魂，指的是肉体。

别只顾贪欢，别一味哀怨；
人生的道路该另有目标——
去实干吧，让每一个明天
看我们都比今天站得更高。

艺业需恒久，而光阴只一晃。
我们的心尽管勇敢、坚毅，
却仍旧像那丧鼓在闷响，
一声声送我们走向坟地。

世界就是辽阔的大战场，

译文四

人 生 礼 赞

勿用悲伤的诗句对我吟唱：
人生只不过是梦幻一场！
因为沉睡中的灵魂如同死去，
万事万物并非看上去那般模样。

人生实实在在！人生充满期望！
人生的目标决不是坟场；
"你来自尘土，必归于尘土"，
但灵魂决不是如此消亡。

一味享乐，一味悲伤，
哪里是我们既定的目标和方向？
而要行动起来，让每一个明天
见证我们在更高的起点上。

艺海无涯，时光飞逝，匆匆忙忙，
我们的心，尽管勇敢而坚强，
却如那阵阵低沉的鼙鼓，
把我们通向坟墓的哀乐奏响。

在人世间那广阔的战场，

笔 记

原　文	译文一	译文二
In the bivouac of life, Be not like dumb, driven cattle! Be a hero in the strife!	在生命的露宿的营地上， 别作默默无声、任人驱使的牛羊， 要在战斗中当一名闯将！	在人生征途的野宿营帐， 别像默默的牛羊任驱赶！ 要争取做英雄，能征惯战！
Trust no Future, howe'er pleasant! Let the dead Past bury its dead! Act—act in the living Present! Heart within, and God's o'erhead!	莫信托未来，不管它怎样欢畅！ 让逝去的岁月将死者埋葬！ 行动吧，就在活着的此刻行动！ 胸内有红心，头顶有上苍！	将来再美好也别空指望！ 让死的过去把死的埋葬！ 干！在活生生的现在就干！ 胸中是赤心，上帝在云端！
Lives of great men all remind us We can make our lives sublime, And, departing, leave behind us Footprints on the sands of time;	伟大人物的生平把我们提醒， 我们能使我们的一生变得高尚， 在离开人间时，也能让足印 遗留在我们身后的时间的沙滩上。	伟人的生平向我们指出： 我们能使此生超群脱俗—— 一朝逝去，时间的沙滩上 将留下我们的脚印行行。
Footprints that perhaps another, Sailing o'er life's solemn main, A forlorn and shipwrecked brother, Seeing, shall take heart again.	呵，足印！也许另一位弟兄， 当他航行在生命庄严的海洋上， 不幸遇难，看见了这些足印， 他就会使勇气重新增长。	在庄严的生活之海航行， 也许有兄弟会遭到不幸， 会因为航船沉没而绝望—— 但见那脚印，又变得顽强。
Let us, then, be up and doing, With a heart for any fate; Still achieving, still pursuing, Learn to labour and to wait.	那么让我们振奋起来行动吧， 我们准备迎接任何命运的风浪； 永远要有所作为，不断追求， 学会劳动，也学会等待和期望。	让我们挺起身，行动起来， 凭对付任何命运的胸怀， 不断去收获，不断去追求； 永远在学着苦干和等候。
	（黄新渠　译）	（黄杲炘　译）

译文三

人生要随时准备去战斗,
做一个英雄去英勇奋战!
不要像被人驱使的哑牲口!

别指望未来,不管它多欢乐;
让已逝去的岁月也去它的蛋吧!
上帝在头上,丹心在胸窝,
干吧,抓住活泼泼的现在干吧!

伟人的一生都是好榜样——
我们能使得人生崇高而伟大。
即使死去,在时间的沙滩上,
也会有我们的脚印留下。

也许,在人生严峻的大海上,
有某个兄弟在扬帆远去,
突然遭了难,他已经绝望,
看到那脚印又鼓起了勇气。

那就让我们奋发有为吧,
要决心去跨过任何障碍;
不断地探求,点滴地积累,
要学会工作,还要坚持不息。

(黄一宁 译)

译文四

在人生那坎坷的露营地上,
勿做默默无语、任人驱使的牲口!
要勇于斗争,做一名闯将!

勿寄望于未来,不管令人多欢畅!
让逝去的岁月将过去埋葬!
行动吧——就在活生生的现在!
火红的心在胸膛,仁慈的上帝在天上!

伟人的一生为我们树立了榜样,
我们因此让生活变得更加高尚,
一旦我们逝去,留在我们后面的
是一串串脚印在时间的沙滩上。

脚印也许被另一位兄弟看见,
他正在人生那庄严的海上扬帆,
突然间遇到海难而孤立无助,
因此而将生活的信心重新点燃。

咱们鼓足勇气,立即行动起来,
去接受命运的挑战,永不言败;
我们永远进取,我们永远追求,
我们学会劳作,我们学会等待。

(李明 译)

笔 记

三 诗歌翻译的批评与赏析练习

原 文

Nothing Gold Can Stay

Nature's first green is gold,
Her hardest hue to hold.
Her early leaf's a flower;
But only so an hour.
Then leaf subsides to leaf.
So Eden sank to grief,
So dawn goes down to day.
Nothing gold can stay.

(Robert Frost)

译文一

凡是金的怎能光华长留

大自然最初的绿芽是金子,
但这种颜色最难保持。
她的叶子起先花一般秀丽,
但只能维持一个小时。
叶子退化成繁叶满枝,
而乐园跌入愁苦人世,
黎明坠毁变成白昼,
凡是金的怎能光华长留。

（赵毅衡 译）

译文二

美景转头空

新绿胜锦绣,
无奈最难留。
嫩叶如花香,
有几许春光?
秋风扫落叶,
仙境亦萧瑟。
天明催醒梦,
美景转头空。

（朱明海 译）

第十五章 "When You Are Old" 汉译文的批评赏析

一 关于 "When You Are Old"

　　"When You Are Old" 这首爱情诗是爱尔兰诗人叶芝（1865—1939）在 29 岁时写的。就在五年前的 1889 年，诗人遇见了爱尔兰民族自治运动的领导人之一、著名的女演员毛特·冈（Maud Gonne）。叶芝对她一见倾心，并忠贞不渝，但他的爱一再遭到她的拒绝。后来，毛特·冈嫁给了同她并肩战斗的麦克布莱德少校。23 年之后，即 1916 年，麦克布莱德少校在斗争中献身，叶芝再次向她求婚，但仍然遭到拒绝。可以想象，这种遭受巨大打击之后诗人所经历的爱的痛苦和悲伤是何等巨大！但叶芝却无怨无悔，因为在他的心灵深处，毛特·冈就是"永恒的女性"，是真善美的化身，是爱情的信仰和理想的象征。也正是这一点，成为了诗人创作这首诗的灵感和激情的源泉。叶芝终生爱慕着毛特·冈，并为她写了许多诗。《当你老了》就是其中一首。从这首诗可以看出，叶芝并没有表达自己遭到她的拒绝之后的痛苦，而是表达了自己对爱情的专一和执着。诗中没有华丽的辞藻，没有甜蜜的柔情，甚至听不到一句爱的誓言。诗人用略带悲哀的语调，诉说着不可挽回的爱情。至多，他表达了他的悲哀，因为心中的爱人辨不出真伪，而当她能分辨真伪的时候，他们都已老去，天各一方，鸳梦难圆。

　　作为译者，务必要了解诗人的情感历程，进而将这首诗的深意和神韵充分挖掘出来，并通过中英两种语言的巧妙契合，以优雅舒缓的语调，将诗人那在流动和飘逸中透出的一抹淡淡哀伤，温婉亲切、真挚平静地向其佳人倾诉出来。

二 "When You Are Old" 原文及四种汉译文

原文

When You Are Old

When you are old and gray and full of sleep,

And nodding by the fire, take down this book,

And slowly read, and dream of the soft look

Your eyes had once, and of their shadows deep;

How many loved your moments of glad grace,

And loved your beauty with love false or true,

But one man loved the pilgrim Soul in you,

And loved the sorrows of your changing face;

And bending down beside the glowing bars,

Murmur, a little sadly, how Love fled,

And paced upon the mountains overhead,

And hid his face amid a crowd of stars.

译文一

当你老了

当你老了,白发苍苍,睡意朦胧,
在炉前打盹,请取下这本诗篇,
慢慢吟诵,梦见你当年的双眼
那柔美的光芒与青幽的晕影;

多少人真情假意,爱过你的美丽,
爱过你欢乐而迷人的青春,
唯独一人爱你朝圣者的心,
爱你日益凋谢的脸上的哀戚;

当你佝偻着,在灼热的炉栅边,
你将轻轻诉说,带着一丝伤感:
逝去的爱,如今已步上高山,
在密密星群里埋藏它的赧颜。

(飞白 译)

译文二

当你年老时

当你年老,鬓斑,睡意昏沉,
在炉旁打盹时,取下这本书,
慢慢诵读,梦忆从前你双眸
神色柔和,眼波中倒影深深;

多少人爱你风韵妩媚的时光,
爱你的美丽出自假意或真情,
但唯有一人爱你灵魂的至诚,
爱你渐衰的脸上愁苦的风霜;

弯下身子,在炽红的壁炉边,
忧伤地低诉,爱神如何逃走,
在头顶上的群山巅漫步闲游,
把他的面孔隐没在繁星中间。

(傅浩 译)

译文三

当你老了

当你老了,头白了,睡意昏沉,
炉火旁打盹,请取下这部诗歌,
慢慢读,回想你过去眼神的柔和,
回想它们昔日浓重的阴影;

多少人爱你青春欢畅的时辰,
爱慕你的美丽,假意或真心,
只有一个人爱你那朝圣者的灵魂,
爱你衰老了的脸上痛苦的皱纹;

垂下头来,在红光闪耀的炉子旁,
凄然地轻轻诉说那爱情的消逝,
在头顶的山上它缓缓踱着步子,
在一群星星中间隐藏着脸庞。

(袁可嘉 译)

译文四

当你韶光已逝时

当你韶光已逝,头发灰白,睡意沉沉,
倦坐于炉火旁,请取下这本诗集,
慢慢品味,去追忆你那曾经温柔的眼神,
去追忆你的双眸那深邃的影子。

多少人爱恋过你那青春飞扬的时刻,
爱恋过你的美丽,是出自真心或者假意,
但唯有一人爱的是你那朝圣者般的灵魂,
爱的是你渐渐衰老的脸上那愁苦的皱纹。

你曲着背,在熊熊燃烧的炉火旁,
凄凄然,你低语呢喃,爱神怎么会逃逸,
爱神怎么会漫步于巍巍群山之间,
爱神怎么会将容颜隐没于繁星万点。

(李明 译)

笔 记

三 诗歌翻译的批评与赏析练习

原 文

To a Young Lady

Sweet stream, that winds through yonder glade,
Apt emblem of a virtuous maid—
Silent and chaste she steals along,
Far from the world's gay busy throng:
With gentle yet prevailing force,
Intent upon her destined course;
Graceful and useful all she does,
Blessing and blest where'er she goes;
Pure-bosom'd as that watery glass,
And Heaven reflected in her face.

(William Cowper)

[1] yonder glade 那边的林中空地
[2] apt emblem 合适的标记
[3] gay busy throng 忙忙碌碌，快活喧闹的人群

译文一

致一位年轻女士

蜿蜒流过那树林的清溪，
才能同贤淑的姑娘相比——
恬静高洁，悄悄地流淌，
远离着世上繁华的地方；
她力量柔婉却难以抗拒，
专注于自己命定的目的，
做的一切又美又有用处，
到处造福又到处受祝福；
胸怀纯净得像清澈明镜，
苍天在她面上得到反映。

（黄杲炘 译）

译文二

致一位年轻女士

涓涓的溪流流过远处林中的空地，
那是对一位贤淑姑娘贴切的比拟——
她寂静无声、圣洁纯真，悄悄前进，
她远离喧嚣，远离忙忙碌碌的人群：
她那动人的温柔具有无比的威力，
她一心一意追寻自己命定的足迹，
她所做的一切不仅优雅而且有益，
她所到之处便福音一路、受人祝福；
她胸怀纯净，犹如那面清澈的明镜，
将上天映射到她那张美丽的面容中。

（李明 译）

第十六章 《江雪》《清明》英译文的批评赏析

一 关于《江雪》

《江雪》的作者柳宗元是唐宋八大家之一。据史料记载，《江雪》创作于诗人谪居永州期间。在永州，残酷的政治迫害，艰苦的生活环境，加之几次无情的火灾，严重损害了他的健康，竟至到了"行则膝颤、坐则髀痹"的程度。这首诗就是他借助歌咏隐居山水的渔翁，来寄托自己清高孤傲的情怀，抒发政治上失意的苦闷和压抑，表达诗人永贞革新失败后，虽处境孤独，但仍傲岸不屈的性格。诗中客观境界的幽僻更能体现出作者落寞孤寂的心情。

这是一首押仄韵的五言绝句，"千山鸟飞绝，万径人踪灭。"这两行的意思是：所有的山上，都看不到飞鸟的影子；所有的小路，都没有人的踪影。"孤舟蓑笠翁，独钓寒江雪。"这两行的意思是：（在）孤零零的一条小船上，坐着一个身披蓑衣，头戴斗笠的老翁，在大雪覆盖的寒冷江面上独自垂钓。全诗用简单而细腻的语言描绘出了一幅寒江雪钓图：千山万径都没有人烟鸟迹，天地间只有一个渔翁在江雪中独自垂钓。

写雪景而前三句不见"雪"字，纯粹运用烘托之笔，一片空灵，更加突出了独钓的孤舟。诗人淡墨轻描，渲染出一个洁静绝美的世界。北京大学吴小如教授这样解读《江雪》："首先，诗人用'千山''万径'这两个词，目的是为了给下面两句的'孤舟'和'独钓'的画面作陪衬。没有'千''万'两字，下面的'孤''独'两字也就平淡无奇，没有什么感染力了。其次，山上的鸟飞，路上的人踪，这本来是极平常的事，也是最一般化的形象。可是，诗人却把它们放在'千山''万径'的下面，再加上一个'绝'和一个'灭'字，这就把最常见的、最一般化的动态，一下子给变成了极端的寂静、绝对的沉默，形成一种不平常的景象。因此，下面两句原来是属于静态的描写，由于摆在这种绝对幽静、绝对沉寂的背景之下，倒反而显得玲珑剔透，有了生气，在画面上浮动起来、活跃起来了。"

张海鸥（2000：300，301）则认为《江雪》写的是静态，"诗人运用了对比、衬托的手法：千山万径之广远衬托孤舟老翁之渺小；鸟绝人灭之阒寂对比老翁垂钓之生趣；画面之安谧冷寂衬托人物心绪之涌动。孤处独立的老翁实际是诗人心情意绪的写照。"

二 《江雪》原文及四种英译文

原文	译文一	译文二
江雪	**Fishing in Snow**	**River Snow**
千山鸟飞绝，	From hill to hill no bird in flight;	These thousand peaks cut off the flight of birds
万径人踪灭。	From path to path no man in sight.	On all the trails, human tracks are gone.
孤舟蓑笠翁，	A lonely fisherman afloat	A single boat—boat—hat—an old man!
独钓寒江雪。	Is fishing snow in a lonely boat.	Alone fishing chill river snow.
（柳宗元）	（许渊冲 译）	(Gary Snyder 译)

三 关于《清明》

《清明》是一首千百年来传诵不断的小诗。但要将这首小诗翻译成英文却非易事。笔者手头有好几个译本，但不同译本对于其中的文字又有不同的理解。在我看来，要翻译好这首诗，在很大程度上要对诗中的"路上行人"有一个正确理解。下面这段文字，也许可以对这个问题做一个很好的脚注：

公元581年，隋文帝杨坚建立隋朝，结束了南北朝分裂的局面，继而又被大唐帝国取代。唐太宗"贞观之治"造福于民，生产力得到极大发展，物资增加，粮食储积，酒业大大推进。市肆腾踊，酒旗纷飘，汾州杏花村，在唐代是由军事重镇太原通往皇城西安的途径要地，无论文武百官，各地武举诗人，乡土访学，凡路经者都闻香下马，一饮为快，因此，酿造技术发展特别迅速。杏花村人在名酒"汾清"的基础上，采用了熟料拌曲，乾和入瓮发酵，蒸馏制酒的办法酿出的酒，清澈如水，酒香纯厚，酒度较高，最易点燃，在酒史上创造了第一家蒸馏白酒。

译文三

The birds have flown away from every hill.
Along each empty path no footprint seen.
In his lone skiff his bamboo garments screen
An aged fisher from the snowstorm chill.

(Fletcher Myriad 译)

译文四

Snow River

O'er mountains and mountains could be seen no birds
Along paths and trails could be found no footprints
An old man with a rain cape and a rain hat
Is fishing alone in a single boat in the snow river.

(李明 译)

杏花村白酒出现后，很快传遍了南北。起初，民间见其易燃，称其为火酒或烧酒，又有人称"汾白酒"，汾州官府称之为汾酒，村民为区别他所产却称"杏花白"。这时，酒名传进朝内，试饮绝佳，令州进贡。因其酿造技术新奇，尤为乾和入瓮，故定名为"乾酿"，又名"乾和"。从此杏花村乾酿酒又称为"汾州贡酒"。

美酒飘香，引来了更多的客商和访酒文人、诗人。他们赞誉汾酒，写下了不朽的佳句，唐朝诗人李白、杜甫都来过汾阳，分别留下了《留别西河刘少府》（西河为汾阳古称）、《过宋员外之问旧庄》（宋之问为初唐诗人，汾阳人，与沈期章齐名，并称"沈宋"。"旧庄"即诗人的汾阳故居宋家庄村）。根据民间传说，李白、杜甫饮过杏花酒，写过杏花诗，只是诗稿遗失。但这种说法，值得进一步考证。

唐朝名将郭子仪因平安史之乱战功赫赫，唐肃宗赞誉："吾之家国由卿再造。"入朝后授郭为"汾阳王"。一代中兴名将之封地，全国著名贡酒的所在地，使汾阳、杏花村声名鹊起，成为晚唐仁人志士一个重要的旅游景点。

晚唐著名诗人杜牧就是其中的一位。杜牧是一位既悲叹自己生不逢时又立志报国、力挽晚唐颓靡之势的有识之士，对已故 40 余年的一代名将郭子仪充满了景仰之情。因此，这位陕西人 20 多岁便出游各地，体察民情，寻访名胜，考察要地。他东渡黄河，来到汾阳，寻访郭子仪故地，抒发自己的报国雄心，来到并州、代州等军事要地考察，并写下了《并州道中》的诗句。在他途经名酒产地杏花村时，写下了这首千古传诵、妇孺皆知的题为《清明》的诗。

　　诗人在细雨濛濛的清明节，怀着对一代名将的缅怀，"行役苦吟"，思醉遣乏，遇牧童给他指出卖酒的村落，就是"汾州贡酒"的产地杏花村。诗歌体现了诗人独自一人游历的生活景况。在宋代，由于交通工具逐步先进，杏花村可四通八达，杏花村酒更为知名，"甘露堂""醉仙居""杏花春"以及各姓酒记旗牌高挂。这时汾酒仍称为"乾酿""乾和"或"甘露"。每年贡酒，由甘露堂等大酒肆提取，故宋代张能臣《酒名记》中有"汾州甘露堂最有名"的记载。

　　笔者也曾比较和赏析过这首小诗的各种译文。这里，我想谈谈自己的感受。

　　首先，对"清明"的翻译就目前来看能找到的英译文有以下十余种：The Pure Brightness Day、The Day of Mourning for the Dead、The Mourning Day、All Souls' Day、All Souls' Festive Day、Clear and Bright、Pure Brightness、the Qingming Festival、Day of Tomb-Worship、Spring Festival 和 The Late Spring Festival Day。虽然译法有如此之多，但没有一个比较理想的翻译。若用 festive 或 festival 来翻译，都有一种"欢乐"和"喜庆"气氛的联想，这与本诗的意境不相符合。但若用西方的 All Souls' Day 来翻译，则指十一月二日"万灵节"。该节日为罗马天主教为亡灵祈祷超度的节日。这与我国上坟扫墓的清明节相比，宗教色彩太浓，在时间上也迥异，只在纪念死者这一点上是相似的。（郭著章、江安、鲁文忠，1994：230-231）而若使用颇具我国传统文化色彩的 The Pure Brightness Day 或 the Qingming Festival 来翻译"清明"则需要较大篇幅的注解才能解决问题，这又不利于诗歌的翻译。这里所引译文中，译文一将其作了非专有名词处理，文化隔阂因此消除（毛荣贵，2005：136），对"杏花村"这个在本诗中不属于确指的名词也译成了非专有名词，即杏花盛开的村庄（hamlet nestling amidst apricot blossoms）。这为整首诗的英文行文扫清了障碍。译文二将"清明"译为 the Mourning Day，文化隔阂没有消除，给英译文读者带来阅读困难。

第二是对于"路上行人"这个意象该如何理解，也让译者颇费斟酌。从所收集到的译文看，对其翻译有以下几种：I、the mourner、the men and women、pedestrians、travelers。这里的译文一为杨宪益、戴乃迭夫妇所译，译文二为许渊冲所译。他们分别使用的是 travelers 和 the mourner。我以为，不管是用 travelers along the road 还是用 the mourner 以及 the men and women 和 pedestrians，都与此诗的意境显得有些不太关联，尤其是无法同诗的第三行和第四行构成一个具有连贯性的语篇。可以说，翻译好"路上行人欲断魂"是关系到整个语篇是否具有连贯性的关键所在。在这一点上，译文一和译文二都翻译得不够成功。下面来看看吴钧陶先生的英译文（郭著章等，1994：230）：

It drizzles thick on the Pure Brightness Day;
I travel with my heart lost in dismay.
"Is there a public house somewhere, cowboy?"
He points at Apricot Bloom Village faraway.

吴钧陶先生的英译文不仅在语篇的连贯性方面做得很成功，而且在意、形、音三方面都同原文具有较高程度的相似。特别突出的一点是：吴译有和原诗同样的韵式，但显得自然，无因韵害义之毛病（郭著章等，1994：231）。笔者很赞同这一评价。

对于"酒家"的翻译，译文一使用的 tavern 不够恰当，因为 tavern 一词属古老用法，而且主要为"客栈"（inn）之意，给人的印象好像是在传达"我"要"投宿"而非意欲借酒消除心中的哀愁之意。译文二使用 wineshop 一词比译文一要好，但吴钧陶译文中使用的 public house 更为确切。在对第三行诗的翻译上，译文二使用被动语态不可取，它不符合原文语言平实的语气，也让读者读来别扭。另外，该诗行英译文中的 to drown his sad hours 属超额翻译，它过于直白地明示了原文的意义而使得原文韵味全无，读者读来犹如受人嚼过之馍。在全诗最后一行的翻译中，译文一使用了 nestling，此词用于此的确很妙，但却多此一举，删除该词可使译文更加精练。译文二对此诗行的翻译还算差强人意。

综合上述讨论，笔者对《清明》一诗进行了重译（译文四）。

四 《清明》原文及四种英译文

原文	译文一	译文二
清　明	**In the Rainy Season of Spring**	**The Mourning Day**
清明时节雨纷纷，	It drizzles endless during the rainy season in spring,	A drizzling rain falls like tears on the Mourning Day;
路上行人欲断魂。	Travelers along the road look gloomy and miserable.	The mourner's heart is going to break on his way.
借问酒家何处有，	When I ask a shepherd boy where I can find a tavern,	Where can a wineshop be found to drown his sad hours?
牧童遥指杏花村。	He points at a distant hamlet nestling amidst apricot blossoms.	A cowherd points to a cot'mid apricot flowers.
（杜牧）	（杨宪益、戴乃迭　译）	（许渊冲　译）

五 诗歌翻译的批评与赏析练习

原文	译文一	译文二
春　怨	**A Lover's Dream**	**A Complaint in Spring**
打起黄莺儿，	Oh, drive the golden orioles	Drive orioles off the tree
莫教枝上啼；	From off our garden tree!	For their songs awake me
啼时惊妾梦，	Their warbling broke the dream wherein	From dreaming of my dear
不得到辽西。	My lover smiled to me.	Far off on the frontier.
（金昌绪）	(Fletcher Myriad　译)	（许渊冲　译）

译文三

The Pure Brightness Day

It drizzles thick on the Pure Brightness Day;

I travel with my heart lost in dismay.

"Is there a public house somewhere, cowboy?"

He points at Apricot Bloom Village faraway.

（吴钧陶　译）

译文四

The Pure Brightness Day

It drizzles on end on the Pure Brightness Day in spring;

I feel gloomy on my way from graveyard mourning.

Where can I have a drink to drown my sorrow, I ask a herdsboy.

He points to a hamlet far 'mid apricot blossoms.

（李明　译）

笔　记

原　文

少年不识愁滋味，
爱上层楼，
爱上层楼，
为赋新词强说愁。

而今识尽愁滋味，
欲说还休，
欲说还休，
却道天凉好个秋。

（辛弃疾《丑奴儿》）

译文一

Young I was, and ignorant of the taste of care;

Alone I loved to mount the stairs,

Alone I loved to mount the stairs,

And in new verses my imagined woes declare.

Now I've learned all the bitterness of life's fare,

Never would I hint my despair,

Never would I hint my despair,

Murmuring instead: Ah autumn, how cool and fair.

（冯世则，2005：275）

译文二

In my young days,

I had tasted only gladness,

But loved to mount the top floor,

But loved to mount the top floor,

To write a song pretending sadness.

And now I've tasted

Sorrow's flavors, bitter and sour,

And can't find a word,

And can't find a word,

But merely say, "What a golden autumn hour!"

（林语堂　译）

第十七章 《再别康桥》英译文的批评赏析

一 关于《再别康桥》

康桥是英国剑桥大学所在地。诗人徐志摩（Tsemon Hsu）曾于 1920 年 10 月至 1922 年 8 月游学于此。在剑桥大学的经历成为徐志摩一生的转折点。正是康河的水，开启了诗人的心灵，唤醒了蛰于其内心那诗人的天命，正如他后来在其散文《吸烟与文化》中所说的：我的眼是康桥教我睁的，我的求知欲是康桥给我拨动的，我的自我意识是康桥给我胚胎的。

《再别康桥》是诗人于 1928 年故地重游之后在归国途中所作，展现了诗人重返康桥的真切感受。不过，据说当时徐志摩所留下的是英文版的《再别康桥》，目前的这首汉语版的《再别康桥》是当时一位不知名的中国人翻译过来的。

汉语版的《再别康桥》共七节，每节四行，每行两顿或三顿，不拘一格而又法度严谨，韵式上严守二、四押韵，读来抑扬顿挫、朗朗上口，节奏犹如涟漪般荡漾开来，既是虔诚的学子寻梦的跫音，又契合诗人感情的潮起潮落，有一种独特的审美快感。

此诗是一首写景的抒情诗，所抒发的情感有三：留恋之情、惜别之情和理想幻灭后的感伤之情。

第一节诗可概括为：节奏舒缓，动作轻盈，情意缠绵，哀愁淡淡。最后的"西天的云彩"，为下文的描写布下绚丽的色彩。所以，第一节诗为整首诗定下了基调。

第二节诗实写康河之美，其中"金柳"中的"柳"在古诗里谐音"留"，为"留别""惜别"之意。康河之美给诗人留下深刻印象，一切牵挂用"在我心头荡漾"概言之，简洁形象。诗人在此运用了比拟（拟人、拟物）手法，并与第三节诗紧密联系在一起：

"软泥上的青荇，油油的在水底招摇；在康桥的柔波里，我甘做一条水草。"

这一节突出了康河的明静和自由自在。自由和美正是徐志摩所孜孜以求的东西。诗人在此还表现出一种爱心：那水草好像是在欢迎诗人的到来。这一节诗与中国古诗有着非常相似的地方，这便是物我合一。如果说第二节是化客为主，那么，第三节就是移主为客了。诗人充分做到主客交融、物我难忘。

第四节是全诗的转折点："那榆荫下的一潭，不是清泉，是天上虹，揉碎在浮藻间，沉淀着彩虹似的梦。"这节诗运用虚实结合的手法："实"是景物的描写，"虚"是象征手法的运用。一潭水很清澈，霞光倒映下来，"不是清泉，是天上虹"。这一片红光是实写。可潭水上漂浮着许多水藻，挡住部分霞光，零零碎碎的，有的红，有的绿，好像彩虹被揉碎一般，非常形象生动。这个"揉"写得非常生动，同时也预示着自己梦想的破灭。诗人的梦想于1927年破灭。

　　第五节诗是徐志摩对往昔生活的回忆与留恋。他在康桥生活了两年。那时，他有自己的理想，生活很充实，对未来怀着希望。所以，他用"一船星辉"来比喻那时的生活，具有象征意味。

　　可是，过去已成历史，现实却令人哀伤，所以，"悄悄是离别的笙箫，夏虫也为我沉默，沉默是今晚的康桥。"这第六节诗是情感的高潮，充分展现了徐志摩对康桥的情感，也集中表现了他离别康桥的惆怅。"悄悄是离别的笙箫"运用了暗喻手法。箫声低沉、哀怨，而笛声则悠扬、欢悦，所以，用"箫"来比喻"悄悄"，说明了诗人的心境。接下来的是"夏虫也为我沉默，沉默是今晚的康桥。"诗歌讲究精练、忌讳重复，可在这首诗中，诗人一再重复"沉默""悄悄""轻轻"，这种高频率选词的运用，起到了不断强化的修辞效果，最终凸显了诗人所渲染的气氛。另外，"沉默"是人最深的感情。说"沉默是今晚的康桥"，康桥尚且如此，诗人又何以堪呢？这样描写，正好反衬了诗人对康桥的感情非常深厚。

　　最后一节："悄悄的我走了，正如我悄悄的来，我挥一挥衣袖，不带走一片云彩。""云彩"有象征意味，代表彩虹似的梦，它倒映在水中，但并不能够带走。因此，再别康桥不是和他的母校告别，而是同给他一生带来最大变化的康桥文化进行告别，是再别康桥的理想。

　　《再别康桥》这首诗，充分体现了新月诗派所追寻的"三美"：绘画美、建筑美、音乐美。音乐美是徐志摩最强调的，其中第一句和最后一句是反复的，加强节奏感，且其中的词是重叠的，如"悄悄""轻轻"。再者，每句诗均换了韵，因为感情是变化的，所以不是一韵到底的。再是音尺，"轻轻的我走了"，分别为"三字尺""一字尺"和"二字尺"。这符合徐志摩活泼好动的性格。再就是压韵。所谓建筑美，一、三句诗排在前面，二、四句诗低格排列，空一格错落有致，建筑有变化。再者，一、三句短一点，二、四句长一点，这显出视觉美。音乐是听觉，绘画是视觉，视觉美与听觉美融通，读起来才会感觉好。绘画美即是词美，如"金柳""柔波""星辉""软泥""青荇"，这些形象都非常具有色彩，而且有动态感和柔美感。

　　这三者结合起来，徐志摩追求"整体当中求变化，参差当中求变异"，显示出新月诗的特点和个性，概括为：柔美幽怨的意境，清新飘逸的风格。

　　这首诗表现出诗人高度的艺术技巧。诗人将具体景物与想象糅合在一起构成诗的鲜明生动的艺术形象，巧妙地把气氛、感情、景象融合为意境，达到了景中有情、情中有景的艺术效果。诗的结构形式严谨整齐、错落有致。诗的语言清新秀丽，节奏轻柔委婉，和谐自然，伴随着情感的起伏跳跃，犹如一曲悦耳徐缓的散板，轻盈婉转，拨动着读者的心弦。《再别康桥》可谓是"音乐美""绘画美""建筑美"的完美结合，堪称是徐志摩诗作中的绝唱。

二 《再别康桥》原文及四种英译文

原文

再别康桥

轻轻的我走了，
正如我轻轻的来；
我轻轻的招手，
作别西天的云彩。

那河畔的金柳，
是夕阳中的新娘；
波光里的艳影，
在我的心头荡漾。

软泥上的青荇，
油油的在水底招摇；
在康河的柔波里，
甘心做一条水草！

那榆荫下的一潭，
不是清泉，是天上虹；
揉碎在浮藻间，
沉淀着彩虹似的梦。

寻梦？撑一支长篙，
向青草更青处漫溯；
满载一船星辉，
在星辉斑斓里放歌。

译文一

Saying Goodbye to Cambridge Again

Very quietly I take my leave
As quietly as I came here;
Quietly I wave good-bye
To the rosy clouds in the western sky.

The golden willows by the riverside
Are young brides in the setting sun;
Their reflections on the shimmering waves
Always linger in the depth of my heart.

The floating heart growing the sludge
Sways leisurely under the water;
In the gentle waves of Cambridge
I would be a water plant!

That pool under the shade of elm trees
Holds not water but the rainbow from the sky;
Shattered to pieces among the duck weeds
Is the sediment of a rainbow-like dream?

译文二

Moving softly I am going away,
Just like I came to here in the same way;
Moving softly I am waving my hand,
Part with clouds in west sky with no delay.

Along riverside, the golden willows,
Are brides in the splendid setting-sun glow;
In twinkling waves, flowery reflection,
Is rippling in depth of my heart and soul.

Green duckweeds grasping on soft mud firmly,
Are swaying on riverbed glossily;
In gentle ripples of Cambridge River,
I'm a slender water plant willingly!

The pool located under elm shadow,
Is not a clear spring, but the sky rainbow;
Rubbed to pieces in the floating algae,
With dream precipitating like rainbow.

译文三

Saying Farewell to Cambridge Again

Quietly I'm taking my leave
In much the same way as I came.
Quietly I wave my farewell
To the clouds in the western sky.

The golden willow by the river
Is a bride in the setting sun.
Her reflection in the shimmering waves
Remains etched forever in my mind.

The green grass on the soft riverbed
Sways glossy in the waters deep.
With gentle waves of Cambridge River,
How I wish to be a waterweed!

The pool under the elm tree shade
Is no longer a pool but a rainbow
Shattered in the water with duck-weed
But keeping alive that rainbow-like dream.

译文四

Goodbye Again, Cambridge!

I leave softly, gently,
Exactly as I came.
I wave to the western sky,
Telling it goodbye softly, gently.

The golden willow at the river edge
Is the setting sun's bride.
Her quivering reflection
Stays fixed in my mind.

Green grass on the bank
Dances on a watery floor
In bright reflection.
I wish myself a bit of waterweed
Vibrating to the ripple
Of the River Cam.

That creek in the shade of the great elms
Is not a creek but a shattered rainbow.
Printed on the water
And inlaid with duckweed,
It is my lost dream.

原 文	译文一	译文二
但我不能放歌， 悄悄是别离的笙箫； 夏虫也为我沉默， 沉默是今晚的康桥！ 悄悄的我走了， 正如我悄悄的来； 我挥一挥衣袖， 不带走一片云彩。	To seek a dream? Just to pole a boat upstream To where the green grass is more verdant Or to have the boat fully loaded with starlight And sing aloud in the splendor of starlight. But I can't sing aloud Quietness is my farewell music; Even summer insects heap silence for me Silent is Cambridge tonight! Very quietly I left As quietly as I came here; Gently I flick my sleeves Not even a wisp of cloud will I bring away. （无名氏　译）	Pursue dreams? Punt a barge-pole long indeed, Freely upstream towards the greener weed; Pole a boat fully loaded with starlight, T' sing freely in bright starlight is my need. But I cannot happily n freely sing, I just play flute secretly when parting; Summer insects keep silent for me too, Cambridge remains silent this evening. Very peacefully I'm going away, Just like I came to here in the same way; I flick my sleeves gently and casually, From west sky I don't take a cloud away. （宋德利，2014：176-178）

译文三	译文四	笔　记
To hunt a dream? I pull a long punt-pole To bring my boat into grass greener still. With a boat full of starlight I sing loud with my heart and soul. But now I just cannot do so As quietness is what I seek in farewells. Even summer insects keep quiet for me As quiet also is tonight's Cambridge! Quietly I'm taking my leave In much the same way as I came. With a flick of my sleeves I go, And never will I take a cloud away. 　　　　　　（李明　译）	Hunting a dream? Wielding a long punting pole I get my boat into green water, Into still greener grass. In a flood of starlight On a river of silver and diamond I sing to my heart's content. But now, no, I cannot sing With farewell in my heart. Farewells must be quiet, mute, Even the summer insects are silent, Knowing I am leaving. The Cambridge night is soundless. I leave quietly As I came quietly. I am leaving Without taking so much As a single piece of cloud. But with a quick jerk of my sleeve I wave goodbye. 　　　　(Tsemon Hsu 英文原诗？)	

三 诗歌翻译的批评与赏析练习

原　文	译文一	译文二
向晚意不适， 驱车登古原。 夕阳无限好， 只是近黄昏。 （李商隐《乐游原》或《登乐游原》）	With twilight shadows in my heart I have driven up among the Lo-Yu Tombs To see the sun, for all his glory, Buried by the coming night. （Witter Bynner　译）	Towards evening my soul was disquieted, And I urged my carriage up to this ancient plateau. The setting sun has boundless beauty; Only the yellow dusk is so near. (R. Kotewell & N. Smith　译)

第五部分

演讲翻译的批评赏析

一 关于演讲及演讲词

演讲是一门语言艺术。它的主要形式就是"讲",即运用有声语言并追求言辞的表现力和声音的感染力;同时还要辅之以"演",即运用面部表情、手势动作、身体姿态乃至一切可以理解的体态语言,使讲话"艺术化"起来,从而产生一种特殊的艺术魅力。

作为供演讲使用的演讲词,是社会生活中经常使用的一种文体,它可用来宣传政治主张,发表个人见解,交流彼此的思想,因而往往具有强烈的呼唤功能。由于演讲词是事先准备的口述书面材料,故从性质上讲,它既不同于日常的即兴谈话,也不同于纯粹的书面文体。演讲词在遣词造句上,需要通俗易懂,形象生动,但在结构安排上需要严谨缜密。换言之,演讲词具有独特的文体特点,即:语言通俗平易,句式短小,读来朗朗上口;结构清晰明了,逻辑严谨缜密;篇章安排紧凑,层次分明。(荆素蓉,2001:46)

为取得语言通俗平易,同听众拉近距离的效果,演讲者往往既运用消极的修辞手段,又运用积极的修辞手段来达到目的。比如,演讲者因演讲时需要直接面对听众,故在称谓词的使用方面,多使用单数第一人称 I 开始演讲,接着便使用复数第一人称的 we 和 us,并使之成为整个演讲中出现频率最高的人称代词。通过这种称呼语的选用,演讲者把自己归入到听众这个群体当中,视自己为他们的一员,这便让听众在心理上拉近了同演讲者的距离,从而使演讲内容的可接受性大大提高。如在《葛底斯堡讲话》中,林肯虽居总统要职,但在演讲中却自始至终以 we 和 us 来称呼听众,从而唤起包括林肯总统在内所有美国人空前的责任感。只有极少数情况下演讲者与听众代表截然不同的势力,"你"和"我"分得很清楚的时候,演讲者才使用 you。

除使用上述消极的修辞手段之外,演讲者还运用积极的修辞手段。这些积极的修辞手段包括比喻(simile and metapor)、对照(contrast)、对偶(antithesis)、蝉联(anadiplosis)、层进(climax)、排比(parallelism)、反复(repetition)等,其中最有代表性的是排比和反复。排比是英语和汉语中都喜欢使用的修辞手段。它由结构相似,意义和语气一致的词、词组、短语或句子排列成串而形成一个整体。这些修辞手段的运用,可以通过对听众感官的刺激而强化演讲的感染力,从而取得演讲者所期望的最终效果。

二 演讲词翻译的原则

演讲词的文体特点非常独特,因此,在对演讲词进行翻译时,就需要遵循同其他文体不一样的翻译原则。以下这些翻译原则可作为演讲词的翻译原则:

一是完整性。即将演讲原文作为一个整体看待,将演讲词的开头、中间以及结尾的铺陈和它们之间的格局翻译得逻辑缜密。

二是清晰性。即将演讲原文中通俗生动的语言在译文中也要译得通俗生动;演讲原文中使用了朴素的语言，译文中也要使用朴素的语言；演讲原文中使用了形象的语言，译文中也要使用形象的语言；演讲原文中使用了幽默的语言或警句，译文中也要尽可能使用幽默的语言或警句。

三是跌宕起伏。即作为译者，应该将原文中的那种有张有弛、有起有伏的表达效果在译文中充分体现出来。

四是灵活性。即译者应本着"不走失原意，力求其易懂"的原则，对于那些在译入语中阙如或由于文化差异而无法再现的表达形式及修辞手段，进行灵活处理。

总之，一篇演讲词，无论长短，其特点就是讲道理，摆事实。译者在翻译过程中应该把原文鲜明的观点译得透彻，严密的例证译得准确，深厚的感情译得感人。当然，译者不同于原作者，他在翻译时不能像写作一样可以随心所欲地自由发挥。因此，在这四个基本原则中，完整清晰是跌宕灵活的基础；而后者则是前者的升华。通俗地说就是，译者灵活的前提必须是要不走失原意，要忠实于原作者。这一点应该是译者在做任何文体的翻译时必须遵循的基本原则，演讲词翻译当然也不例外。（荆素蓉，2001：48）

第十八章 "Gettysburg Address" 汉译文的批评赏析

一 关于 "Gettysburg Address"

　　1863 年 7 月 3 日，联邦军在宾夕法尼亚州葛底斯堡的胜利标志着美国内战的关键转折点。联盟军的罗伯特·更·李将军侵占宾夕法尼亚，曾希望以此来分割北方并打击北方的士气，以便迅速结束这场战争。葛底斯堡战役是一场流血最多的战役。联邦军损失二万三千人，而南方联盟军伤亡失踪的士兵达二万八千人。北方对葛底斯堡的胜利欢欣鼓舞。四个月后林肯总统到葛底斯堡战场访问，为这场伟大战役的阵亡将士墓举行落成仪式。这篇演说是在 1863 年 11 月 19 日发表的。

　　林肯的葛底斯堡演说是美国文学中最漂亮、最富有诗意的文章之一。虽然这是一篇庆祝军事胜利的演说，但它没有好战之气；相反地，这是一篇感人肺腑的颂辞，赞美那些做出最后牺牲的人，以及他们为之献身的那些理想。

　　林肯的讲话是极简短、极朴素的。这往往使那些滔滔不绝的讲演家大瞧不起。

　　葛底斯堡战役后，决定为死难烈士举行盛大葬礼。掩葬委员会发给总统一张普通的请帖，他们以为他是不会来的，但林肯答应了。既然总统来，那一定要讲演的，但他们已经请了著名演说家艾佛瑞特来做这件事，因此，他们又给林肯写了信，说在艾佛瑞特演说完毕之后，他们希望他"随便讲几句适当的话"。这是一个侮辱，但林肯平静地接受了。两星期内，他在穿衣、刮脸、吃点心时也想着怎样演说。演说稿改了两三次，他仍不满意。到了葬礼的前一天晚上，还在做最后的修改，然后半夜找到他的同僚高声朗诵。走进会场时，他骑在马上，仍把头低到胸前默想着自己的演说辞。

　　那位艾佛瑞特讲演了两个多小时，将近结束时，林肯不安地掏出一副旧式眼镜，又一次看他的讲稿。他的演说开始了，一位记者支上三脚架准备拍摄照片，等一切就绪的时候，林肯已经走下讲台。这段时间只有两分钟，而掌声却持续了 10 分钟。后人给以极高评价的那份演说辞，在今天译成中文，也不过 400 字。

　　林肯的这篇演说是英美演说史上著名的篇章，其思想的深刻，行文的严谨，语言的洗练，确实是不愧彪炳青史的大手笔。尤其是其中的第二段，建议加以仔细分析，其语义的承转，结构的安排，甚至包括句式的使用，无一不是极尽推敲之作。

　　这篇演说充分表现出林肯总统在怀念先烈的同时，对这个新生国家的万世长存充满了信心和希望。演讲词开门见山并立即转入正题，文字洗练，没有任何多余的赘言和楔子；结尾语气坚定，给听众留下了感情奔放、情深意切、逻辑严密、生动有力的深刻印象。

二 "Gettysburg Address" 原文及四种汉译文

原 文

Four score and seven years ago our fathers brought forth on this continent a new nation, conceived in liberty, and dedicated to the proposition that all men are created equal.

Now we are engaged in a great civil war, testing whether that nation, or any nation so conceived and so dedicated, can long endure. We are met here on a great battlefield of that war. We have come to dedicate a portion of that field as a final resting place for those who here gave their lives that this nation might live. It is altogether fitting and proper that we should do this.

But, in a larger sense, we can not dedicate—we can not consecrate—we can not hallow—this ground. The brave men, living and dead, who struggled here, have consecrated it far above our poor power to add or detract. The world will little note nor long remember what we say here, but it can never forget what they did here. It is for us, the living, rather, to be dedicated here to the unfinished work which they who fought here have thus far so nobly advanced. It is rather for us to be here dedicated to the great task remaining before us—that from these honored dead we take increased devotion to that cause

译文一

八十七年前,我们的先辈在这个大陆上建立起一个崭新的国家。这个国家以自由为理想,以致力于实现人人享有天赋的平等权利为目标。

目前我们正在进行异常伟大的国内战争。我们的国家或任何一个有着同样理想与目标的国家能否长久存在,这次战争就是一场考验。现在我们在这场战争的一个伟大战场上聚会在一起。我们来到这里,将这战场上的一小块土地奉献给那些为国家生存而英勇捐躯的人们,作为他们最后安息之地。我们这样做是完全恰当的,应该的。

然而,从深一层的意义上说来,我们没有能力奉献这块土地,没有能力使这块土地变得更加神圣。因为在这里进行过斗争的,活着和已经死去的勇士们,已经使这块土地变得这样圣洁,我们的微力已不足以对它有所扬抑了。我们今天在这里说的话,世人不会注意,也不会记住,但是这些英雄业绩,人们将永志不忘。我们后来者应该做的,是献身于英雄们曾在此为之奋斗、努力推进、但尚未竟的工作。我们应该做的是献身于他们遗留给我们的伟大任务。我们的

译文二

八十七年前,我们的先辈在这个大陆上建立了一个以自由为理想、以人人平等为宗旨的新国家。现在我们正进行一场大内战,考验这个国家,或者任何一个主张自由平等的国家,能否长久存在。

我们在这场战争的一个大战场上集会,来把战场的一角献给为国家生存而牺牲的烈士,作为他们永久安息之地,这是我们义不容辞、理所当然该做的事。

但是,从更深刻的意义来说,我们不能使这一角战场成为圣地,我们不能使它流芳百世,我们不能使它永垂青史。因为在这里战斗过的勇士们,活着的或死去的,已经使这一角战场神圣化了,我们微薄的力量远远不能为它增光,或者使它减色。世人不会太注意、也不会长久记住我们在这里说的话,但是永远不会忘记他们在这里做的事。因此,我们活着的人更应该献身于他们为之战斗并且使之前进的未竟事业。

我们更应该献身于我们前面的伟大任务,更应该不断地向这些光荣牺牲的烈士

188 翻译批评与赏析 Translation Appreciation and Criticism

译文三

　　八十又七年以前，我们的先辈在这片大陆上建立起了一个新国家，她孕育于自由之中，致力于人人生来平等的主张。

　　现在，我们正在进行一场意义重大的内战。这场内战，正考验着我们这个或其他孕育于自由、主张人人生来平等的每一个国家，能否长久存在下去。

　　今天，我们聚集在这场战争的一个伟大战场上，要将这个战场上的一片土地，奉献给那些在此为了国家的生存而捐躯的人们，作为他们最终的安息之地。我们这样做是完全恰当的，我们这样做是完全合理的。

　　但是，从更严格的意义上说，我们是不能够奉献这片土地的。我们更不能够圣化、更不能够神化这片土地。那些曾经在这里战斗过的勇士们，活着的和死去的，都已将这片土地圣化了。我们的微薄之力，是远远不能够使这片土地增光或者减色的。世界可能不会太注意，也不会永久记住我们在这里所讲的话，但它永远不会忘记勇士们在这里所做的付出。

　　现在倒是该轮到我们，轮到我们活着的人，在这里致力于这项未竟事业的时候了。这项未竟事业，那些曾经在此战斗过的人们已经非常崇高地推进到了现阶

译文四

　　八十七年前，我们的先辈在这座大陆上建立了一个崭新的国家，她以自由为立国之本，并致力于这样的奋斗目标，即人人生来都具有平等权利。

　　现在我们正在进行一场伟大的内战，这场战争能够考验我们的国家，或任何一个具有同样立国之本和同样奋斗目标的国家，是否能够持久存在。我们在这场战争的一个伟大的战场上相聚在一起。我们来到这里，是为了将这战场上的一块土地作为最后的安息之地献给那些为国捐躯的人们。我们这样做是完全恰当的，也是完全应该的。

　　然而在更广的意义上说，我们没有能力来奉献这块土地，我们没有能力来使这块土地更加神圣。在这里战斗过的，仍然健在或已经牺牲的勇士们，已经使这块土地变得如此神圣，我们微不足道的能力已不足以增加或减少它的圣洁了。世人也许不会注意，也不会长久地记住我们在这里所说的话，却永远也不会忘记这些勇士们在这里做出的崇高业绩。更加重要的是，我们仍然活着的人应该献身于在这里战斗过的勇士们曾高尚地推进、却终于未竟的工作。我们应该献身于他们留给我们的伟大任

笔记

第五部分　演讲翻译的批评赏析　189

原文	译文一	译文二
for which they gave the last full measure of devotion; that we here highly resolve that these dead shall not have died in vain; that this nation, under God, shall have a new birth of freedom; and that government of the people, by the people, for the people, shall not perish from the earth. (Abraham Lincoln, "Gettysburg Address")	先烈已将自己的全部精诚付与我们的事业，我们应从他们的榜样中汲取更多的精神力量，决心使他们的鲜血不致白流。我们应该竭诚使我国在上帝的护佑下，自由得到新的生命；使我们这个民有、民治、民享的政府永存于世。 （石幼珊 译）	学习他们为事业鞠躬尽瘁、死而后已的献身精神，更应该在这里下定决心，一定不让这些烈士的鲜血白流，这个国家在上帝的保佑下，一定要得到自由的新生，这个民有、民治、民享的政府，一定不能从地球上消失。 （许渊冲 译）

三 演讲翻译的批评与赏析练习

原文	译文一	译文二
I am happy to join with you today in what will go down in history as the greatest demonstration for freedom in the history of our nation. Five score years ago, a great American, in whose symbolic shadow we stand signed the Emancipation Proclamation. This momentous decree came as a great beacon light of hope to millions of Negro slaves who had been seared in the flames of withering injustice. It came as a joyous daybreak to end the long night of captivity. But one hundred years later, we must face the tragic fact that the Negro is still not free. One hundred years later, the life of the Negro is still sadly crippled by the manacles of segregation	一百年前，一位伟大的美国人签署了解放黑奴宣言，今天我们就是在他的雕像前集会。这一庄严宣言犹如灯塔的光芒，给千百万在那摧残生命的不义之火中受煎熬的黑奴带来了希望。它之到来犹如欢乐的黎明，结束了束缚黑人的漫漫长夜。 然而一百年后的今天，我们必须正视黑人还没有得到自由这一悲惨的事实。一百年后的今天，在种族隔离的镣铐和种族歧视的枷锁下，黑人的生活备受压榨。一百年后的今天，黑人仍生活在物质充裕的海洋中一个	我很高兴同你们一道参加今天的集会，这次集会为自由而进行，它将永垂青史。 现在，我们正站在一位伟大的美国人的雕像前。一百年前，正是这位伟大的美国人签署了《解放黑奴宣言》。这是一个庄严的宣言，它犹如伟大的灯塔，给千百万一直在摧残生命的不义之火中备受煎熬的黑人奴隶们带来了希望的光芒。它犹如欢乐的黎明，结束了黑人们受奴役的漫漫长夜。可是一百年之后的今天，我们还要面对这样一个悲惨的事实：黑人仍然没有得到自由！ 一百年之后的今天，黑人们仍然要戴着种族隔离的镣铐

译文三	译文四	笔 记
段。现在倒是该轮到我们在这里献身于摆在我们面前的伟大任务的时候了。从这些光荣牺牲的人们的身上，我们要不断汲取忠诚，去献身于他们为之付出最后一片赤诚之心的事业。在这里，我们要庄严承诺，烈士们的鲜血不会白流。我们这个国家，在上帝的庇佑之下，一定会获得自由的新生。我们这个产生于民、管理依民、施政为民的政府一定会永世长存。 （李明 译）	务：这些值得尊敬的先烈们为了自己的事业竭尽忠诚、鞠躬尽瘁，我们应当继承他们的遗志，为我们的事业奉献更多的至诚。在此，我们下定决心，更努力使他们的鲜血不会白流，决心使我们的国家在上帝的护佑下在自由中获得新生，决心使我们这个民有、民治、民享的政府永世长存。 （姚媛 译）	

原 文	译文一	译文二
and the chains of discrimination. One hundred years later, the Negro lives on a lonely island of poverty in the midst of a vast ocean of material prosperity. One hundred years later, the Negro is still languishing in the corners of American society and finds himself an exile in his own land. So we have come here today to dramatize an appalling condition. In a sense we have come to our nation's capital to cash a check. When the architects of our republic wrote the magnificent words of the Constitution and the Declaration of Independence, they were signing a promissory note to which every American was to fall heir. This note was a promise that all men would be guaranteed the inalienable	穷困的孤岛上。一百年后的今天，黑人仍然萎缩在美国社会的角落里，并且意识到自己是故土家园中的流亡者。今天我们在这里集会，就是要把这种骇人听闻的情况公诸于众。 就某种意义而言，今天我们是为了要求兑现诺言而汇集到我们国家的首都来的。我们共和国的缔造者草拟宪法和独立宣言的气壮山河的词句时，曾向每一个美国人许下了诺言。他们承诺给予所有的人以生存、自由和追求幸福的不可剥夺的权利。	和种族歧视的枷锁，仍然在过着悲惨而畸形的生活。一百年之后的今天，黑人们仍然生活在贫穷的孤岛上，而孤岛的周围却是物质富足的汪洋大海。一百年之后的今天，黑人们仍然在美国社会的各个角落里呻吟，并且发现自己竟然在自己的土地上是漂泊的浮萍，无处是自己的家。 我们今天到这里集会，就是要把这种骇人听闻的情况公之于众。从某种意义上说，我们今天来到祖国的首都，是要求兑现诺言的。当共和国的缔造者们写下《宪法》和《独立宣言》中那气壮河山的词句时，他们就是在签署一项每个美国人都会继承的"期票"。

原　文

rights of life, liberty, and the pursuit of happiness. It is obvious today that America has defaulted on this promissory note insofar as her citizens of color are concerned. Instead of honoring this sacred obligation, America has given the Negro people a bad check which has come back marked "insufficient funds".

But we refuse to believe that the bank of justice is bankrupt. We refuse to believe that there are insufficient funds in the great vaults of opportunity of this nation. So we have come to cash this check—a check that will give us upon demand the riches of freedom and the security of justice.

We have also come to this hallowed spot to remind America of the fierce urgency of now. This is no time to engage in the luxury of cooling off or to take the tranquilizing drug of gradualism. Now is the time to rise from the dark and desolate valley of segregation to the sunlit path of racial justice. Now is the time to open the doors of opportunity to all of God's children. Now is the time to lift our nation from the quicksands of racial injustice to the solid rock of brotherhood.

It would be fatal for the nation to overlook the urgency of the moment and to underestimate the determination of the Negro. This sweltering summer of the Negro's legitimate discontent will

译文一

就有色公民而论，美国显然没有实践她的诺言。美国没有履行这项神圣的义务，只是给黑人开了一张空头支票，支票上盖着"资金不足"的戳子后便退了回来。但是我们不相信正义的银行已经破产。我们不相信，在这个国家巨大的机会之库里已没有足够的储备。因此今天我们要求将支票兑现——这张支票将给予我们宝贵的自由和正义的保障。

我们来到这个圣地也是为了提醒美国，现在是非常急迫的时刻。现在决非侈谈冷静下来或服用渐进主义的镇静剂的时候。现在是实现民主的诺言的时候。现在是从种族隔离的荒凉阴暗的深谷攀登种族平等的光明大道的时候。现在是向上帝所有的儿女开放机会之门的时候。现在是把我们的国家从种族不平等的流沙中拯救出来，置于兄弟情谊的磐石上的时候。

如果美国忽视时间的迫切性和低估黑人的决心，那么，这对美国来说，将是致命伤。自由和平等的爽朗秋天如不到来，黑人义愤填膺的酷暑

译文二

这张期票许诺：所有人都被赋予生存、自由和追求幸福的权利，这些权利是不可剥夺的。但是到今天，就有色公民而言，美国显然没有兑现这张期票。美国没有履行这项神圣的义务，而是给黑人开了一张假支票，支票上印着"资金不足"的字样被退了回来。但是，我们拒绝相信正义的银行已经破产，拒绝相信在我们这个有着巨大机会宝库的国家中会出现资金短缺的现象。

我们来到这里就是要兑现这张支票——这张在我们的要求之下将赋予我们自由这笔财富和正义得以保障的支票。我们来到这片圣地，也是想提醒美国人现在这一时刻的极端紧迫性。现在不是奢谈冷静下来或者服用渐进主义的镇静剂的时候。现在是从种族隔离的阴暗而荒凉的深谷中爬到种族平等的光明大道上的时候。现在是向所有上帝的儿女们开放机会之门的时候。现在是把我们的祖国从种族不平等的流沙中拯救出来并置身于手足情谊的坚实磐石上的时候。

如果美国忽视"现在"这个时间的紧迫性，低估黑人们的决心，那对美国来说将是致命的。如果充满自由与平等的凉爽的秋天不到来，黑人们的这个义愤填膺的酷暑就不会过去。一九六三年不是一个终点，

原文	译文一	译文二
not pass until there is an invigorating autumn of freedom and equality. Nineteen sixty-three is not an end, but a beginning. Those who hope that the Negro needed to blow off steam and will now be content will have a rude awakening if the nation returns to business as usual. There will be neither rest nor tranquility in America until the Negro is granted his citizenship rights. The whirlwinds of revolt will continue to shake the foundations of our nation until the bright day of justice emerges.

But there is something that I must say to my people who stand on the warm threshold which leads into the palace of justice. In the process of gaining our rightful place we must not be guilty of wrongful deeds. Let us not seek to satisfy our thirst for freedom by drinking from the cup of bitterness and hatred. We must forever conduct our struggle on the high plane of dignity and discipline. We must not allow our creative protest to degenerate into physical violence. Again and again we must rise to the majestic heights of meeting physical force with soul force.

The marvelous new militancy which has engulfed the Negro community must not lead us to distrust of all white people, for many of our white brothers, as evidenced by their presence here today, have come to realize that their destiny is tied up with our destiny and their freedom is inextricably bound to | 就不会过去。一九六三年并不意味着斗争的结束，而是开始。有人希望，黑人只要消消气就会满足；如果国家安之若素，毫无反应，这些人必会大失所望的。黑人得不到公民的权利，美国就不可能有安宁或平静。正义的光明的一天不到来，叛乱的旋风就将继续动摇这个国家的基础。

但是对于等候在正义之宫门口的心急如焚的人们，有些话我是必须说的。在争取合法地位的过程中，我们不要采取错误的做法。我们不要为了满足对自由的渴望而抱着敌对和仇恨之杯痛饮。我们斗争时必须永远举止得体，纪律严明。我们不能容许我们的具有崭新内容的抗议蜕变为暴力行动。我们要不断地升华到以精神力量对付物质力量的崇高境界中去。

现在黑人社会充满着了不起的新的战斗精神，但是我们却不能因此而不信任所有的白人。因为我们的许多白人兄弟已经认识到，他们的命运与我们的命运是紧密相连的，他们今天参加游行集会就是明证。他们的自 | 而是一个起点。那些希望黑人们只需消消气就会满足的人一定会突然惊醒，一定会后悔莫及的——只要美国让此事回复到原来的状态。只有黑人们被赋予公民的权利，美国才会有太平与宁静。

充满正义的光明的日子一天不到来，反叛的旋风就会继续动摇整个美国的基础。但是，对于那些正站在通向那温暖的正义殿堂之门的人们，我有话要对你们说。在争取合法地位过程中，我们一定不要因采取不正当行为而成为历史的罪人。我们一定不要以痛饮苦难和仇恨之杯为代价来满足对自由的渴求。

我们在斗争时必须永远达到既有尊严又有纪律的崇高境界。我们不能够容忍我们那富于创造性的抗议活动退化为暴力行动。一遍又一遍地，我们要达到以精神的力量去赢得物质的力量这种崇高的境界。

一直以来，整个黑人社会在弥漫着新一轮的非凡战斗精神，但这不能够让我们对所有白人都持怀疑态度，因为我们的许多白人兄弟——有他们出席今天的集会为证——已经认识到，他们的命运与我们的命运紧密相连，他们的自由与我们的自由息息相关。 |

原 文

our freedom.

We cannot walk alone.

And as we walk, we must make the pledge that we shall march ahead.

We cannot turn back.

There are those who are asking the devotees of civil rights, "When will you be satisfied?" We can never be satisfied as long as the Negro is the victim of the unspeakable horrors of police brutality. We can never be satisfied as long as our bodies, heavy with the fatigue of travel, cannot gain lodging in the motels of the highways and the hotels of the cities. We cannot be satisfied as long as the Negro's basic mobility is from a smaller ghetto to a larger one. We can never be satisfied as long as a Negro in Mississippi cannot vote and a Negro in New York believes he has nothing for which to vote. No, no, we are not satisfied, and we will not be satisfied until justice rolls down like waters and righteousness like a mighty stream.

I am not unmindful that some of you have come here out of great trials and tribulations. Some of you have come fresh from narrow cells. Some of you have come from areas where your quest for freedom left you battered by the storms of persecution and staggered by the winds of police brutality.

译文一

由与我们的自由是息息相关的。我们不能单独行动。

当我们行动时，我们必须保证向前进。我们不能倒退。现在有人问热心民权运动的人，"你们什么时候才能满足？"

只要黑人仍然遭受警察难以形容的野蛮迫害，我们就绝不会满足。

只要我们在外奔波而疲乏的身躯不能在公路旁的汽车旅馆和城里的旅馆找到住宿之所，我们就绝不会满足。

只要黑人的基本活动范围只是从少数民族聚居的小贫民区转移到大贫民区，我们就绝不会满足。

只要密西西比仍然有一个黑人不能参加选举，只要纽约有一个黑人认为他投票无济于事，我们就绝不会满足。

不！我们现在并不满足，我们将来也不满足，除非正义和公正犹如江海之波涛，汹涌澎湃，滚滚而来。

我并非没有注意到，

译文二

我们不能够单独行动。我们行动时，一定要保证向前行进。我们不能够倒退。现在有人在询问热心民权运动的人，"你们什么时候才会满意？"

只要我们那奔波劳累而疲惫的身体不能够在公路旁的汽车旅馆和城市里的旅馆里找到安顿之所，我们就绝不会满意。

只要黑人们的基本活动范围只限于从小贫民区到大贫民区，我们就不会满意。

只要密西西比州有一个黑人不能投票选举，纽约市里有一个黑人认为他投票没有意义，我们就绝不会满意。

决不会的！决不会的！我们现在不会满意的，我们将来也不会满意，除非正义恰似江水滚滚而来，除非公正犹如汹涌的波涛，势如破竹。

我并非没有注意到，今天参加集会的人当中，你们有些人历尽了苦难和折磨；有些人刚刚从窄小的牢房中解脱出来；有些人则来自这样一些地方：在那里，你因追求自由而受到暴风雨般的迫害使得你心力交瘁，你因追求自由而受到警察狂风般野蛮行径的摧残使得你步履蹒跚。一直以来，你们都是人为痛苦的长期受难

原　文	译文一	译文二
You have been the veterans of creative suffering. Continue to work with the faith that unearned suffering is redemptive. Go back to Mississippi, go back to Alabama, go back to South Carolina, go back to Georgia, go back to Louisiana, go back to the slums and ghettos of our northern cities, knowing that somehow this situation can and will be changed. Let us not wallow in the valley of despair. I say to you today, my friends, that in spite of the difficulties and frustrations of the moment, I still have a dream. It is a dream deeply rooted in the American dream. I have a dream that one day this nation will rise up and live out the true meaning of its creed: "We hold these truths to be self-evident: that all men are created equal." I have a dream that one day on the red hills of Georgia the sons of former slaves and the sons of former slave owners will be able to sit down together at a table of brotherhood. I have a dream that one day even the state of Mississippi, a desert state, sweltering with the heat of injustice and oppression, will be transformed into an oasis of freedom and justice. I have a dream that my four children will one day live in a nation where they will not be judged by the color of their skin but by the content of their character.	参加今天集会的人中，有些受尽苦难和折磨；有些刚刚走出窄小的牢房；有些由于寻求自由，曾在居住地惨遭疯狂迫害的打击，并在警察暴行的旋风中摇摇欲坠。你们是人为痛苦的长期受难者。坚持下去吧，要坚决相信，忍受不应得的痛苦是一种赎罪。 让我们回到密西西比去，回到阿拉巴马去，回到南卡罗来纳去，回到乔治亚去，回到路易斯安那去，回到我们北方城市中的贫民区和少数民族居住区去，要心中有数，这种状况是能够也必将改变的。我们不要陷入绝望而不可自拔。 朋友们，今天我对你们说，在此时此刻，我们虽然遭受种种困难和挫折，我仍然有一个梦想。这个梦想是深深扎根于美国的梦想中的。 我梦想有一天，这个国家会站立起来，真正实现其信条的真谛："我们认为这些真理是不言而喻的：人人生而平等。" 我梦想有一天，在乔治亚的红山上，昔日奴	者。你们一定要坚持这样一种信念：不该忍受的痛苦一定要得到补偿。 回到密西西比州去吧，回到阿拉巴马州去吧，回到乔治亚州去吧，回到路易斯安那州去吧，回到我们北方城市中的贫民区和少数民族居住区去吧，带着这样一个信念：这种状况会得到改变的，这种状况一定会得到改变。我们不要沉沦于绝望的低谷。 今天我要对你们说，朋友们，此时此刻，我们虽然遭受种种困难和挫折，我仍然有个梦想。这个梦想深深地扎根于美国梦中。 我梦想有一天，这个国家会直起身子，赋予自己的信条以真正的意义："我们坚信这个真理不言而喻：人人生而平等。" 我梦想有一天，在乔治亚州那红色的山顶上，昔日奴隶的儿子和昔日奴隶主的儿子将能坐在一块儿，共叙兄弟情谊。 我梦想有一天，甚至连密西西比这个在空中充满着非正义和压迫的沙漠之州，也会转变成自由和正义的绿洲。 我梦想有一天，我的四个孩子将生活在一个不是以他们的肤色，而是以他们的品格优

原文	译文一	译文二
I have a dream today! I have a dream that one day the state of Alabama, whose governor's lips are presently dripping with the words of interposition and nullification, will be transformed into a situation where little black boys and black girls will be able to join hands with little white boys and white girls and walk together as sisters and brothers. I have a dream today! I have a dream that one day every valley shall be exalted, every hill and mountain shall be made low, the rough places will be made plain, and the crooked places will be made straight, and the glory of the Lord shall be revealed, and all flesh shall see it together. This is our hope. This is the faith with which I return to the South. With this faith, we will be able to hew out of the mountain of despair a stone of hope. With this faith we will be able to transform the jangling discords of our nation into a beautiful symphony of brotherhood. With this faith we will be able to work together, to pray together, to struggle together, to go to jail together, to stand up for freedom together, knowing that we will be free one day. And this will be the day—this will be	隶的儿子将能够和昔日奴隶主的儿子坐在一起，共叙兄弟情谊。 我梦想有一天，甚至连密西西比州这个正义匿迹，压迫成风，如同沙漠般的地方，也将变成自由和正义的绿洲。 我梦想有一天，我的四个孩子将在一个不是以他们的肤色，而是以他们的品格优劣来评价他们的国度里生活。 我今天有一个梦想。 我梦想有一天，阿拉巴马州能够有所转变，尽管该州州长现在仍然满口异议，反对联邦法令，但有朝一日，那里的黑人男孩和女孩将能与白人男孩和女孩情同骨肉，携手并进。 我今天有一个梦想。 我梦想有一天，幽谷上升，高山下降，坎坷曲折之路成坦途，圣光披露，满照人间。 这就是我们的希望。我怀着这种信念回到南方。有了这个信念，我们将能从绝望之巅劈出一	劣来评判他们的国度里。 今天我有个梦想。 我梦想有一天，阿拉巴马州会变成另一个样子，而不是目前这种连州长都是满口持反对意见并极力主张废除联邦法令的状况。我梦想那时黑人男孩和黑人女孩将能够同白人男孩和白人女孩手牵着手，像兄弟姐妹一样共同并进。 今天我有个梦想。 我梦想有一天，河谷会升平，山脉变平地，崎岖的山地变成平原，曲折的道路变成通途，上帝的光辉会显灵，全人类会沐浴于上帝的光辉之中。 这就是我们的希望。这就是我回到南方所怀有的信念。 怀着这个信念，我们一定能够从绝望的高山上劈出一块希望之石。 怀着这个信念，我们一定能够把这个国家中刺耳的嘈杂声变成一支洋溢着手足情谊的优美的交响曲。 怀着这个信念，我们一定能够一起工作，一起祈祷，一起斗争，一起坐监狱，一起维护自由，因为我们知道，我们终将有一天会获得自由的。

原 文	译文一	译文二
the day when all of God's children will be able to sing with a new meaning: "My country, 'tis of thee, sweet land of liberty, of thee I sing. Land where my fathers died, land of the pilgrim's pride, From every mountainside, let freedom ring." And if America is to be a great nation, this must become true. So let freedom ring from the prodigious hilltops of New Hampshire. Let freedom ring from the mighty mountains of New York. Let freedom ring from the heightening Alleghenies of Pennsylvania! Let freedom ring from the snowcapped Rockies of Colorado! Let freedom ring from the curvaceous peaks of California! But not only that: Let freedom ring from Stone Mountain of Georgia! Let freedom ring from Lookout Mountain of Tennessee!	块希望之石。有了这个信念，我们将能把这个国家刺耳争吵的声音，改变成为一支洋溢手足之情的优美交响曲。 有了这个信念，我们将能一起工作，一起祈祷，一起斗争，一起坐牢，一起维护自由；因为我们知道，终有一天，我们是会自由的。 在自由到来的那一天，上帝的所有儿女们将以新的含义高唱这支歌："我的祖国，美丽的自由之乡，我为您歌唱。您是父辈逝去的地方，您是最初移民的骄傲，让自由之声响彻每个山岗。" 如果美国要成为一个伟大的国家，这个梦想必须实现。让自由之声从新罕布什尔州的巍峨峰巅响起来！让自由之声从纽约州的崇山峻岭响起来！让自由之声从宾夕法尼亚州阿勒格尼山的顶峰响起来！ 让自由之声从科罗拉多州冰雪覆盖的洛基山响起来！让自由之声从加利福尼亚州蜿蜒的群峰响起来！不仅如此，	那一天，上帝的所有儿女将会以新的意义放声歌唱："我的祖国，您是自由的乐土，我为您歌唱。您是我父辈安息的地方，您是最初移居美国的公民的骄傲，您要让自由之声响彻每一道山岗。" 如果美国要成为一个伟大的国家，这个梦想必须实现。 所以， 让自由之声响彻新罕布什尔州巍峨的山巅吧！ 让自由之声响彻纽约州的巍巍群山吧！ 让自由之声响彻宾夕法尼亚州高耸入云的阿勒格尼山吧！ 让自由之声响彻科罗拉多州冰雪覆盖的落基山脉吧！ 让自由之声响彻加利福尼亚州婀娜多姿的山峰吧！ 还有， 让自由之声响彻乔治亚州的石头山吧！ 让自由之声响彻田纳西州的观景峰吧！

原　文	译文一	译文二
Let freedom ring from every hill and every molehill of Mississippi.

From every mountainside, let freedom ring.

When we let freedom ring, when we let it ring from every village and every hamlet, from every state and every city, we will be able to speed up that day when all of God's children, black men and white men, Jews and Gentiles, Protestants and Catholics, will be able to join hands and sing in the words of the old Negro spiritual:

"Free at last! Free at last!

Thank God Almighty, we are free at last!"

(Martin Luther King, "I Have a Dream") | 还要让自由之声从乔治亚州的石巅响起来！让自由之声从田纳西州的瞭望山响起来！

　　让自由之声从密西西比的每一座丘陵响起来！让自由之声从每一片山坡响起来！

　　当我们让自由之声响起来，让自由之声从每一个大小村庄、每一个州和每一个城市响起来时，我们将能够加速这一天的到来，那时，上帝的所有儿女，黑人和白人，犹太教徒和非犹太教徒，耶稣教徒和天主教徒，都将手携手，合唱一首古老的黑人灵歌："终于自由啦！终于自由啦！感谢全能的上帝，我们终于自由啦！" | 让自由之声响彻密西西比州的每一道山丘吧！

　　让自由之声响彻每一道山岗吧！

　　当我们让自由之声响起来的时候，当我们让自由之声在每一个村庄、每一个部落、每一个州、每一个城市响起来的时候，我们一定能够加速这一天的来临：这一天，所有上帝的孩子们，黑人和白人，犹太人和非犹太人，新教徒和天主教徒，将能够手挽着手，合唱一首古老的黑人灵歌："终于自由啦！终于自由啦！感谢全能的上帝，我们终于自由了！"

（李明　译） |

原　文	译文一	译文二
Hillary Clinton's DNC Remarks DENVER, August 26, 2008

I am honored to be here tonight. A proud mother. A proud Democrat. A proud American. And a proud supporter of Barack Obama.

My friends, it is time to take back the country we love. | 希拉里在民主党全国代表大会上的演讲（部分）

　　今天晚上我很有幸，作为一个自豪的妈妈、一个自豪的民主党人、一个自豪的美国人、一个自豪的Barack Obama的支持者而站在这里。 | 希拉里在民主党全国代表大会上的演讲（部分）

　　今晚我很荣幸，以一个自豪的母亲、自豪的民主党人、自豪的美国人、自豪的巴拉克·奥巴马的支持者的身份，站在这里。

　　朋友们，现在正是收回我 |

原 文	译文一	译文二

原文

Whether you voted for me, or voted for Barack, the time is now to unite as a single party with a single purpose. We are on the same team, and none of us can sit on the sidelines.

This is a fight for the future. And it's a fight we must win.

I haven't spent the past 35 years in the trenches advocating for children, campaigning for universal health care, helping parents balance work and family, and fighting for women's rights at home and around the world … to see another Republican in the White House squander the promise of our country and the hopes of our people.

And you haven't worked so hard over the last 18 months, or endured the last eight years, to suffer through more failed leadership.

No way. No how. No McCain.

Barack Obama is my candidate. And he must be our President.

Tonight we need to remember what a Presidential election is really about. When the polls have closed, and the ads are finally off the air, it comes down to you—the American people, your lives, and your children's futures.

译文一

我的朋友们,该把我们热爱的国家接管过来了。

无论你们投票选我还是选 Obama,现在应该为了同一个目的把我们党团结在一起。我们是同一个团队,我们任何人都不能袖手旁观。

这是一场基于未来的战斗,这是一场为了胜利的战斗。

在过去的 35 年中,我一直为了孩子们而呼吁,为了普及每个人的医疗保健而竞选,帮助父母平衡工作与家庭的关系,为妇女在家庭与单位的权利而努力——我们不想看到另一个共和党人坐在白宫浪费我们国家的承诺和人们的希望。

你们在过去 18 个月中以前所未有的精神努力工作,在过去 8 年中受尽了煎熬,再也不能忍受一个更加失败的领导。

不可能,没有理由,不需要 McCain。

Obama 是我的候选人,他必须当选我们的总统。

今天晚上我们需要回忆总统选举的深刻内涵。当投票结束、广告消失,就轮到

译文二

们所热爱的国家的时候了。

不管你们是投我的票还是投巴拉克的票,现在正是为了一个共同的目的团结一心的时候。我们同舟共济,我们当中,没有人有理由袖手旁观。

这是一场致力于未来的战斗,也是一场我们必须取得胜利的战斗。

过去 35 年中,我一直战斗在第一线,为孩子们的利益到处呼吁,为普罗大众的卫生保健四处活动,为天下父母平衡工作与家庭之关系提供帮助,为国内乃至全世界妇女们的权利而奋斗……(我做这一切的目的),不是想看到白宫里又出现一个共和党人,糟蹋我们的国家作出的承诺,糟蹋我们的人民寄予的希望。

在过去一年半中,你们那么拼命地工作,在过去八年中,你们忍受了苦难,其目的不是要历经更加失败的领导而遭受痛苦。

那绝对不行!那无论如何不行!绝对不能是麦凯恩。

巴拉克·奥巴马就是我选的总统。他必须是我们的总统。

今晚我们需要回顾一下选举总统的意义所在。当投票

原　文	译文一	译文二

原文：

For me, it's been a privilege to meet you in your homes, your workplaces, and your communities. Your stories reminded me everyday that America's greatness is bound up in the lives of the American people—your hard work, your devotion to duty, your love for your children, and your determination to keep going, often in the face of enormous obstacles.

You taught me so much, you made me laugh, and ... you even made me cry. You allowed me to become part of your lives. And you became part of mine.

I will always remember the single mom who had adopted two kids with autism, didn't have health insurance and discovered she had cancer. But she greeted me with her bald head painted with my name on it and asked me to fight for health care.

I will always remember the young man in a Marine Corps T-shirt who waited months for medical care and said to me: "Take care of my buddies; a lot of them are still over there. ...and then will you please help take care of me?"

I will always remember the boy who told me his mom worked for the minimum wage and that her employer had cut her hours. He

译文一：

为你们美国人、你们的生活、你们的未来而努力了。

对我来说，优先考虑在你们家、你们车间、你们社区接见你们。你们的故事每天都在提醒我，美国的伟大与美国人的生活紧紧相连，你们的努力工作，你们的对责任的献身，你们对孩子们的爱，你们持之以恒的决心，经常面对巨大的阻力。

你们教会了我太多的东西，你们使我笑，你们也使我哭泣。你们允许我成为你们生活中的一部分，你们也变成了我生活中的一部分。

我经常想起一个单身妈妈，她孤单地养活着两个小孩，没有医保还发现身患癌症。但是她在没有头发的头顶上写上我的名字，请求我为医保而努力。

我经常想起一个等候数月等待医疗、身穿海军陆战队T恤的青年人，他对我说："照顾好我的伙伴，他们很多人仍在那里等待，你能也帮助照料我吗？"

我经常想起一个小男孩，他告诉我他妈妈挣最低工资，其老板克扣她数小时的工资。他说不知道未来其家庭会怎么样。

译文二：

结束、最终不再进行广告宣传时，总统选举就意味着你们——意味着美国人民，意味着你们的生活，意味着你们孩子的未来！

对我来说，在你们的家、你们的工作地、你们的社区见到你们，一直都是我的荣幸。你们的经历曾每天让我想起，美国的伟大同美国人民的生活密切相连——生活中的你们，工作上兢兢业业，忠于职守，热爱自己的孩子，并且在面临巨大挑战时，仍然坚毅地奋然前行。

是你们教会了我这些，是你们让我笑，……是你们甚至让我哭。是你们让我成为你们生活中的一部分，而你们也成为我生活中的一部分。

我永远不会忘记那位收养了两位自闭症孩子、自己没有医疗保险并发现自己患上了癌症的单身母亲。而她却以涂上我名字的光头向我问候，并要求我继续为卫生保健努力。

我永远不会忘记那位穿着海军陆战队T恤的年轻人，他等了数月的医疗护理并告诉我："去照顾我的伙伴们吧。他们有很多人还在那里呢。那烦请您能帮我这个忙吗？"

我永远不会忘记曾告诉我他母亲拿着最低工资去工

原文	译文一	译文二
said he just didn't know what his family was going to do. I will always be grateful to everyone from all fifty states, Puerto Rico and the territories, who joined our campaign on behalf of all those people left out and left behind by the Bush Administration. To my supporters, my champions—my sisterhood of the traveling pantsuits—from the bottom of my heart: Thank you. You never gave in. You never gave up. And together we made history.	我总是感谢来自50个州和Puerto Rico及其辖区的每一个人，他们加入我们的选举，代表着每一个被布什政府遗弃的那些人们。 我从内心感谢你们，我的支持者，我的拥护者，我的穿旅游便服的姐妹们。 你们从来没有屈服，你们从来没有放弃。我们一起改变了历史。	作，而她的雇主却克扣她小时数的那个男孩。他说他就是不知道他家将怎样过活。 我要永远感激来自美国五十个州、来自波多黎各、来自联邦属地的每一个人。是他们代表了被布什政府忽视和忘记的所有人加入了我们的竞选活动。 对我的所有支持者，对我的拥护者——旅游时穿着便服的姐妹们——从内心深处，我要说：谢谢你们！ 你们未曾屈服。你们未曾放弃。你我一起，我们创造了历史。 （李明　译）

第六部分

信函翻译的批评赏析

一 关于信函

"书信是生命的安慰。"这是法国启蒙运动思想家伏尔泰的名言。"烽火连三月,家书抵万金。"这是中国诗圣杜甫的名句。关于书信,黄继忠(1987: v-x)先生在其翻译的《名人书信一百封》之中作了很好的归纳和总结:

> 书信,对于人生,有着重要意义。在家的父母收到游子远方的来信,会立刻释念;出门在外的丈夫,在收到妻子的平安家报,会顿时欣慰无比;热恋中的情侣,在收到心上人的情书,会感到如饮琼浆、甘甜无比;亲朋挚友,当收到相互间的来信,通过书信相互学习、相互切磋、相互帮助、相互鼓励、相互支持、共同探索人生奥秘、相互倾诉心中烦恼,无不令人感到快慰,其乐融融。

书信,对于人生,有着巨大魅力。对此,法国12世纪时的多情女子艾绿伊思(Heloise)在给爱人阿伯拉(Peter Abelard)的信中说得非常透彻:"有什么感情是书信所不能抒发的呢?书信有灵魂;书信能说话;书信具有表达喜怒哀乐的一切本领;书信具有各种激情的全部烈焰;书信能使激情上升,就跟当事人本身在场一样;书信具有语言的全部温柔与细腻,有时甚至具有语言所望尘莫及的大胆表达力。书信最初发明时,就是为了安慰像我这样的寂寞的人服务的!……自从丧失了见到你、占有你的那种实质性乐趣之后,我只有在你的书信中寻求安慰,以弥补这种损失于万一。在书信中,我可以读到你最圣洁的思想。"

书信,是印证历史的源泉。美国著名史学家卡尔·贝克(Carl Becker)曾说:"历史大事记,人类所作所为的记载,均是比较丰富和充足的。然而,关于产生这些事件的心理状态的记载,关于可供我们剖析隐藏在公诸于世的宗旨以及既定行动纲领后面的那些复杂的本能和感情的记载却非常缺乏。人们作这类研究所需要的是一些私人文字——回忆录和(最主要的是)书信。因为在书信中,人们总是自觉或不自觉地流露出隐藏在内心深处的行为动机来。"由此可见,书信对于史学家们来说是多么的弥足珍贵啊!

书信的作用就在于:它向我们揭示出历史上重大事件下面渺小的一面,同时还提醒我们:历史曾经一度是实实在在的生活。书信告诉我们,名人在最典型、最光辉和最可怕的时刻的生活情况:有充满激情的生活,有赤裸裸的生活,有困厄危亡中的生活,有登峰造极时的生活。通过这些书信,我们不但可以印证历史事件,还可以看到人物的性格特点和脾气。有时在一封信中,一个伟人有血有肉的形象会活生生地呈现在我们面前。读这些书信时,我们的感情也往往不由自主地为大人物的感情所左右。

可见,书信是历史和现实的见证和反映。

二 书信的翻译

在实际生活中,我们见到最多的是商务书信。但商务书信不是我们这里要关注的对象。这里我们所关注的是在西方已经成为一种准文学形式的书信。作为准文学形式的书信,有着很高的文学价值和美学价值。这类书信有很多。比如在中国,晋朝时李密为侍奉祖母而向皇帝推辞官职的《陈情表》、诗人李白的《与韩荆州书》、司马迁的《报任安书》、李陵的《答苏武书》、诸葛亮的前后《出师表》等,都曾经是脍炙人口的书信。

由于书信主要用于传达个人情感,故它主要具备情感功能。翻译时,最为重要的是把握写信人的口吻和语气,将写信人的情感充分传达出来。因篇幅所限,我们这里选取了英国文学史上最为著名的书信之一《致切斯菲尔德伯爵书》("Letter to Lord Chesterfield")以及《致儿子的一封信》("A Letter to My Son")作为书信翻译赏析和练习。

第十九章 "Letter to Lord Chesterfield" 汉译文的批评赏析

一 关于 "Letter to Lord Chesterfield"

"Letter to Lord Chesterfield" 是一封信函，出自常被称为约翰逊博士（Dr. Johnson）的塞缪尔·约翰逊（Samuel Johnson, 1709—1784）之手。约翰逊是 18 世纪英国著名散文家、文艺批评家和辞书编撰家，英国古典主义代表人物之一。他的前半生名不见经传，真正让他名扬天下，并确立其文坛地位的是他编纂的辞典 *A Dictionary of the English Language*。这部辞典在当时有巨大影响力，对英语语言的规范化使用起到了巨大作用，堪称英语发展史上的里程碑。

编纂这部词典的过程非常艰苦。在当时的英国文坛，文人要想成名，必须要有达官显贵引荐和提携，即必须要有名人作为 patron（恩主，提携人）。当时最显赫的内阁大臣切斯菲尔德伯爵（Earl of Chesterfield）就是这样一位十分有名的"恩主"。约翰逊也将目光投向了他。早在 1747 年，约翰逊就有编纂一本英语辞典的计划，但因工程艰巨，自己的景况又十分窘迫，他便将编纂计划呈送给切斯菲尔德伯爵，希望获得支持与赞助。不料切斯菲尔德伯爵并不看好这一计划。约翰逊几次登门求见，均未被理睬。遭受冷遇的约翰逊并未灰心和气馁，而是自立更生，苦苦奋斗了七年，终于完成这部鸿篇巨制。

然而就在辞典即将出版之际，切斯菲尔德伯爵突然抢先在当时的一家拥有广大读者群的报纸《世界报》上，连续发表了两篇赞美约翰逊词典的文章，旨在暗示自己是约翰逊词典的幕后赞助人。这让约翰逊十分愤怒，于是便写下了这封文笔犀利的信作复。这封信语言精练、结构严谨、寓意深刻、措辞柔中带刚，看似卑微，却语带讥讽，堪称散文中的精品，是英国散文中不可多得的佳作。"此文在欧洲文学史上被看作是作家的'独立宣言'。欧洲文人被迫'摧眉折腰事权贵'的历史，开始了一个崭新的转折。"（张继华，2004：27）

约翰逊的这封信，让我们看到了一位满身傲骨的书生在权势面前那像松柏一般挺拔的浩然气节。

"Letter to Lord Chesterfield" 原文及四种汉译文

原文

Letter to Lord Chesterfield

(7th February 1755)

My Lord,

I have been lately informed, by the proprietor of *The World*, that two Papers, in which my Dictionary is recommended to the Public, were written by your Lordship. To be so distinguished, is an honour, which, being very little accustomed to favours from the Great, I know not well how to receive, or in what terms so acknowledge.

When, upon some slight encouragement, I first visited your Lordship, I was overpowered, like the rest of Mankind, by the enchantment of your address; and could not forbear to wish that I might boast myself Le vainqueur du vainqueur di la terre—that I might obtain that regard for which I saw the world contending; but I found my attendance so little encouraged, that neither pride nor modesty would suffer me to continue it. When I had once addressed your Lordship in public, I had exhausted all the art of pleasing which a retired and uncourtly scholar can possess. I had done all that I could; and no Man is well pleased to have his all neglected, be it ever so little.

译文一

致切斯菲尔德伯爵书

伯爵大人：

近日从《世界报》馆主得知，该报刊载了两篇文章，对拙编词典颇多举荐溢美之词，这些文章据悉均出自阁下您的手笔。承蒙您如此的推荐，本应是一种荣耀，只可惜在下自来无缘得到王公大人的青睐，所以真不知道该如何来领受这份荣耀，也不知道该用些什么言辞来聊表谢意。

回想当年，也不知哪来的勇气，我竟第一次拜访了大人阁下。我像所有的人一样，深为大人的言谈风采所倾倒，不禁玄想他年能口出大言"吾乃天下征服者之征服者也。"——虽知此殊荣是举世学人欲所得，仍希望有朝一日能侥幸获取。然而我很快发现自己的趋走逢迎根本没有得到鼓励。不管是出于自尊也好，自矜也好，我反正无法再周旋下去。我本是一个与世无争、不善逢迎的书生，但那时我也曾用尽平生所学的阿谀逢迎的言辞，当众赞美过阁下。能做的一切我都做了。如果一个人在这方面付出的一切努力（不管是多么微不足道）受到完全的忽视，他是绝不会感到舒服的。

译文二

致切斯菲尔德伯爵书

大人阁下：

顷得《世界报》馆主告知，该报近日揭载二文，对拙编词典，颇有扬善褒荐之词，闻皆出自阁下手笔。厚爱如此，理当引为大幸。奈何在下不惯贵人垂青，茫然不知何以领受、何辞致谢。

忆当年，在下小蒙鼓励，竟斗胆初谒公门。大人之言谈风采，语惊四座，令人绝倒。使在下不禁谬生宏愿：他日或能自诩当世："吾乃天下征服者之征服者也。"——举世学人欲夺之殊荣，或竟鹿死我手！孰料余自度不复干谒此途，自尊与自卑，皆勿与论也。余本一介书生，不善谄辞，不尚交际，而曾一度当众致语阁下，可谓罄尽取悦文饰之辞。仆思已尽犬马之劳，虽功效绵薄，又何甘辛劳遭逢白眼之遇也。

回想当初侍立君堂，甚或见逐门首，忽焉七载飞去。斯年以来，吾力排艰辛，独撑大业，无援手相助，无片言相许，无一

译文三

最近《世界报》老板向本人透露，阁下曾两度在报上撰文，向公众推荐本人的辞典。对于平时极少受到大人物青睐的我来说，获此殊荣真不知该如何领受，如何措辞来表示感谢。

回顾当年我受到些许鼓励，初次拜见阁下时，我也和世人一样，为阁下那非凡的谈吐所深深地折服；不禁奢望能自命为征服世界者的征服者，能够获得阁下的那世人趋之若鹜的关注。但本人的求见竟屡遭冷遇，以至无论是自尊心还是羞耻心都不允许我再勉强行事了。但本人一度公开向阁下讨教时，我竭尽了一个与世无争、不善逢迎的书生所可能有的讨好手段，可谓不遗余力。对于自己所付出的全部努力遭到如此冷遇，无论这种努力是如何微不足道，任何人都会为之愤然的。

伯爵阁下，从我恭候接

译文四

1755年2月7日

伯爵大人阁下：

近闻《人世间》主人言：阁下曾二度撰文，将仆之辞典推荐于世，曷胜荣幸。然仆生平鲜蒙贵人恩典，是以受宠若惊，不知何以答谢。

昔者偶为人言所动，初度造府晋谒；于君之谈吐，一似世人之倾慕无已。实望一登龙门，身价十倍；并冀能博得阁下之青睐，此天下人争相罗致者也。然仆之趋候，颇遭冷遇；其后遂裹足不前，半以孤芳自赏，半以自惭形秽也。仆本一介寒士，不求闻达于世，不善逢迎之术。前者于大庭广众之间得与阁下共语，曲尽所能，以期取悦于君，终不可得。人之竭尽绵薄，辱遭鄙夷而复能怡然自得者，鲜矣哉！

忆昔伫候于外室，见拒于侯门，岁月荏

笔 记

原 文	译文一	译文二
Seven years, My Lord, have now past, since I waited in your outward Rooms, or was repulsed from your Door; during which time I have been pushing on my work through difficulties, of which it is useless to complain, and have brought it, at last, to the verge of Publication, without one Act of assistance, one word of encouragement, or one smile of favor. Such treatment I did not expect, for I never had a Patron before. The Shepherd in Virgil grew at last acquainted with Love, and found him a Native of the Rocks. Is not a Patron, My Lord, one who looks with unconcern on a Man struggling for Life in the water, and, when he has reached ground, encumbers him with help? The notice which you have been pleased to take of my Labours, had it been early, had been kind; but it has been delayed till I am indifferent, and cannot enjoy it; till I am solitary, and cannot impart it; till I am known, and do not want it. I hope it is no very cynical asperity not to confess obligations where no benefit has been received, or to be unwilling that the Public should consider me as owing that to a Patron, which Providence has enabled me to do for myself.	大人阁下，从我第一次候立于贵府门下，或者说被您拒于门外时算起，已经7年过去。7年多来，我一直苦苦地撑持着我的编撰工作。这些苦楚，现在再来倾诉，已经没有用处。所幸我的劳作而今终于快要出版，在这之前我没有获得过一个赞助的行为，一句鼓励的话语，一抹称许的微笑。我固然不曾指望这样的礼遇，因为我从未有过一位赞助人。 维吉尔笔下的牧童最后终于和爱神相识，这才发现所谓爱神只不过是岩穴土人而已。 大人阁下，有的人眼见落水者在水中拼命挣扎而无动于衷，等他安全抵岸之后，却才多余地伸出所谓援手，莫非这就叫赞助人么？大人而今忽有雅兴来关照在下的劳作，这原本是一桩美意，只可惜太迟了一点。迟到我已经意懒心灰，再无法快乐地消受；迟到我已经孤身一人，无从与家人分享；迟到我已经名闻海内，再不需阁下附丽张扬。我既然本来就没有得到过实惠，自然毋需怀感恩之心；既然是上帝助我独立完成这桩大业，我自然不愿让公众产生错觉，似乎我曾受惠于某一赞助人。但愿上面这番话不致被认为太苛刻、太不近人情。 我已经在根本没有所谓学术赞助人赞助的情况下使自己	笑相期。幸得终竟成功，付梓在即。当此时，发怨尤之词，恐无益也。然余实从未曾知遇提携之人，自不曾指望过蒙受恩惠。 维吉尔笔下牧童终与爱神相识，方知爱神原只是草野之夫。 设有人于溺水者奋命中流之际，漠然相对，视若无睹，伺其安全抵岸，方忽急伸援手，反增累赘，所谓赞助人也者，莫非即此辈耶？ 大人而今忽有雅兴垂顾拙编，倘恩泽当初，犹可称善；奈何此惠顾姗姗来迟，我已心灰意冷，受之谅无深趣；我已鸳鸯失伴，有乐无人与共；我已名播天下，再不需阁下扬誉之辞！在下当初既不曾蒙恩，今朝亦无须感德；天帝既助我独成大业，今何敢欺世惑众，默认身后有所谓莫须有之赞助者？在下言辞或有苛刻不敬，还望海涵。 余自承担此编撰业以来，从未获所谓赞助者分毫，亦使大业行将告竣，纵或杀青之际倍感艰难无助，余亦绝无失望之心。奢望赞助之美梦，梦破多

译文三

见却被拒之门外至今,已历时七载。在此期间,我加紧字典的编纂,个中艰难,自不必说。如今终于幸告杀青,行将出版。在此期间未受一桩资助的善行、一句鼓励的言辞,甚至一缕赞同的微笑。这些待遇本人向来就未敢奢望,因为我从来就没有过什么"恩主"!

维吉尔故事中的牧童终于认清了爱神原来是个生长在荒山乱石间的野人。

伯爵阁下,难道恩主能是这样一个人吗——在落水者拼命挣扎呼救时他无动于衷,而当落水者抵达岸边时他却以帮助相累?倘若阁下对我的关注来得早些,那么它会是亲切的。可惜这种关注却姗姗来迟,直到我已心如死水,不能消受;直到我已孤居独处,无法与人共享;直到我已功成名就,不再需要什么关注。没有受到任何恩惠,自然也就没有什么答谢可言。既然上帝赐我独立完成这项工作,我当然也就不愿让公众认为它应该归功于什么"恩主"。我想这样做也不算什么非礼吧!

我在没有什么学术权威恩赐的情况下已将工作

译文四

苒,春秋七易。七岁之间,仆励志孟晋,披荆斩棘,致力于辞书之编著;个中艰辛,今日言之何益?所幸功垂于成,刊行在即,其间未尝获君一臂之助,一言之勖,一笑之惠。惟此等殊遇,原非所期,盖仆生平迄未受恩主之惠。

弗吉尔诗中之牧者,其后终得稔悉"爱童"之为人,方知其为铁石心肠之辈也。

伯爵阁下:见人挣扎于水中则漠漠然袖手旁观,见其安然登岸则遽遽乎殷勤相助,此非恩主之为人乎?阁下于拙著之锦注,若在昔年,诚不失为美意;惜乎姗姗其来迟,今仆已兴味索然,难以欣赏;仆已孑然一身,无人分享;仆已薄有声名,不劳垂颐矣。且仆既未受惠于人,自不欲天下人误以为恩主所赐;此言谅不致失之于尖酸刻薄耳。

仆自编纂辞书以还,既未受惠于任何学术赞助人于前,则

第六部分 信函翻译的批评赏析

原 文	译文一	译文二
Having carried on my work thus far with so little obligation to any Favourer of Learning, I shall not be disappointed though I should conclude it, if less be possible, with less; or I have been long wakened form that Dream of hope, in which I once boasted myself with so much exultation, My Lord, Your Lordship's Most Humble, Most Obedient Servant. Sam. Johnson.	的工作完成到目前这个地步，那么，尽管我将要在更艰难无助的情况下——假如还有可能更艰难无助的话——完成全稿，我也绝不会感到沮丧。因为我已经早就从那个赞助的美梦里幡然猛醒；曾几何时，我还在那梦中得意非凡地自诩是 大人您门下最卑微 最驯顺的仆人 塞缪尔·约翰逊 1755年2月7日 （辜正坤　译）	年；堪笑曾几何时余亦曾梦中顾盼自雄、自诩为 大人您门下最卑微 最驯顺之奴仆 塞缪尔·约翰逊 一千七百五十五年二月初七日 （辜正坤　译）

三 信函翻译的批评与赏析练习

原 文	译文一	译文二
A Letter to My Son Dear Seth, You're only three years old, and at this point in your life you can't read, much less understand what I'm going to try to tell you in this letter. But I've been thinking a lot about the life that you have ahead of you, about my life so far as I reflect on what I've learned, and about my role as a dad in trying to prepare you for the trials that you will face in the coming years.	致儿子的一封信 亲爱的塞斯， 你现在仅仅3岁，此刻你还不识字，更不用说让你去理解我接下来想在这封信里对你所说的话了。但是我已经苦思冥想了好久，关于你即将面临的人生以及我的生活，我反思我所学会的；思考一个父亲的职责，力图让你为未来岁月中即将面临的困难做好充分准备。	致儿子的一封信 亲爱的塞斯， 你现在只有三岁，此刻还不识字，更不用说能明白我在这封信中想对你说的话。但一直以来，我对这几件事情作了诸多思考：你未来的生活、就我对自己所领悟到的一切反思过后我自己的生活，以及在努力让你应对未来岁月所面临的各种考验时我作为父亲的职责。

译文三

推进至此，在工作行将完成之际我更不期望得到什么点滴的恩惠，即使这种可怜的恩惠是可能的话。因为我早已从自己的黄粱美梦中清醒。在这个美梦中，我曾一度极为得意地夸耀过自己是

阁下最谦恭的
最忠实的仆人
塞缪尔·约翰逊

（张继华 译）

译文四

于今大功垂成之日，即无丝毫恩赐于后，亦当不以为憾耳。盖仆昔时固尝陶醉于希望之美梦，今则猛醒久矣。

仆
塞缪尔·约翰逊
顿首再拜

（黄继忠 译）

笔 记

原 文

You won't be able to understand this letter today, but someday, when you're ready, I hope you will find some wisdom and value in what I share with you.

You are young, and life has yet to take its toll on you, to throw disappointments and heartaches and loneliness and struggles and pain into your path. You have not been worn down yet by long hours of thankless work, by the slings and arrows of everyday life.

译文一

你今天并不能理解这封信的含义，但是某一天，当时机成熟，我希望你能在我与你分享的内容当中找寻到些许的智慧和价值。

你还很年轻，生命还尚未开始摧残你，没有在你的人生道路上布置失望、伤心、孤独、挣扎和苦痛。你还没有被漫长的乏味工作，被日常生活的打击搞得筋疲力尽。

因此，谢天谢地吧。你

译文二

眼下你还理解不了这封信的含义，但有一天等你明白事理时，我希望你能在我同你分享的这一切当中，找寻到些许智慧与价值。

你还年轻，生活中的酸甜苦辣你尚未品尝到，人生道路上的各种失望、悲伤、孤独、挣扎与痛苦你尚未体验到。你还没有因长时间没有回报的工作而精疲力竭，没有因日常生活的风刀霜剑而心力交瘁。

仅凭这一点，你要感恩。

原文	译文一	译文二
For this, be thankful. You are at a wonderful stage of life. You have many wonderful stages of life still to come, but they are not without their costs and perils.

I hope to help you along your path by sharing some of the best of what I've learned. As with any advice, take it with a grain of salt. What works for me might not work for you.

Life Can Be Cruel

There will be people in your life who won't be very nice. They'll tease you because you're different, or for no good reason. They might try to bully you or hurt you.

There's not much you can do about these people except to learn to deal with them, and learn to choose friends who are kind to you, who actually care about you, who make you feel good about yourself. When you find friends like this, hold on to them, treasure them, spend time with them, be kind to them, love them.

There will be times when you are met with disappointment instead of success. Life won't always turn out the way you want. This is just another thing you'll have to learn to deal with. But instead of letting these things get you down, push | 正处在人生一个美妙的阶段。还有很多美妙的阶段会来到你面前，但是都不是唾手可得的，你都得付出代价，经历风险。

我希望通过分享一些我所学到的最好的道理能帮助你走好人生路。至于任何建议，且把它当作佐料，因为适合我的并不一定适用于你。

生活会很残酷

你的生活中一定会有并不友好的人。他们耻笑你因为你不同，而没有更好的理由。他们可能会欺负你或者伤害你。

对这种人你除了学会和其接触无计可施，同时你也要学会择友，选择那些对你友善的，那些真正关心你的，那些令你对自己感到很好的人做朋友。当你寻找到像这样的朋友，就一定要坚守这份友谊，珍惜他们，花些时间和他们在一起，友善的对待他们并爱他们。

有时你会遭遇挫折而非成功。生活并不总会如你所愿。这是另一件你需要学会处理的事情。但你要挺住向前，而不是让这些事让你陷入低谷。接受挫败并学会坚 | 你正处在人生美妙的阶段。未来，你还会经历很多人生美妙的阶段，但这些阶段都需付出代价、历经风险。

我希望，在分享我人生领悟的点滴中，你的人生道路更加平坦。就像对其他建议一样，你就有所保留地接受它吧，因为适合于我的并不一定适合于你。

生活有时会很残酷

在你的生活中，一定会有人很不友好。由于你突出，或者不一定有什么原因，他们会取笑你。他们还可能故意欺侮你或伤害你。

对于这种人，除学会对付他们，你无计可施。你要学会与对你友善的人交朋友，与真正关心你的人交朋友，与令你感到自在的人交朋友。一旦交上这样的朋友，就要同他们打成一片，就要珍视他们，就要在他们身上花时间，就要对他们友善，就要热爱他们。

你会碰到挫折而非成功的时候。生活并非总是以你希望的方式呈现。这正是你要学会应对的另一件事情。但不要让这些事情把你弄得垂头丧气，而应勇往直前。要接受失望，学会坚持，学会追寻梦想，哪 |

原文

on. Accept disappointment and learn to persevere, to pursue your dreams despite pitfalls. Learn to turn negatives into positives, and you'll do much better in life.

You will also face heartbreak and abandonment by those you love. I hope you don't have to face this too much, but it happens. Again, not much you can do but to heal, and to move on with your life. Let these pains become stepping stones to better things in life, and learn to use them to make you stronger.

But Be Open to Life Anyway

Yes, you'll find cruelty and suffering in your journey through life … but don't let that close you to new things. Don't retreat from life, don't hide or wall yourself off. Be open to new things, new experiences, new people.

You might get your heart broken 10 times, but find the most wonderful woman the 11th time. If you shut yourself off from love, you'll miss out on that woman, and the happiest times of your life.

You might get teased and bullied and hurt by people you meet … and then after meeting dozens of jerks, find a true friend. If you close yourself off to new peo-

译文一

持,不畏风险地追求你的梦想。学会把消极转化为积极,之后你就能做的好得多。

你同样会面临心碎时刻以及你深爱的人的抛弃。我希望你无须经历太多此类事件,但如果不幸发生了,再一次,除了慢慢愈合心中的创伤并继续下去你的生活,你别无选择。让这些痛苦成为你通向更美好生活的垫脚石,并学会利用它们让自己更坚强。

**但无论如何,
都要张开双臂拥抱生活**

是的,在你的生命历程中你会遇到残酷,煎熬……但不要让这些让你拒绝接受新鲜事物。不要逃避生活,不要躲藏,抑或封闭自己。拥抱新鲜事物,经历全新体验,接触新的人。

你或许心碎了十次,但是在第十一次找到至爱。如果你把自己关在爱的门外,你就会错过这个女子,和你生命中最快乐的时光。

你可能会被你遇到的人耻笑、欺负、伤害……而在见了一打这种稀奇古怪的人后,你会找到一个真正的朋友。如果你拒绝接触新人群,并不向他们敞开心扉,

译文二

怕处处充满陷阱。学会将消极因素转为积极因素,你就会生活得更滋润。

你还会面对难忍的悲伤,遭受你钟爱的人的抛弃。但愿你不必经历太多的这类事件,但这类事情偶尔会发生。同样,除慢慢愈合心灵的创伤并继续生活下去,你无计可施。就让这些痛苦成为你获取生活中更美好事物的探路石,并学会运用它们,使自己更坚强。

但要尽情拥抱生活

的确,在你的生命历程中,你一定会遇到严酷的现实,遭受痛苦的经历……但不要让这个封住你接受新鲜事物的心灵。不要逃离生活,不要将自己躲藏封闭起来。要去拥抱新鲜事物,接受新的体验,见识新的人物。

或许有十次你都伤透了心,但第十一次你却找到了你至爱的女人。如果封闭自己,远离恋爱,你就会错过这个女人,错过你生活中最快乐的时光。

你可能会受到所遇见的人的取笑、欺侮和伤害……而在遇见这帮愚蠢的人之后,你会找到真正的朋友。如果拒绝见

第六部分 信函翻译的批评赏析

原　文	译文一	译文二
ple, and don't open your heart to them, you'll avoid pain ... but also lose out on meeting some incredible people, who will be there during the toughest times of your life and create some of the best times of your life. You will fail many times but if you allow that to stop you from trying, you will miss out on the amazing feeling of success once you reach new heights with your accomplishments. Failure is a stepping stone to success. **Life Isn't a Competition** You will meet many people who will try to outdo you, in school, in college, at work. They'll try to have nicer cars, bigger houses, nicer clothes, cooler gadgets. To them, life is a competition—they have to do better than their peers to be happy. Here's a secret: Life isn't a competition. It's a journey. If you spend that journey always trying to impress others, to outdo others, you're wasting your journey. Instead, learn to enjoy the journey. Make it a journey of Happiness, of constant learning, of continual improvement, of love. Don't worry about having a nicer	你会避免受伤……但是同时也失去了认识这些不可思议的人的机会，他们会在你生命最困难的时刻陪伴着你，并带给你人生当中最美好的时光。 你会失败多次但是如果你让失败打倒了你，不再努力，你就会错过那种当你达到新高度的难以言喻的成就感。失败是成功之母。 **生命不是一场竞赛** 你会遇到一些人，他们总是试图超过你，在中学，大学，在工作中。他们想要拥有更好的车，更大的房子，更好的衣物，更酷的小玩意。对他们来说，生命就是一场竞赛——他们不得不比同辈做得更好来让自己感到快乐。 这里有一个秘诀：生命并不是一场竞赛。而是一段旅程。如果你在途中一直都试图给他人留下深刻印象，超过别人，那你就浪费了这段旅程。与之相反，学会享受它，让之成为快乐之旅，永恒的学习之旅，持久的进步之旅以及爱之旅。	识新的人物，拒绝向他们敞开心扉，你的确会避开痛苦……但同时，你也没有机会去结识那些了不起的人。这些人会在你生命中最艰难的时刻陪伴你，给你创造出人生最美妙的音符。 你会不止一次地遭受失败，但如果你让失败阻挠你进行新的尝试，你就无法领略一旦你以惊人的成就达到新的高度时那种妙不可言的成功的感觉。失败是成功的探路石。 **生活并非竞赛** 中学时，大学时，工作中，你都会遇到很多人，他们总想着要超过你。他们总想着要买更好的车、更大的房子、更高级的服装、更酷的生活用品。对他们来说，生活就是竞赛——他们所追求的快乐就是胜过同辈。 这里的秘诀是：生活并非竞赛。生活是旅程。在这个旅程中，如果你总是想方设法彰显自己，想方设法超过他人，你是在浪费这段旅程。恰恰相反，你要学会享受这段旅程，要让这段旅程成为快乐之旅、不断学习之旅、永远进步之旅、奉献爱心之旅。 不要为拥有一辆更昂贵的

原　文	译文一	译文二
car or house or anything material, or even a better-paying job. None of that matters a whit, and none of it will make you happier. You'll acquire these things and then only want more. Instead, learn to be satisfied with having enough—and then use the time you would have wasted trying to earn money to buy those things … use that time doing things you love. Find your passion, and pursue it doggedly. Don't settle for a job that pays the bills. Life is too short to waste on a job you hate. **Love Should Be Your Rule** If there's a single word you should live your life by, it should be this: Love. It might sound corny, I know … but trust me, there's no better rule in life. Some would live by the rule of success. Their lives will be stressful, unhappy and shallow. Others would live by the rule of selfishness—putting their needs above those of others. They will live lonely lives, and will also be unhappy. Still others will live by the rule of righteousness—trying to show the right path, and admonishing	不要为拥有一辆更好的车或一所更好的房子或者任何物质的东西，即便是一份薪水更高的工作操心。这些根本无足轻重，也不会使你快乐。你可能在拥有了这些之后只是想要更多的。与之相反，学会满足你已经拥有的——然后学会利用你原本想要浪费在为挣钱买这些东西的时间去做你真正热爱的事。 找到你的激情，坚持不懈地追求它。别让自己被一个还债的工作所累。生命太短暂了，更不可将之浪费在你所厌恶的工作上。 **爱应该成为你的生活准则** 如果让一个词成为你的生活支撑的话，那它应该是爱。也许这听来已是老生常谈，我也清楚……但是请信任我，再没有更好的生活准则了。 一些人以成功作为生活准则。他们的生活会很紧张，不开心并且很浅薄。 另一些人的生活准则是个人利益——他们将个人需要置于他人需要之上。他们孤独一生，终究也不会快乐。 还有一些人他们为正义而生——努力展示其道路的正确性，并试图劝服任何一	汽车、一套更高档的房子、一件更高级的实物，甚至一份收入更高的工作而焦躁不安。这些没有一样举足轻重，没有一样会使你更加快乐。你会获得这一切的，然后你只会期望更多。不能这样，要学会对自己所拥有的足够的东西感到满足——然后，利用好你浪费在拼命赚钱来购买那些东西上的时间……利用那个时间去做你喜欢做的事情。 寻找激情，不懈地去追求激情。不要从事仅仅是还债的工作。人生苦短，没有时间浪费在令人讨厌的工作上。 **爱应该就是你的法则** 如果要选择唯一的一个词语来支撑你生活的话，这个词语应该是：爱。我知道，这听起来也许是老生常谈，……但请相信我，生活中再也没有更好的法则。 有些人靠成功的法则生活。于是，他们生活得紧张、缺乏快乐、非常浅薄。 另一些人靠自私的法则生活——他们将个人需要置于他人之上。他们过着孤独的生活，也没有快乐可言。 还有一些人则以正义的法则生活——他们尽力昭示正

原 文	译文一	译文二
anyone who doesn't live by that path. They are concerned with others, but in a negative way, and in the end will only have their own righteousness to live with, and that's a horrible companion.

Live your life by the rule of love. Love your spouse, your children, your parents, your friends, with all of your heart. Give to them what they need, and show them not cruelty nor disapproval nor coldness nor disappointment, but only love. Open your soul to them.

Love not only your loved ones, but your neighbors … your co-workers … strangers … your brothers and sisters in humanity. Offer anyone you meet a smile, a kind word, a kind gesture, a helping hand.

Love not only neighbors and strangers … but your enemy. The person who is cruelest to you, who has been unkind to you … love him. He is a tortured soul, and most in need of your love.

And most of all, love yourself. While others may criticize you, learn not to be so hard on yourself, to think that you're ugly or dumb or unworthy of love … but to think instead that you are a wonderful human being, worthy of Happiness and love … and learn to | 个不以正义为生活准则的人。他们关心他人，却以一种消极的方式，最终怀抱追寻一生的正义而终，而正义却是一个糟糕的伴侣。

用爱支撑你的生命。爱你的妻子，你的孩子，你的父母亲，你的朋友，全心全意地去爱。给与他们你所需要的，不要流露出任何残忍，不赞同，冷漠或者失望，只有爱。向他们敞开灵魂。

不仅仅爱你深爱的人，也要爱你的邻居……你的同事……甚至陌生人……他们是你广义上的兄弟姐妹。给你遇到的任何一个人一个微笑，一句善语。一个友好的姿势，一只援助之手。

不仅仅爱邻居和陌生人……也要爱你的敌人。对你最残酷的人，对曾经对你不善的人……爱他。他是一个备受折磨的灵魂，最需要你的爱。

最重要的是爱你自己。当别人批评你时，学着不要强加自己，去认为自己丑，笨或者不值得去爱……而要想着自己是一个很完美的人，值得拥有幸福和真爱……并学会爱现在的自己。

最后，要知道我爱你并 | 道，并告诫那些偏离正道而生活的任何人。他们关心他人，却以消极的方式，最终只会抱着自己的正义终其一生，这个正义成了可怕的伴侣。

要用爱的法则去生活。爱你的配偶，爱你的孩子，爱你的父母，爱你的朋友，全心全意地。将他们需要的给他们，展现给他们的不是残忍，不是否定，不是冷漠，不是失望，而只是爱。要向他们敞开心扉。

你要热爱的不仅仅是深爱你的人，还有你的邻居……你的同事……陌生人……普天下的兄弟姐妹。对于你碰到的任何人，不要吝惜一个微笑、一句善言、一个友好的姿势、一只援助之手。

你热爱的不仅仅是邻居和陌生人……还要爱你的敌人。那个对你最残酷的人，那个一直对你不友好的人……你要去爱他。他是一个备受煎熬的人，他最需要你的爱。

而最重要的，就是要热爱你自己。别人会批评你，但你要学会不对自己苛刻，要学会不认为自己丑陋、愚笨或不值得爱……相反，你要学会认为自己就是一个出类拔萃的人，是一个值得拥有幸福和爱的人……要学会热爱之所以是你的这个你自己。 |

原　文

love yourself for who you are.

Finally, know that I love you and always will. You are starting out on a weird, scary, daunting, but ultimately incredibly wonderful journey, and I will be there for you when I can. Godspeed.

译文一

且永远都会。你即将开启一段有点奇怪，令人害怕，令人心悸但最终很不可思议的奇妙旅程，我永远会支持你。祝万事如意。

译文二

最后，你要知道我爱你，我永远地爱你。你即将开启的是一段充满奇特、布满荆棘、经受磨难但终将奇妙无比的旅程。只要有可能，我都会与你相伴。祝你一路平安。

（李明　译）

第七部分

戏剧翻译的批评赏析

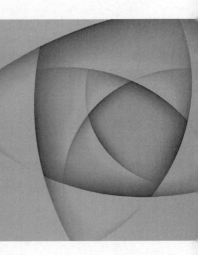

一 关于戏剧

"戏剧"一词在英语中有两个对应语，即 drama 和 theatre。前者侧重戏剧的文学性或可阅读性（readability），后者侧重它的舞台性或可表演性（performability）。正是这种文学性或可阅读性和舞台性或可表演性，铸就了戏剧的双重特性。

"戏剧"有广义和狭义之分。广义的戏剧有戏曲、话剧、歌剧等，狭义的戏剧专指话剧。在西方，戏剧主要是指狭义的戏剧，即话剧。而在中国，19 世纪之前的各类剧种均属戏曲体系，19 世纪 40 年代起，引入了西方的戏剧形式。故现代中国戏剧泛指戏曲、话剧和歌剧等。

戏剧的内涵非常丰富，它运用文学、导演、表演、音乐、美术等艺术手段来塑造人物并反映社会生活。因此，我们可以将戏剧定义为"一种以剧本为基础，通过演员的表演，运用舞蹈、音乐、美术等多种艺术手段来塑造人物形象，反映社会生活的综合性的舞台艺术"（党争胜，2008：83）。

中国晚明时期戏剧评论家王骥德在论及戏剧创作时认为，剧作家在创作戏剧时要充分把握戏剧的"全体力量"。这种"全体力量"包括结构安排、情节线索、情感意蕴、语言文字、格律声韵、艺术真实以及表演性等美学要素（党争胜，2008：87）。

二 戏剧的翻译

戏剧翻译的主体是剧本。剧本是一种独特的文学体裁，融合了小说、诗歌、散文、评论等文体特点。剧本不仅是舞台演出的蓝本，同时也可单独作为文学作品来阅读。

翻译界曾就戏剧翻译应侧重剧本文本的翻译，还是以舞台表演为最终目的进行过长期争论。英国翻译理论家彼得·纽马克认为：基于剧本的最终目标是搬上舞台，因此戏剧翻译应保持语言简洁、台词口语化、适合在舞台上表演或朗诵；同时，译文还要符合目的语观众的接受心理和文化习惯，即不能对原文中的双关语、歧义句以及有关文化现象进行注释，也不能为了保留原文的地方语言特色而音译某些词语。否则，台下的观众会觉得无趣，台上的演员也因效果不佳而脸上无光（金鑫，2009：553）。

文化学派的代表人物苏珊·巴斯奈特也认为戏剧翻译者要注重"舞台表演性"，即戏剧翻译不同于其他文学翻译，译者不仅要进行书面文本之间的语言转换，还要考虑剧本潜在的"动态表演性"。剧本不是静态的文本，而是要搬到舞台上演出，用剧本上的文字（台词）来进行对话和表演，这就要求剧本台词读起来顺口，听众听起来顺耳（金鑫，2009：553）。

因此，正如刘肖岩（2004）所认为的，戏剧翻译的特点是由戏剧的舞台性所决定的。戏剧翻译同其他文学体裁翻译的区别在于：1）戏剧服务的对象是剧院观众而非一般读者。2）戏剧融"视觉艺术"和"听觉艺术"于一体，观众既可看见舞台表演又可听见演员言说，但因戏剧舞台受时空限制，故观众在欣赏戏剧时多数时候是"听"大于"看"的。而要在这种转瞬即逝的时间内让观众一听便能理解，戏剧翻译的语言就需通俗易懂。3) 戏剧具有无注释性。另行加注是其他文学体裁在翻译过程中涉及文化现象时的处理方法，但戏剧翻译通常没有加注的可能性，而必须采取灵活的方式将应加注的地方在文内处理。4) 戏剧语言需具通俗性。戏剧既然是舞台表演艺术，人物语言就要适合舞台演出，即译文对白要便于演员言说，也便于观众理解，这就要求所使用的语言具备通俗化和口语化的特点。归纳起来可以说，戏剧翻译实际上是用笔译的方式寻求口译的效果（胡显耀、李力，2009：257）。

第二十章 An Ideal Husband 汉译文的批评赏析

一 关于 An Ideal Husband

　　一百多年以前，奥斯卡·王尔德创作的两出喜剧相继在伦敦首演，一时轰动英国文坛。剧中充满了妙语警句，令人入耳难忘。这两出喜剧就是《理想丈夫》(An Ideal Husband)与《不可儿戏》(The Importance of Being Earnest)。

　　王尔德剧中的人物，大致可分成互为对照的两类：其间不是道家的正邪之别，而是美学的雅俗之分。正人君子、淑女贤媛一类，在道德上当然属于正方，但在风格上却未必是雅人。反之，浪子名士、浪女刁娃一类，在道德上不属正派，但在风格上却未必是俗客。《理想丈夫》里的齐氏伉俪，皆属前一类，而《不可儿戏》则完全超越了道德纠纷，原则上一切角色都不正派，只有配角劳小姐是个小小例外。至于杰克和亚吉能这对浪子，加上关多琳和西西丽这对刁妮，当然都属于后一类。每逢正主在场，多半言语无味，一到反客开口，妙语警句就如天女散花，飘逸不滞，绝无冷场。王尔德的名言大半是由他们说出来的。

　　《理想丈夫》讲述的是大约 18 世纪 80 年代发生在英国伦敦贵族阶层的故事。年仅 30 余岁的罗伯特·切尔顿爵士，因才华出众和品格正直而身居参议院经济委员会副主席一职，掌握着英国重大投资项目提案在国会是否获得通过的表决权；同时他还一表人才，娶了一名出身高贵的妻子。妻子不仅容貌美丽、气质高雅，而且品格正直、追求完美。他俩彼此深深相爱，罗伯特正是她心目中的理想丈夫。然而有一天，当一个名叫彻弗莉夫人的女人出现在他们生活中时，罗伯特的美好仕途和理想丈夫的角色受到了严重威胁。阴险狡诈的彻弗莉夫人为谋取私利，通过一小部分议员向国会提交了投资开发阿根廷运河的议案。但是，当得知该议案将遭到罗伯特否决时，彻弗莉夫人利用手中掌握的罗伯特年轻时所犯错误这一把柄，试图逼迫罗伯特同流合污。罗伯特清楚地知道，如果他向彻弗莉夫人之流屈服，国家和人民的利益将蒙受损失，而如果为了维护正义而反对该投资议案通过，他将身败名裂，并失去心爱的妻子。

　　果然，在妻子率先得知丈夫有着不可告人的历史污点后，当即将他扫地出门，罗伯特承受了这个重大打击，并仍然义无反顾地坚决与彻弗莉夫人进行斗争，在国会审议投资提案会上，他带着略显疲惫的面容和悲壮的眼神，大义凛然地表明自己的观点："我认为这是一个很好的提案（全场哗然）——但这是对舞弊者而言的很好——这是个舞弊案。一些有钱人总想更加有钱，而置国家、民族和大多数穷人的利益不顾，提出这个根本不值得投资的项目，我坚决反对！"顿时，全场响起热烈的掌声和欢呼声。

站在旁听席上的妻子和彻弗莉夫人也为之动容。会后，彻弗莉夫人或许是良心发现，或许是看到大势已去，当即向罗伯特表示认输，放弃了对他的威胁。妻子则认识到"理想丈夫"的含义是，在人性上未必完美，但在人格上却真正崇高。

剧中，罗伯特代表正义和崇高理想所作的英勇斗争，不仅战胜了邪恶，维护了民众利益，

二 An Ideal Husband 原文片段及四种汉译文

原 文	译文一	译文二
An Ideal Husband (excerpt) Oscar Wilde	理 想 丈 夫	理 想 丈 夫
Sir Robert Chiltern (hereinafter referred to as S): Mrs Cheveley, you cannot be serious in making me such a proposition!	齐　谢太太，您不可能是当真的吧！	齐爵士　薛太太，你不会当真向我提出这种要求吧！
Mrs Cheveley (hereinafter referred to as M): I am quite serious.	谢　我可是当真的。	薛太太　我可完全当真。
S: [*Coldly.*] Pray allow me to believe that you are not.	齐　[冷冷地] 我不相信。这哪能当真哪！	齐爵士　（冷然）请容我相信你不是当真。
M: [*Speaking with great deliberation and emphasis.*] Ah! But I am. And if you do what I ask you, I … will pay you very handsomely!	谢　[一字一板、语气庄重] 我的确是当真的。如果您照我的意思做，我会……重重的酬谢您！	薛太太　（语气极为郑重而又强调）啊！我可是当真的。只要你照我的话去做，我……就会重重地酬谢你！
S: Pay me!	齐　酬谢我？！	齐爵士　酬谢我！
M: Yes.	谢　对了。	薛太太　没错。
S: I am afraid I don't quite understand what you mean.	齐　我恐怕不明白您的意思。	齐爵士　只怕我不懂你的意思。
M: [*Leaning back on the sofa and looking at him.*] How very disap-	谢　[向后靠在沙发上，望着他] 唉，那我就大失	薛太太　（靠在沙发上望着他）太令人失望了！我

还获得了政府对他的提升,任命他为内阁成员,他的妻子也回到了他的怀抱,从而实现了美好的爱情。

《理想丈夫》演绎的是一曲理想人生的赞歌。

译文三	译文四	笔　记
一个理想的丈夫	一个理想的丈夫	
罗伯特·切尔突恩爵士(以下简称切爵士)　谢弗利太太,您提出这样的建议,是跟我开玩笑吧!	罗伯特·奇尔顿爵士(以下简称奇爵士)　谢弗利太太,你向我提出这样一个要求,一定不能是严肃的吧!	
谢弗利太太(以下简称谢太太)　我说的是当真的话。	谢弗利太太(以下简称谢太太)　我是非常严肃的。	
切爵士　(冷淡地)请允许我相信,您说的不是当真的话!	奇爵士　(冷冷地)还是让我相信你是不严肃的好。	
谢太太　(语气相当强调)哦!但我说的是当真的话。而且,如果您做了我要求您的一切,我……一定给您一笔巨额报酬!	谢太太　(用非常慎重和强调的口气说)呵!可我的确是严肃的。如果你按我所要求的做了,我会……会付给你非常大的一笔款子!	
切爵士　给我报酬!	奇爵士　付给我钱!	
谢太太　是的。	谢太太　是的。	
切爵士　只怕我完全不懂您的意思。	奇爵士　我担心我压根没有听懂你的意思。	
谢太太　(仰靠在沙发上,看着他)多么令我失望!我	谢太太　(背靠在沙发上看着他)多么让人失望啊!我	

原文	译文一	译文二
pointing! And I have come all the way from Vienna in order that you should thoroughly understand me.	所望了！我老远从维也纳来，为的就是让您明白我的意思。	还老远从维也纳赶来，就为了使你完全明白我的意思。
S: I fear I don't.	齐 我恐怕真的不明白。	齐爵士 只怕我还是不懂。
M: [*In her most nonchalant manner.*] My dear Sir Robert, you are a man of the world, and you have your price, I suppose. Everybody has nowadays. The drawback is that most people are so dreadfully expensive. I know I am. I hope you will be more reasonable in your terms.	谢 [泰然自若、极其冷淡地] 齐爵士，您是个老于世故的人，相信您也有个价钱的。现在人人都有价钱，可惜大多数人都太贵了，我自己也是这样。希望您不会要价过高吧。	薛太太 （状至冷漠）我的好爵士，你是见过世面的人，想必你也有身价吧。这年头人人都有价钱的。毛病是多半都贵得要命。我知道我自己就如此。只希望你的条件开得比较公道。
S: [*Rises indignantly.*] If you will allow me, I will call your carriage for you. You have lived so long abroad, Mrs. Cheveley, that you seem to be unable to realise that you are talking to an English gentleman.	齐 [愤慨地站起来] 我们就到此为止吧，我替您把马车叫来。谢太太，您大概在国外呆得太久了，好像不知道，您是在跟一个英国绅士说话呢。	齐爵士 （愤然起身）如果你不反对，我这就去把你的马车叫来。你在国外住得太久了，薛太太，似乎不了解你这是在对一位英国绅士说话。
M: [*Detains him by touching his arm with her fan, and keeping it there while she is talking.*] I realise that I am talking to a man who laid the foundation of his fortune by selling to a Stock Exchange speculator a Cabinet secret.	谢 [用扇子拦着他的手臂，并且一直不放下] 我知道在跟谁说话。这个人，曾经把内阁机密出卖给一个股票投机家，然后才抖起来的。	薛太太 （用扇子点住他的手臂不让他走，把话说完才收回扇子。）我只了解，跟我说话的人，当年是靠了把内阁的机密卖给证券交易所的投机户，才发迹起家的。
S: [*Biting his lip.*] What do you mean?	齐 [咬着嘴唇] 你是什么意思？	齐爵士 （咬唇）你这是什么意思？
M: [*Rising and facing him.*] I mean that I know the real origin of your wealth and your career, and I have got your letter, too.	谢 [起身面对着他] 我意思就是，我知道你的财富、你的地位，都是怎么来的。而且，我手里还有你的信呢！	薛太太 （起身面对他）我的意思是，我知道你的财富和事业的真正来源，而且你的信也在我手里。
S: What letter?	齐 什么信？	齐爵士 什么信？

译文三	译文四	笔 记
远路风尘从维也纳而来，目的是要您完全懂得我。	老远从维也纳来，为的就是让你完全理解我的。	

译文三

切爵士　恐怕我不能懂得。

谢太太　（态度相当冷淡）亲爱的罗伯特爵士先生，我想，您是个老于世故的人，您有您的价格。如今每个人都有自己的价格。买卖不能成交的障碍，在于大多数人索价太高了。我知道我就是。我希望您的价格公道些。

切爵士　（愤然地起身）要是你允许的话，我为你准备马车了。谢弗利太太，你在国外生活了那么多年，所以你似乎不能意识到，你在和一个英国绅士说话。

谢太太　（用扇子挡着他肩膀，拦住他，她边说边保持这种架势）我意识到我在和一个人说话，他把内阁机密出卖给一个证券交易所的投机商，由此发了大财。

切爵士　（紧咬嘴唇）这是什么意思？

谢太太　（起身，面向他）我的意思是，我知道你是怎样发财致富的，而且我有你写的那封信。

切爵士　什么信？

译文四

奇爵士　恐怕我理解不了啊。

谢太太　（完全一副漠然的样子）我亲爱的罗伯特爵士，你可是世界级人物，有你自身的价值，我认为。当今之日，谁都有自己的价值。退却就意味着大多数人身价百倍了。我知道我是的。我希望你说话更加理智一点。

奇爵士　（生气地站起来）你要是允许我，我这就给你叫马车。你在国外生活得时间太长了，谢弗利太太，你好像没有明白你是在和一个英国绅士讲话吧。

谢太太　（用她的扇子点住他的臂，说话时一直用扇子顶在那里）我明白我在和一个通过向股票投机商出卖内阁秘密而平步青云的人讲话。

奇爵士　（咬着嘴唇）你这话什么意思？

谢太太　（站起面对着他）我的意思是说我知道你发家致富和飞黄腾达的真正根源，我手里还拿着你的那封信呢。

奇爵士　什么信？

原文	译文一	译文二
M: [*Contemptuously.*] The letter you wrote to Baron Arnheim, when you were Lord Radley's secretary, telling the Baron to buy Suez Canal shares—a letter written three days before the Government announced its own purchase.	谢 [轻蔑地] 你写给安乐文的信呗。那时候，你是外交大臣赖德利勋爵的秘书，你写信教他买进苏伊士运河的股票，是在政府宣布收购之前三天。	薛太太 （蔑然）你写给安海男爵的那封信，教他买进苏伊士运河的股份——这封信是在政府宣布官买运河股份的三天前写的，当时你正做赖德利勋爵的秘书。
S: [*Hoarsely.*] It is not true.	齐 [声音嘶哑地] 根本没这回事。	齐爵士 （声音沙哑）没有这回事。
M: You thought that letter had been destroyed. How foolish of you! It is in my possession.	谢 你以为那封信已经销毁了吧！傻瓜！在我手上呢。	薛太太 你以为那封信已经销毁了。你真蠢！信在我手里。
S: The affair to which you allude was no more than a speculation. The House of Commons had not yet passed the bill; it might have been rejected.	齐 你说的这件事不过是正常的商业投机而已。那时候，下议院还没通过收购议案，说不定会否决呢。	齐爵士 你指的那件事，不过是推测而已。那议案当时下议院还没有通过；也许都会被否决掉。
M: It was a swindle, Sir Robert. Let us call things by their proper names. It makes everything simpler. And now I am going to sell you that letter, and the price I ask for it is your public support of the Argentine scheme. You made your own fortune out of one canal. You must help me and my friends to make our fortunes out of another!	谢 哼，齐爵士，这可是一场骗局呀。我们还是实话实说吧，这样就什么问题都简单多了。现在我要把这封信卖给您，而您要付的代价，就是凭外务次官的身份支持阿根廷运河计划。您是靠运河发的财；现在，您得帮我和我的朋友也靠运河来发财！	薛太太 那根本是骗局，齐爵士。我们不如直说吧，还是这样干脆些。现在我打算把那封信卖给你，我要的代价就是，你得公开支持阿根廷计划。以前你靠一条运河发了财。现在你得帮我跟我的朋友靠另一条运河发财！
S: It is infamous, what you propose—infamous!	齐 你这样做法太卑鄙了！你太卑鄙了！	齐爵士 简直可耻，你这提议——太可耻了！
M: Oh, no! This is the game of life as we all have to play it, Sir Robert, sooner or later!	谢 哪儿的话呀！齐爵士，人生如赌博嘛，我们大家早晚总得玩它一手哇！	薛太太 哦，算了吧！人生本来就是游戏，齐爵士，你我迟早都得玩的！
	（张南峰 译，1990）	（余光中 译，1998）

译文三	译文四
谢太太 （傲慢地）你写给安海姆男爵的那封信。你做拉德利勋爵的秘书时，曾经告诉这位男爵，要他买进苏伊士运河的股票——英国政府宣布买下苏伊士运河公司股票的前三天，你写了一封泄密信。	**谢太太** （傲慢地）你写给安海姆男爵的那封信，那时你还是拉德利勋爵的秘书，告诉安海姆男爵购买苏伊士运河的股票——一封在政府宣布自己购买股票三天前发出去的信。
切爵士 （声音嘶哑）没有那回事。	**奇爵士** （嗓子嘶哑地）根本不是事实。
谢太太 你还以为那封信早被毁掉了。你好笨啊！它落在我手里了。	**谢太太** 你满以为那封信毁掉了。你多么傻呀！它现在在我的手里呢。
切爵士 你提到的这件事，至多不过是一种推测，众议院还没有通过这份提案；它可能被否决。	**奇爵士** 你提到的那件事当时不过是一种投机。下议院还没有通过那个提案；它还可能被否决。
谢太太 罗伯特爵士先生，这是一个骗局。让我们还它的真面目吧，这样事情就简单化了。现在我打算把那封信卖给你，我要的代价是：你公开地支持阿根廷运河计划。你曾经在一条运河上发了财，你必须帮助我和我的朋友们，在另一条运河上发财！	**谢太太** 它是一个骗局。让我们按事情的正确名字叫它们好了。这样一切都简单多了。现在我要把这封信卖给你，我所要的价钱就是你公开支持那个阿根廷计划。你从一条运河里发了家。你一定要帮助我和我的朋友从另一条运河里交交好运！
切爵士 这是不体面的，你提出的事——是不体面的！	**奇爵士** 那是无耻之举，你所提议的——是无耻之举！
谢太太 不！罗伯特爵士先生，这是人生的赌局，我们迟早都得赌上一赌！	**谢太太** 哦，不！这是我们大家迟早都要玩的游戏，罗伯特！
（钱之德 译，1983）	（马爱农、荣如德等 译）

三 戏剧翻译的批评与赏析练习

原 文	译文一	译文二
The Importance of Being Ernest (excerpt) Oscar Wilde	认真为上	不可儿戏
Jack: Charming day it has been, Miss Fairfax.	杰 今天天气真好哇，费芬斯小姐。	杰克 费小姐，今天天气真好啊。
Gwendolen: Pray don't talk to me about the weather, Mr. Worthing. Whenever people talk to me about the weather, I always feel quite certain that they mean something else. And that makes me so nervous.	温 威尔丁先生，请你别跟我谈天气好不好？人家一跟我谈天气，我就觉得他们肯定另有企图，心里就紧张起来。	关多琳 华先生，求求你别跟我谈天气。每逢有人跟我谈天气，我都可以断定，他们是别有用心。于是我就好紧张。
Jack: I do mean something else.	杰 我的确是另有企图哇。	杰克 我是别有用心。
Gwendolen: I thought so. In fact, I am never wrong.	温 我早料到了。其实啊，我从来不会错的。	关多琳 果然我料中了。说真的，我向来料事如神。
Jack: And I would like to be allowed to take advantage of Lady Bracknell's temporary absence ...	杰 请你让我借费芬斯夫人暂时不在的机会……	杰克 巴夫人离开片刻，请容我利用这时机……
Gwendolen: I would certainly advise you to do so. Mama has a way of coming back suddenly into a room that I have often had to speak to her about.	温 我劝你抓紧一点儿，妈妈有个坏习惯，老爱突然跑回房间里来，我都不知道说了她多少遍了。	关多琳 我正要劝你如此。我妈妈老爱突然闯回人家房里来，逼得我时常讲她。
Jack: [*Nervously*] Miss Fairfax, ever since I met you I have admired you more than any girl ... I have ever met since ... I met you.	杰 [战战兢兢地]费芬斯小姐，我认识你以后……立刻就爱上你了。我认识你以后……认识的女孩子当中……没有一个比你更令我倾心了。	杰克 （紧张地）费小姐，自从我见你以后，我对你的爱慕，超过了……自从我见你以后……见过的一切女孩子。

原文	译文一	译文二
Gwendolen: Yes, I am quite aware of the fact. And I often wish that in public, at any rate, you had been more demonstrative. For me you have always had an irresistible fascination. Even before I met you I was far from indifferent to you. [*Jack looks at her in amazement.*] We live, as I hope you know, Mr. Worthing, in an age of ideals. The fact is constantly mentioned in the more expensive monthly magazines, and has reached the provincial pulpits I am told: and my ideal has always been to love someone of the name of Ernest. There is something in that name that inspires absolute confidence. The moment Algernon first mentioned to me that he had a friend called Ernest, I knew I was destined to love you.	温 哦，我早就知道了。我还常常嫌你不够露骨呢。要是你怕难为情，也起码应该趁着人多的时候露骨一点儿嘛。我老是觉得，你有一种无法抗拒的魅力。甚至还没认识你以前，我就对你发生感情了。[杰克十分诧异地望着她]威尔丁先生，大概你也知道，我们生活在一个人人充满理想的时代。这说法在高级漂亮的月刊里都常常提到的，听说现在还传到了乡间呢。而我的理想向来就是要爱上一个名叫任真的人。这名字里有一种东西，令人一听就充满信心了。想当初，奥哲能第一次告诉我，他有一个叫任真的朋友，我立即就知道我是注定要爱上你的了。	关多琳 是呀，这一点我很清楚。我还时常希望，至少当着众人的面，你会表示得更加露骨。你对我，一直有一股不能抵抗的魅力。甚至早在遇见你之前，我对你也绝非无动于衷。(杰克愕然望着她) 华先生，我希望你也知道，我们是生活在一个理想的时代。这件事，高级的月刊上经常提起，据说已经传到外省的讲坛上了；而我的理想呢，一直是要去爱一个名叫任真的人。任真这名字，绝对叫人放心。亚吉能一跟我提起他有个朋友叫任真，我就知道我命里注定要爱你了。
Jack: You really love me, Gwendolen?	杰 你真的爱我吗，温黛琳？	杰 克 你真的爱我吗，关多琳？
Gwendolen: Passionately!	温 还爱得很深哪！	关多琳 爱得发狂！
Jack: Darling! You don't know how happy you've made me.	杰 亲爱的，你不知道你使我多么幸福哇！	杰 克 达令！你不知道这句话令我多开心。
Gwendolen: My own Ernest!	温 噢，我的任真哪！	关多琳 我的好任真！
Jack: But you don't really mean to	杰 可是，你不是说，要是	杰 克 万一我的名字不

原　文	译文一	译文二
say that you couldn't love me if my name wasn't Ernest?	我不叫任真，你就不爱我吧？	叫任真，你不会当真就不爱我了吧？
Gwendolen: But your name is Ernest.	温　不过你是叫任真哪。	关多琳　可是你的名字是任真呀。
Jack: Yes, I know it is. But supposing it was something else? Do you mean to say you couldn't love me then?	杰　是啊，我知道哇。不过要是我叫别的名字呢？那，你不会就不爱我了吧？	杰　克　是呀，我知道。可是万一不是任真呢？难道你因此就不能再爱我了吗？
Gwendolen: [*Glibly.*] Ah! That is clearly a metaphysical speculation, and like most metaphysical speculations has very little reference at all to the actual facts of real life, as we know them.	温　[口若悬河地] 嗐，你可问得太玄了！这些玄学的问题，和现实生活中我们所认识的现象，往往毫不相干。	关多琳　（圆滑地）啊！这显然是一个玄学的问题，而且像大半的玄学问题一样，和我们所了解的现实生活的真相，根本不相干。
Jack: Personally, darling, to speak quite candidly, I don't much care about the name of Ernest … I don't think the name suits me at all.	杰　亲爱的，坦白说吧，任真这个名字，我自己可不怎么喜欢……任真根本不适合我。	杰　克　达令，我个人，老实说，并不怎么喜欢任真这名字……我觉得这名字根本不配我。
Gwendolen: It suits you perfectly. It is a divine name. It has a music of its own. It produces vibrations.	温　哪儿啦，完全适合哪。任真这个名字好听啊。它有独特的音乐美，既动听又动心哪。	关多琳　这名字对你是天造地设，神妙无比，本身有一种韵味，动人心弦。
Jack: Well, really, Gwendolen, I must say that I think there are lots of other much nicer names. I think Jack, for instance, a charming name.	杰　不过，我还是觉得，有许多名字比任真好多了，好比说吧，我觉得，杰克就很好听。	杰　克　哪，关多琳，坦白地说，我觉得还有不少更好的名字。例如杰克吧，我就认为是很动人的名字。
Gwendolen: Jack? … No, there is very little music in the name	温　杰——克？不行不行。杰——克，根本没有多	关多琳　杰克？……不行，这名字就算有一点韵

原　文	译文一	译文二
Jack, if any at all, indeed. It does not thrill. It produces absolutely no vibrations … I have known several Jacks, and they all, without exception, were more than usually plain. Besides, Jack is a notoriously domesticity for John! And I pity any woman who is married to a man called John. She would probably never be allowed to know the entrancing pleasure of a single moment's solitude. The only really safe name is Ernest.	少音乐美。真的，既不动听，也不动心。我认识好几个杰克，全都那么其貌不扬的，一个也不例外。而且呀，叫杰克的人满街都是，太俗气了。女人最可怜就是嫁个丈夫叫杰克了。冷清宁静那种醉人的乐趣，这种女人永远也享受不到哇。最保险的名字就只有一个任真。	味，也有限得很。说真的，杰克这名字没有刺激，一点儿也不动人心弦……我认识好几个人叫杰克，毫无例外，都特别地平庸。何况，杰克只是约翰的家常小名，实在很不体面。无论什么女人嫁了叫约翰的男人，我都可怜她。这种女人只怕一辈子都没有福气享受片刻的清静。只有任真这名字才真的保险。
Jack: Gwendolen, I must get christened at once—I mean we must get married at once. There is not time to be lost.	杰　温黛琳，我得马上到教堂去领洗、改名……不，我是说，我得马上跟你结婚，一分钟也不能耽搁。	杰　克　关多琳，我必须立刻受洗——我是说，我们必须立刻结婚。不能再耽误了。
Gwendolen: Married, Mr. Worthing?	温　你说什么，威尔丁先生？结婚？	关多琳　结婚，华先生？
Jack: [*Astounded*.] Well … surely. You know that I love you, and you led me to believe, Miss Fairfax, that you were not absolutely indifferent to me.	杰　[大吃一惊] 啊……是……是啊。费芬斯小姐，你知道我爱你；你也令我相信，你对我不是毫无感情的呀！	杰　克　（愕然）是啊……当然了。你知道我爱你，费小姐，你也使我相信，你对我并非完全无情。
Gwendolen: I adore you. But you haven't proposed to me yet. Nothing has been said at all about marriage. The subject has not even been touched on.	温　我很喜欢你，不过你还没有向我求婚呢。结婚这事连提也没提到过呀。	关多琳　我崇拜你。可是你还没有向我求婚呢。根本还没有谈到婚嫁呢。这话题碰都没碰过。
Jack: Well … may I propose to you now?	杰　那……我现在就向你求婚，行吗？	杰　克　那么……现在我可以向你求婚了吗？

原文	译文一	译文二
Gwendolen: I think it would be an admirable opportunity. And to spare you any possible disappointment, Mr. Worthing. I think it only fair to tell you quite frankly beforehand that I am fully determined to accept you.	温 现在可是个大好时机呀，威尔丁先生。而且，为了免得你担心碰钉子，我觉得应该事先跟你交个底，我早就决定答应你了。	关多琳 我认为现在正是良机。而且免得你会失望，我想天公地道应该事先坦坦白白地告诉你，我是下定了决心要——嫁你。
Jack: Gwendolen!	杰 温黛琳！	杰 克 关多琳！
Gwendolen: Yes, Mr. Worthing, what have you got to say to me?	温 啊，威尔丁先生，你有什么要跟我说的呀？	关多琳 是啊，华先生，你要怎么说呢？
Jack: You know what I have got to say to you.	杰 你知道我有什么要跟你说。	杰 克 你知道我会怎么说。
Gwendolen: Yes, but you don't say it.	温 是啊，不过你还没说呀。	关多琳 对，可是你没说。
Jack: Gwendolen, will you marry me? [*Goes on his knees.*]	杰 温黛琳，你嫁给我好吗？〔跪下〕	杰 克 关多琳，你愿意嫁给我吗？（跪下）
Gwendolen: Of course I will, darling. How long you have been about it! I am afraid you have had very little experience in how to propose.	温 当然好了，任真。磨蹭了这么久才说出来，你恐怕是太缺乏求婚经验了。	关多琳 我当然愿意，达令。看你，折腾了这么久！只怕你求婚的经验很有限。
Jack: My own one, I have never loved anyone in the world but you.	杰 亲爱的温黛琳哪，这个世界上，除了你之外我还没爱过别人哪。	杰 克 我的宝贝，世界之大，除你之外我没有爱过别人。
Gwendolen: Yes, but men often propose for practice. I know my brother Gerald does. All my girl-friends tell me so. What wonderfully blue eyes you have, Ernest! They are	温 我知道哇，不过男人是经常为了练习而求婚的呀。我哥哥就经常练习；我认识的女孩子全都这么说的。任真哪，你的蓝眼睛真漂亮。蓝得那	关多琳 对呀，可是男人求婚，往往是为了练习。我知道我哥哥杰罗就是这样，我所有的女朋友都这么告诉我的。你的眼睛蓝得

原　文	译文一	译文二
quite, quite blue! I hope you will always look at me just like that, especially when there are other people present.	么水灵灵的，多可爱呀。但愿你以后就永远这么看着我，特别是在大庭广众之中。 （张南峰　译，1990）	好奇妙啊，任真！真的好蓝，好蓝啊。希望你永远像这样望着我，尤其是当着别人的面。 （余光中　译，1998）

附 录

翻译批评与赏析文章

一 *Pride and Prejudice* 三种汉语译文对比赏析

1. 前言

《傲慢与偏见》是 18 世纪末 19 世纪初英国女作家简·奥斯汀（Jane Austen, 1775—1817）的代表作。奥斯汀是一位不动声色的反讽艺术家，她用清新、秀丽、细腻的语言，描绘着平凡生活中的平凡人物——以日常生活中的琐事为描述对象，以一个女性的敏感视角观察着生活，并用精雕细琢式的写作技巧表达出来，这就是她独特的创作风格。简·奥斯汀一生的感悟，融汇在她的六部小说里面，分别是《傲慢与偏见》《理智与情感》《曼斯菲尔德庄园》《爱玛》《诺桑觉寺》和《劝导》。其中《傲慢与偏见》是她所创作的第一部小说，也是奥斯汀作品中最成功、最受欢迎的作品。毛姆曾经说："我相信，广大的读者已经认定《傲慢与偏见》是奥斯汀的杰作"。反讽，是奥斯汀小说的一种主要艺术手段，是她领悟世界的一种主要方式。而她的反讽手法在《傲慢与偏见》中发挥得淋漓尽致，她用极为细腻的手笔风趣地反映了 18 世纪末到 19 世纪初处于保守和闭塞状态下的英国乡镇生活和世态人情，展现给读者一部社会风俗喜剧佳作，为后人所津津乐道。小说大量运用了嘲讽语调和巧妙的喜剧手法，常以风趣诙谐的语言来烘托人物的个性特征，这种艺术创新使她的作品独具特色。英国著名文学家和评论家基布尔（T. T. Keb-ble）指出，"简·奥斯汀是一位喜剧艺术家"，并认为她"在纯粹喜剧艺术方面仅次于莎士比亚"。

2. 作者背景及写作风格

简·奥斯汀于 1775 年 12 月 16 日出身于英国乡村的一个中产阶级家庭，她知识渊博的父亲，和出身于贵族家庭的母亲，十分重视对子女的教育和培养。奥斯汀虽然没有上过正规学校，但在父母的教导下，她从小就博览群书，16 岁左右就开始写作。奥斯汀终身未婚，一生中与之交往的大都是些乡间的乡绅、淑女、中小地主以及牧师等人物。她一生所接触到的人，以及他们恬静、舒适的乡村生活给了她创作的灵感。1796 年，简·奥斯汀创作了她的第一部小说《第一印象》，并于 1813 年以《傲慢与偏见》为名发表，这部作品一反 18 世纪后期感伤小说的流行内容和矫揉造作的写作方法，生动地采用喜剧手法表达了对生活的严肃批评，一经发表，便引起了轰动。小说中展现的乡村邻居的舞会、串门喝茶、家宴和平常琐碎的谈话，全部都是生活中的琐事，然而正是这些从另一个侧面反映了当时的乡村生活和英国文化背景，深刻映射出了 18 世纪末 19 世纪初英国的社会状况和世态人情，是当时西方文化的一个缩影。著名作家毛姆曾评论："描绘的尽是日常生活的事物，但每当我读完一页，就想知道下一页的故事。"可见奥斯汀在对人物和故事的描写方面有着极深的造诣。

反讽是简·奥斯汀最为拿手的写法，她在《傲慢与偏见》中将这一艺术运用得炉火纯青。作者用她独特的视角和语言，嘲笑着当时的社会，讥讽着当时的生活。李建军在《小说修辞研究》中说："反讽是作者洞察了表现对象在内容和形式、现象与本质等反面复杂因素的背离状态并为了维持这一状态而采取暗含嘲弄，使用否定义，使其具有隐蔽性质的一种委婉幽隐的修辞策略。"由此可见，反讽是作家创作时用来洞察社会真相，揭示现实的一种叙事技巧。简·奥斯汀小说中丰富、娴熟的反讽手法使她的小说充满幽默感，她以轻快的笔触揭示生活在她周围的那些人身上可笑而又可爱的怪癖和缺点，把人物的内心活动和思想感情表现得更为细腻，使作品更具艺术美感及艺术震撼力，正是用这样的一种技巧包装着她的作品。简·奥斯汀让读者在品尝她作品的时候像是喝着一杯咖啡，苦涩之中带点甜味儿，在甜中又透露着淡淡的苦涩。这种从语言表象到深层态度的张力结构无疑使得这部作品具有巨大的理解审美空间，用奥斯汀独特的角度去观察人性，读者可以从中读出可笑、愚蠢与荒谬，从而得到教育与启迪——这种喜剧反讽是作家对充满矛盾、谬误的现实世界的嘲弄，但仍不缺乏对未来的憧憬。

在《傲慢与偏见》中，作者把反讽这一写作手法运用于人物的塑造和故事的发展中。开篇第一句便告诉读者"一个举世公认的真理"——凡是有钱的单身男子，必定要娶一位妻子。这个看似可笑的"真理"在整个故事中不断地被证明，从班纳特太太急于嫁出她的五个女儿，到最后"有情人终成眷属"，一个看似"谬论"的"真理"，在一个头脑简单、行为乖张，处处遭到奥斯汀嘲讽的人物——班纳特太太的坚持下，竟然变成了现实。这一精彩的呼应让人在哭笑不得之中充分领略到简·奥斯汀的反讽艺术。著名文学评论家刘易斯就曾这样评价简·奥斯汀："奥斯汀小姐的伟大之处，即她那绝妙的戏剧性力量，比斯哥特的一切都更近似莎士比亚的最伟大的特点。"

3. 译作对比分析

塑造人物"大概是奥斯汀最感兴趣、最拿手的本领"，她把反讽主要集中于人物的塑造上。《傲慢与偏见》最吸引人之处，是它为读者展现的形形色色、栩栩如生的人物形象。E.W.福斯特把小说人物分为"扁形人物"（Flat Characters）和"圆形人物"（Round Characters）。"扁形人物"指的是那些次要的没有浓墨重彩描写的角色，他们往往是一些简单的，直接受到作者嘲弄讽刺的人物。在《傲慢与偏见》中，"扁型人物"的主要代表就是小说女主人公伊丽莎白的母亲班纳特太太。奥斯汀在刻画人物时，采用了难度较大的"戏剧表现"手法，不是直接描写人物的外部特征，而是由他们各自亮相，让他们把自己充分地展示出来。在小说的第一章中，奥斯汀就把班纳特太太这一典型的"扁型人物"描写得出神入化，短短几个对话，便把一个头脑简单、肤浅饶舌的乡村妇女活生生地带到读者面前。由此可见，人物对话是小说不可或缺的组成部分，是塑造人物、推动情节发展的有效助推器。在传统翻译中，译者一般只注意到人物话语本身，关注翻译是否符合人物身份以及个性特征等，他们认为只要把对话内容翻译出来便可以传达原文所要传达的意思，但随着文体学的兴起，批评家渐渐开始关注人物话语的不同表达方式。作者选择什么样的表达方式呈现人物的语言和思想，都会产生不同的文体效果，对文本风格的形成起着重要的作用。因此，在文学翻译，特别是小说翻译中，译者应对体现叙述风格的话语或思想的不同表现方式给予特别的关注并尽力再现，否则，译文就不可能表现出与原作同样或尽可能相类似的文体风格，甚至可能会扭曲原作风格。所以，不同的表达方式,包括句式的变化、直接引语和间接引语的应用等所产生的迥异功能对小说表达和加强主题意义、美学效果起到了重要的作用。因此,译者在翻译的过程中应当特别重视作者的描述方式,不要轻易地改变作者的表达方式,否则便有可能会改变作者的写作风格和文章的美学效果。

《傲慢与偏见》这部书在国内有多个译本,每个译本都力求把书中的精髓呈现给中国的读者,但是翻译具有多译性和多元性的特征,翻译的标准既对立又统一,如科学性与艺术性、忠实性与创造性等等,每个译者对原著的理解不同,翻译出来的效果必然也不一样,本文选取了比较有代表性的三个译作——王科一(1980年版)、孙致礼(1990年版)和李明(2006年版)进行对比分析。三位译者都是翻译界的佼佼者,他们对原著的把握都相当的准确到位,但是毕竟两个不同国家的文字之间总会有距离,译者的理解与文风跟原作品的内容和形式之间也必然有些差距,另外译者也未必总能非常准确的表达出自身的体会,因此,在翻译的过程中三位译者对文章内容、形式等方面的处理各有侧重,处理方式也不尽相同,笔者现将原文与译文对照分析如下,试图找出更加贴近奥斯汀写作风格的翻译。由于文章篇幅限制,这里只对该书第一章的某些片段进行分析对比。

奥斯汀通过《傲慢与偏见》运用反讽批评了当时社会一味追求金钱和地位的婚姻观。小说一开场,作者就用了言语反讽把主题烘托出来。文章的第一句话就点明了这篇文章的主旨,整个故事围绕着这样"一句话"在有条不紊的进行着,而奥斯汀的反讽艺术,在第一、二段就得到了体现:

It is a truth universally acknowledged that a single man in possession of a good fortune must be in want of a wife.

However little known the feelings or views of such a man may be on his first entering a neighborhood, this truth is so well fixed in the minds of the surrounding families, that he is considered as the rightful property of some one or other of their daughters.

第一句话充分展现了作者的幽默,她跟读者开了个小小的玩笑:当大家都看到 a truth universally acknowledged 的时候,就会不约而同地想到一些大道理,会以为奥斯汀要说些哲学理论,但是当读者继续往下看的时候,不由得忍俊不禁,因为这样一个 truth 竟然是 a single man in possession of a good fortune must be in want of a wife,这就达到很好的喜剧效果,把一个大家都习以为常的观点放在"真理"这样的包装之下,反而让人觉得这是一个"谬论"了。下面让我们来看看几位译者的翻译是否达到了原文的效果:

王科一译(以下简称王译):凡是有钱的单身汉,总想娶位太太,这已经成了一条举世公认的真理。

孙致礼译(以下简称孙译):有钱的单身汉总要娶位太太,这是一条举世公认的真理。

李明译(以下简称李译):寰宇间有这样一条公认的真理:凡腰缠万贯的单身汉一定会娶

一个媳妇儿。"

单从内容上看，三位译者都把奥斯汀所要表达的意思给表述出来了，但是在表达形式上却不尽相同。原作者使用的是一句完整的从句，尤其是"公理"的内容部分，a single man in possession of a good fortune must be in want of a wife 有一气呵成的效果，而 in possession of a good fortune 和 be in want of 的使用也产生了一些咬文嚼字和夸张的效果，那么从这个角度看来，王译的"凡是有钱的单身汉，总想娶位太太"和孙译的"有钱的单身汉总要娶位太太"就显得不那么玩味了，而李译的"凡腰缠万贯的单身汉一定会娶一个媳妇儿"则比较准确地传达了原文的效果，使这样一条公理看起来严肃但却惹人发笑。而在句式的应用上，王译和孙译都不约而同的把"一条举世公认的真理"置后了，这样也符合中文的表达方式，但是都不如李译的前置翻译，因为李译的翻译达到了奥斯汀的反讽效果：看起来是严肃的话题，拆开包装后看到的却是如此通俗的认识。

第一句看似是对事实的描述，可能会引起读者的广泛认同，但作者紧接着却说 he is considered as the rightful property of some one or other of their daughters，一下子就把要讽刺批评的主题烘托出来了。第二句是个长句，而对长句的翻译主要体现在句子的逻辑关系上，三个译者都能较好地理清句子中的逻辑关系，其中以李译最为准确，他把 this truth is so well fixed in the minds of the surrounding families 翻译成"（但）由于这一条真理在周围人们的心中早已根深蒂固"显然比王译的"（可是,）既然这样的一条真理早已在人们心目中根深蒂固，因此……"和孙译的"这条真理还真够深入人心的"来得贴切。而 rightful 一词,显然翻译成"理所应当"或"理所当然"都比"合法的"要恰当。

既然有了前面两段的铺垫，而小说的主题也揭示了出来，那么接下来就轮到小说的两位主要人物出场。这两个人并不是主角，但在小说的发展中起到了推动的作用。这就是女主人公的父母，班纳特夫妇。对人物的塑造往往离不开对人物语言、行为举止和心理活动的描写，该作品的开篇就是两大配角——班纳特夫妇的对话，奥斯汀借助生动的人物对话，生动地刻画出一个肤浅饶舌的乡村妇人和一个幽默内敛的乡绅。在第一章中，奥斯汀运用了大量的对话描写，其中包括直接引语和间接引语的应用。直接引语，指的是原封不动地引用人物话语使读者有一种如临其境、如闻其声的感觉，因此也就产生一种申丹教授所说的"音响效果"，而当直接引语和间接引语交替使用的时候，便产生了一种对比强烈、亮暗分明的视觉和听觉效果。而奥斯汀正是运用这种描写方式对她小说中典型的"扁型人物"进行嘲讽。让我们看看这样一段对话：

"My dear Mr. Bennet," said his lady to him one day, "have you heard that Netherfield Park is let at last?"

Mr. Bennet replied that he had not.

"But it is," returned she, "for Mrs. Long has just been here, and she told me all about it."

Mr. Bennet made no answer.

在这段对话中，班纳特太太的语言始终是以直接引语的形式出现，而班纳特先生则是用间接引语描写的。这样两种形式的对话同时出现，就给了我们一个极强的对比：一个喋喋不休，一个爱理不理。让我们看看三个译本：

王 译：

有一天，班纳特太太对她的丈夫说："我的好老爷，尼日斐花园终于租出去了，你听说过没有？"

班纳特先生回答道，他没有听说过。

"的确租出去了，"她说，"朗格太太刚刚上这儿来过，她把这件事的底细，一五一十地都告诉了我。"

班纳特先生没有理睬她。

孙 译：

"亲爱的贝纳特先生，"一天，贝纳特太太对丈夫说："你有没有听说内瑟菲尔德庄园终于租出去了？"

贝纳特先生回答道，没有听说。

"的确租出去了，"太太说道，"朗太太刚刚来过，她把这事一五一十地全告诉我了。"

贝纳特先生没有答话。

李 译：

"我说老爷子，"一天，贝纳特太太对丈夫说，"您听说了吗？内瑟菲尔德庄园终于租出去了。"

贝纳特先生说没有听说过。

"但真的租出去了，"贝纳特太太说，"因为朗格太太刚来过这儿，她把出租的事情全都告诉我了。"

贝纳特先生没有理会。

孙译和李译都采用了原文的表达顺序，把班纳特太太说话的内容放在句首，这样就给读者一个"未见其人先闻其声"的效果，一下子就把这个多嘴的妇人带到读者的面前，故事的叙述显得生动形象。而王译则以传统的"讲故事模式"进行记叙，这样就显得太过平淡，也无法烘托出这个人物的形象。而对于班纳特先生的回答，三位译者的翻译颇为相似，但细究之下，便会发现李译更好地把班纳特先生对于他太太要说的消息的冷漠态度表现出来，这主要体现在句子的长度上。王译用了"班纳特先生回答道，他没有听说"（13个字加逗号），孙译则用了"贝纳特先生回答道，没有听说"（12个字加逗号），相比之下，李译显得简洁明了："贝纳特先生说没有听说过"（11个字，且无断句），读李译的翻译就能体会到班纳特先生的漠不关心。下面一段对话也是如此。只有把人物对话的强烈对比展现出来，才能更好地体现奥斯汀的反讽艺术。

也正是有了班纳特先生的冷漠，才有了下面班纳特太太的抓狂：

"Do not you want to know who has taken it?" cried his wife impatiently.

班纳特先生终于开口了，而他说的话无异于一个"邀请"（invitation）。

"You want to tell me, and I have no objection to hearing it."

This was invitation enough.

王　译："既是你要说给我听，我听听也无妨。"

这句话足够鼓励她讲下去了。

孙　译："既是你想告诉我，我听听也无妨。"

这句话足以逗引太太讲下去了。

李　译："是你想告诉我的，我就听你讲吧。"

这句话足够打开她的话匣子。

李译的"我就听你讲吧"较好地传达了班纳特先生有些无奈的态度，为下文交代这对夫妇微妙的关系作一个铺垫，也是对班纳特先生因为美貌而娶了这么一个难缠的老婆的嘲讽，这就延续了奥斯汀的风格。而王译和孙译的"听听也无妨"则没有这层意思了。另外对 This was invitation enough 的翻译，把 invitation 翻译成为"鼓励"或"逗引"都不够形象，而李译用的"打开……话匣子"则很好地体现出班纳特太太喋喋不休的特点。

最终，班纳特太太把她所听说的小道消息一股脑儿地倒了出来之后，也说出了她对这一消息感到如此振奋的原因：

"… What a fine thing for our girls! … You must know that I am thinking of his marrying one of them."

王　译："……真是女儿们的福气！"

"……我正在盘算，他要是挑中我们的一个女儿做老婆，可多好！"

孙　译："……真是女儿们的好福气！"

"……告诉你吧，我正在思谋他娶她们中的一个做太太呢！"

李　译："……这对我们的几个女儿可是大好事呀！"

"……您就没有想到我正盘算着他能娶走我们的一个女儿吗？"

其中，把 fine thing 翻译成"大好事"显然要比"福气"来的贴切，而对 You must know that I am thinking of his marrying one of them 的翻译，也是李译的比较贴切，因为说"娶走我们的一个女儿"更能描绘出班纳特太太嫁女儿的急切心理，从而呼应了开头的那条"举世公认的真理"，而用"盘算"也比"思谋"来得准确，因为"思谋"给读者感觉像是在密谋一件不好的事情。

由于班纳特太太把她的意图说得如此明显,班纳特先生"爱挖苦人"的特点也被激发出来,他狠狠地嘲笑了自己的太太:

"I see no occasion for that. You and the girls may go, or you may send them by themselves, which perhaps will be still better, for as you are as handsome as any of them, Mr. Bingley might like you the best of the party."

这句话也达到了一个极强的反讽效果:本来是一个年老色衰、头脑简单的妇人,硬是给说成了"和女儿们一样有姿色、会惹人喜欢"的人。

王 译:"我不用去。你带着女儿们去就得啦,要不你干脆打发她们自己去,那或许倒更好些,因为你跟女儿们比起来,她们哪一个都不能胜过你的美貌,你去了,彬格莱先生倒可能挑中你呢。"

孙 译:"我看没有那个必要。你带着女儿们去就行啦,要不你索性打发她们自己去,这样或许更好些,因为你的姿色并不亚于她们中的任何一个,你一去,宾利先生倒作兴看中你呢。"

李 译:"我看没这个必要。你和女儿们去吧,或者你让她们自己去可能会更好些,因为你跟她们一样美丽动人,你跟她们去,彬格莱先生有可能最喜欢你呢。"

对于文中 as handsome as any of them 的翻译,显然忠于原文的翻译"跟她们一样美丽动人"要比其他两个强,这样忠于原文的翻译更能凸显奥斯汀的反讽艺术。而对于 Mr. Bingley might like you the best of the party 的翻译,王译的显然比孙译的好些,但仍不如李译的贴近原文。班纳特先生的这句嘲讽,也是奥斯汀对书中这个"扁型人物"的嘲讽,而奥斯汀对班纳特太太嘲讽得越多,与小说的结局——班纳特太太的愿望得以实现形成了越为强烈的对比,这样更能让读者体会到奥斯汀的反讽艺术。

4. 结束语

这三位译者的译文都很好地将小说的内容翻译了出来,但是对于小说风格的翻译,则主要依靠对原著表达形式的重视。如果译文只为了传达原文的意思,而忽略了原文特定语言表达形式所产生的文体效果,这种翻译就或多或少地歪曲了原作风格,对原作的艺术价值造成了一定的损失,这势必也影响了译文读者对原文的理解和欣赏。因此,译作者必须充分认识到译文与原作风格统一的重要性,这样有助于更加准确地传递原文的内涵,最大限度地保持原文的艺术价值。

(广东外语外贸大学 2009 级 MTI 周末班学生　陈樱之)

二、*Gone with the Wind* 三种汉语译文对比赏析

Gone with the Wind 是美国著名女作家玛格丽特·米歇尔创作的一部带着伤感怀旧情怀

的小说。它以美国南北战争为背景，重点刻画了一位外表迷人、内心冷酷、性格坚强、头脑精明、命运坎坷的南方佳人的艺术形象。小说塑造的棱角分明的人物，和由于人物各自不同的性格和道德观造成的命运的巨大差别，使小说跌宕起伏，引人入胜。自 1936 年出版以来，这本书就好评如潮，并于 1937 年获得普利策奖。

该小说至今已有多个译本出现，比较著名的有傅东华先生 1940 年的译本，陈廷良先生 1990 年译本及戴侃、李野光 1990 年译本等。本文拟从翻译策略、语言风格及表达手段等方面对这三个译本的第一章开头两个自然段进行对比赏析。

1. 从翻译策略上看

小说开头两个自然段，其内容是通过对女主人公——Scarlet O'hara 的外貌及穿着打扮等细节进行描写，为人物的进一步描写及故事情节的展开作铺垫。因此对这两段意思的传达是非常重要的，逐字逐句的翻译很难达到好的效果。

(1) 归化和异化

下表为三个译本中对第一章前两个自然段人名及地名的翻译：

原　文	傅　译	陈　译	戴、李译
Scarlett O'hara	郝思嘉	斯佳丽·奥哈拉	思嘉·奥哈拉
The Tarletton	汤家	塔尔顿家	塔尔顿家
Georgia	（未译）	佐治亚	佐治亚
Stuart Tarletton	汤司徒	斯图特	斯图尔特
Brent Tarletton	汤伯伦	布伦特	布伦特
Tara	陶乐	塔拉	塔拉
Atlanta	饿狼陀	亚特兰大	亚特兰大

归化是傅译最显著的特征，尤其表现在人名地名的翻译上。从上表可以看出，陈译和戴、李译属于异化。十九世纪四五十年代，在人们对中国以外的事物缺少了解的情况下，傅先生为了让译文符合中国读者的文化意识，有意将人名和地名译成了颇具中国色彩的名字，这点是可以理解的。不过，随着越来越多外来文化传入中国，常用的人名地名有了它们约定俗成的译法，大部分是忠实于原文的音译。这时，我们会感到陈廷良对人名地名的翻译更妥帖更自然。

对人名地名的翻译，陈译和戴、李译基本相同。但我认为，"斯佳丽"比"思嘉"要好一些，一则"斯佳丽"与原文 Scarlet 达到音合；二则对中国人来说，名字也能反映出一个人的特征，中国的读者也习惯于把人名与人相联系，"斯佳丽"这个名字读起来更生动，更能体现 Scarlett 大胆、爱美、虚荣等特点。

值得提及的一点是，傅译中 Georgia 这个地名并没有译出，我认为不应该。在原文中，

Georgia 是一个很重要的地方,是主人公生长生活的地方。因为它位于美国南部,所以太阳很热,这是第一自然段中皮肤要保养的原因。

除了专有名词外,傅译中还有一些词运用了归化策略。比如第一自然段中 her thick black brows 译成"两撇墨墨的娥眉",第二自然段中 new green flowered-muslin dress 译成"新制的绿色花布春衫"。"娥眉"和"春衫"一词都具有很浓的中国文化色彩。这两个短语在陈译和戴、李译中分别是"两道又浓又黑的剑眉"和"绿花布的新衣"(陈译),"两撇墨黑的浓眉"和"新做的绿花布衣裳"(戴、李译)。陈译"剑眉"亦是归化译法,具中国色彩。总体上看,傅译中的描写有个人想象的因素在里面,描写得更生动一些,中国读者能根据描述在脑海中形成符合中国人审美习惯的魅力佳人的形象,不过让人感觉是"中国佳人"而不是"美国佳人"。

(2) 分句

三个译文都用到了分句的翻译策略,这是由于中英文在句型结构、思维方式及语言习惯等方面的不同所致。原文第二自然段有一句中间没有标点符号的复合长句:

Her new green flowered-muslin dress spread its twelve yards of billowing material over her hoops and exactly matched the flat-heeled green morocco slippers her father had recently brought her from Atlanta.

傅 译:她身上穿着一件新制的绿色花布春衫,从弹簧箍上撑出波浪纹的长裙,配着脚上一双也是绿色的低跟鞋,是她父亲新近从饿狼陀买来给她的。

陈 译:她穿着那件绿花布的新衣,裙箍把用料十二码波浪形裙幅铺展开来,跟她父亲刚从亚特兰大给她捎来的平跟摩洛哥羊皮绿舞鞋正好相配。

戴、李 译:她穿一件新做的绿花布衣裳,长长的裙子在裙箍上波翻浪涌般地飘展着,配上她父亲新近从亚特兰大给她带来的绿色山羊皮鞋,显得分外相称。

几位译者皆把原文的长句分成短句表达,对原文的语序、结构和表达方式作了一些必要的调整,使之符合中文的句子表达结构和中国人的思维习惯,易于理解。

这里要说的是,原文句子中主句的动词是 spread 和 matched,我认为这是原文要突出的内容;brought 这个动作是分句中的,是次要内容。傅译的句子似乎更强调的是"是她父亲新近从饿狼陀买来给她的"这个分句,我认为不贴切;陈译和戴、李译把"展开／飘展"、"正好相配／分外相称"作为重点表达,因此更妥帖些。

(3) 增词

增词是为了增强译文句子的连贯性,将原意更明白准确地传达给读者,它往往是与分句结合使用的。我们来看看三个译本使用增词的情况。

原 文:In her face were too sharply blended the delicate features of her mother, a Coast aristocrat of French descent, and the heavy ones of her florid Irish father.

傅 译：<u>原来这位小姐脸上显然混杂着两种特质：一种是母亲给她的娇柔，一种是父亲给她的豪爽。因为她母亲是一个法兰西血统的海滨贵族，父亲是一个皮色深浓的爱尔兰人，所以遗传给她的质地难免不调和。</u>

陈 译：她脸蛋上极其明显地融合了<u>父母的容貌特征</u>，<u>既有</u>母亲那种沿海地区法国贵族后裔的优雅，<u>也有父亲那种肤色红润的爱尔兰人的粗野，</u>……

戴、李 译：她脸上混杂着<u>两种特征</u>，<u>一种是她母亲的娇柔</u>，<u>一种是她父亲的粗犷</u>，前者属于法兰西血统的海滨贵族，<u>后者来自浮华俗气的爱尔兰人，</u><u>这两种特征显得不太调和。</u>

下划线部分是原文没有而译者增加的词句。在对比中我们看到，傅译增词较多，加上了一些解释的成分，是为了便于读者理解。虽然有将近一半是译者增添上去的，但读起来并不啰嗦。戴、李译和傅译的区别不大，增词方面基本相同。陈译的句子简洁流畅，并运用合句的方法把与下一句 But it was an arresting face, pointed of chin, square of jaw 译成一句话："……不过这张脸还是挺引人注目的，尖尖的下巴颏儿，方方的牙床骨儿。"陈译没有增加太多的词却能把原文内容基本上表达完整，读起来亦很连贯。我认为从整个句子结构上说，陈译相对叫好一些。对于一些细节及选词方面，将在下文评析。

总体上看，傅译采用增词策略较多，除了上面谈到的，还有很多处用了增词方法。比如将 her eyes were her own（第二自然段末）译成"至于那一双眼睛，那是天生给她的，绝不是人工改造得了的。"而陈译和戴、李译并没有增词。

当然，除了以上三种策略外，还有一些策略（合句、减词、词性转换等）是三种译本采用的，笔者在此不一一列举。

2. 从语言风格及表达手段上看

从整体风格上说，傅译中的汉语地道，句子、短语通常较短，根据汉语习惯选择主语，常采用"话题 + 评论"的结构，语体方面呈现出口语化。对于英语特有而传统汉语无对应的句型，如 …never would, or could…，傅东华跳出形式，只译内容，根据汉语表达方式使用平行结构加以重写，使之易于理解，增强了译文的可读性。

陈译在语言结构方面较另外两个译本更接近原文，在用汉语清楚表达原文内容和意义的基础上力求达到形似。可以看到，在第一章第一、二自然段中，有几处句子使用的是与原文句子结构形似的长句，比如原文第一句 Scarlett O'Hara was not beautiful, but men seldom realized it when caught by her charm as the Tarleton twins were 的译文为："斯佳丽·奥哈拉长得并不美，但男人们一旦像塔尔顿家孪生兄弟那样给她的魅力迷住往往就不大理会这点"。句子结构基本上与原文一致。

戴、李译在语言风格上与陈译相似，不过在一些表达上借鉴了傅译的手法。笔者认为三个译本的差异是由于译本的历史、社会和文化语境不同造成的。前一个是 1940 年译的，属于最早的译本，后两个是 1990 年译的，历史背景、语言发展和读者群不同，翻译的目的、语言的选择就略有不同。

下面我们对三个译本中一些语言及词的选择作一下具体的赏析。

书名 Gone with the Wind 通常译为《飘》或《乱世佳人》，Gone with the Wind 的字面意思是"随风而逝"。傅东华先生把它首译为《飘》，笔者认为"飘"这个字深切体现了原著的内涵，反映了主人公生活经历、社会及情感的动荡和不安定，并表达出原著的浪漫气息。既与原题 Gone with the Wind 达到神似，又充满诗意。在傅译本前言中，译者解释道："飘的文学意象是回旋的风，像是狂风。原文中风更有狂风的意思。飘同时也有飘走的意思，所以也就包含了 gone 的意思。所以我觉得这一个词就能表达出原著名字的内涵。"《乱世佳人》这个题目是译者的一个陈述，对主人公及历史背景的概括性陈述，虽缺少诗意但是一目了然，这样译也是可以的。

原文开头第一句关于 beautiful 的翻译上，傅译本和陈译本都译做"美"，戴、李译本则译为"漂亮"。笔者在朗文词典中查到：beautiful 表示美丽的、优美的，在描写人的外貌时，比 pretty、handsome、good-looking 和 attractive 都要强烈得多。从词典解释的意思中我们知道，beautiful 是优雅的、最高标准的接近于完美的"美"，从作者在后面对 Scarlett 的容貌描述来看，她并未达到如此完美，但这并不意味着她不漂亮。所以笔者认为，beautiful 应翻译成"很美"或"十分美"，翻译成"漂亮"和作者的原意不合。

原文第一自然段第二句中，too sharply 是贬义，表示对 Scarlett 面部特征一定程度上的否定——即她所遗传的母亲的 delicate features 和父亲的 heavy features 体现在她脸上并不和谐，而 But 后面的内容又表示肯定——她的面貌有吸引人的地方。这是一种先抑后扬的表现手法。三个译本对这两句话都作了相应的处理，傅译本和戴、李译本用"混杂""不调和"反映 too sharply 的意思，陈译本中译成"极其明显地融合"并没有把 too sharply 表达出来，不过后面在描述她父亲面部特征的时候用了"粗野"一词，算是表示贬义或否定，但是远没有达到原文要表现的强度。

原文 slightly tilted at the ends，傅译"眼角微微有点翘"；陈译"稍稍有点吊眼梢"；戴、李译"稍稍翘起的眼角"。吊眼梢带有一点贬义，不合原义，"眼角微翘"要好一些。另外戴、李译在此句后面增加了一句原文中并没有说到的："显得别具丰韵"，我觉得多此一举，完全没有必要。

原文 The dress set off to perfection the seventeen-inch waist, the smallest in three counties, and tightly fitting basque showed breasts well matured for her sixteen years，对于该句，作者主要描述的是 Scarlett 的 waist 和 breasts，perfection 一词的使用意味着那身衣服使她的十七英寸腰显得很美，实际上主要强调的是"腰美"。傅译"她的腰围不过十七英寸，穿着那窄窄的春衫，显得十分合身"主要强调的是"春衫合身"，与原文要表达的有点出入；陈译"她的腰围只有十七英寸……那身衣服把她的腰肢衬托得更见纤细"强调"腰肢纤细"比较接近原意，但"纤细"并不能表现 perfection；戴、李译"她的腰围不过十七英寸……衬托得恰到好处。"又比陈译更贴切一些。tightly fitting basque 傅译用"紧紧绷着……"表示 tightly fitting；陈译"熨贴的紧身上衣……裹得……"；戴、李译"……绷得紧紧的……"。"绷"字在这里使用得不恰当，有点"过窄"不合身的感觉，只有陈译表达了 fitting 这个词。

原文最后两句：The green eyes in the carefully sweet face were turbulent, willful, lusty with life, distinctly at variance with her decorous demeanour. Her manners had been imposed upon her mother's gentle admonitions and the sterner discipline of her mammy; her eyes were her own。

傅 译：她那双绿色的眼睛虽然嵌在一张矜持的面孔上，却是骚动不宁的，慧黠多端的，洋溢着生命的，跟她那一副装饰起来的仪态截然不能相称。原来她平日受了母亲的温和训诲和嬷嬷的严厉管教，这才把这副姿态勉强造成，至于那一双眼睛，那是天生给她的，绝不是人工改造得了的。

陈 译：精心故作娇憨的脸上那对绿眼睛爱动、任性、生气勃勃，和她那份端庄的态度截然不同。原来她一贯受到母亲的谆谆告诫和黑妈妈的严格管教才勉强养成这副礼貌；她那双眼睛才显出她的本色呢。

戴、李 译：那双绿色的眼睛尽管生在一张故作娇媚的脸上，却仍然是骚动的，任性的，生意盎然的，与她的装束仪表很不相同。她的举止是由她母亲的谆谆训诫和嬷嬷的严厉管教强加给她的，但她的眼睛属于自己。

之前对女主人公外貌、衣着、动作的单纯描写都是在为这两句由表及里的评价作铺垫，笔者认为译好这两句话是很重要的。carefully sweet 的字面意思是"谨慎而甜美的"，其中暗含着 Scarlett 为迎合世俗而被动地压抑其本性的成分。笔者会把 in the carefully sweet face 译为"看似谨慎甜美的脸上"，并认为三个译本对此处两词的翻译与原文有些出入。对 turbulent, willful, lusty with life 的翻译，傅译"慧黠多端的、洋溢着生命的"不贴切；陈译"爱动"一词并不能表达出 turbulent 的意思，用于描述眼睛时，turbulent 应译为"不安分的"为好；戴、李译"生意盎然"，此词用于描写人则不准确，译为"充满活力"好一些。distinctly at variance with her decorous demeanour 一句，傅译"一副装饰起来的仪态"，下划线部分是增词，不过我觉得没有必要；陈译"态度"一词用得不贴切。manners 一词戴、李译的"举止"用得较好，但"强加给她的"这种说法程度太过了，笔者这里会译为"她得体的举止是由于母亲一直以来的谆谆教诲和黑嬷嬷的严格管教才勉强形成的，但她的眼睛透露了一切"。

三个译本都是经典之作，翻译家们通过对原文的深刻研读和理解，译出一篇行文流畅、通俗易懂的小说，并让主人公以鲜活的形象跃然于译作中，这是实属不易。不同的译作具有不同的风格，但不可否认三个译本都是那个时期优秀的译作。

（广东外语外贸大学高级翻译学院 2007 级研修生　覃源）

三 "The Author's Account of Himself" 三种汉语译文对比赏析

钱钟书曾经说:"一国文字和另一国文字之间必然有距离,译者的理解和文风跟原作品的内容和形式之间也不会没有距离,而且译者的体会和自己的表达能力之间也时常有距离",而且,翻译具有多译性和多元性的特点。文学翻译的重要特点是多译性,对于一部文学作品而言,不可能只有唯一的翻译。另外,翻译的标准既对立又统一,如科学性与艺术性、忠实性与创造性。这就是为什么同一文本会产生各种各样的译本的原因所在。

《作者自叙》在国内有多种译本,林纾和魏易、夏济安、高健、隋兵、李明等都对该文进行了翻译。对于译本比较的方法,杨晓荣提出了比较好的分类方法。"不同译本之间的比较除了是两种语言文化系统之间的比较之外,还有属于同一种语言文化系统内部的比较"(杨晓荣,2005:84)。杨晓荣把译本比较分为横向比较和纵向比较,横向比较又分为"以一译本为主,其他译本为次"和"两种(或者两种以上)译本平行比较",纵向比较也分"同一译者不同时期的译本比较"和"不同译者不同时期的译本比较"(杨晓荣,2005:85)。笔者采用了横向比较的方法,主要使用"以一译本为主,其他译本为次"的比较方法,从中选出三篇具有代表性的译文进行对比和评析。由于国内已经有学者对夏译和高译作过评析,所以我主要侧重分析李明的译文,并且将李译与夏译和高译进行对比分析。

《作者自叙》是一篇优美的散文。凡散文都会讲究意境、韵味和文采。《作者自叙》可谓是达到了"形美""神美""音美"之效果,做到了形散而神不散,灵活而不越轨,自由而有准绳,随意而又精粹。该文以抒情为主、记叙为辅。对于记叙性散文,阅读也好,翻译也好,都"要把握记叙线索,通过对人物、事件、场景的分析,去发现作者对生活的独特感受和深切体验,揭示主题思想;对抒情性散文则要把握作者思想感情发展的脉络,要剖析文章的议论和描写,特别是要揭示其中的寓意,从字里行间发现含而不露的感情。"(黄秀根,1998:42)本文所对比的三位译者,即夏济安(以下简称夏译)、高健(以下简称高译)和李明(以下简称李译)在翻译《作者自叙》时,对该篇以抒情为主、记叙为辅的散文都有比较全面的理解和把握。无论是从内容上,还是风格上,三位译者对译文的处理都比较成功。从整篇文章的传情达意方面来看,三位译者的译文都很好地再现了原文的意韵;从思想内容和语言文字以及表现手法上的处理来看,三位译者各有侧重,各有千秋。现将原文和译本逐段对照分析如下。

原文第一段描写了作者少年时代旅游的经历及真切感受。第一句话即开门见山、点出主题,对整篇文章起着提纲挈领的作用,突出了作者对景、人、俗等三个方面的喜好。从对整段文字的处理来看,夏译发挥了中文成语和四字语的优势,使用了如"奇风异俗""穷乡僻壤""耄老硕德""踵门求教"等。夏译把 strange characters and manners 翻译为"奇风异俗",较之高译"异地人物及其风习"要言简意赅一些。高译虽然属于一一对应的直译,但夏译的"奇风异俗"与原文仍有差异,不够具体化。李译则对该句进行分译,即将 observe 分别译成"见识"和"考察"以便同各自的宾语"人物"和"习俗"进行搭配。因此,李译的"见识异地的人物，考察他乡的习俗"准确到位，而且字数对应，朗朗上口，很好地将原文两个并列名词准确传达了出来。对于 foreign parts and unknown regions 的翻译，夏译的"穷乡僻壤"过于具体，原文并没有表明"穷乡僻壤"的意思。高译的"偏僻之所与罕至之地"较夏译略胜一筹，但不及李译的"罕至之地，未名之域"来得确切。对于 to the frequent alarm of my parents, and the emolument of the town-crier 的翻译，李译和夏译运用了"语用引申"（喻云根，1996：30）的翻译方法，具体明确地解释了 emolument 所代表的意义，从而使原文潜在的意义明示化，便于读者理解。而高译虽然也贴近原文，但其意不如李译和夏译显豁。对于 town-crier，高译的"市镇报讯员"太泛，夏译的"镇上的地保"过于归化，这一点在喻云根的分析中也提到，相比之下，李译的"街头公告员"更准确达意。另外，夏译中所使用的"耋老硕德"和"踵门求教"两个短语用词过于雕琢，这与欧文所善于运用的不虚饰的文体有些不相称。欧文所使用的文字简洁优美，用词不事雕琢，所以这些词的使用反而有伤原文的娓娓自如，从而在一定程度上妨碍了"抑扬有致，亦庄亦谐"（刘和平，2002）的原文风格的再现，不及李译的"与那里德高望重者以及大人物进行交谈"来得平实自然，更容易为目的语读者所喜闻乐见。第七句 by noting their habits and customs 在夏译中被漏掉了，李译和高译更准确。最后一句夏译将 many a mile 误译为"一哩"，是没有理解 many a 的意思是"许多"，由于对该词理解不当，所以造成误译。高译的"远山之巅"不如夏译的"很远很远地方的一个山头"以及李译的"最远处一座山的山顶"确切，但高译将 many a mile of terra incognita 译为"无名广土"有点牵强。李译将 astonish 用"惊叹"来表达要比高译用"惊悟"以及夏译用"吃惊"更好，更能体现作者的感情和原文的意蕴，因为翻译就是再现原文的过程，在再现原文的过程中，译者需要通过依照原文的"显像结构"来选择最符合语境的词语，好的词语能够让读者产生美好的联想，这也是原作的目的所在，所以选词在翻译过程中特别重要。所以对于这句话，李译比较成功，更能体现作者对"天地之大"的感叹，与原文的意境相一致。

如果再细嚼原文，就会发现这段文字由八句话构成，其中有七句是以 I 起头。当然，这在英语中是十分自然的，因为英语是主语突出（subject-predominant）的语言，汉语则是话题突出（topic-prominent）的语言。如果将所有以 I 开头的英语句子都翻译成保留同样多的主语"我"的汉语句子，就会显得重复啰嗦，而且会使译文变得平淡甚至浅陋，翻译腔就会变得很重，译文就难以达到预期效果。在这个问题的处理方面，夏译先后用了五个宾语前置句，使文章既有生气又符合原文作者的口吻。另外，作者用了很多大词来描绘童年的经历，如 observe、converse、terra incognita 等，这种做法是通过用词和思想上的反差来取得一种幽默效果，译者如果把作者故意使用的手段误解为目的而追求用词古雅，不问其效果，就会有失原文的风格。根据刘重德的观点，由于文学作品是"语义、隐喻和文体上的创造"，"外延和内涵意义话语成分相互混杂"，近似于"一种语言游戏"，因此首先要求翻译与解释性或联想性的循环操作相关联，并要求译者与原作者之间有密切的反馈。其次要求译者不仅能"靠惯常的翻译能力，而且必须充分调动他的组合本领"（刘重德，1998：120），所以翻译对译者素质要求很高，译者需要有很高的悟性和语言感悟能力，才能达到奈达所提出的"功能对等"。

第二段共有三句话。第二句中的 books of voyage and travels 夏译为"游记旅行之类"，不如李译和高译的确切。第三句 How wishfully would I wonder... 高译为"我往往怀着多么渴慕的心情漫步在……"和夏译的"我到码头四周去游荡"用的均是过去时态，而过去时态表明的是事情已经发生，但原文所表达的是一种还没有实现的愿望。这样，高译和夏译就把未然视为已然，错误地理解了原文作者的意图。李译"我多么渴望"不仅准确传达了原文的意思，而且能激起读者一种美好的想象，意境十分柔美。而且李译所用的叠词，如"迢迢""一艘艘""渐远渐小"等更能传达原作的神韵。可见，再现原文其实是很不容易的，译者需要"将从原文的审美接受中获得的'显象结构'物化为语符"（刘重德，1998：365），这是和意象分不开的，并且要求形成更鲜明、更生动的意象，而李译在传达原文意象方面做得非常成功。

第三段第一句的高译"稍就理性之范""却适足使之更其固定"虽然译出了大意，但是文字过于雕琢，晦涩难懂，不符合汉语读者的语言习惯。而夏译将此句用分号隔开来翻译为"渐渐的纳入理性的规范；但是本来只是空泛的憧憬，现在变成确定的心愿了"，准确得体地传达了原意。李译巧妙地用了一个让步状语从句："……尽管这种阅读和思考使得这种道不清、说不明的爱好趋于理性化"，意思传达准确，而且逻辑清楚。对于 vague inclination 的翻译，相对于高译"渺茫的向往"和夏译"好玩的性情"，李译采用"说不清、道不明的爱好"要显得更为准确和明晰，这说明译者吃透了原文模糊词语的具体所指。而且李译将 brought into more reasonable bounds 译为"趋于理性化"，要比高译的"稍就理性之范"和夏译的"纳入理性的规范"更合乎汉语的表达习惯，更加自然。第二句夏译、高译和李译都传达了原句的完整意义，但高译过于讲究用词华丽，比如"此帮却可谓得天独厚，世罕其俦"，不够自然。另外，对 charms of nature 的翻译，高译为"大自然的妩媚"缩小了词语意义的范畴，正如喻云根在分析时提到，"妩媚"属于阴柔之类，此词与语境不符，通常考察一个词用得是否合理，要参照该词所出现的语境。语境一般包括语言语境（linguistic context），亦称 co-text（上下文），情景语境（situational context）和文化语境（cultural context）。这些因素都是在翻译时选词要考虑的，对照下文罗列的英国风光的佳处，妩媚仅是英国景色特点的一个方面，而非全部，不能犯以偏概全的错误。李译和夏译则是比较准确可取的译法。

第三段第三句是描写美国绮丽风光的长句，作者连续使用了八个平行结构勾勒出了美国那美不胜收的风光。该平行结构前后联系紧密，语气贯通，能够深入浅出地增加句势，增强说服力，突出了所要强调的内容。三家译文都采用了排比句式来翻译，手法各异但能达到同样的神韵，但在某些用词上，三家译文各有高下。夏译用了"（5个）美国有……，美国的大河……美国的森林……美国的天空……"。较之高译的"（8个）试想她那"和李译的"（8个）她那"的排比句式，夏译看上去是在罗列美国的风光，他所采用的是"有"字引导的存在句。该句式往往是用来表示所存在的具体客观事实，很少带有个人的感情色彩，让读者读起来感觉作者是在以一个旁观者的身份来观察美国的风光，读不出原作中欧文作为一个美国人对祖国美好风光的无限热爱。高译的"试想她那……"和李译的"她那……"都用了拟人手法，把美国比作一个美丽的少女，频频使用"她"。这就拉近了作者和祖国的距离，也更好地传达了欧文那丰富的思想感情，因此夏译所体现出的自豪感没有高译和李译所体现的自豪感强烈和淋漓尽致，而且李译和高译均采用了八个短小精致的排比句式，这样既干净利落，又把作者对于祖国大好河山的无限热爱充分地传达了出来，而且高译和李译的选词很到位，善用叠词，如李译使用的"绿草茵茵""滔滔"和四字短语或成语以及动感非常强烈的词语，以创造视觉形象、听觉形象和触觉形象，真正取得了"美在心物联系"的效果。可以说，高译和李译均能给读者一种美好的联想，并且能达到心的共鸣，他们的译文与原文有异曲同工之妙，从而使读译文的汉语读者能像读原作的英语读者那样产生同样的情愫和联想。

  对于第三句的翻译，由于高译和李译在句式上相似，所以我想借此机会重点将两者的译文进行对比分析。对于 Her mighty lakes, like oceans of liquid silver，高译为"试想她那银波荡漾、与海相若的浩渺湖面"，李译为"她那烟波浩渺的湖泊，犹如银光闪烁的大海"，显而易见，高译为一个由两个四字短语修饰的名词短语，而李译先用一句短语，再把其他修饰成分放在其后作补充，后者的意境更加柔美，前者气势稍微雄厚些，但显得有些突兀，不及后者流畅。对于 Her mountains, with the bright aerial tints，高译为"那晴光耀眼，顶作天青的巍峨群山"，李译为"她那绵延不绝的群山，巍峨耸立，苍翠欲滴"，李译将 bright aerial tints 具体化了，并且使用了"绵延不绝"这个增益成分，原文虽无文字表达，但内涵其意，属于合理的增益成分，而且李译将两个四字短语放在名词后作补充修饰成分，显得更有气势，更贴近原作的气韵。对于 Her valleys, teeming with wild fertility，高译为"那粗犷而富饶盈衍的峡岸溪谷"，李译为"他那沟壑纵横的山谷，草木茂盛，鸟兽欢腾"，相比较之下，对 wild 一词，高译为"粗犷"，"富饶盈衍"比较抽象，不如李译的传神和有动感。李译真正能激起读者美好的联想，更好地传达原作的意象。其实文学翻译的审美和再现就是从文字到意象，又从意象到文字的过程。所以，刘重德认为，译者要有深厚的笔力、再创造的才能和技巧，才能把心灵里流动的有生命的情感和生动、跳跃的"象"再现给译文读者，而李译在这方面做得的确很到位。对于 Her tremendous cataracts, thundering in their solitudes，高译和李译都把 solitudes 译为"阒寂"，两者选词的功夫可见一斑。对于余下几句的处理，高译和李译都很有技巧，用词不仅准确而且生动。只是在句式上，我更倾向于李译的句式，两个四字短语放在名词之后显得更有气势，更具原文情致。对最后一句 no, never need an American look beyond his own country for the sublime and beautiful of natural scenery 的翻译，高译为"——不，在自然景物的壮丽方面，美国人从不需要舍本土而远求"，高译将 sublime and beautiful 统译为"壮丽"，加上上述的 charms 译为"妩媚"，两者其实从词的本身意义来看是有很大差别的，因而使全段的内在联系变得很模糊。而李译的"美丽而壮观"既忠于原文又准确。李译将 no 的翻译处理得很巧妙，译为"——的确"，这要比使用"——不"更符合目的语读者的习惯。李译增添了"自然景色在美国应有尽有"，这属于合理的增益成分，有效传达了原文作者所流露出的自豪感。综观全段，李译的处理更有技巧，读起来更有一气呵成的感觉，与原作气韵最相符合，是难得的佳译。

从第四段开始，作者话锋一转，描写欧洲的吸引力。第一句是全段的主题句。第二句李和夏译处理得比较灵活，而高译则比较拘谨。但夏译所增加的"而美国所未必有者"有些晦涩，不及李译所使用的三个排比句"那里可以读到……，那里可以享受到……，那里可以体验到……"，这样表达更加连贯、自然。第三句是一个表示对照的对偶句，三家虽都采用了不同的翻译方法，但都传达了原作之意。夏译和高译用了一些表示转折关系的连词如"可是""却"等，使欧洲和美国的对比关系比较明显地显现了出来，而李译由于受到原文的束缚，没有很明确地体现两者的对比关系，如果适当加上一些连词，会使语篇衔接得更好，更连贯一些。高译的"我的本国充满着青年的远大前程"有失自然，但他灵活地在此句和下句加上"就连"，使两句的语义关系衔接得更紧密。而夏译在下句中加了"你到了欧洲，不必进博物馆"，原文无此意，有画蛇添足之嫌，李译和高译更贴近原作。第五句破折号后有五个并列的不定式短语，表达了作者的强烈渴望。而夏译将其译为对往事的一般记叙，显得没有气势，看不出"渴望"的意韵，体现不出作者的情感。高译和李译都比较成功，李译用了六个"渴望着"的平行结构，并用六个破折号，把作者的强烈的渴望生动地烘托了出来，而且破折号的使用使作者的感情好像河水一般，滔滔不绝，不可收拾，很生动形象地将作者的渴望之情溢于言表。

第五段作者转而写对拜会欧洲名人的热望。Besides all this 夏译增添了"除了游览外"，把作者所指更明确地表达了出来，比较可取。第二、三句写美国的伟人。An ample share of this, 夏译为"几个"，高译为"不知凡几"，李译为"无数"，作为艺术语言，都可视为确切的翻译。第三句中的 in my time, 夏译"尽量找机会"属误解；高译为"平生"，李译为"在我一生中"都正确。从语言上讲，李译比高译的语言更顺，更符合汉语读者的语言习惯。如高译"常被他们弄得暗无颜色""往往有为小人物所难堪者"，均不如李译的"更令他感到难堪的了"流畅通顺。第五句结构比较复杂，夏译与高译都比较准确，夏译为"咱们赫德逊河流域的土丘既然比不上人家阿尔卑斯山的高峰，咱们的大人物比起欧洲的伟人来，至少也得矮一个头"。而李译为"欧洲的伟人一定同美国的伟人一样高贵，这就像阿尔卑斯山的山顶之于欧洲同哈得逊河的高地之于美国。"从意思的传达来看，夏译与李译的译文有出入，意思相左。夏认为美国的伟人比不上欧洲的伟人，而李译认为两者一样高贵。联系上下文，前句"谈到所有的动物在美国都会退化，人类也不例外"，后句"因此我想"表明前句是原因，后句是结果，既然人类不例外，那么美国的伟人在美国也会退化。另外，就这个类比本身来看，欧洲阿尔卑斯山的顶峰本来就比美国的哈得逊的高地要高，作者拿这个例子作类比，是为了说明欧洲的伟人要比美国的伟人高明，这就是为什么后句提到的欧洲人要不可一世的原因，即使他们在本国是小人物，但他们自己觉得很伟大，这也是为什么作者一直想去拜访欧洲伟人的原因。试想，如果理解成两者一样高贵，此句就不能和前句构成因果关系，显然李译理解有出入。由于欧文来自荒蛮的、未开化的新大陆，他对英国充满了感情，字里行间都流露出了他对英国的热爱,虽然美国也是他的祖国,作者也在下面一句描述了英国人的不可一世,带有讽刺意味,但这正是激起作者想要拜访欧洲的原因所在,他去拜访英国就是想更清楚地了解自己的祖国,因为一个人只有到了国外,他也才能更清楚地了解自己的祖国。高译把这句模糊化了,没有明确指出两者的关系,让读者去领悟,也是比较可取的翻译技巧。最后一句李译比夏译和高译处理得更好,夏译和高译用词雕琢,如夏译用"忝为",高译用"恭游上国"。另外,在高译的"我要立志恭游上国……以便见见我这已经凋残的后裔所出生的那个巨人民族"表达中,高将 degenerated 译为"凋残",将 gigantic 译为"巨人",与原文相左,而且句子的意思前后矛盾,"上国"在这里指英国,而"巨人民族"指美国,去英国见美国是否自相矛盾呢?这句话李译的也是自相矛盾的,和高译是一样的意思,都没有夏译的准确。

第六段作者仍然由"游"写起,《见闻札记》一书的特点也非常巧妙地由"游"字引出。第一句中的 my roving passion,夏译为"游历欲",李译为"游历的热望",这都要比高译的"漂泊"恰当。第三句夏译发挥更多,模糊了原句的语义中心。高译为"而仅仅是徘徊于众多版画店窗前的探幽寻胜的谦卑嗜者的一种闲眺",不及李译的语言通俗连贯,而且高译的"时而美物写生,……"这部分并没有能够体现原作者的意图。译者在翻译时,要"全身心、全人格、全灵魂地进入作品之中,最终与对象所传达的内在生命结构达到相契与共通。"(邓新华,1991:31)。作者在这里其实不只是在讲画,而是通过这个比喻来介绍自己的观察方式与习惯。不全心投入到翻译中,想作者之所想,不和作者融为一体,就很难把握作者的真实意图,李译使用"时而""时而",效果比较好。第四句夏译遗漏了 their port-folios filled with sketches 的意义。高译"拣出"与原意不符。第五句三家翻译都比较理想。第六句和第七句是由一个比喻紧密联系起来的句群,夏译处理句子比较灵活,他从句群着眼,将 I fear… 这部分意义置于句末,逻辑更清晰,读来丝毫无斧凿痕迹,而且使得原文作者所要传达的意思更加彰显。高译未能打破原文句群的格局,比较刻板。根据傅雷的主张,再现原文的意义、精神和效果是翻译的第一要义,翻译不能拘泥于原文的形式。他的翻译名言是:以效果而论,翻译应当像临画一样,所求的不在形似而在神似。所以高译给人一种"不化"之感,而李译读来更顺,有一种浑然一体的感觉,语句衔接自然。

总而言之,三篇译文都有诗一般的情调,画一般的妩媚。除了部分需要调整之外,都可以被看作是很好的译文。

从语言风格来看,夏译和李译在抓住原作的风格特征之后,敢于摆脱原作的形式束缚,大胆发挥汉语之优势,在用词上信手拈来,简单却意义隽永。句式上犹如讲故事一般娓娓道来,以万变应神韵之不变,便于读者的理解入"境"。凡是对原文进行直译有碍传达内容、有碍传达自然风格的句式,夏译都作了调整,绝大部分效果是相当好的,但夏译措辞过于随便,长句较多。高译对原作的调整幅度不大,特别是在句式的选用上没作太多调整,而是力图以切近原作的形式来移植原作的风格,加之用词倾向于使用古雅的词句,因此不少句子显得过于刻板,而且有些用词腐儒腔过重,整体效果不如夏译和李译。李译的句式也比较灵活,其显著特点是用词平实但意义隽永，读来很流畅自然，符合现代读者的语言习惯，其译文也做到了"行文从容不迫，抑扬有致，笔触轻盈而趣味盎然"，其语言功底可谓相当扎实，是笔者力推之作。

可见，译者在翻译时，必须经历感觉经验层次活动和理性认识活动。翻译人员需要较强的语言"解码能力"，很强的"艺术感知能力"、"想象和思维的能力"、"丰富的感性经验存库"。（刘重德，1998：365）。看翻译作品的优劣，就要看作品的审美价值。邓新华（1991）认为："由语言结构包容在内的作品精神气质如意境、神韵、气势、情态、韵味、风貌等，这是一些非物质形态的、非直观的审美要素，它构成最高审美境界，具有重要的审美价值。"所以我们评析译文的质量，必须考虑到以上各个方面。

就本文而言，三位译者都吃透了原作的审美情趣和读者的审美需求。笔者对三篇文章欣赏的同时，又从词句等层面上互相参照，加以评析。由于翻译者所处时代背景不同，加上个人认识的局限性，三个译本都有需要改进的地方。笔者认为，学习翻译和翻译理论，如能结合翻译理论来对翻译作品进行赏析，就能使我们的理论水平和实践水平在赏析中得以提高。这是学习翻译的有效途径之一，对翻译方法研究、翻译批评和翻译实践都有重要意义。

（广东外语外贸大学高级翻译学院 2005 级硕士研究生　覃芙蓉）

四　对"Altogether Autumn"两种译文的比较评析——兼论多种译本"批评"的方法论

1. 引言

《中国翻译》2000 年第 1 期刊登了'99 全国暑期英汉翻译高级讲习班英译汉练习原文——"Altogether Autumn"，并附陆谷孙教授的参考译文与讲习班学员周仁华的习作，旨在使读者从典型译作中进行比较、学习和借鉴，理论联系实际，以便更好地推动翻译理论研究的开展和提高实践水平。笔者拟对两种译文作一比较评析，并以此引出多种译本"批评"（亦称"评析"）的方法论研究等问题。目前有关译作的评析文章大多限于对单句或片断的讨论，且流于随感式、印象式的评析方式，缺乏系统观念，未能将其作为切入点反思一些重要的翻译理论问题。随着构建翻译学呼声渐高，译学界对翻译学的理论构建提出了许多富有建设性的提议（黄龙，1988；刘宓庆，1999a；黄振定，1999），但均未提到多种译本"批评"的系统方法研究。翻译"批评"的方法论涉及对翻译理论与实践的关系的辩证认识，而脱离理论指导的译作"批评"不具有系统的客观实证性，无助于全面揭示翻译活动的本质及探讨其规律。笔者在《论构建翻译学的若干理论问题》（曾亦沙，2000）一文中针对这种现象提出将多种译本"批评"的方法论研究纳入翻译学基础理论的研究范畴。本文拟在确立系统"批评"参数的基础上对两种译文作一评析，以期引起译学界对多种译本"批评"的理论模式作进一步探讨，共同推动翻译学理论的全面发展。

2. 系统评析参数与论证理据

多种译本"批评"以完整的语篇（或译本）为评析对象，注重整体性和系统性，因而其方法论的一个重要原则就是要确定一个系统参数。首先是宏观层次的参数，即根据原作题材、文体功能及其目的确定相应的翻译原则。如文学作品摹物状景、刻画人物、塑造形象、表现情感，具有审美功能，翻译的目的是向接受语读者译介异域民族不同的社会生活、文化思想、观念等，译文应以忠实于原文为主。如果是广告、投资指南、商务函电、经济合同等材料，其翻译原则应侧重于以接受语的语言习惯与读者的接受心理为主。客体性质不同，目的有异，原则要求有所侧重，评析方法和重点也就有别。其次，"辨义为翻译之本"（王宗炎，1984），译者在翻译过程中面临着对原作操作单位潜在意义的辨析与选择，因此多种译本的评析应反映译者（创造性地）传达了何种层次上的意义，并试图揭示译者在操作过程中潜在的心理表征和理据，这就需要建立一组可供描写、可供操作和可供实证的微观层次的意义参数，并需将其与整个语篇结构系统结合起来，考察整体框架内文本意义互动特征和表现规律。胡塞尔说过"逻辑永远探讨理想的客体"。刘宓庆在《当代翻译理论》（1999a）一书中也指出翻译理论研究应突出其"对策性"。多种译本评析所选择的对象应是那些具有针对性和典型意义的语篇（或译本），"批评"的宗旨不在于以指出所比较译文的正误或差异为归宿，而在于审视这些译文的正误或差异成因背后行为主体的主、客观思维运动形式与特征，并由此反思一些重要的译学理论问题。比如，对文学翻译的评析应着重探讨那些能揭示文学翻译艺术的本质特征和译者主观（艺术表现）和客观（艺术再现）的艺术创造性形象思维的"运动形式"，及通过比较评析阐释"科学性"在文学翻译中与艺术性的互动关系。

3. 本文的系统评析参数

"Altogether Autumn"为散文，属于文学作品的范畴，其功能是借景抒情，我们将"信、达、雅"作为评析的原则参数。笔者在（曾亦沙，2000）中指出翻译原则与标准在翻译学系统理论中的功能区别，将"信"（忠实）的标准具体化为 18 种"意义参数"。本文将这些意义参数视为多种译本评析的系统参数，在下面讨论中将用到语境意义、（概念）逻辑意义、形象意义、情感意义、内涵意义、风格意义等参数。其中形象意义和情感意义是对文学作品译本进行评析不可或缺的重要参数因子，它们反映了翻译艺术与科学性最本质的区别。而语境参数则提供一种更广视域内的论证理据，它有助于更好地揭示翻译活动科学性的本质特点和规律。语境参数因子分为言内和言外语境两个次系统。言内语境是一种上下文语境，又分为言语形式（语言结构形式）和言语内容（主题、段旨、句意）。上下文语境相互依存和相互转化，言语形式与言语内容有机地统一在一定的语言单位之中，内容决定形式，形式反作用于内容；主题、段旨、句意等互相区别又紧密联系。言外语境又称情境语境，由语言运用相关的社会环境、自然环境、交际场合（及意图、内容、方式）、交际双方的特点等构成。这些因子又含有若干更小的结构因子，如交际双方的特点就包括各自的思想、性格、身份、教养、处境、心情及双方关系等，而双方关系又由社会角色、交际地位、情感距离、信息背景等构成。这些宏、微观层次的参数因子对文本意义有制约功能、解释功能、生成功能（段曹林，2000）。

4. 对"Altogether Autumn"两种译文典型译例的评析

1) 情感意义（参数）

例(1)：对题目 Altogether Autumn 译文的评析

陆译："人间尽秋"。译文以"尽秋"译 Altogether Autumn（altogether 意为 wholly 或 completely）是概念意义层次的对应，而增译"人间"二字是对"尽"的语义扩展，同时也顺应"达"。"人间尽秋"为四字结构，结构均衡、节奏稳定、富有乐感，这是汉民族对本族语语言文字结构的一种审美感。从审美心理及效果看，"人间尽秋"在读者心理图景中激活的"形象意义"凸现为"广袤大地，一片金秋"，是对原文抽象概念意义的一种写实和渲染。译文将"秋"对大自然的物化作用表现出来，具有静态的审美感。孤立地看，译文在形、音、意三方面胜于原文。

周译："挡不住的秋天"。译文没将 altogether 译出，而"挡不住的"为"无中生有"，译者何有此译？有何理据可言？我们试对译者潜在的心理表征或理据作一深究，以寻找行为主体在翻译操作过程中主观能动性和客观制约性互动作用的心理轨迹，探讨翻译艺术创造性的本质特征。"秋"是人类对自然现象的一种理性概念认识，是对一年中特定时间段的标识。"秋"在自然界表现为一种逐渐推进的时间流，其存在是以时间的物化作用的形式为人们所认识的，即大地万物的外形由绿变黄及气温的由暖变冷的渐变过程，是不以人的意志为转移的且无法抗拒的自然现象。因此，译文"挡不住的"实质上是对原文概念本质内容的深掘，将其动态的特征突显出来，其理据在于原文前三段文字内容的提示，是一种段旨对微观层次操作单位意义生成与制约的功能体现。从译者思维过程的运动形式看，这是译者对原文操作单位的一种"艺术再现"。所谓翻译的"艺术再现"是指"译者对原作中那些外在的可以直观的各种事物的形象描绘"（曾亦沙，2000）。从艺术效果看，"挡不住的秋天"具有动态的审美感，是翻译艺术创造性形象思维的一种典型体现。

综上所述，陆译和周译突出的是形象意义。下面我们将这一微观层次的操作单位置于语篇宏观系统内作进一步分析，从深层次考察翻译活动中"信"的多层次内涵的体现。

概言之，语篇题目是具有高度概括的宏观结构，是对全文内容的高度抽象和概括，提示文章主旨（theme-highlighted），对读者具有预期的逻辑导向作用。原文 altogether 一词运用巧妙，状景亦或寓情？景的描写和情的表现是文学作品审美功能的两个重要范畴，也是翻译艺术论赖以存在的理论基础的核心因素，对情与景的解读需要译者的艺术创造性形象思维。原作者通过对景的描写抒发情感，写景亦寓情，所谓情景交融，表"情"是第一位的，也正如刘勰所说的："故情者，文之经，辞者，理之纬"（《文心雕龙·情采》）。从整个语篇看，前三段写"秋"景，主要描绘园中之"秋"景和近处之"秋"景，揭示了"秋"的自然运动形式；中间四段则是作者追忆每到秋天和小女儿在园里种球茎植物那种幸福欢乐的美好时光及女儿的音容笑貌，表现的是有女儿"相伴"（I had her around）左右的欢乐之情；后两段既写女儿很快长大成人不能相伴左右并由此而产生距离（We no longer chattered away from one subject to another）的惆怅感，又写女儿每到此时定打电话来谈及下种的事，而母女俩都只能以怀旧的心情（nostalgia）念及从前的种种欢乐和感受，以至于幻想有一种时间机器，带她们回到从前（To go back, just for a day），这是多么强烈的情感表现！从语篇功能看，文章最后一段起到点题和对题目的照应作用，是通过对"秋"这一给人们带来收获和欢乐及下播希望之种的特殊季节的中介，表达了母女间那种浓浓亲情及母女俩对园中之"秋"的那种眷恋情怀。Altogether Autumn 的内涵在此处得到照应和体现：Whenever Autumn approaches, the mother and daughter have strong sentimental longing wholly (or completely) for the garden where they enjoyed their most joyful moments。但从陆译和周译的逻辑导向看，"人间尽秋"给读者的心理预期是：文章很可能是描写一种基于广阔背景之上的异域秋景，内容以描绘秋景为主；"挡不住的秋天"则可能意味着秋天的必然到来，万物难挡秋的步伐。总之，两种译文都没能把原文两个特定人物的情感意义揭示出来，"忠实"的是局部操作单位的概念意义和附加于概念意义之上的"形象意义"。笔者将其试译为"情系金秋"（原文主要指园中之"秋"），其理据是语篇宏观结构的主旨参数对微观层次操作单位意义生成与制约的功能体现，是对更大一级语篇单位的"信"。

例（2）：with all the enthusiasm and joyfulness of her age（见原文第4段）/ wonder about, so happily, carefree, calling out, little voice, chattering, watched deliberately（见原文第5段）

这是通过母亲的眼睛对小女儿的音容笑貌的描写，母爱之情流露无遗。陆译为"女儿怀着她那年龄特有的全部踊跃和欢乐""兴高采烈又无忧无虑地满园子跑""用尖细的嗓子一遍又一遍聒噪着""留意审视孩子"。译文"她那年龄特有的全部踊跃和欢乐"欠生动形象（且语句有"欧化"味）；"聒噪"意为"声音杂乱，吵闹"（《新华词典》），英语释义为 noisy or clamorous，是一种不和谐的声音，加上"尖细的嗓子"，使得小女儿的形象并不招人喜欢；"审视"则有"感情不外露地端详"的内涵意义，使读者觉得母女间有一种距离感，未能有效表达原作中的母亲那种抑制不住的喜爱之情。再看看周译："带有浓厚的兴趣和欢呼雀跃的心情""兴高采烈、无忧无虑地四处转悠""稚嫩的声音""嘴里念念有词""特别观察"，译文将一个天真稚气、惹人喜爱的小女孩形象生动地刻画出来，字里行间洋溢着母亲对女儿的喜爱之情。

2）形象意义（参数）

例（3）：Pulling out all the annuals which nature has allowed to erupt in overpowering purple, orange and pink, a final cry of joy. That would almost be murder, ...（见原文第1段）

陆译："把一年生植物强行拔起，掐死造化恩赐的紫绛、橘黄和浅红这一片烂漫，阻断自然界的最后欢声，简直无异于谋杀。"译文表达生动、形象、准确。特别是将 erupt 分译为两个动词（掐死、阻断）体现了灵活的技巧运用。"自然界"（最后欢声）的增译，是译者对花卉情感观照的深层次挖掘：一年生花草的花朵绽放是其生命的高潮体现，花开时间虽短，但它们聚集了毕生之精华为的却是这瞬间的辉煌,而这瞬间的辉煌就是它们在大自然中展现的最后的"无言的欢声",作者又怎能忍心去"阻断"它们那"最后的欢声"?译文在生动有效再现原作形象意义的同时,也将作者所寓寄的情感表现出来,具有很强的艺术感染力。周译未能把握原作深层次的寓意,将 a final cry of joy 略去不译,joy 则化作副词修饰前句中的花儿:"……把那些欢畅地绽放着紫色、橙色、粉红色花朵的花儿给拔除掉,大自然只给了它们一次生机,拔除它们几乎无异于谋杀。"

例(4):…gazing at the huge mysterious shadows the trees conjured up on the green meadows, the cows languidly flickering their tails. Everything breathes an air of stillness, the silence rent by the exuberant colors of asters, dahlias, sunflowers and roses.(见原文第 2 段)

陆译:"一边注视着树木在绿油油的草地上投下一幢幢诡谲的黑影,还有倦慵地甩动尾巴的牛群。一片静谧,唯有紫苑、大丽菊、向日葵和玫瑰的浓艳色彩似在撕裂四下的沉寂。"

上文中,作者希望"但愿眼下的好天气会持续下去",怎样的好天气?下文接着描绘了暮夏初秋静谧的美丽景色。但是,"一幢幢诡谲的黑影"("诡谲"意为"奇异多变")会让读者产生何种审美心理?有太阳才有树影,阳光明媚下的树影怎样奇异变幻?原文 Everything breathes an air of stillness 集视觉、听觉意象于一体,表现效果很生动,译文却将其抽象化为"一片静谧",未能忠实传达原作独特的具有审美艺术效果的综合形象意义。"……浓艳色彩似在撕裂四下的沉寂"虽取"信"于原作的修辞手法,但从文体功能和语境制约因素看却与整个上下文组构的画面不协调,未能产生和谐的审美感,这种修辞手法在汉语译文中显得较生硬。笔者认为,文学翻译的"信"应具有动态性,局部操作单位有时受更大一级语言单位(语境参数)的制约。

周译:"一边呆望着树木在绿油油的草坪上聚集起来的庞大而神秘的影子,呆望着懒洋洋地摇动着尾巴的牛儿。万物都在呼吸恬静的空气,静谧中穿透着紫苑、大丽菊、太阳花和玫瑰花的浓郁芳香。"这是一幅画面连贯流畅、意境和谐的自然美景,它诉诸于读者的视觉、听觉、嗅觉等多种感官,使读者仿佛身临其境,感受到大自然的美,具有很强的艺术感染力。译者运用艺术创造性形象思维,将 rent by(被……撕裂)变通地译为"静谧中穿透着",再增译"芳香"与上文的"万物呼吸恬静的空气"相照应,呼吸恬静的空气,也是在呼吸鲜花的浓郁芳香,衔接十分自然且合乎逻辑,这是翻译创造性"艺术再现"的典型体现,生动地传达了原作的形象意义。此外,译文连用两个"呆望着",形象地再现了作者那种"出神"思绪融于自然景物之中的外观神态和内心情感。

3) 逻辑意义(参数)

例(5):…evaporating the mist on the grass, butterflies and wasps appear and cobwebs glisten against windows like silver lace.(见原文第 3 段)

陆译"阳光……将雾霭化作蒸汽,在草地上升腾""蛛网犹如丝带,挂在窗前闪出银光"

有两处值得推敲。一是"雾霭"为飘浮于低空的一种非常微小的水粒（原文的 on the grass 修饰 mist，为后置定语），蒸汽也是一种非常微小的水粒，但蒸汽常指水的蒸发或是太阳将雨后潮湿的土壤里的水分蒸发。如果说将雾霭再化作蒸汽在升腾，即是从一种微小水粒转化为另一种微小水粒的物理过程，这是一种怎样的自然现象？二是蛛网挂在"窗前"是一个怎样的位置？令人难以想象。周译更符合逻辑："将笼罩在草地上的雾气蒸发一空，……窗棂上蜘蛛网如同银色的花边在闪闪发光"。

4) 风格意义（参数）

作家的风格体现于富有个性的用词与遣句，译作的风格也同样体现于译者选词用句的倾向性。从两种译文看，陆译用词富有文采，讲求修饰，特别是双音节词和四字结构的使用，驾轻就熟，信手可拈。如：残夏、倦慵、凛冽、凝结、绕膝、缅想、幽闭；寿终正寝、树叶犹盛、光鲜可人、婆娑轻摇、不绝如缕、凄风苦雨、直面现实、恣意幻想、自得其乐、天南海北、尚不知晓等，这些是典型的描写性甚浓的文学语汇。而与之相应的周译却用的是近于口语化的叙述性语言：季夏为时不多的光阴、懒洋洋地、开始变得寒冷、到处都是、陪伴、怀念、远离尘嚣的；温柔地死去、树儿郁郁葱葱的、丰满而气派、轻轻地摇落着、像不停地飞舞的、秋天的风暴、直率干脆的现实主义者、从不沉迷幻想、热衷于沉浸在遐思中、一个话题接着一个话题地、没有半点意识。

在句式上，陆译追求语句的简练，如"一片静谧"就是对原文生动形象的语句的抽象压缩。又如"贝贝种""娃娃种"（周译为"球茎花宝宝""球茎花娃娃"）以及尽量避免"地"的使用（括号内为周译）：亲密依偎（温情地拥抱）、一遍又一遍聒噪（声音不停地传过来）、白桦婆娑轻摇（白桦轻轻地摇落）、不再有天南海北的闲聊（我们不再是一个话题接一个话题地聊个没完）等。陆译总计 1 101 个字，体现出译者简练的书面语言风格；而周译则达 1 278 个字，体现出流畅的口头语言的特征。

就风格而言，陆译具有明显的个性化。这种个性化的成因是由译者自身学识的构成、丰富的语汇、用语习惯及不愿译文表达流于"一般化"的思维定势所决定的。如只比较译文，陆译文字的表现力要强于周译，具有深厚的汉文化底蕴。陆谷孙教授以其深厚的中、英文功底，在翻译过程中措词用句驾轻就熟，原作中即使一些平常语句，他也能立即从其语汇中调动出不同一般的表达方式。如他将原文第一段中的 …creaky crust that causes them to wither; a very gentle death 译为"蒙无知觉中自行凋零，和婉地寿终正寝"（周译为"使它们慢慢凋零，温柔地死去"）。但从原作风格看，译者如片面追求这种"不一般化"效果，有时难免造成局部操作单位"义"与"意"的失"真"，文学味浓的语汇和口语化的语言夹杂一起，使读者吟颂起来觉得不大流畅自然，缺乏整体风格上的和谐性。原作以第一人称自述，用词浅显易懂，语句明快，文字有口语化的省略形式，读来亲切朴实，就像是对朋友倾诉衷肠，这种潜在的交际对象决定了原作近似口语化的语言风格。陆译过多的文学描写性语汇使得原作朴实的语言风格变得"文气横秋"，从而塑造了一个近似学者型的"母亲"（如"带来秋的凄风苦雨""直面现实"等措辞），可以说，译文中"母亲"的形象有一部分乃译者的化身。

反观周译，则无明显个性化。译文语汇和行文比较朴实，没有刻意寻求雕饰，而正是这种不求表现的风格使得译文明快流畅，在整体风格上与原文比较和谐一致，但过多使用"地"的句式等则显得有点生硬。周译之所以与陆译形成反差主要出于以下因素：一是除了译者学识和驾驭双语能力的差异外，其翻译经验的不足在客观上使他不能在表达上做到游刃有余（如第 5 段中的 ..., between an infant and a toddler, with such a round little tummy 周译为"个头介于不会走路的婴孩和蹒跚学步的儿童之间：她还有一个溜圆溜圆的肚子呢。"陆译则处理得巧妙自然："出了襁褓，挺了个圆滚滚的小肚子开始蹒跚学步。"），因而在操作过程中没有那种个性化的"表现欲"，而在主观上有"亦步亦趋"（此处指"忠实"）的努力。但难能可贵的是译者能从大处着眼，小处着手，有几处译文突破了表面上的"忠实"，考虑到了局部和整体风格上的和谐性，可圈可点。

5. 小结

限于篇幅，本文未能对译文中的典型译例一一加以讨论。上述几个方面的评析不一定准确，仅供译者参考，其目的在于反思一些重要译学理论问题，并由此引出多种译本"批评"的宗旨、对象和研究方法等问题。此外，由此生发的一些相关问题也值得进一步讨论。如同一题目三种不同译法体现的是文学翻译的艺术性还是科学性？多种译本"批评"的方法论研究还涉及对有代表性的译者群体的译作风格的研究，探讨特定群体内不同译者译作的共性和个性的体现，以此引出对"归化"和"异化"的比较认识及翻译理论的原则性与实践中的"现象性"的辩证关系的问题，并由此探讨翻译批评理论的职能等等。简言之，开展多种译本"批评"是通过对同一原作不同译本的差异性进行系统研究，进而探讨不同行为主体潜在的心理表征和理据，揭示特定译者个体或群体在翻译实践中主、客观思维形式、思维特征及运作方式。对典型译作的比较评析不仅有助于我们进一步认识翻译活动的本质，而且能以此作为客观实证的切入点，反思一些译学理论问题，推动翻译学理论的构建，值得译学界同仁的重视。

（广东外语外贸大学国际商务英语学院教授 曾利沙）

五 翻译中的信息缺失与作用补偿

1. 前言

翻译是特殊的语言交际过程。关联理论（Relevance Theory）从语言哲学、认知心理学、交际学等角度对语言交际进行解释，其研究涉及翻译领域，大大促进了译文的准确性和适应性。Sperber 和 Wilson（1995）认为交际是一个"示意—推理"的过程（ostensive-inferential process）：信息发布者提供明示信息；信息接受者根据所获得的信息进行推理，揣测意图。因此，语言交际过程是一个非论证性的逻辑过程。信息的接受者在获得信息后能否认知其义，主要取决于交际中隐含在话语中的深层含义,不仅要靠信息接受者通过特定语境进行猜测,有时候也需要信息交互的双方相互有所了解。因为译者所面对的读者不是个别人,而是一群具有不同文化、不同阶层、不同背景、不同思维方式的人,所以在翻译时需要强化"示意—推理"的过程,对一些可能失去明示作用的信息作出策略性的处理,特别要注意语言的环境和深层含义。

"Altogether Autumn"是一篇借景抒情的散文,讲述作者与女儿在金秋时节一同种下球茎植物的往事,表达了作者对往昔的美好回忆和对女儿的深情思念。本文拟就关联理论在传达语篇意义方面的作用展开研究,并以陆谷孙和李明各自翻译的"Altogether Autumn"两个汉译文本的部分译文为研究对象,揭示运用关联理论有助于在翻译实践中译出更贴近原文含义的译文,同时也可在一定程度上解决译文中所产生的一些因不同文化差异而导致的理解上的障碍。

2. 关联理论与翻译

Ernst-August Gutt 率先提出将关联理论与翻译结合起来进行研究。各界学者对其进行了深入研究,充分肯定认知语境、互明、推理性给翻译带来的新启示,并不断拓展关联翻译论,国内学者包括何自然、赵彦春、冉永平、李寅、罗选民、何三宁等。关联理论要求译者从潜在的认知语境中选择合适的语境假设,从原文的语音层、句法层、语义层和语用层等语言或交际层面中推断原文的意图(熊学亮,2007:87-88)。刘靖之先生在《文化翻译论纲》中认为,翻译其实就是"原文 + 原文文化背景 + 译文 + 译文文化背景 + 原文作者的气质和风格 + 译者的气质和风格"的混合体。由此可见,确保翻译文本信息的效度和信度需要考虑诸多因素。

翻译实质上就是跨文化的信息传递,是译者用语言重现原作的文化活动。Gutt 认为翻译最好是作为交际来处理。在翻译过程中,由于是两种语言和两种文化的交流,难免会造成信息阻塞和原文语义的流失,翻译就是一个关联重构的过程,在这个过程中将遇到关联性缺失的问题(冉永平、张新红,2007:109-110)。即使译文中有明确含义的信息,也会由于译语读者不同的文化而产生不同的解读和理解。例如,"钟馗"一词,在汉语中是指为民间驱鬼逐邪的门神,在翻译过程中如果只是译成"Zhong Kui",外国人一定无法理解。因此,需在翻译过程中补充说明 In the folklores, Zhong Kui drive away ghosts and evils for the people. It is quite popular to paste the portrait of Zhong Kui up to doors at the Dragon Boat Festival on the fifth day of the fifth lunar month。

3. "Altogether Autumn" 两种汉语译例的对比分析

例(1):标题——Altogether Autumn

译文一:人间尽秋

译文二:秋天感怀

分析:分析语篇标题有助于揭示主题倾向或意图性(戴莉莎,2007:111-112)。Altogether 是个重要信息，在本文中的意思是 totally、always。作者选用此词有多重意思的表达：Altogether 说明此时不仅接近深秋尾声，而且是女儿少年时代的结束，具有高度概括的功能。母女关系由"儿童—成人模式"转变为"成人—成人模式"后，母亲追忆往昔秋日，怀念着女儿年幼时母女相处的美好时光，这时光一去不复返。作者用 Altogether 阐明主题，抒发无奈情思，同时引导读者产生预期的心理感受。"人间尽秋"四个字充分地描述了无奈的意味，且"人间"二字点出主题信息是人物之间的关系，可谓传神。但由于"人间尽秋"的意思外延较大，不读全文恐难了解这种无奈实际是一种亲情，容易让人直观地臆测文章内容为某种消极甚或令人颓废的事物。相比之下，"秋天感怀"四字让人直接感受到秋意中的怀旧情绪，与内文意境统一，能激发起译文读者的共鸣，与整个语篇主旨有逻辑地贯通。

例 (2)：It's time to plant the bulbs. But I put it off as long as possible because planting bulbs means making space in borders which are still flowering. Pulling out all the annuals which nature has allowed to erupt in overpowering purple, orange and pink, a final cry of joy.

译文一：到了栽种球茎植物的时候了。我却是能拖则拖，因为栽种球茎得在园篱处腾出空间，而此时篱上仍开着朵朵鲜花。把一年生植物强行拔起，掐死造化恩赐的绛紫、橘黄和浅红这一片烂漫，阻断自然界的最后欢声。

译文二：眼下到了栽种球茎的好时光，但我却能拖就拖，因为要栽种球茎的话，就意味着要在开满鲜花的狭长花坛中腾出空地来，就意味着要把这些一年生植物连根拔起，而这些植物此时正接受着大自然的恩赐在尽情地绽放各种色彩——紫色、橙色、粉红等，这是它们最后的欢声。

分析：任何语篇都受其主题的控制和支配，对词义语境化内涵的理解与解释都必须以反映主题的宏观命题结构为依据，每一个语段在反映主题信息的时候都应具备整体连贯性（陈忠华，2004：181-187）。a final cry of joy 充分体现出生命最后的欢愉。译文一使用一系列动词"拔起、掐死、阻断"，简洁连贯，但"强行""掐死"等词语容易让译文读者产生不协调的认知，不利于反映语篇主旨——母女深情。译文二将重点放在描述尽情绽放的植物，用"就意味着……"两个排比句表达作者内心的犹豫，从爱花人的视角显示作者内在的宽厚与柔情，从语篇的微观层次上与宏观主题达成一致。

例 (3)：That would almost be murder, and so I'll wait until the first night frost anaesthetizes all the flowers with a cold, creaky crust that causes them to wither; a very gentle death.

译文一：简直无异于谋杀。所以我要等待第一个霜降之夜，等待花瓣全部沾上一层冷冽的霜晶，蒙无知觉中自行凋零，和婉地寿终正寝。

译文二：连根拔掉它们无异于谋杀。所以我要等到第一个霜降之夜，那时，所有的花儿将被寒霜麻醉，那冰冷的、嘎吱作响的霜层会让它们慢慢凋零，会让它们温柔地逝去。

分析：假设该句的语境是让花儿随着深秋季节的变化自行萎谢。译文一遣词精美，诸如

"沾上霜晶""蒙无知觉"等都体现了译者深厚的文学功力。译文二充分表现了对原文的"信"的功能，同时具备相当的画面美感，行文柔美流畅兼具母性情怀，与后文相呼应。原文 a very gentle death 体现了作者的爱怜之意，gentle 修饰 death 属于移觉的修辞手法，意在说明死得温柔体面自然，译文二用"逝"字完整地表达了这层意思。

例（4）：Suddenly I think of my youngest daughter, living now in Amsterdam. One day soon she will call and ask, "have you planted the bulbs yet?" Then I will answer teasingly that actually I'm waiting until she comes to help me. And then we will both be overcome by nostalgia, because once we always did that together.

译文一：突然，我想到如今客居阿姆斯特丹的幼女。这两天，她定会打电话来问："球茎植物种下了吗？"随即我会用打趣的口吻回答说，老妈正等着她来帮忙下种呢。接着母女双双陷入怀旧的情思，因为从前有段时间我们总是合作下种的。

译文二：突然，我想起了此时正生活在阿姆斯特丹的小女儿。过一两天，她一定会打电话来问："球茎种好了吗？"我会打趣地告诉她，我正等着她来帮忙呢。接着，我们俩就会沉浸在怀旧的思绪中，因为以前有一段时间，我们总是一起种球茎。

分析：作者的意图与原作的内容、结构、措辞之间存在关联性制约（Hatim & Mason, 2001）。本文从此处开始脱离铺陈性的状景描述，开始叙事。在该语段的信息处理中，读者形成以主题为中心的认知整合结构，事件的开始与发展存在着某种关联，景物的铺陈衬托出亲情的背景，感怀之意愈显浓烈。语境对选词择义产生影响。由于母女之间的人物关系非常亲密，不适合使用专业化术语，因此将 the bulbs 译为"球茎"应该比"球茎植物"更合适。

例（5）：It was one of the last afternoons I had her around because her place in school had already been reserved.

译文一：生活中女儿绕膝的下午不多了，因为学校已给她留出一个名额。

译文二：当时她已报到准备上学了，她能伴我身边只剩最后几个下午了。

分析：语境含义的流失和流变是由于在翻译过程中，译者所构建的语境联系并不能激发起读者对语境含义的洞悉，无法推出隐性结论，无法获得译者想通过构建这般语境来表达的新信息（曾文雄，2007：67-68）。例如，reserve a place in school 不是"预定名额"，而是"上学报到"。从达意上看，"学校给她留出名额"意思模糊，令人不甚明了缘由。从上下文的关联性来看，译文二能体现原文整体的逻辑感。另外，将 had her around 译为"伴我身边"比"女儿绕膝"更合适。

例（6）：She wandered around so happily carefree with her little bucket and spade, covering the bulbs with earth and calling out "Night night" or "Sleep tight", her little voice chattering constantly on.

译文一：她带上自己的小桶和铲子，兴高采烈又无忧无虑地满园子跑，给球茎培掩泥土的同时，用尖细的嗓子一遍又一遍聒噪着"晚安，晚安"或是"睡个好觉"。

译文二：她提着小桶，拿着铲子，兴高采烈、无忧无虑地满园子里跑，一会儿给球茎掩土，一会儿喊着"夜晚来临了"或"睡个好觉吧"。那稚嫩的声音一遍又一遍地传来。

分析：译文二将 carefree with 分别译为两个动词"提着……，拿着……"；现在分词短语 covering … and calling 用"一会儿……一会儿……"的并列结构表达。在遣词上，"稚嫩的声音"显然比"尖细的嗓子"更加符合幼童的人物特征。

例 (7)：She discovered "baby bulbs" and "kiddie bulbs" and "mummy and daddy bulbs" — the latter snuggling cozily together.

译文一：她还分别发现了"贝贝种"和"娃娃种"，还有"妈妈爸爸种"，后者指的是那些亲密依偎的球茎种。

译文二：她还会区分"球茎宝宝""球茎娃娃"和"球茎爸妈"。"球茎爸妈"是指那些亲密依偎在一起的球茎。

分析：原文中的一些语境假设在译文中会产生削减和消失的现象，这会造成交际中断（陈治安，2000：190-192）。如本句，discover 除了"发现（find out）"，还有"注意到（notice）"的意思，此处取后者。那么，译文二译为"她还会区分"比译文一"她还分别发现了"更为妥帖。其次，"种"有两种读法：一是读上声，一是读去声。读上声是名词，读去声是动词。试比较"这是贝贝的球茎种"（读上声）和"贝贝种球茎"（读去声）。很明显三岁半的幼儿更有可能熟悉的应该是去声的读法而不是上声的读法。从句法结构看，上声的读法导致汉译句子结构为：主语名词+谓语动词。英语原句的结构为：名词+名词。从功能等效看，译文一和原文略有出入，不如译为"球茎宝宝""球茎娃娃"和"球茎爸妈"好。

例 (8)：Never once dreamy, her hand in her pockets; no longer happily indulging her fantasies.

译文一：从不把双手插在口袋里想入非非，再不靠恣意幻想而自得其乐。

译文二：她从不将手插入衣袋，沉溺于梦幻之中，也不再沉浸于遐想之中而自得其乐。

分析：作者在原文中认为读者已经知晓的部分若是译文读者在理解时的盲区，在译文中就应该略加提起和修补，不应不加变通直译字面含义（胡庚申，2005：101-102）。never once dreamy 意思是"从不沉溺于梦幻之中"，her hand in her pockets 作为独立结构修饰主句 never once dreamy。原文 hand 为单数形式，似不应译为"双手"；但是 pockets 为复数形式，令人费解，一只手如何插进多个口袋？此处原文究竟是描述性文字还是具有引申意义？是否具有深层语义的内涵？短语 keep one's hand in one's pocket 意思是"偷懒不做事"，而 (be prepared to) put one's hand in one's pocket 意思是"准备用钱或出钱"。相比较，前一短语的语义和本文有相交点。如果 hand in one's pocket 可以理解为偷懒不做事，那么 Never once dreamy, her hand in her pockets 则可译为"她从不手插口袋无所事事地沉溺于梦幻之中"。

例 (9)：The schoolgirl developed long legs, her jaw line changed, she had her hair cut.

译文一：女学生的双腿变得修长，下颏的轮廓线变了，要上理发店剪发了。

译文二：女学生的双腿变得修长了，下颌变得有轮廓了，也注意理头发了。

分析：两个译文的不同之处一为 her jaw line changed，一为 she had her hair cut。译文一"下颏的轮廓线变了"，变得怎样并未说明；译文二说明"下颌变得有轮廓了"语义明确。译文一"要上理发店剪发了"与原文时态上有差别。时态是否有必要译出？笔者认为不译出时态会产生歧义，最好把时态表达出来。

4. 结语

关联理论是翻译受众的直接需要，也是对译者的更高要求（何自然，1996：39-43）。一篇好的译文不仅需要将原文的含义尽可能表达出来，在词语和句型结构的选择使用上也需多加注意，避免造成读者额外的解读负担。对不同的原文材料，应采用不同的语言风格。针对在翻译过程中所产生的关联缺失现象，可以采取的策略首先是信息意图和交际意图的关联重构，即对其进行重新匹配。对于译文和原文含义的不同，需要进行修改。其次是语境假设充实，即对原文隐藏、表意不明确或是一些在特定文化中才有的语言符号和专有内容进行适当的补充说明。最后是语境含义的显示，即是将原文中的缺失信息通过译文表现出来。由此可见，译者若非具备深厚的理论基础和审美能力，很难做到出神入化的翻译境界。

（佛山职业技术学院　万颖）

六　张培基先生的英译文《落花生》赏析

原文具备 1) 信息功能，描述了作者童年时代的一个小小生活片断，说明了落花生的特点和用途；2) 美感功能，原文笔调朴实无华、清新自然，没有华丽的词藻，与原文的内容、格调相映成趣，因而具有强烈的艺术感染力；3) 表情功能，表现了作者身处旧社会的污泥浊流而洁身自好、不慕虚名的思想境界；4) 祈使功能，作者从落花生的平凡而有用，谈到做人的道理，寓哲理于字里行间："人要做有用的人，不要做伟大的、体面的人。"短短的两句话，古朴素静却含意深远，给人以启迪，让人明白做人的道理。

张培基先生在英译时以保持原作娓娓讲故事的朴素风格为要，遣词造句通俗简洁，朴实无华，最大限度地再现了原文信息，达到了与原文极其相似的功能。具体分析如下：

原文共二十四句，译文也只有二十八句，多数句子是句对句地译出，有些句子因英语的语法特点加了相应的关联词，另一些句子则根据英语的表达习惯而相应调整了语序，从而使译文读来流畅、自然、地道。例如：

原文：母亲说："让它荒芜着怪可惜，既然你们那么爱吃花生，就辟来做花生园罢。"

译文：Mother said, "It's a pity to let it lie waste. Since you all like to eat peanuts so much, why not have them planted here."

原文前半句"让它荒芜着怪可惜"非常口语化，文字浅显易懂，风格朴实无华，译文照顾到英语语言习惯，用 it 作形式主语，采用 It's a pity to do… 的句型，to let it lie waste 既符合原义，又是地地道道的英语，也符合原文古朴素雅的风格。原文后半句的一部分"就辟来做花生园罢"实质上是一个表示建议的句子。在英语口语中，表示建议可以用 1) Why don't you do…? 2) Why not do…? 3) You'd better do… 4) Let's do… 等来表达，但用哪一个更符合上下文和语境呢？张先生作了最佳的选择，因为用第一种过于正式，第三、四种语气都显平淡，而且没有商量的口气。当然，这句话的英译文若稍作变动，以 Why not plant some here? 译出，则更直截了当、更口语化。

下面一句译文也十分精彩：

原文：我们几姊弟和几个小丫头都很喜欢——买种的买种，动土的动土，灌园的灌园；过不了几个月，居然收获了！

译文：That exhilarated us children and our servant girls as well, and soon we started buying seeds, ploughing the land and watering the plants. We gathered in a good harvest just after a couple of months!

原文被分译成两句。"我们几个姊弟和几个小丫头都喜欢"，喜欢的是什么呢？喜欢的是妈妈提出的好建议。这句话本可以译作 All of us children and servant girls liked the idea very much，但这样行文会使篇章的衔接不顺。张先生采用语篇衔接中的代词 that 替换法，用代词 that 替代母亲所说的话，并用点睛之笔 exhilarate 一词活灵活现地在"我们"的脸上写满了笑意。原文有破折号，译文中以 and soon 来承上启下，传达了原文中破折号的隐含意义。"买种的买种，动土的动土，灌园的灌园"，这一系列动作反映出"我们"的急迫心情和忙忙碌碌的景象。为了传达这层含义，张先生在动词 start 之后分别用了 buying、ploughing 和 watering 三个动词的 -ing 形式。我们知道，动词 start 之后亦可直接用动词不定式作宾语，但张先生取 -ing 形式而舍弃不定式的形式，突出表现"我们"忙碌的景象。"居然"一词乍看在译文中似乎漏译了，但通过 good 一词以及 just after 和句末的感叹号，充分地再现出了这一层含义。

原文：母亲把花生做成好几样的食品，还吩咐这节期要在园里的茅亭举行。

译文：Mother made quite a few varieties of goodies out of the peanuts, and told us that the party would be held in the thatched pavilion on the peanut plot.

汉语里的"把"字句是常用句式，"把"字有多种含义，这里的"把"是"利用""从……中"之意，张先生使用 make sth. out of sth. 的搭配，准确地译出了原文的含义。另外，汉语中多使用主动语态，而英语中则多使用被动语态，因而"这节期要在园里的茅亭举行"以 the party would be held in the thatched pavilion on the peanut plot 译出，非常符合英语的表达习惯。

原文：那晚上的天色不大好，可是爹爹也到来，实在很难得。

译文：It looked like rain that evening, yet, to our great joy, Father came nevertheless.

"天色不大好"是地道的口语，译为 It looked like rain 既是地道的英文，又符合原义。"实在很难得"译为 to our great joy 初看上去似乎与原文相去甚远，但仔细品读则妙不可言，令人不能不赞叹张先生驾驭汉英两种语言的能力。

原文：无论何等人都可以用贱价买它来吃；都喜欢吃它。

译文：Peanuts are so cheap that anyone can afford to eat them. Peanuts are everyone's favourite.

原文是一句话，前半句与后半句以分号隔开，译文以分号为界分别译作两个句子。在汉译英时有时主语是很难确定的，原文这句话的主题很明确，所谈论的是花生，因而张先生选取了 peanuts 作主语。可以说，这个汉语句子翻译的成功与否关键在于主语的选择上。正因为张先生对主语的这一正确选择为他翻译整个句子扫清了障碍，使得所译出的句子文通句顺，地道流畅。原文"都喜欢吃它"使用了动态动词，英译文为 Peanuts are everyone's favourite，译文以静态动词传译原文的动态动词，十分传神。

原文：这小小的豆不像好看的苹果、桃子、石榴，把它们的果实悬在枝上，鲜红嫩绿的颜色，令人一望而发生羡慕的心。它只把果子埋在地底，等到成熟，才容人把它挖出来。

译文：Unlike nice-looking apples, peaches and pomegranates, which hang their fruit on branches and win people's instant admiration with their brilliant colours, tiny little peanuts bury themselves underground and remain unearthed until they are ripe.

原文是两个句子，译文以一个句子译出，这在翻译上称为合译。这两句话是将小小的豆（即花生）同好看的苹果、桃子、石榴对比，显示出花生不慕虚名、追求平凡的品质。这是原文中极重要的信息。可以看出，张先生对该句的选词是经过仔细推敲的。"这小小的豆"显示出说话人对花生的怜爱之意，要表达"小小的"这层意思还真不容易，张先生将 tiny 和 little 放在一起，花生的"小巧"和"可爱"的形象便跃然纸上。但这句英译文的美中不足是使用了一个较长的非限定性定语从句，显得过于正式和书面化。英语中由 while 引导的状语从句可以用于表示比较，因此笔者建议改译为：

While nice-looking apples, peaches and pomegranates hang their fruit on branches and win people's instant admiration with their brilliant colours, tiny little peanuts bury themselves underground and remain unearthed until they are ripe.

原文：所以你们要像花生，因为它是有用的，不是伟大、好看的东西。

译文：So you must take after peanuts because they're useful though not great and nice-looking.

汉语里的"像"是静态动词,译文以动态动词短语 take after 译出。这反映出在汉民族文化里,人们习惯于将花生的品质作为一面镜子,对照自己进行比较,因而是"静态的";而在英美文化中,当有一个值得学习的榜样时,就要马上采取行动,故以动态动词短语译出。"因为它是有用的,不是伟大的、好看的东西"这句话在用词、句式上平凡得像尘土,但却含有深刻的哲理,寓做人的道理于其中。英译文亦文字简洁、晓畅,读来朴素自然。

原文:那么,人要做有用的人,不要做伟大、体面的人了。

译文: Then you mean one should be useful rather than great and nice-looking.

许地山先生的《落花生》这篇抒情散文到这里可谓是"卒章显其志"了,他托物言志,直抒胸臆,颂美斥丑,给人以很强的艺术感染力,读罢使人了解许先生的为人,同时也顿悟他为何以"落华生"为笔名自喻了。

原文中的"要做……,不要做……"在译文中以 should be... rather than... 译出,简洁明快,是地道的英语,同时又符合原义。

原文虽短,但直接引语较多,汉语里"某某人说""某某人回答道"等多用在直接引语之前而毫无单调、不连贯之感,但在英语中,若将 Someone says/said 之类的话一律置于直接引语之前,则会显得异常地单调,而且影响语篇的衔接和连贯,这反映了汉英两种语言在表达方式上的差别。张先生在翻译这一语言现象时,非常注意英语的表达习惯和语篇的衔接与连贯,将 someone says/said 之类的话或置于直接引语之前,或置于直接引语中间,或置于直接引语之后,灵活多变,使得译文读起来一气呵成,如行云流水,毫无斧凿的痕迹。

综上所述,张先生非常成功地再现了原文的信息功能、美感功能、表情功能和祈使功能,很好地传达了原文完整的意义。译文语言流畅地道、通俗简洁、古朴素静,堪称"意义相符、功能相似"的典范之作。

(李明,1997)

七 从原文作者内心出发,把握作者感情走向——复译《荷塘月色》有感

1. 关于《荷塘月色》

《荷塘月色》是现代散文家朱自清先生的杰作。该文文中有画,画中有情,情景交融,文采炳焕,自然贴切,出神入化,宛如一幅传世名画,让人陶醉,又如一杯百年陈酿,令人心旷神怡。正因其艺术魅力无穷,该文"赢得一批一批知音,招来一代一代读者"(罗新璋,1991:29),也正因其艺术特色,赢得一个个译者将其译成英文。在这些译者中,或因被其艺术魅力所吸引,于是"不免技痒"而"自得其乐"地再译,或因对完美的追求而精益求精,重新翻译(罗新璋,1991:29)。这种在已有译本基础上对某个源语文本进行重新翻译的做法

在译学上叫做"复译"或"重译"。

2. 关于复译

复译在英语中称为 retranslation，可指三种形式的翻译：一是回译（back translation），指将甲种语译入乙种语，以后又再作为素材引用从乙种语译回到甲种语，或从第三第四语种译回到原始语种（林煌天，1997：303）；二是重译（indirect translation），即译文不是直接来自最初的原文，而是通过第三种语言的转译作品翻译而来（Almberg, 1995: 925），如英国诗人菲茨杰拉德（Edward Fitzgerald）将波斯诗人莪默·伽亚谟（Omar Khayyam）的《鲁拜集》（The Rubaiyat of Omar Khayyam）从波斯语翻译成英语后，我国诗人郭沫若、黄克孙又将英语的《鲁拜集》译成汉语的《鲁拜集》，即属重译；三是复译本身，在英语中叫做 new translation 或 multiple translations（Almberg, 1995: 925）。英文中之所以有两个英语表达形式，是因为复译可以是译者对自己以往旧译的修正润色（罗新璋，1991：29），这种复译在英语中可叫做 new translation；也可以是先前已有他人译本，但"后来的译者自己觉得可以译得更好，就不妨再来译一遍"（林煌天，1997：219），这样就有了多种译本的存在，因而英语叫做 multiple translations。

3.《荷塘月色》英译之我见

笔者手头有三个《荷塘月色》英译本：一是王椒升的英译文；二是朱纯深的英译文；三是杨宪益、戴乃迭的英译文。笔者在为我校翻译专业高年级学生开设的"翻译批评与赏析"课上选取了三位译家对《荷塘月色》的英译文进行对比赏析，同时也根据自己对原文的理解并"取旧译的长处，再加上自己的新心得"（罗新璋，1991：30）对这篇散文进行了复译。但翻译的性质决定了翻译似乎永远是一门令人遗憾的艺术，"后来未必居上"，可是，只要复译者能够提供自认为的有一定"建构性的译文"，那也算是在"使译文能一步步地更接近原文语境意义，实现'成功一种近于完全的定本'"（郑诗鼎，1999：47）的道路上尽了自己的绵薄之力。

我以为，作为译者，要译好《荷塘月色》，除了要具备扎实的英汉两种语言的基本功之外，还要从原文作者内心出发，把握作者感情走向，采用"走内线"（梁宗岱语）方式，才有可能创造"神来之笔"，把文章译得声色并茂。

原文开头第一句"这几天心里颇不宁静"开门见山，确立了原文的"文眼"，"开宗明义地点出即将展开的下文所包含的心理取向和精神意义"（朱纯深，1994），给整篇文章定下基调。作为译者，只有首先把握住原文的基调，才有可能在语气等各方面传达得更为贴切。《荷塘月色》写的是朱自清任教于清华大学——尤其是 1927 年 1 月自白马湖接眷北来后就住于清华园西院时日常生活的一个片断。作者此时心绪骚动不宁，正如他自己所述，当时"心中常觉有一点除不去的阴影"，"心里是一团乱麻，也可以说是一团火。"至于他那乱麻一团的心绪到底由什么引起，众说纷纭，见仁见智。但笔者认为，这主要归因于作者自己平凡的日常生活无法满足其创造性的浪漫冲动，于是就只好艺术地进入其既有的思想轨道，审美地"跳过"

生命的狭小"圈子",这样便有了荷塘月色下的爱欲景观,一个安抚自然生命之律动和超越文化生命之凡庸的精神"白日梦",一个寄寓了朱自清的生命哲学的思想文本(高远东,2001)。

作者在原文开头并没有点明作者自己——"我",从而使得视点模糊化。从文体学意义上讲,这显然有利于创造一种积极的读者认同和读者参与——因为没有用"我"作主语的潜台词可以是"我已设定你认识我,但你不知道有关我这几天的心境,我给你说的就是这事"(朱纯深,1994)。在将这句话翻译成英语时,由于英语是主语显著的(subject prominent)语言,我们就不得不考虑选择什么来充当主语的问题。原文可以看作是省略主语"我"的句子,因而将该句翻译成英语时可以使用人称代词 I 作主语,谓语则可以用心理动词 feel 或连系动词 be 来充当。但刚好翻译这句话也可以使用 The last few days 或 These (few) days 作主语,谓语动词使用 find 这种结构。本人更倾向于使用后一种英文句式,因为它具有更加浓郁的英语味道,同时还能表达只有上苍才知"我"心这层涵义,为下文中作者为什么选择回到大自然的怀抱寻求片刻安宁作铺垫。

对于"颇不宁静"四个字,表面上看似轻描淡写,实则言轻意重,一个"颇"字,真乃一字千钧,作者当时沉闷、压抑、彷徨、烦躁,有如"一团乱麻"的浓重哀愁跃然纸上。在英语中到底用什么表达才能再现它们的意义呢?我以为,用 restless(焦躁不安)、uneasy(心神不定)、upset(苦恼的,难过的,失望的)均不能够较为全面地表达出作者此时内心深处那异常复杂的心境。其实,英语中的 turmoil 一词,其意义为 a state of confusion, disorder, uncertainty, or great anxiety(《COBUILD 英汉双解词典》),可用于描写人那纷繁复杂、有如乱麻一团的心绪,用 be quite in turmoil 来传达"颇不宁静"之意比较精当。

此外笔者发现,翻译《荷塘月色》时,如何在英译文中再现原文动词的时态是一个不得不面对的问题。汉语里的动词没有时态标志,因而可以信手拈来轻松地使用,而一旦将汉语里的句子翻译成英语,就不得不考虑如何标示动词的时态了。这个问题在翻译第一段时就立即凸现出来。原文读上去具有"历史现在时"(historical present tense)之感,但如果将第一段完全译为历史现在时,又觉得与下文的行文有一些不相称之处,因为作者肯定是在观赏荷塘之后完成该散文写作的。由于汉语在时态的表达上同英语具有很大差别,译者只好根据需要,勉强地交替使用一般现在时和一般过去时,这样,原文所具有的"历史现在感"在译文中使用一般过去时时已经失落,这是跨语言翻译中经常出现的令人遗憾的情况。

在作者交代完自己"心里颇不宁静"之后,一个重要的意象"月光"出现了。文章写道:忽然想起日日走过的荷塘,在这满月的光里,总该另有一番样子吧。这里,作者对于荷塘这个不同于家庭的自然世界,产生了一种期待,希望它与"日日走过"的荷塘"有些不同"。显然,作者准备借助"月光"来移情。对于该句,我以为应进行分译,分译后的英译文前后两句中间用冒号隔开,冒号后面的句子借助情态动词 must 来表示作者对月色下荷塘景色的推断和期盼:...I suddenly thought of the lotus pond I pass by every day: on such a fully-moonlit night, it must assume a different outlook。但杨宪益夫妇将其译成 ...it struck me how different the lotus pond I pass every day must look under a full moon，对此我不敢苟同。因为这样翻译在意义的传达上似乎前言和后语搭配有些不协调，因为在"it struck me / occurred to me + 从句"这类结构中，从句中所描述的如果是事实，整个句子在语意上就显得比较合乎逻辑，但如果从句中所表示的是一种推测，就令人感觉与前面的 it struck me / occurred to me 在意义上似乎出现了逻辑搭配上的毛病。

"月亮渐渐升高了"一句表示家庭生活的景象耐人寻味地黯淡了下来："墙外马路上孩子们的欢笑已经听不见了"，妻也迷迷糊糊地哼着眠歌，进入梦乡。这样，最后一丝与日常生活的联系也被切断，于是作者便准备走上一条出世游仙之路，"我悄悄地披了大衫，带上门出去"。在此，我要特别谈一谈这最后一句的翻译。由于下文第二段是以"沿着荷塘，是一条曲折的小煤屑路"开头，那么如何将第一段中最后一句的翻译同下文第二段开头衔接起来至关重要。如果我们只是根据原文的语序亦步亦趋地将其翻译成英文，就无法同第二段开头衔接起来。正是基于这样的考虑，我将该句翻译为：And quite quietly, I put on my long gown, left the door on the latch and made my way towards the pond。这样，"带上门出去"实际上就被改写为 made my way towards the pond。我认为，这样翻译既没有偏离原文的意义，又为下文的衔接和行文作了充分考虑。

那么，如何翻译第二段开头呢？首先我们知道，一个语篇的每个自然段通常包含多于一个句子的组合。"在一个'句子组合'内，各句之间就有一个相互联系、衔接、照应、过渡的问题，因为，这样的一段话语，不仅仅是合乎语法的句子的连续，而且首先是思想发展的连续"（徐盛桓，1982：2）。一段话语如此，一篇文章更是如此。《荷塘月色》是一篇美文，文章里的思想发展具有很强的连续性，这是汉语这种具有意合特点的语言使然的。然而，如果英语译文的行文同原文一一对应，毫不考虑英文的表达方式，就会使译文读来佶屈聱牙，没有英语的味道。在翻译《荷塘月色》时尤其要特别注意。正因为我在上文最后一句提到了 the pond，第二段的开头才可以顺理成章、自然流畅地使用 Along the pond 这个主位[3]来行文，这样表达既可以前后照应，又可以使译文形式富于变化，丰富多彩。我在翻译原文第六段"荷塘的四面，远远近近，高高低低都是树……"时，更是充分考虑到英语的行文而对每个句子里的主位作了慎重选择或在相应地方作了增词翻译，以保证主位的选择符合在此语境下语言交际的需要，保证上下文之间"相互联系、衔接、照应"和顺利"过渡"。

《荷塘月色》之所以成为一篇美文，还得益于文章从一开始就大量使用叠音词，并取得良好音响效果："蓊蓊郁郁""远远近近""高高低低"的树，"阴森森"的道路，"淡淡"的云和月光，"曲曲折折"的荷塘，"田田""层层"的荷叶，"亭亭"的舞女，"粒粒"明珠，"缕缕"清香，

---

[3] 根据 Halliday 的观点，一个句子除可按照句法结构划分为主语和谓语外，还可根据语言交际功能划分为主位和述位。主位是交际双方的已知信息，述位是发话人要传递的新信息，为听话人所不知。主位和述位可以同主语和谓语完全一致，也可以完全不一致，如在译文 Along the pond winds a narrow cinder footpath 中，Along the pond 是主位，但在句法结构中它是状语。

叶子"密密"地挨着，流水"脉脉"地流淌，月光"静静"地泻下来，还有那"薄薄"的雾，"弯弯"的杨柳，"隐隐约约"的远山等等。这些叠音词，分布在文章的各个地方，读来跌宕反复，朗朗上口，听来悦耳无比，犹如"大珠小珠落玉盘"，给人以无限美好的遐想。翻译这篇散文，可不能不考虑对它们进行恰当处理。英语中的叠音词只有少数几个，其数量同汉语相比可谓小巫见大巫，而且，汉语中的叠音词在绝大多数时候都无法找到英语中的对等语。

那么，到底如何在英译文中再现汉语里的叠音呢？在我看来，就《荷塘月色》而言，对叠音词的翻译主要有以下方法：1) 译意法：迷迷糊糊地哼着眠歌（sleepily humming a cradle song），虽然月光是淡淡的（though the moonlight is in a thin, whitish veil），曲曲折折的荷塘上面（all over the pond with its winding margin），脉脉的流水（the rippling water）；2) 头韵（alliteration）法：悄悄地，我披了大衫（And quite quietly, I put on my long gown），阴森森的（(it is) somewhat somber），亭亭的舞女的裙（flared skirts of fair lasses dancing gracefully），峭楞楞如鬼一般（looked gloomy and ghost-like），弯弯的杨柳（the weeping willows）；3) 类韵（assonance）法：荷塘四面，长着许多树，蓊蓊郁郁的（Around the pond grows a huge profusion of trees, exuberant and luxuriant），叶子本是肩并肩密密地挨着（the leaves have been jostling and overlapping），荷塘四面，远远近近、高高低低都是树（Around the lotus pond could be seen trees here and there, anywhere and everywhere, most of them willows）；4) 增加名词复数词尾 -s 表意法：田田的叶子（a field of trim leaves），层层的叶子中间（upon layers of leaves），缕缕清香（breaths of fragrance）；5) 组合表意法：树色一例是阴阴的，乍看像一团烟雾（The trees were all enshrouded in such heavy gloom that they looked like a heavy mass of mist at first sight）；6) 简化表意法：月光如流水一般，静静地泻在这一片叶子和花上。薄薄的青雾浮起在荷塘里。（The moonlight, like a cascade, was flowing down quietly to the leaves and flowers and a light blue mist shrouded the pond.），树梢上隐隐约约的是一带远山（Above the treetops loomed faintly distant hills）。

除使用叠音词外，原文中还充满了比喻、拟人、对偶、通感等多种修辞手法，长句和短句交错出现，文字活泼清新，使得该文很自然地就能达到"石蕴玉而山辉，水怀珠而川媚"的效果。作为译者，应该尽自己最大努力去再现这一切。原文中的比喻和拟人到处都是，恰到好处地将它们在英译文中再现出来是每个译者应绞尽脑汁去做的事情，但对很多比喻和拟人的英译，都会涉及措词（wording）问题，这一点将在下文中作进一步讨论。那么，如何处理原文中对偶的翻译呢？对于原文中对偶的翻译，我认为完全可以将其翻译成英语中的对偶句，如可将"我爱热闹，也爱冷静；爱群居，也爱独处。"翻译成 I enjoy a tranquil life as well as a bustling one; I enjoy being in solitude as well as being in company。这样翻译，可以使译文完全能够取得同原文一样的效果。关于通感，原文中主要有两个。第一个在原文第四段：……微风过处，送来缕缕清香，仿佛远处高楼上渺茫的歌声似的。原文第四段文字清雅动人，描写荷花的形态栩栩传神。这是该段的最后一句，微风送来荷花的"缕缕清香"本来属嗅觉范畴，可作者笔锋一转，把它描写成听觉的愉悦，嗅着花香变换成仿佛听见"远处高楼上渺茫的歌声"。嗅觉与听觉相通更加衬托出花香的曼妙、温馨与缥缈（李鑫华，2003：66）。其实，这句话完全可以直接用明喻（simile）这一修辞手法将原文中通感所传达的意义传达出来：When a breeze passes, it wafts breaths of fragrance, which are like faint singing drifting from a far-away building. 第二个通感在原文第五段：……塘中的月色并不均匀；但光与影有着和谐的旋律，如梵婀玲上奏着的名曲。光与影本来是视觉，但此时在朱自清先生笔下却又一次成了听觉上的感受，光与影组成了"和谐的旋律"，如"梵婀玲上奏着的名曲"（李鑫华，2003：67）。这样的通感根据原文进行忠实的翻译，就能取得同原文一样的效果：The moonlight was not evenly distributed over the pond but there was a harmonious combination of light and shade, which was as rhythmic as a famous melody played on a violin.

再者，凡读过《荷塘月色》的人，一定不会不注意到文中所出现的两个"忽然想起"。第一个出现在第一段，第二个出现在第七段。对于这两个"忽然想起"的翻译，我认为应根据原文语境来选词组句。第一个"忽然想起"出现在"今晚在院子里坐着乘凉，忽然想起日日走过的荷塘"中。显然，"忽然想起"在这里是一个主动的有意行为，翻译时可通过语态选择来体现这层含义。我将该句译为：I suddenly thought of the lotus pond I pass by every day. 而第七段中的"忽然想起"则是作者在欣赏完荷塘那如诗如画的世界，情绪从原来那亦真亦幻的超然境界回到眼前现实中来时而荡开的一笔——忽然想起六朝时采莲的盛况。这个"忽然想起"是由一定的诱因引起的，即由观赏到眼前的荷塘月色而诱发出的作者的遐想。这一点在翻译时必须体现出来。通观上下文，该句仍然使用 I 充当主语比较恰当，因此，将该句译为被动语态比较合适：Then I was suddenly reminded of the lotus-seed plucking, which was an old custom in areas south of the Changjiang River.

与此同时我们还注意到，在第二个"忽然想起"之后，朱自清毫不忌讳地大段引用《采莲赋》和《西州曲》，这是颇为意味深长的：它不仅意味着人物心理历程的转折和高潮，意味着抒写内容从自然转向了文化，而且使其"夜游"荷塘的意义更加明白地得以揭示：作者披着月光，一路进入"荷香月色"的爱欲境界，在相互感应中思想、感受、行动，只是眼见一切虽被"拟人化"，但它毕竟只是纯粹的自然景致，并非真正的人的活动；而作为"江南旧俗"的"采莲"就不同，它可是地地道道的人类自己的"热闹"和"风流"。

在所引用文字中提到的"六朝"和"江南"在传统文学中往往与富庶、繁华、物质享受的享乐主义相联系，不会给人以礼教管束异常森严之印象；而梁元帝更是风流无限，其诗文称艳一时，风格浮靡。作者所引《采莲赋》一段，正是描写情窦初开之少男少女，在采莲季节相互嬉戏打闹，把生产劳动变成爱情风会。作者直接援引此赋里的华丽文字，当然意味着作者对"采莲"习俗之肯定，对这种"顺遂"人的爱欲的"六朝文化"充满了向往。最后作者引用南北朝民歌《西洲曲》这首以"采莲"隐喻男女爱情，寄托一个女子思念所爱男子的情歌，为自己的精神"白日梦"雁过无痕地作结（高远东，2001）：采莲南塘秋，莲花过人头；

低头弄莲子，莲子清如水。掀开所引用文字的冰山一角，便能发现作者含蓄省略的重要内容：开门郎不至，出门采红莲。……置莲怀袖中，莲心彻底红；忆郎郎不至，仰首望飞鸿。④

可以说，《荷塘月色》并非为写景而写景，也非对江南"采莲"旧俗发无端之幽思，作者把对景物的精确印象和自己内心深处幽远绵长的情怀融为一体，情随景生，景随情移，真乃"一切景语皆情语也"。（罗雪松，2000）

因此，如何翻译好第二个"忽然想起"后面的内容，尤其是作者所援引的《采莲赋》和《西洲曲》里的内容，也特别重要。我以为，如果把《采莲赋》和《西洲曲》同作者此时的心情联系起来，就可以使译文大为增色，也可以将作者的意图和用心较为充分地传达出来。作者从《采莲赋》中所援引的内容为：

于时妖童媛女，荡舟心许。鹢首徐回，兼传羽杯。棹将移而藻挂，船欲动而萍开。尔其纤腰束素，迁延顾步。夏始春余，叶嫩花初，恐沾裳而浅笑，畏倾船而敛裾。

从形式上看，原文是一首赋，译成英语时，需要以诗歌形式，即以分行的形式来呈现原文信息比较可取。另外，译文还要考虑到押韵，主语选择的正确性，语序、意义传达的准确，所描述情景的传神等问题。在参照朱纯深先生和杨宪益夫妇的英译文后，我的译文如下：

Charming boys and fair maidens

Row their boats in mutual understandings;

They veer their prows slowly,

But pass the wine cups swiftly;

When they pull the oars,

They are easily caught in algae;

When they row their boats,

The duckweed apart floats;

The maidens with slender waists

Are girdled with plain silk

And turn round watchfully and with grace.

It is late spring and early summer

When leaves are tender green and flowers blooming;

---

④《西洲曲》是南北朝民歌，原文很长，朱自清只援引了其中的四句，全文为：忆梅下西洲，折梅寄江北。单衫杏子红，双鬓鸦雏色。西洲在何处？两桨桥头渡。日暮伯劳飞，风吹乌桕树。树下即门前，门中露翠钿。开门郎不至，出门采红莲。采莲南塘秋，莲花过人头。低头弄莲子，莲子清如水。置莲怀袖中，莲心彻底红。忆郎郎不至，仰首望飞鸿。鸿飞满西洲，望郎上青楼。楼高望不见，尽日栏杆头。栏杆十二曲，垂手明如玉。卷帘天自高，海水摇空绿。海水梦悠悠，君愁我亦愁。南风知我意，吹梦到西洲。

They giggle for fear of wetting their silk,

They draw in their skirts lest the boats tilt.

我以为，用上述方式翻译原文可以较为细腻地再现原文信息，同时也基本上能够将作者的意图和用心蕴涵于字里行间。有心的读者能否将上面的英译文同原文进行比照，然后自己进行评价呢？

在翻译《西洲曲》时，恐怕译者最先碰到的问题就是如何翻译这个"曲"字了。朱纯深先生将其译为 Ballad of Xizhou Island，王椒升先生将其译为 West Islet Ditty，杨宪益夫妇将其称为 poem，用 West Islet 表示"西洲"之意。我以为，将这里的"曲"译为 ballad 比较准确。且看《COBUILD 英汉双解词典》对三种译文中所使用的三个词的解释：

A **ballad** is 1) a long song or poem which tells a story in simple language and which often has lines which are repeated at the end of each verse. 2) a slow, romantic, popular song.

A **ditty** is a short and simple song or poem; an old-fashioned word, sometimes used humorously.

A **poem** is a piece of writing in which the words are chosen for their beauty, sound, or imagery and carefully arranged, often in short lines which rhyme.

在翻译"采莲南塘秋"等四句时，英语中毫无疑问需要增加主语，根据《西洲曲》的内容和最后四句："海水梦悠悠，君愁我亦愁。南风知我意，吹梦到西洲"，译文需选择第一人称作主语。在主语的选择上，杨宪益夫妇没有选择第一人称单数而选择第三人称复数 they，这应该说是误译。朱自清所援引的这四句我认为应这样翻译：

In autumn I pluck lotus seeds in the South Pond

With lotus flowers high above my head.

Lowering my head, I pluck lotus seeds

Which are as green as the water underneath.

最后我要着重强调的是，上文已讲到，《荷塘月色》的文字清新活泼。这除得益于上面所谈到的方方面面之外，还得益于作者措词的准确和精当。作为译者，要使用一个精当的词语来传递原文信息，很多时候往往需要从几个同义词语中选择出最为适合上下文或语境的那一个。到底选择哪个词语才能够妥帖地再现原文信息呢？我认为，这一定要依据原文语境从语义和语用两个层面进行考虑。在此，我想列举几例笔者在翻译《荷塘月色》过程中所认为的比较精当的选词、短语或句式（注意原文和英译文中的粗体文字），以就教于方家。

墙外马路上孩子们的欢笑已经听不见了——the laughter of children playing had died away from the **alleys** beyond our wall（"马路"，选择了 **alleys** 而没有选择 road、street、lane 与之对应）

我悄悄地披上大衫——And quite quietly, I put on my long **gown**（"大衫"，选择了 gown，没有选择 coat、overcoat 与之对应）

这一片天地好像是我的——I seem to have this bit of the universe **all in my possession**（没有选择 This bit of the universe seems to belong to me 的句式）

我爱热闹，也爱冷静；爱群居，也爱独处——I enjoy a **tranquil** life as well as a **bustling** one; I enjoy being **in solitude** as well as being **in company**

微风过处，送来缕缕清香——When a breeze passes, it **wafts** breaths of fragrance

这时候叶子与花也有一丝的颤动，像闪电般，霎时传过荷塘的那边去了——Instantly, **a slight tremble thrills through** the leaves and flowers, like a streak of lightning, flashing across the whole field

这些树将一片荷塘重重围住——These trees **had the pond entirely enveloped**

这时候最热闹的，要数树上的蝉声与水里的蛙声——The creatures that **were full of vitality** at the moment, however, were the cicadas that were chirping on the trees and the frogs that were croaking in the water

这样想着，猛一抬头，不觉已是自己的门前——Deep in such thoughts, I suddenly looked up, only to find myself **at the door of my house**

这最后一句"自己的门前"即"自己的家门口"，既可译为 at the gate of my home，也可译为 at the gate of my house，"home 和 house 这两个词语到底选择哪一个，取决于译者对原文作者朱自清此时对"家"的态度的理解。如果家对他来说是一个温馨的庇护所，就选择 home；如果家对他来说是一个不一定有温馨但又必须回去的地方，就选择 house。

4. 结语

以上是本人在复译《荷塘月色》时的所思所想。复译《荷塘月色》，我不敢说自己像许渊冲先生复译《约翰·克利斯朵夫》那样，是为了使人"知之、好之、乐之"（转引自许钧，2002：24），但我完全可以说自己是同他一样，复译是为了"自得其乐"。许渊冲先生在傅雷之后复译《约翰·克利斯朵夫》时，遵循了四个原则：一是翻译时对照傅雷译本，发现其长处；二是尽量胜过傅译，形成自己的风格；三是在有关字句的处理上，即使认为傅雷译得好，也尽量在原文提供的创造空间里寻找新的表达；四是在个别词句的传译上，如傅雷的翻译是独特而唯一的，那只有承认自己不如他，借用他的"译法"。（转引自许钧，2002：25）我在复译《荷塘月色》时，对朱纯深先生、王椒升先生以及杨宪益夫妇的译文也同样遵循了许渊冲先生所提出的上述复译原则，但愿我这次的尝试能够在一定程度上，使原文和译文"有着和谐的旋律"。

八　"A Psalm of Life" 三种汉语译文对比赏析

1. 思想内容

"A Psalm of Life"四句一节，共计三十六句，分为九节。第一、二节，针对"人生如梦"的颓废论调，开宗明义地指出"人生是实在的，人生不是虚无"。第三、四、五节进一步指出，既然生活不是梦，那就要抓住现在去实干，去行动。第七、八两节以伟人的榜样来激励人们，要在"时间的沙滩上"留下脚印，以给后来者鼓舞。最后一节以更为激昂的声调总括全诗，首尾呼应，在"不断去收获，不断去追求"的强音中结束全诗。三篇译作，都能准确地把握诗人的思想脉搏，以慷慨激昂的笔调，完整地再现了原诗的思想内容，但在具体细节处理上，各家又表现了不同的特点。

具体细节处理的不同，主要表现在表层结构（即字面意义，或称表层意义）的转化上。根据乔姆斯基（Avram Noam Chomsky）的转换生成语法理论，同一种深层意义（或称深层结构），不仅在不同的语言中具有不同的表层结构，即使在同一语言中，不同作者、不同译者所使用的表层结构也有较大差别。对于译者来说，同一作品不同译本间的表层结构的差异，不仅是两种语言结构的不同造成的，更主要的是由于作者的审美情趣、艺术修养及翻译观的不同。由于这些差异，不同译者在同一翻译过程中采用的技巧也就不尽相同。下面我们将从词语的增加、形象及句式的改变等方面来分析这三位译者表层结构的调整以及深层结构的表达。

1) 增词

增词主要是为了调整诗行的节奏和韵律，照顾汉语双音节化的特点，也有的是为使意义更清楚，或增加一些富有"诗意"的词语，有时候这几个方面的因素都有。但这一切都必须有一个前提，即不增加深层结构的信息量。

第二节 Was not spoken of the soul 一行，黄新渠（以下简称"渠"）译为"但这是指肉体，灵魂并未死亡"，黄一宁（以下简称"宁"）译为"那不是说灵魂，指的是肉体"，都增加"肉体"等词。推究起来，大概主要是为了增加音节，照顾韵脚并使意义更为清楚。"指的是肉体"之意，是在深层结构中已含有的，并不是凭空添加，因此这样做还是合理的。黄杲炘（以下简称"炘"）虽然未加"肉体"之类，为了音节的缘故也把原句给拉长了，译成了十个音节，意义也很突出。

第四节中 drums 一词，为了节奏的缘故，炘译成了"鼙鼓"，加了一个同义的"鼙"字，渠译成了"鼓声"，加了一个"声"字，形象有所转换；宁译成了"丧鼓"，但他并没有加词，而是把后一行的 funeral 提到了前面。另外，炘译在"鼓"前加了"一些"，渠译加了"阵阵"，宁译在"鼓"后加了"一声声"。这一切，都是出于节奏整齐的考虑而加上了一些不影响深层意义的词语。

再如，第六节中 heart 一词，炘、渠、宁分别译成了"赤心""红心""丹心"，增加了一个色彩形容词，这主要是受汉语双音节化的限制而加上的，因为单独一个"心"字读起来节奏上就不那么流畅了。

2) 改变形象，转换视角

译文中有不少改变原文形象或视角之处。这些改变，一般是出于"诗意"的考虑，有时也是为了照顾押韵。比如第二节中炘把"坟墓"译为"一抔黄土"，使用了借代手法，大概是由于"一抔黄土"更能引起中国人的联想，更富有意蕴，当然也有节奏的因素在内，因为炘译把每行诗都规定为十个音节，但若单纯出于节奏的考虑，他也许会用"一座坟墓"，但形象感就比不上"一抔黄土"了。第三节中，宁把 Find us farther than today 译为"看我们都比今天站得更高"，以"高"易"远"，属于视角的转换。汉语喜用高度来表示进步，所谓"步步高""更上一层楼"即是。这里以"高"易"远"，应是出于这种考虑，当然，用"高"也押韵。

以上是转换得好的地方，但也有改得值得商榷之处。如 With a heart for any fate 句，炘保留原文形象译文为"凭对付任何命运的胸怀"，虽然节奏不那么流畅，却还尚能达义，而宁则把 fate 转化为"障碍"，译为"要决心去跨过任何障碍"似嫌力度不够，形象上也相差较远，不如渠译"准备迎接任何命运的风浪"更有力度，更能传达原句慷慨激昂的气势。

3) 句式的改变

对原文表层意义的偏离，还表现在句式的改变上，如原文是正说的，译文改为反说；原文是反说的，译文改为正说；原文为短语的，译文改为句子等等。

第二句中 Life is earnest 原为正说，炘、宁二译都改成了反说，分别译为"它决非虚度""人生不是虚无"，深层意义都保持不变。第三节中 Not enjoyment, and not sorrow, / Is our destined end or way 本是否定的陈述句，宁译改为两句，一句为否定的祈使句，一句为肯定的陈述句，成了"别只顾贪欢，别一味哀怨；/ 人生的道路该另有目标"，而炘、渠则按原句式译出，不过颠倒了一下诗行。这句诗按原句式或按原顺序直译似很难译好，需改变句式或顺序，才能传达出深层意义来。

译文中也有个别因表层结构的改变而导致深层意义改变之处，如宁译第一节最后两行，把 And things are not what they seem 译为"肉体也不再是原来的姿容"，无论表层还是深层都与原意不符。又如宁译第六节，把 Let the dead past bury its dead 译为"让已逝的岁月去它的蛋吧！"对表层改动过大，深层也不尽相同。原文是化引《圣经新约·马太福音》上的话，"又有一个门徒对耶稣说，'主啊，容我先回去埋葬我父亲'，耶稣说：'任凭死人埋葬他们的死人，你跟从我吧！'"宁译完全抛弃了这个典故，与原诗差距较大，似不足取。

从以上分析中我们可以看到，对于原作思想内容的忠实，可以表现为表层意义上的忠实和深层意义的忠实。对深层意义的忠实是绝对标准，对表层意义的忠实是相对标准。在许多情况下，译作对表层意义是不忠实的，它可以有不同于原文的表达方式，有不同的视角，不同的词语，不同的句式。为了更好地忠实于深层意义，译者可针对不同的情况，对表层意义进行适当的增词、减词，改变形象，变换句式等。对表层意义的忠实与偏离都是以忠实于作者原作的深层意义为标准的。

在对原作思想内容的忠实上，有时候会遇到一个棘手的问题，即原作由于作者的疏忽或其他原因，在内容上出现了明显的错误，这时候是应该保留这一错误呢，还是应给予修正？《人生颂》第五节就存在这么一个问题。这一节有一处比喻，把世界比作战场，人生比作营帐，号召人们不要做"默默无声、任人驱使的牛羊"，"要在战斗中当一名闯将"。著名学者朗斯伯里（Thomas R. Lounsbury）认为这节诗有语病：战场上有"斗争"（strife），宜做英雄，自然很有道理，但在"露宿营"（bivouac）里，大家都是同生共死的战友，也有"斗争"，也要在"斗争"中做英雄，就说不过去了，而且，在军营里，服从命令乃是军人的天职，诗句却让人不要做"默默无声、任人驱使的牛羊"，就更说不过去了。诗人大概只顾慷慨陈词，陶醉于字句的铿锵而忽视了其意义上的和谐。面对这么一个问题，三译的处理方式是有所不同的。忻、渠二译采取了将错就错、照译不误的做法，宁译则给予修正，把"露宿营"一行去掉，含糊地改成"人生要随时准备去战斗"。这两种处理方法，站在不同的角度来看，应该说各有道理，但都不太令人满意。比较好的办法大概是加注，将错就错也好，见错就改也好，都应该加注说明，给读者一个明白的交待。

上面我们谈了三译在思想内容上不同的处理方法以及对原诗的忠实程度。总的说来，三译对原诗的思想内容都传达得准确无误（偶有一两处例外），令人满意，尽管采用的表层结构偶有不同，但深层结构是相同的，这是译诗最基本的出发点，三译在这方面做的可以说是比较成功。

2. 艺术风格

风格一词在使用时含义不太一致，有的用它指作品所表现出的一种总的境界、神韵和气势，而把作品的形式特点（如韵律、节奏、诗行等）与修辞特点排除在外；有的则用它指作品思想内容除外的一切形式上、修辞上的特点以及由此形成的作品的境界、气势和神韵。考虑到作品的形式特点和修辞特点是作品风格的构成因素，对于所谓的"神韵"的分析也离不开这些特点，我们采用风格的后一种说法，即广义的风格意义。

《人生颂》节奏整齐明快，音韵自然和谐，语言简朴流畅，句式上反复咏叹，层层深入，读起来抑扬顿挫，铿锵有力，形成了一种昂扬奋进、慷慨激昂的格调。直抒胸臆的表达方式使诗作感情真挚、浓郁，比喻、引用、双关、对称等修辞方法的运用，又弥补了形象感不足的缺陷。这一切，都使全诗流动着一股蓬勃奋进、乐观向上的内在气势，读之如浴阳光，如沐春风，令人热血沸腾。难怪当年有人读了此诗之后，消沉之气一扫而光，打消了自杀的念头。翻译时要注意体现出原诗的这些风格特征。

1) 形式特点

诗歌的形式特点，指的是诗作在运用音韵、音节、节奏以及建行分节等方面所表现出的特点。对于诗歌形式的翻译，译界历来有着不同的、甚至是针锋相对的意见，对于诗歌翻译的争论，几乎全集中在这一点上。从大的方面说，有主张以诗译诗的，有主张以散文译诗的；主张以诗译诗的，又有格律体和自由体之分；格律派之中，有主张严格按原诗格律的，有主张自创一套格律的，也有站在这两极之间，主张基本按原诗格律，中间可以有所破格的。我们所选的这三首译作，都是以新体格律诗来译的，但对格律的具体处理有所不同。

朗费罗极为重视诗歌形式的构建，讲究节奏韵律，技巧娴熟。《人生颂》为四行体诗，韵式为最常见的 abab 式，无一破格之处，阴韵阳韵大体上交替使用，每节一三诗行含四个抑扬格音步，二四行含三个半音步，最后半个为一重读音节，整齐之中稍有变化，严谨而不失活泼，读起来起伏有致，有着完美的音响效果。要想把这种效果完美地再现出来是很不容易的。

在押韵上，炘译使用的一律是 aabb 韵式。这是一种典型的汉语韵式，产生的音乐效果足可与原诗媲美，且更符合汉语读者的欣赏习惯。脚韵使用的多半是 an、ang、ai 等声音响亮的阳韵，读起来朗朗上口，颇能传达出原诗的气势。渠译使用的是一三不论、二四押韵的 abcb 韵式，且从头到尾押的一律是响亮的 ang 韵，因此音乐效果也很强，很适合传达那种激昂的情绪。宁译则采用了与原诗同样的韵式，除第五节为 abcb，第九节为 abac 外，其余全是 abab 韵。一般说来，这种韵较难押，汉语中用的也不多，但其韵律之美却是无可否认的。与炘、渠二人相同的是，宁也有意识地使用一些响亮的元音，如 ang、an、a 等。总的来讲，三位译者虽然各自使用的韵式不同，但其达到的音乐效果却是金声玉振，难分轩轾。

节奏上，原诗是很整齐、流畅的，每节四行，一三行为八音节，二四行为七音节三个半音步，多半为抑扬格，中间略有变化，这样就使得原诗节奏整齐而不呆板，谨严而又活泼。这种节奏，汉语是无法模仿照搬的。汉语自有自己的节奏形式——"顿"。每顿由数量大致相等的音节构成（一般是二至三个），顿与顿之间有一定的停顿，停顿的反复出现就构成了汉诗节奏。出现的频率愈高，节奏感就愈明显，愈强烈；各行顿数越一致，诗歌的节奏就越整齐。这就是汉诗的节奏规律。在所选的三篇译文中，各译家都自觉地利用停顿来形成自己的节奏，基本上取得了与原诗类似的效果。

炘译每行都保持十个音节，分为四顿，每顿二至三个音节，有时略有变化，但顿数不变，整齐谨严的程度堪与原诗媲美。宁译每行十至十二个音节，分为五顿，个别诗行亦可读成四顿，节奏的谨严与鲜明似不在原诗之下。相比之下，渠译的节奏就不如炘、宁那么严谨，他每行八至十二个音节不等（第七节第四行多达十四个音节，但其中的代词"我们"明显多余，去掉后仍有十二个音节），有四顿有五顿。尽管不那么严谨，但停顿是很明显的，且有一定的规律可循，因此也有很明显的节奏感。

原诗除使用有规律的轻重音节交替来形成节奏外，还运用了大量的平衡对称的句式来增强节奏感。如：

Life is real! Life is earnest!

Not enjoyment, and not sorrow

Art is long, and time is fleeting

In the world's broad field of battle

In the bivouac of life

Heart within, and God o'erhead

Still achieving, still pursuing

这些诗句中平衡对称的结构及其鲜明的节奏感，在译文中大都得到了体现。如：

忻　译：

　　　　学艺费光阴，时日去匆忙

　　　　在风云世界的广阔战场

　　　　在人生征途的野宿营帐

渠　译：

　　　　你来自尘土，必归于尘土

　　　　既不是享乐，也不是悲伤

　　　　艺术长久，韶光飞逝

宁　译：

　　　　你本是尘土，复归于尘土

　　　　别只顾贪欢，别一味哀怨

　　　　艺业需恒久，而光阴只一晃

限于篇幅，难于一一列举。以上是译得好的，但也有不太理想的，如忻译"人生多真切，它决非虚度"，渠译"永远要有所作为，不断追求"，没有译出那种对称的美。

2) 修辞特点：

诗歌的修辞特点是构成诗歌语言风格的重要因素，即使在《人生颂》这样文字平直、明白如话的诗作里，也存在着大量的修辞手段，如明喻、暗喻、双关、隐喻等，给平直的语言增添了丰富的意蕴，简朴之中透着生动形象。译文也在重现原诗修辞特征方面作出了努力，取得了突出的效果。

明喻：全诗有两处明喻：like muffled drums 和 Be not like dumb, driven cattle，三译都按明喻准确译出。

暗喻：本诗暗喻较多，如：

Life is but an empty dream.

the dead Past

dust thou art

the world's broad field of battle

the bivouac of life

the sands of time

life's solemn main

三译基本上都按暗喻译出，仅个别处除外。如宁译"灵魂睡去如同死去一般"化暗喻为明喻，"已逝的岁月"化暗喻为含修辞格的正常语言；炘译渠译"你来自泥尘""你来自泥土"化暗喻为正常语言。

引用：引用之多是本诗另一重要特色。引用分明引和暗引，本诗皆为暗引，内容多为格言式警句。诗人对所引原文作了灵活的变动，使之适合于本诗的韵律与节奏，其贴切自然，可谓天衣无缝。据黄杲炘译文所注，原文有六处使用了暗引：

(1) For the soul is dead that slumbers,

And things are not what they seem.

此话最早见于第一个用拉丁文字写寓言故事的罗马寓言家费得鲁斯（公元前15?- 公元50?）的作品。此后也常被人们引用。

(2) Dust thou art, to dust returnest

语出《圣经·旧约·创世纪》3章19节。

(3) Art is long, and time is fleeting

与此意义相同的句子，最早见于希腊几何学家希波克拉底（活动于公元460年前后）的著作。

(4) Funeral marches to the grave

类似的句子出自英国十七世纪剧作家鲍蒙特（1584-1616）、弗莱彻（1579—1625）的作品：我们的生命只是我们向坟墓的行进过程。

(5) Let the dead Past bury its dead.

语出《圣经·新约·马太福音》8章22节。

(6) With a heart for any fate.

类似的诗句见拜伦《致托马斯·穆尔》第一节：这儿有个对付任何命运的胸怀。

这些引用，巧妙地与原诗融为一体，意蕴丰富，启人思索，给诗歌增添了丰富的内含，加强了诗作的表现力和感染力。译文中不同程度地反映了这一特点，许多引语也被译成了精炼生动的格言诗句，如：

炘：学艺费光阴，时日去匆忙

渠：艺术长久，韶光飞逝

宁：艺业需恒久，而光阴只一晃

炘译对引语内容一般都按字面译出，且附以脚注便于读者查对。渠译也是按字面译出。宁译对个别引用改动过大，以至失去本来面目。

双关：本诗有两处使用了双关修辞。一处在第四节 Our hearts-like muffled drums, are beating …, beating 既指心的跳动，又指敲鼓的动作，一语双关。汉语中没有既指心跳又指敲鼓的词，只好借助比喻迂回表达，保留其意义。另一处在第七节，departing 既可指离开、分别，又可指死去。炘译为"一朝逝去"，似较能表达 departing 的两重意义；渠译为"离开人间"，含有离开之意，但整体上还是偏重于死去，不是双关；宁译干脆弃"离开"而仅译"死去"。

叠映：Let the dead Past bury its dead。dead 一词叠用，突出了表意重点，增强了诗句的节奏感和表现力，给人以深刻的印象。炘译把它完整译出："让死的过去把死的埋葬"，渠、宁则未能译出这一特点。

诗中还出现了其他一些修辞方式，这里不拟讨论。需要指出的是，某些修辞方式是很难译出的，尤其是牵涉到语言本身的特点时。翻译时不必过于拘泥，免得因辞害意。此三译已准确地译出了绝大多数修辞方式，应该说是比较成功的。

3) 总体风格

总体风格指的是诗作从思想内容到格律形式以至修辞炼句等各方面表现出的总的气势、韵致和境界，是人对欣赏主题的审美把握。本诗以积极向上的思想内容，直抒胸臆的表达方式，铿锵有力的音韵节奏，简洁朴实而又生动活泼的语言特色，形成了一种慷慨激昂的艺术情调，充满了阳刚之气，读来如战鼓催征，令人振奋。

三篇译文应该说基本上达到了这个效果，思想内容以直抒胸臆的表达方式再现得完整准确，字里行间流露出真挚的感情，格律整齐规范，音乐响亮有力，句间停顿快慢适中，修辞方式再现准确。这一切，使译诗产生了与原诗基本接近的效果。

通过以上分析，我们可以看到，炘、渠、宁三译，尽管在细节处理上有所不同，但其在思想内容、格律形式、修辞特征等方面却有着与原诗相近的效果，且有些方面与原诗相比毫不逊色。如果说有差异，那就是渠译在音节、节奏上没有原作那么整齐，宁译在思想内容上有一两处与原文距离过大。当然，由于语言本身的原因，在意义、韵律、节奏、修辞等各方面都要兼顾的情况下，三译中可能都存在一些不尽如人意之处，比如某些词句在语音上可能不如原诗自然和谐，读起来可能诗意不浓。这是翻译的局限，诗译者的无奈，也是读者的不幸。我们不能期望译作在各个方面、各个层次都达到与原诗一样的境界，这只能是一个理想。能够在内容与风格两方面达到与原作大致相似的效果，我们说，这就已是很不错的译作了。

(喻云根，1996，83-94)

九 "The Gettysburg Address" 三种译文的对比赏析

1. 前言

"The Gettysburg Address" 是 1863 年林肯在葛底斯堡国家烈士公墓落成典礼上做的著名演讲（姚银燕，2007）。演说词通常都有一定的特点，如语言通俗易懂，朗朗上口；结构清晰明了，逻辑缜密；篇章安排紧凑，层次分明等。林肯这篇讲话极其简短朴素，全篇总共十个句子，267 个词，演说时间只有两分钟，但演讲稿手稿后来收藏在美国国会图书馆，被看做是演说词中的最高典范和优秀的文学杰作（荆素蓉，2001）。

本文将从文本类型及语言功能的角度对 "The Gettysburg Address" 三个中译本进行对比评析，三个译本分别为姚媛译本——选自朱刚主编《英语演说词精品》，江怡译本——选自陈冠商主编《英语背诵文选》，李明译本——选自李明主编《翻译批评与赏析》。K. Reiss 将语篇按文本类型分为信息类文本、表情类文本以及呼吁类文本。那么相应的这三种文本在语言上就分别具有信息功能、表情功能及呼吁功能。而 Reiss 又指出很多文本其实都不止具有一种文本类型特征，如正式演说就是这三种类型的杂合（Munday, 2001）。"The Gettysburg Address" 是一篇庆祝军事胜利的演说，同时也是一篇感人肺腑的颂词（李明，2006），既是对那些为国捐躯的烈士的贡献表示肯定，又表达作者的赞美敬佩之情，同时也呼吁全国人民一起行动，共同完成烈士未完成的事业。因此，可以说 "The Gettysburg Address" 在语言上同时具备了信息、表情、呼吁等功能。本文将从这三个功能出发对三个译本进行评析，以求使译文与原文做到"功能相似，意义相符"(similarity in function and correspondence in meaning)（陈宏薇，1996）。

2. 信息功能

根据 Reiss 的观点，The TT (Target Text) of an informative text should transmit the full referential or conceptual content of the ST (Source Text). The translation should be in "plain prose" without redundancy and with the use of explicitation when required。(Munday, 2001) 也就是说信息类文本是表意文本，译文应准确传达原文意义，陈述原文事实，在语言上既做到信息对等同时也要简洁、明了。

三个译本从这一功能上来说，都基本抓住了原文信息，但也有一些信息理解或传达不准确之处。Four score and seven years ago our fathers brought forth on this continent, a new nation, conceived in Liberty, and dedicated to the proposition that all men are created equal 是原文第一句，开门见山直入正题，conceived、dedicated 两个词指出国家之信仰。姚译："87 年前，我们的先辈在这块大陆上建立了一个崭新的国家，她以自由为立国之本，并致力于这样的奋斗目标，即人人生来都具有平等权利。"此处译者将 conceived in Liberty 和 dedicated to the proposition 分别译为"以自由为立国之本""致力于……奋斗目标"用词不当,在理解上似乎有误。自由并不是其立国之本,而是随着国家的创立同时产生的,至于"人人生来都具有平等权利"也不能认为是奋斗目标,而是美国整个民族的信仰和行为准则,所以译者在对信息的理解和传达上出现了偏差。相对来说,江译和李译的"孕育于自由之中""奉行……原则""致力于……主张"更达意。

第二段第一句:…, testing whether that nation, or any nation so conceived and so dedicated, can…,这里的分词 testing 三个译本有不同的理解。姚译为"……这场战争能够考验我们的国际……",用分词表达一种能力;蒋译为"……以考验这个国家……",表目的;而李译"这场内战正考验着我们……",用分词表伴随状态。可以看出李译的理解是正确的,译文与原文在意义上对等。另外,so conceived and so dedicated 是呼应原文第一句的,姚因对第一句理解有误,造成此处同样对信息表达不准确,其译文"……具有同样立国之本和同样奋斗目标的国家……"不恰当。

从 We have come to dedicate a portion of that field, as a final resting place for those who here gave their lives that this nation might live 这一句的译法,也能看出三位译者对信息的理解以及传达信息的能力。从字面上看,a portion of that field 似乎就是江译所指的"战争的一部分"。然而,战争的一部分怎么能作为安息之所?只有战场的一部分才可以。比较三个译文,李译"战场上的一片土地"最佳。该句后面一部分用 for 表目的,包含了两个从句。笔者认为应按照信息功能所提到的,在简洁、不冗余的情况下做到信息对等,因此,姚译"……献给那些为国捐躯的人们"比另外两个译本更简单明了。同样的问题也存在于对以下这句的翻译:The brave men…, have consecrated it, far above our poor power to add or detract。姚译:"……,我们微不足道的能力已不足以增加或减少它的圣洁了。"虽然译文信息传达准确,但在表达上却显得有点啰嗦,读来也不够通顺,不及江译和李译简洁、流畅。

接下来这句 …, but It can never forget what they did here,姚译在信息传达上也不准确,将 what they did here 译为"……在这里做出的崇高业绩",使原本的意思太过具体化;而江译"……这些勇士在这里做过的事"又显得过于平淡;李译对此的处理非常恰当,"……勇士们在这里的付出"既不脱离原文意思,又突显了勇士的功劳。此外,后面一句 It is for us, the living, … who fought here have thus far so nobly advanced,姚译增译了"更加重要的是,……"这不符合信息功能对等的原则,是多余的。而且,姚译将 nobly advanced 译成"高尚地推进",这种字对字的翻译既显生硬同时也没有体现原文的隐含意义。此处江译"……勇士们以崇高的精神向前推进而尚未完成的事业"是比较合适的译文。

3. 表情功能

The TT of an expressive text should transmit the aesthetic and artistic form of the ST. The translation should use the "identifying" method, with the translator adopting the standpoint of the

ST author。（Munday, 2001）以上是对 Reiss 所指另一类文本即表情类文本的描述。表情类文本中，不仅作者感情丰富，同时文章形式也具有美感。体现在语言功能上应做到形式与原文一样优美，感情与作者一样真挚。

第一句开头 Four score and seven years，三个译文都用了阿拉伯数字 87，笔者认为原文用词很正式，作者是想以此来渲染气氛，表达内心情感。因此将"87"改为"八十七"更能起到传情的效果。

再看第三段第一句 ...we cannot dedicate—we cannot consecrate—we cannot hallow—this ground，作者用三个破折号连接三个排比句，语气和感情都很强烈。译者应该注意原文的这些特点，不仅要在感情上同时也要在译文形式上与原文贴近，增强感染力和艺术性。姚译为"……我们没有能力来奉献这块土地，我们没有能力来使这块土地更加神圣。"译者将近义词 consecrate 和 hallow 合起来译成"更加神圣"，这样虽然简洁，却明显少了原文的气势，更不能全面体现作者的思想感情。作者用三个动词来强调"我们"不能做什么，是要强调烈士所作的贡献之大，是为下文作铺垫的。李译"……我们是不能够奉献——我们是不能够圣化——我们是不能够神化——这片土地的"比其他两个译文都要略胜一筹，其情感的宣泄更接近原文效果。不过笔者认为如果去掉李译三个排比句中的"是"以及最后一个"的"，读起来似乎更通顺。

接下来一句 The brave men, living and dead, ... 是对前面一句的照应和解释，"我们"不能够"奉献、神化"这片土地是因为烈士们"已经把这块土地神化了。这片土地的神圣是远非我们的微薄之力所能增减的。"这里感情得到进一步升级，表达作者对那些为国做出贡献的人们的崇高敬意。姚译和江译在感情的流露和语言的表达上都不及李译。如姚将 living 译为"仍然健在……"，用词不恰当；江把 The brave men、living and dead 合起来译为"那些曾在这里战斗过的勇敢的生者与死者……"，这样显得感情不够强烈。李译用关联词"不管……还是……"对"那些曾经在这里战斗过的勇士"表示强调，既使前后连贯同时感情也很突出。

4. 呼吁功能

The TT of an operative text should produce the desired response in the TT receiver. The translation should employ the "adaptive" method, creating an equivalent effect among TT readers。这是对呼吁类文本功能的概述，Reiss 认为呼吁类文本的功能应该是唤起听众做出所需反应。因此译者也应该关注译文所达到的呼吁效果。

第二段最后一句 It is altogether fitting and proper that we should do this，作者用了两个近义词 fitting、proper 表达强烈的情感，呼吁全体民众应该行动起来，因为这是必须要做的。此处，语言的表情和呼吁功能都得到明显体现。作者既以此来表达自己对烈士的尊敬，同时也是在号召听众作出回应，以产生共鸣。江译："……是理所当然、恰如其分的。"仅用两个成语翻译 fitting 和 proper，显得力量不够，感情稍嫌平淡，达不到共鸣的效果。姚译："我们这样做是完全恰当的，也是完全应该的"，其中两个"完全"使感情得到了凸显，比江译气势要强。

李译:"我们这样做是完全恰当的,我们这样做是完全合适的。"用两个排比句来强调感情,加强号召力和感染力,呼吁功能得到完全体现,译得很到位。

对 It is for us, the living, rather, to be dedicated here to… 这一句的处理,李译可谓精彩绝妙。该译文不仅在此处另起一段表示强调,同时在句式上也是气势非凡,激励着广大民众。如"是该轮到我们,轮到我们所有活着的人……",对词语的重复加强了感染力。

最后一句是整个演说的精华之处,也是作者感情的高潮。句子很长,作者通过这样一个长句,运用一连串的从句和排比将感情渲染到极致,同时强烈的呼吁效果也达到了顶峰。三位译者在此句的翻译上各有千秋,都通过句式及对相应词语的重复来传达作者的这种呼吁和号召。如姚译"我们下定决心……,决心……,决心……";江译"我们要……,要……,要……"感情都很强烈。李译虽然句式没有这么整齐,但整体来看,气势丝毫不亚于前面两个译本,即三种译文都达到了与原文在呼吁功能上的相似对等。不过,最后一个分句…that government of the people, by the people, for the people… 的翻译值得深入研究。大多数译者包括读者都理所当然的认为这里应该翻译成"民有、民治、民享",然而李译却为"……归人民所有、由人民管理、为人民服务……",初看觉得不如前面译文顺口,然细细想来才发现译者的细心与用意。本文开头也提到,演说词是口述的演讲稿,因此语言大都简单明白。最后这一分句,如果作为书面材料,译为"民有、民治、民享"当然非常合适,可是演说面对的是听众,很可能有许多听众都不清楚到底是哪三个词语,这样就会造成理解上的差异,呼吁的效果自然会大打折扣。李译却通俗易懂,读来也很通顺,因而笔者认为此处李译最为恰当。

5. 结语

总之,从语言的信息、表情、呼吁这三个功能出发分析这三个译本,最后得出结论,无论是在意思的准确性和明了性方面,还是对感情的传达或是对听众的情感号召方面,李译都比其他两个译本略胜一筹,真正做到了与原文"功能相似,意义对等",是非常不错的译文。

(广东外语外贸大学高级翻译学院 2007 级硕士研究生 邓娟)

辜正坤对"Letter to Lord Chesterfield"两种译文的译注

文章作者及背景介绍:

塞缪尔·约翰逊(Samuel Johnson, 1709-1784),18 世纪英国文坛巨匠,著名的散文家、文艺批评家和辞书编撰家。早年曾就读于牛津大学,后因生计而中途辍学,遂以卖文为生,开始了艰难的文学创作生涯。早期多从事翻译和诗歌创作,还主办过多由自己撰稿的《漫游者》杂志(The Rambler)。约翰逊较有影响的著述有《诗人传》(Lives of the Poets),诗集《人类欲望的虚幻》(Vanity of Human Wishes),以及小说《拉塞勒斯》(Rasselas)等。

不过真正确立了约翰逊文坛地位的是他编纂的辞典 A Dictionary of the English Language。这部辞典在当时有很大的影响力，对英语的规范化使用起到了巨大的作用，堪称英语发展史上的一个里程碑。本文所要介绍的就是该辞典出版前发生的一个小插曲。

背景是这样的：在当时的英国文坛，文人要想成名，必须要有达官显贵的引荐、提携，即必须有名人作为保护人，英语称 patron（恩主，提携人）。当时的内阁大臣，自命为文人 patron 的切斯特菲尔德伯爵（Earl of Chesterfield）就是这样一位显赫的人物。此人集贵族、政客、作家头衔于一身，深受文人们的崇拜。当时作为一介穷儒的约翰逊也未能免俗，想把成名的希望寄托于某个大人物。他早在 1747 年就拟就了编纂一本英语辞典的计划，但工程之艰巨使他感到有些力不从心。于是他便把该计划呈交给切斯特菲尔德，希望得到他的赞许与资助。不料几次奔走求见，均未被理睬。约翰逊求助无望，但并未气馁。他卧薪尝胆，孤军奋战，披沥七载，终于完成了这部划时代的鸿篇巨著。然而就在辞典即将出版之际，切斯特菲尔德忽然在报上撰文公开推荐并吹捧约翰逊的辞典。其贪天之功、沽名钓誉之心昭然若揭。约翰逊得此消息，十分气愤，当即写了这封文笔犀利、气势雄浑的信作为答复，对切斯特菲尔德的势利行径进行了无情的揭露与抨击。该信语言精练，结构严谨，寓意深刻，字字珠玑，实为英国散文中不可多得的名篇。由此也可见约翰逊散文风格之一斑。约翰逊此举也标志着文人依附权贵时代的结束。

翻译此文的理论准备：

根据翻译标准多元互补论，翻译本身具有多种功能（或曰目的性）：如模拟信息功能，揭示思维模式功能，审美娱乐功能或丰富译入语功能等。其次，具体翻译标准之所以是多元的，还在于人类审美趣味的多样化及读者和译者的多层次等。（参见拙著《中西诗鉴赏与翻译》，湖南人民出版社，1998，pp. 193-251。）

我们先从模拟信息来看。要模拟信息，先要弄清原作的信息存在原型。信息存在原型与信息存在的时空关系紧密相连。从时空关系看，原作（源语作品）写于 1755 年的英国，正值英国古典主义文风盛行的时候。作者约翰逊即当时有代表性的古典主义作家，其散文正如李赋宁先生所言"既具有拉丁散文的典雅、气势和音调的铿锵，又兼备英文散文的雄健、朴素和简练。"再从当时中英对应时空关系来看，1755 年前后的中国正值清朝乾隆年间，当时正是桐城派散文相当流行的时候。同期文学大师有郑板桥、吴敬梓、全祖望、曹雪芹、袁枚、纪昀、蒋士铨、赵翼、钱大昕、王文治、姚鼐、翁方纲、李调元、高鹗等。假如由上述中的任何一位大师来翻译约翰逊的文章，我们自然会期望他们把这位同时代人的大作译成颇为高雅的文言文（即使不是地道的桐城派文风），而绝不是白话文，这是毫无疑义的。因此，为了能最大限度地近似中英时空对应关系，较为理想的处理手段就是把它译成比较雅致的文言文。这就等于在风格方面定了一个翻译标准。

然而，站在读者的角度来看，我们现在的翻译主要是为当代人服务。不用说，当代人在时空关系上已经和约翰逊所处时代有了 255 年的时空错位，因而不能指望当代人能比较充分地体会理解当时的文风,至少对一部分读者来说要做到这一点已经颇不容易。因此,译成白话文,也是符合多数读者层的需要的。更何况今天中国大陆的翻译出版物差不多一律是白话文,绝少看到有新的文言文翻译出版物,所以,译成白话文已经是大势所趋。这就等于在风格上定了第二个翻译标准。

　　再从译者的角度来看。译者抱定的宗旨,往往是声称要"忠实"于原作。如果要真正"忠实"于原作,那么就不能译成白话,因为我们期待古人写的就是古文。如果把王勃的《藤王阁序》译成白话文,那么,无论译者的手段有多高明,原有的那种文采必然是所剩无几了。(当然,现代人也尝试把它们译成白话,但主要是为了帮助不大懂古文的读者理解文意,而非主要为了传输原作的文采。此当别论。)这样看来,若能将约翰逊的原作译成雅致的文言文,看来也是需要的。怎么办呢?若译文以达意为主,译成白话就可以了(何况白话也有一定的文采);若译文以模仿表现原作的古雅风味,则宜译成文言文。若想两者兼得,那就两种译文并存,或者再来一种文白兼具的译文(虽难以讨好,但也不妨一试)。那么,就等于又定了双标准并存或三标准并存了。

　　姑不论其他的许多条件,单就上述的三个角度,在风格上就产生了三个标准。如果面面俱到地加以理论分析(尚包括其他微观处理手段),则必定要建立一个标准系统才能济事。此文主要是为了用作翻译练习,篇幅有限,不能展开阐述,亦不可能将原作按各类标准译成若干种风格。为简便计,此处只提供较普通的文言文和白话文译例各一,聊供参考。

(辜正坤)

参考文献

蔡良骥. 1996. 论艺术氛围. 文艺理论研究（3）: 35-39.
曹雪芹. 1994. A Dream of Red Mansions. 杨宪益，戴乃迭，译. 北京: 外文出版社.
陈冠商. 1998. 英语背诵文选. 上海: 上海外语教育出版社.
陈宏薇. 1996. 新实用汉译英教程. 武汉: 湖北教育出版社.
陈治安. 2000. 语用学: 语言理解、社会文化与外语教学. 重庆: 西南师范大学出版社.
陈忠华. 2004. 知识与语篇理解——话语分析认知科学方法论. 北京: 外语教学与研究出版社.
戴莉莎. 2007. 翻译批评: 宏观和微观的统一. 湖南行政学院学报（6）: 111-112.
戴婉平. 2003. 华盛顿·欧文的散文风格. 云梦学刊（3）: 78-80.
党争胜. 2008. 翻译名篇欣赏. 西安: 西安交通大学出版社.
邓新华. 1991. "品味"的艺术接受方式. 文艺研究（4）: 95.
段曹林. 2000. 系统论与语境研究. 修辞学习（1）: 5-6.
方遒. 2004. 散文学综论. 合肥: 安徽教育出版社.
冯庆华. 1997. 实用翻译教程. 上海: 上海外语教育出版社.
冯世则. 2005. 翻译匠语. 上海: 文汇出版社.
付宁. 2009. 简·奥斯汀在《傲慢与偏见》中的创作风格与艺术成就. 名作欣赏（2）: 104-106.
高远东. 2001.《荷塘月色》——一个精神分析的文本. 中国现代文学研究丛刊（1）: 221-233.
郭著章，江安，鲁文忠. 1994. 唐诗精品百首英译. 武汉: 湖北教育出版社.
韩秀莲，孙慧聪. 2009. 试析《傲慢与偏见》中对"扁平人物"反讽的运用. 电影评价（5）: 110.
何自然. 1996. 翻译要译什么？——翻译中的语用学. 外语与翻译（2）: 39-43.
胡庚申. 2005. 国际交流语用学: 从实践到理论. 北京: 清华大学出版社.
胡显耀，李立. 2009. 高级文学翻译. 北京: 外语教学与研究出版社.
胡裕树. 1985. 大学写作. 上海: 复旦大学出版社.
黄杲炘. 1986. 英国抒情诗100首. 上海: 上海译文出版社.
黄继忠. 1987. 名人书信一百封. 北京: 中国对外翻译出版公司.
黄龙. 1988. 翻译学. 南京: 江苏教育出版社.
黄秀根. 1998. 散文审美教学三步曲. 语文教学与研究（11）: 43.
黄振定. 1999. 翻译学——艺术论与科学论的统一. 长沙: 湖南教育出版社.
简·奥斯汀. 1980. 傲慢与偏见. 王科一，译. 上海: 上海译文出版社.
金鑫. 2009. 带着脚镣在舞台上跳舞——浅析戏剧翻译的双重标准. 人文社科（28）: 562-563.
荆素蓉. 2001. 林肯《葛底斯堡演说》译文比较——浅谈演讲词的翻译原则. 运城高等专科学校学报（4）: 46-48.
老舍. 1984. 谈翻译 // 《翻译通讯》编辑部. 翻译研究论文集（1949-1983）. 北京: 外语教学与研究出版社: 130-132.
老舍. 2001. Camel Xiangzi. 施晓菁，译. 北京: 外文出版社.

李建军 . 2003. 小说修辞研究 . 北京：中国人民大学出版社 .
李凯，付瑞阳 . 2009. 从诗歌的诗趣与意境谈诗歌翻译 . 考试周刊（37）：30-31.
李明 . 1997. 张培基先生的英译文《落花生》赏析 . 中国翻译（4）：38-41.
李明 . 2006. 翻译批评与赏析 . 武汉：武汉大学出版社 .
李庆西 . 1988. 文学的当代性 . 北京：人民文学出版社 .
李鑫华 . 2003. 英语修辞格详论 . 上海：上海外语教育出版社 .
廖四平，张瑜 . 2007. 用心和眼睛传递诠释灵魂的艺术——袁可嘉的外国诗歌翻译 . 中国翻译（2）：51-54.
林煌天 . 1997. 中国翻译词典 . 武汉：湖北教育出版社 .
刘重德 . 1998. 英汉语比较与翻译 . 青岛：青岛出版社 .
刘和平 . 2002. 三位名家对欧文《作者自叙》的翻译 . 上海科技翻译（1）：58-60.
刘宓庆 . 1999a. 当代翻译理论 . 北京：中国对外翻译出版公司 .
刘宓庆 . 1999b. 文化翻译论纲 . 武汉：湖北教育出版社 .
刘宓庆 . 2001. 翻译与语言哲学 . 北京：中国对外翻译出版公司 .
刘肖岩 . 2004. 论戏剧对白翻译 . 北京：中国人民公安大学出版社 .
罗新璋 . 1991. 复译之难 . 中国翻译（5）：29-31.
罗雪松 . 2000. "象牙塔"里的感叹——《荷塘月色》的主题辨析 . 高等函授学报（哲学社会科学版）（5）：22-23.
毛荣贵 . 2005. 翻译美学 . 上海：上海交通大学出版社 .
宁会勤 . 2009. 从《多佛海岸》浅析诗歌翻译 . 读与写：教育教学刊（9）：34.
裴显生 . 1987. 写作学新稿 . 南京：江苏教育出版社 .
钱之德 . 1983. 王尔德戏剧选 . 广州：花城出版社 .
冉永平，张新红 . 2007. 语用学纵横 . 北京：高等教育出版社 .
萨克雷 . 2005. 名利场 . 贾文浩，贾文渊，译 . 北京：北京燕山出版社 .
萨克雷 . 2005. 名利场 . 杨必，译 . 北京：人民文学出版社 .
佘树森 . 1986. 散文创作艺术 . 北京：北京大学出版社 .
申丹 . 2001. 叙述学与小说文体学研究 . 北京：北京大学出版社 .
申丹 . 2004. 视角 . 外国文学（3）：54-63.
沈复 . 1999. Six Chapters of a Floating Life . 林语堂，译 . 北京：外语教学与研究出版社 .
宋德利 . 2014. 译心：我的翻译三宗罪 . 北京：金盾出版社 .
隋荣谊 . 2004. 英汉翻译新教程 . 北京：中国电力出版社 .
王尔德 . 1990. 王尔德喜剧选 . 张南峰，译 . 福州：海峡文艺出版社 .
王尔德 . 1998. 理想丈夫与不可儿戏——王尔德的两出喜剧 . 余光中，译 . 沈阳：辽宁教育出版社 .
王宏印 . 2006. 文学翻译批评论稿 . 上海：上海外语教育出版社 .
王琦 . 2009.《傲慢与偏见》中反讽艺术初探 . 长春理工大学学报（高教版）（1）：81-82.
王宗炎 . 1984. 辨义为翻译之本 . 翻译通讯（4）：4-7.
文军 . 2006. 科学翻译批评导论 . 北京：中国对外翻译出版公司 .
翁世荣 . 1984. 文学写作教程 . 上海：华东师范大学出版社 .
奚永吉 . 2001. 文学翻译比较美学 . 武汉：湖北教育出版社 .

夏洛蒂·勃朗特. 1988. 简·爱. 祝庆英, 译. 上海：上海译文出版社.
夏洛蒂·勃朗特. 1991. 简·爱. 凌雯, 译. 杭州：浙江文艺出版社.
解静莉, 魏金龙, 叶青. 2007. 简·奥斯汀《傲慢与偏见》作品赏析. 科教文汇（2）：161.
熊学亮. 2007. 语言学新解. 上海：复旦大学出版社.
熊学亮, 曲卫国. 2007. 语用学采撷. 北京：高等教育出版社.
徐盛桓. 1982. 主位和述位. 外语教学与研究（1）：1-9.
徐颖. 2008. 小说中人物话语/思想的表达方式及其翻译. 重庆工学院学报（10）：148-150.
许钧. 1992. 文学翻译批评研究. 南京：译林出版社.
许钧. 2002. 作者、译者和读者的共鸣与视界融合——文本再创造的个案批评. 中国翻译（5）：23-27.
许钧. 2009. 翻译概论. 北京：外语教学与研究出版社.
许渊冲. 2000. 唐诗三百首. 北京：高等教育出版社.
杨晓荣. 2005. 翻译批评导论. 北京：中国对外翻译出版公司.
杨正和. 1997. 奥斯丁小说的反讽艺术辨析. 上饶师专学报（5）：79-82.
姚银燕. 2007.《葛底斯堡演说》及其三个中译文的经验功能探讨——功能语言学分析对翻译研究的启示. 山东理工大学学报（社会科学版）（3）：76-79.
喻云根. 1996. 英美名著翻译比较. 武汉：湖北教育出版社.
袁锦翔. 1990. 名家翻译研究与赏析. 武汉：湖北教育出版社.
曾文雄. 2007. 语用学翻译研究. 武汉：武汉大学出版社.
曾亦沙. 2000. 论翻译学研究的若干理论问题——兼论译学研究的辩证观. 外语与外语教学（9）：46-50.
张海鸥. 2000. 唐名家诗导读. 广州：广东人民出版社.
张继华. 2004. 文人独立的宣言——塞缪尔·约翰逊的一封信译析. 大学英语（9）：87-90.
郑诗鼎. 1999. 论复译研究. 中国翻译（2）：43-47.
周仪, 罗平. 2005. 翻译与批评. 武汉：湖北教育出版社.
周兆祥. 2004. 译评：理论与实践 // 黎翠珍. 翻译评赏. 北京：中国青年出版社：3-19.
朱纯深. 1994. 从文体学和话语分析看《荷塘月色》的美学意义. 名作欣赏（4）：79-86.
朱刚. 1998. 英语演说词精品. 北京：北京大学出版社.

Almberg, S. P. E. (1995). Retranslation. In S. Chan & D. E. Pollard (Eds.), *An Encyclopaedia of Translation* (pp. 925-930). Hong Kong: The Chinese University Press.

Austen, J. (1981). *Pride and Prejudice*. New York: Bantam Books.

Cao, Xue-qin. (1958). *Dream of the Red Chamber*. (C. Wang, Trans.). New York: Anchor Books. (Original work published 1765)

Cao, Xue-qin. (1973). *The Story of the Stone*. (D. Hawkes, Trans.). London: Penguin Books. (Original work published 1765)

Hatim, B., & Mason, I. (2001). *Discourse and the Translator*. Shanghai: Shanghai Foreign Language Education Press.

Lao, She. (1979). *Rickshaw: the Novel Lo-t'o Hsiang Tzu*. (J. M. James, Trans.) Honolulu: The University Press of Hawaii. (Original work published 1936)

Lau, Shaw. (1945). Rickshaw Boy. (E. King, Trans.). New York: Reynal & Hitchcock, Inc. (Original work published 1936)

Mair V. H. (Ed.). (2000). *The Shorter Columbia Anthology of Traditional Chinese Literature*. New York: Columbia University Press.

Munday, J. (2001). *Introducing Translation Studies*. London: Routledge.

Shen, Fu. (1983). *Six Records of a Floating Life*. (L. Pratt, & C. Su-hui, Trans.). Middlesex: Penguin Books. (Original work published 1878)

Sperber, D., & Wilson, D. (1995). *Relevance: Communication and Cognition* (2nd ed.). Malden: Blackwell Publishers Ltd.